PRAISE FOR H. W. BRANDS'S

# *Founding Partisans*

### A *Kirkus Reviews* Best History Book of 2023

"The author writes with a sharp and absorbing style, turning what could be a fairly dry topic into a highly readable tale worthy of a cable miniseries with backstabbing characters, high drama, shady deals and huge egos all clashing to determine the course of the new country. For anyone who thinks that gridlock and partisan machinations are a recent development, this book will quickly lay those misconceptions to rest."　　　　　*—New York Journal of Books*

"Mr. Brands has a genius for plotting out real events; a novelist could hardly do better."　　　　　*—The New York Sun*

"As H. W. Brands reminds us in this absorbing new book, partisanship is an ancient, indeed perennial, force in human affairs. From the early hours of the Republic, Americans of good will have struggled to ensure that party feeling be not reflexive but reflective. On that distinction, the Founders understood, hangs the fate of popular government."　　　　　—Jon Meacham,
Pulitzer Prize–winning author of *American Lion*

"An essential book for understanding the foundation of American partisanship."　　　　　*—Kirkus Reviews* (starred review)

"Revolutionary War buffs will relish this."　　　　　*—Publishers Weekly*

"Brands's storytelling prowess preserves the debaters' individual personalities and clearly constructs the grand narrative of the Convention's crafting of one of the political world's greatest documents."
*—Booklist*

## H. W. BRANDS

# Founding Partisans

H. W. Brands holds the Jack S. Blanton Sr. Chair in History at the University of Texas at Austin. He has written more than a dozen biographies and histories, including *The General vs. the President,* a *New York Times* bestseller, and *America First,* his most recent book. Two of his biographies, *The First American* and *Traitor to His Class,* were finalists for the Pulitzer Prize.

*Founding Partisans*

# Founding Partisans

HAMILTON, MADISON,
JEFFERSON, ADAMS
and the Brawling Birth
of American Politics

## H. W. BRANDS

VINTAGE BOOKS
A Division of Penguin Random House LLC
New York

The Library of Congress has cataloged the Doubleday edition as follows:
Names: Brands, H. W., author.
Title: Founding partisans: Hamilton, Madison, Jefferson, Adams and the brawling birth of American politics / H. W. Brands.
Description: First edition. | New York: Doubleday, 2023.
Identifiers: LCCN 2023020138 (print) | LCCN 2023020139 (ebook)
Subjects: LCSH: Founding Fathers of the United States. | United States—Politics and government—1775–1783. | United States—politics and government—1783–1809 | Political culture—United States—History—18th century. | Polarization (Social sciences)—Political aspects—United States—History—18th century.
Classification: LCC E302.5 .B744 2023 (print) | LCC E302.5 (ebook) |
DDC 973.3092/2—dc23/eng/20230428
LC record available at https://lccn.loc.gov/2023020138
LC ebook record available at https://lccn.loc.gov/2023020139

Vintage Books Trade Paperback ISBN: 978-0-593-46903-3
eBook ISBN: 978-0-385-54925-7

*Author photograph © University of Texas*
*Book design by Cassandra Pappas*
*Map by John Burgoyne*

vintagebooks.com

Printed in the United States of America
10  9  8  7  6  5  4  3  2  1

# Contents

# The
# AMERICA
## of the
# FOUNDERS

## 1789

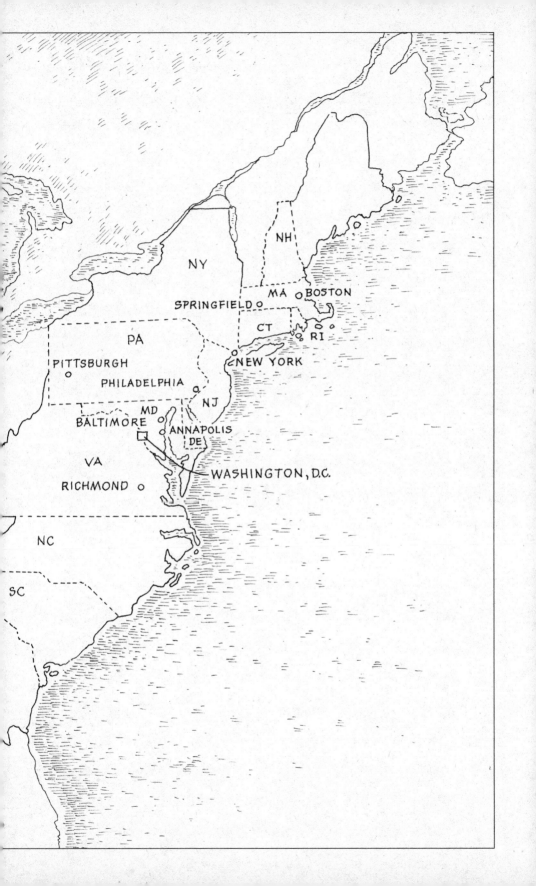

# Prologue

J AMES MADISON WORRIED that the will of the people might yet be denied. The people had rallied to the Republican party in the recent election, replacing Federalists in Congress with Republicans and giving a clear majority to the presidential ticket of Thomas Jefferson. Yet an oversight by the Constitutional Convention—an oversight for which Madison blamed himself as much as anyone—left the result of the presidential contest in doubt. Aaron Burr, the Republican choice for vice president, had tied Jefferson in the electoral vote, and the outcome now rested with the House of Representatives, where the discredited Federalists would render their departing decision.

Some of the Federalists favored Burr, hoping to secure his promise to salvage policies they liked. Others thought they could block both of the Republicans by refusing to give either a majority, thereby throwing the election into confusion from which they might yet emerge victorious. Madison had served in the House for nearly a decade before retiring on account of uncertain health. From the distance of his home in Virginia he monitored the Federalist finaglings and shared his suspicions with Jefferson, the chief of the party the two had created. The Federalists were cynical and unprincipled, Madison told Jefferson, but he hadn't thought them capable of the coup they seemed to be plotting. He still hoped they weren't. "Desperate as some of the adverse party there"—in Washington city, the new national capital—"may be, I can scarcely allow myself to believe that enough will not be found to frustrate the attempt to strangle the election of the people and smuggle into the chief magistracy the creature of a faction," Madison said. "It would seem that every individual member who has any standing or stake in society or any portion of virtue or sober understanding must revolt at the tendency of such a maneuver."

Madison was certain such a scheme couldn't succeed without the connivance of the defeated president, John Adams. He had thought better of Adams. He despised Adams's Federalist policies, the blatantly unconstitutional Alien and Sedition Acts being the most egregious violations of republican liberty; but he had credited the man for honesty. Perhaps he'd been wrong. "Is it possible that Mr. Adams should give his sanction to it if that should be made a necessary ingredient?" he asked Jefferson.

Jefferson had suggested to Madison an overture toward Adams. Jefferson and Adams had once been friends; they had worked together in the Continental Congress on behalf of independence from Britain. But politics had driven them apart these last several years. Their first contest for the presidency, in 1796, had been bitter, with Adams emerging the narrow winner. Their second and most recent contest, in 1800, had been more bitter still. Jefferson beat Adams in electors but hadn't yet won the presidency. Jefferson hoped, for the sake of the country, to mend the partisan wounds.

Madison warned him off. "I would not wish to discourage any attentions which friendship, prudence, or benevolence may suggest in his behalf," he told Jefferson. But they could do the Republican cause no good. Adams had been repudiated. "I find him infinitely sunk in the estimation of all parties," Madison said. Jefferson should keep his distance.


JOHN ADAMS HAD NOT approved the ploy Madison suspected him of. But neither had he rejected it. Perilous times permitted desperate measures. Adams remembered well when he and Jefferson had collaborated on the break from Britain. Adams had insisted that Jefferson draft the Declaration of Independence; Jefferson had asked for Adams's reasons.

"Reason first, you are a Virginian, and Virginia ought to appear at the head of this business," Adams replied. Virginia was the largest of the colonies but lagged behind Adams's Massachusetts in the vigor of its demands for independence. "Reason second, I am obnoxious, suspected and unpopular. You are very much otherwise. Reason third, you can write ten times better than I can."

Yet Adams had always considered himself the better man. Jefferson's facility with words came at the expense of his judgment; Jefferson could justify the most unjustifiable acts. He still defended the French revolution, after all the innocent blood it had shed. He refused to acknowledge the evil inherent in human nature. In the name of democracy he would destroy the institutions that kept human folly within bounds. And now he appeared on the verge of assuming leadership of the American republic.

Adams wasn't sure he could let that happen. "I know no more danger of a political convulsion if a President pro tem of the Senate or a Secretary of State or Speaker of the House should be made President by Congress than if Mr. Jefferson or Mr. Burr is declared such," Adams wrote in reply to a query regarding his position on such possibilities. "The President would be as legal in one case as in either of the others in my opinion, and the people as well as satisfied."

Yet it might not matter. There would have to be another election eventually, and Jefferson would win. "We shall be tossed at any rate in the tempestuous sea of liberty for years to come, and where the bark can land but in a political convulsion I cannot see."


ALEXANDER HAMILTON AGREED that a government headed by Jefferson would end in convulsion for America—which was why he was working so hard to make Jefferson president.

By no means was Jefferson his first choice. Hamilton had difficulty thinking of anyone who would make a worse president than Jefferson. Jefferson was wrong on all the issues confronting America's chief executive. He favored radical France over conservative Britain in the endless struggle between those two European nations. He favored states over the federal government in the contest for power in America. He favored farmers over merchants, debtors over creditors, the countryside over cities, the masses over their betters.

Yet what most irked Hamilton, though he was loath to admit it, was that Jefferson was better at politics than he was. Jefferson posed as the philosopher of Monticello, musing atop his mountain, but in reality he was as cunning and ruthless as anyone in American public life. Hamilton took credit for fashioning the Federalist party in the fight for ratification of the Constitution; no one had done more than he to secure that victory. Yet he refused to give Jefferson credit for constructing the Republican party, because such a negative accomplishment deserved blame rather than credit. The Republican agenda was to undo the good work that had rescued the country from the folly of the Articles of Confederation. The Federalists sought to build America up, the Republicans to tear it down.

Jefferson had begun by bringing Hamilton down. Jefferson's hired libeler had spilled the story of Hamilton's illicit love affair and the blackmail it produced; Hamilton had been compelled to admit the adultery in order to rebut a more damaging Republican charge of embezzlement during his time as treasury secretary.

The scandal left the Federalist party under the leadership of Adams. If Hamilton and Jefferson agreed on anything, it was that Adams was unfit to be president. Jefferson challenged Adams openly, but Hamilton, as a member of Adams's party, had to do so covertly. In Adams's first race for president, Hamilton had worked quietly to get Federalists to rally behind an alternative candidate. The whispering campaign had failed, and Adams had become president.

The second time around, Hamilton came out openly against Adams, publishing a detailed indictment of his qualifications and performance. Again Hamilton hoped to get the Federalists to unite around a party man other than Adams. Again he failed, but this time the victory went to the Republican ticket headed by Jefferson.

Hamilton didn't change his mind about Jefferson's incapacity for sound leadership. "His politics are tinctured with fanaticism," Hamilton wrote to an influential Federalist. "He is too much in earnest in his democracy. . . . He has been a mischievous enemy to the principal measures of our past administration. . . . He is crafty and persevering in his objects. . . . He is not scrupulous about the means of success, nor very mindful of truth. . . . He is a contemptible hypocrite."

And yet he should be made president. The only realistic alternative to Jefferson was Burr. Hamilton distrusted Burr as unprincipled and overly ambitious. But the worst of Burr was that if he became president by the will of the Federalists, he would be seen as one of them, and the disaster that befell America under his administration would be charged against them.

Hamilton was certain a collapse was coming. The Republican majorities in Congress would guarantee it. Better for the Federalists to be far from the scene when it happened. And better for Hamilton.

THOMAS JEFFERSON PROFESSED detachment as the skulduggery unfolded. "I feel no impulse from personal ambition to the office now proposed to me," he wrote to his daughter Mary. If he should lose, he would retire to Monticello in peace.

But the cause of the country required that he *not* lose. His defeat would mean that the American people had been cheated out of their victory. They had voted to reverse the centralizing, antidemocratic policies of the Federalists. "I feel a sincere wish indeed to see our government brought back to its republican principles, to see that kind of government firmly fixed to which my whole life has been devoted," Jefferson told Mary. "I hope we shall now see it so established as that when I retire, it may be under full security that we are to continue free and happy."

As for the office itself, he had no illusions. He had watched the presidency drive George Washington to distraction and then into retirement. He had seen it intensify Adams's stubborn self-righteousness. He had little doubt it would amplify his own faults.

He wasn't proud of the direction politics had taken during the dozen years under the Constitution. With the other founders he had hoped for a politics without parties—a politics of republican virtue. But after Hamilton and the Federalists defined virtue as whatever expanded the reach of the central government and padded the purses of the wealthy, and organized to write their definition into law, he and other defenders of the people had no choice but to organize in opposition. Over time the people looked to him for leadership, and he didn't want to disappoint them. He sometimes puzzled that they thought so highly of him; his career in elective politics, especially as governor of Virginia, had not been much to boast of.

Until recently, the Federalists had been winning. Time and again the Federalist clique had defeated the more numerous but less organized Republicans.

No longer. The Federalists had overreached, and the people had risen up and thrown them from the halls of power. The election of 1800 had been hardly less than a revolution in American politics, second only to the revolution of 1776.

As much as he looked forward to the quiet of retirement, he couldn't turn away at the moment of victory. Besides, for all it was the victory of the people and the principles of republicanism, it was his victory too.

PART I

The Making of a Continentalist

I

ALEXANDER HAMILTON HADN'T INTENDED to father a party and then subvert it; his first goal in politics had been to reform the Continental Congress. Hamilton granted Congress credit for declaring independence from Britain in 1776, but in the war that followed, it did more harm than good, he judged. Its members were idiots, or at least behaved that way. "Folly, caprice, a want of foresight, comprehension and dignity characterize the general tenor of their actions," Hamilton asserted in a letter to George Clinton, the governor of New York, in February 1778.

Hamilton was writing from the headquarters of the Continental Army at Valley Forge amid the worst winter of the Revolutionary War. He had got there by talent and audacity. Born in the West Indies, abandoned by his father, effectively orphaned by the death of his mother, Hamilton had found his way to New York in his teens. He developed a knack for impressing men who could promote his career. George Clinton was one; George Washington was another. Hamilton was clearly going places; at this point he was aide-de-camp to Washington.

"Their conduct with respect to the army especially is feeble, indecisive and improvident, insomuch that we are reduced to a more terrible situation than you can conceive," Hamilton said to Clinton about the members of Congress. They were starving the army. "By injudicious changes and arrangements in the commissary's department in the middle of a campaign, they have exposed the army frequently to temporary want, and to the danger of a dissolution from absolute famine." The situation grew more dire by the day. "Desertions have been immense, and strong features of mutiny begin to show themselves," Hamilton observed. "If effectual measures are not speedily adopted, I know not how we shall keep the army together or make another campaign."

Clinton couldn't tell to what degree Hamilton was speaking for Washington. The sentiments seemed like those of Washington, who too had complained about Congress. But the language was more forthright, indeed disdainful. Like Washington, Clinton had been charmed by Hamilton, but the governor must have asked himself where this brash young immigrant—Hamilton said he was twenty-one; some other evidence suggests twenty-three—had got the idea he knew the business of America's Congress better than its own members did.

Of course he read on. Hamilton explained that even while Congress failed to provide for the rank and file of the army, it let itself be bamboozled by those it made into officers, especially foreigners. "They have disgusted the army by repeated instances of the most whimsical favouritism in their promotions, and by an absurd prodigality of rank to foreigners and to the meanest staff of the army," Hamilton wrote. The foreign officers took advantage of the opportunities Congress afforded them. "It is become almost proverbial in the mouths of the French officers and other foreigners that they have nothing more to do to obtain whatever they please than to assume a high tone and assert their own merit with confidence and perseverance."

Hamilton wondered what had become of the distinguished body of 1776. "America once had a representation that would do honor to any age or nation," he told Clinton. "The present falling off is very alarming and dangerous." Where had the great men gone? "Are they dead? Have they deserted the cause?" Hamilton supplied his own answer: "Very few are dead and still fewer have deserted the cause; they are all except the few who still remain in Congress either in the field or in the civil offices of their respective states."

Hamilton perceived a baneful competition between the states and the central government for talent. The states were winning. "Each state, in order to promote its own internal government and prosperity, has selected its best members to fill the offices within itself and conduct its own affairs," he said. Congress had done nothing to counter the appeal of the states. "This is a most pernicious mistake and must be corrected."

Hamilton struck a note he would play without pause for the rest of his life: the nation must come before the states. "However important it is to give form and efficiency to your interior constitutions and police," he said to Clinton, referring to the states generally, "it is infinitely more important to have a wise general council." If the central government failed, the states would follow. "You should not beggar the councils of the United States to enrich the administration of the several members."

The results of state preference brought the country into disrepute, domestically and especially overseas, Hamilton said. "Realize to yourself the consequences of having a Congress despised at home and abroad. How can the common force be exerted if the power of collecting it be put in weak foolish and unsteady hands? How can we hope for success in our European negotiations if the nations of Europe have no confidence in the wisdom and vigor of the great continental government?"

At last Hamilton acknowledged that he might be speaking out of place. He was, after all, merely an aide-de-camp. He relied on Governor Clinton's discretion. "The sentiments I have advanced are not fit for the vulgar ear, and circumstanced as I am, I should with caution utter them except to those in whom I may place an entire confidence."

AS THE HARROWING WINTER PASSED, Hamilton grew more impatient with Congress, which appeared bent on spoiling what it didn't neglect. "Shall I speak what seems to me a most melancholy truth?" he wrote to Clinton in March. "It is this—that with the most adequate means to ensure success in our contest, the weakness of our councils will, in all probability, ruin us." Congress had tacitly accepted an untruth circulated by the British that Washington was forcing British prisoners to turn coat. "This silences all our complaints against the enemy for a similar practice, and furnishes them with a damning answer to anything we can say on the subject," Hamilton said.

Congress meddled in the exchange of prisoners. "Lately a flag, with provisions and clothing for the British prisoners, with General Washington's passport, was seized at Lancaster," Hamilton reported. "The affair was attended with circumstances of violence and meanness that would disgrace Hottentots. Still more lately, General Washington's engagements with General Howe for an exchange of prisoners have been most shamefully violated." Hamilton granted that opinions could differ on the wisdom of exchanges. "But, admitting this to be true, it is much worse policy to commit such frequent breaches of faith and ruin our national character. Whatever refined politicians may think, it is of great consequence to preserve a national character."

Reputation meant a great deal to Hamilton as a young man on the make. Introducing another theme that would mark his career, he declared that reputation should mean no less to the government of a country struggling for its very existence. "The general notions of justice and humanity are implanted in almost every human breast and ought not to be too freely shocked," he said. If Washington struck a deal with Howe on prisoners, Congress should honor it. America would stand or fall according to the enthusiasm of the American people for the common cause. "I would ask whether in a republican state and a republican army such a cruel policy as that of exposing those men who are foremost in defence of their country to the miseries of hopeless captivity can succeed."

Hamilton again acknowledged that he might be speaking out of turn. But he couldn't *not* speak. "I dwell upon the faults of Congress because I think they strike at the vitals of our opposition"—to Britain—"and of our future prosperity," he said. "I cannot but wish that every gentleman of influence in the country should think with me."

HAMILTON WAS NO idle complainer; he rarely criticized without proposing remedies. Appalled by the fecklessness of Congress, he at once considered how the institution might be improved. He discussed the matter with James Duane, a New York lawyer and member of Congress; Duane was sufficiently intrigued by Hamilton's thinking to ask him to elaborate.

"The fundamental defect is a want of power in Congress," Hamilton declared. He identified three causes. First: "an excess of the spirit of liberty," which made the states jealous of any powers claimed by Congress. Second: "a diffidence in Congress of their own powers," by which that central body had got in the habit of deferring to the states. Third: "a want of sufficient means at their disposal to answer the public exigencies." Here the rub was the inability of Congress to levy taxes on the people; instead it could merely make requests to the states.

Hamilton didn't blame Congress itself entirely. "It may be pleaded that Congress had never any definitive powers granted them and of course could exercise none," he wrote. Yet he wasn't going to let Congress off the hook. The members should have seized power wherever plausible. "They should have considered themselves as vested with full power *to preserve the republic from harm.*" They had declared independence, after all, and were conducting a war. What greater marks of sovereignty were there? Congress should have pushed further into the gray area beyond what was expressly authorized. "Undefined powers are discretionary powers, limited only by the object for which they were given: in the present case, the independence and freedom of America."

The problem, though, ran deeper than the diffidence of the members of Congress. "The confederation itself is defective and requires to be altered," Hamilton told Duane. "It is neither fit for war nor peace." So long as the central government was a mere confederation of sovereign states, it would be no government at all. "The idea of an uncontrollable sovereignty in each state over its internal police"—its internal affairs—"will defeat the other powers given to Congress and make our union feeble and precarious."

In no area did the authority of the states intrude more worrisomely than in the operation of the army. "They should have nothing to do with it," Hamilton said. "The entire formation and disposal of our military forces ought to belong to Congress. It is an essential cement of the union."

Hamilton anticipated objections to his demand for greater central power. "It may be apprehended that this may be dangerous to liberty," he said. But especially in the current crisis, nothing could be more fatuous. "We run much greater risk of having a weak and disunited federal government than one which will be able to usurp upon the rights of the people."

The existence of the states would forever make America's collective existence precarious. "The forms of our state constitutions must always give them great weight in our affairs and will make it too difficult to bend them to the pursuit of a common interest, too easy to oppose whatever they do not like and to form partial combinations subversive of the general one," Hamilton predicted. History revealed the fragility of confederations. The leagues of the Greek republics ought to be a cautionary example for America. "They were continually at war with each other and for want of union fell a prey to their neighbours," Hamilton said. "At length they sunk entirely into contempt."

Modern times corroborated the principle. "The Swiss cantons are another proof of the doctrine," Hamilton said. "They have had wars with each other which would have been fatal to them had not the different powers in their neighbourhood been too jealous of one another and too equally matched to suffer either to take advantage of their quarrels." America's confederation of states would have no such external props. "We are so remote from other nations that we shall have all the leisure and opportunity we can wish to cut each others' throats."

FINANCE WOULD BECOME a fascination with Hamilton. His interest surfaced early. Distributed financial authority was ruining America, he told Duane. "The confederation too gives the power of the purse too entirely to the state legislatures." A government that didn't control its own revenues couldn't control anything. This was where reform of the confederation must begin. "It should provide perpetual funds in the disposal of Congress, by a land tax, poll tax, or the like. All imposts upon commerce ought to be laid by Congress and appropriated to their use." The principle was the most basic in all politics. "That power which holds the purse strings absolutely must rule."

National finance must be controlled by a more powerful national executive. "Congress have kept the power too much into their own hands and have meddled too much with details of every sort," Hamilton said. "Congress is properly a deliberative corps and it forgets itself when it attempts to play the executive." With no separate executive branch—the president was chosen by Congress—there was neither independent energy nor collective memory. "It is impossible such a body, numerous as it is, constantly fluctuating, can ever act with sufficient decision or with system." Most members didn't know enough to act wisely; the others were too corrupt to act honestly.

HOW TO EFFECT his desired reforms? Hamilton proposed "a convention of all the states with full authority to conclude finally upon a general confederation, stating to them beforehand explicitly the evils arising from a want of power in Congress, and the impossibility of supporting the contest"—the war—"on its present footing, that the delegates may come possessed of proper sentiments as well as proper authority to give to the meeting."

Hamilton grew more specific. "The Convention should assemble the 1st of November next"—November 1, 1780—"the sooner, the better; our disorders are too violent to admit of a common or lingering remedy." The goal of the convention should be to bolster the central government at the expense of the states. Hamilton identified the powers Congress should be given: to conduct war, form alliances, levy taxes, control trade, coin money, establish banks and do all the other things any self-respecting sovereign government could do.

In this letter to Duane, Hamilton conceded that he was asking a lot—likely more than the American people were willing to accept at once. Yet he had a plan for that too: a campaign of propaganda to bring them around. "If a convention is called, the minds of all the states and the people ought to be prepared to receive its determinations by sensible and popular writings," he said. The very audacity of his proposal should work in its favor. "There are epochs in human affairs when *novelty* even is useful." The people wanted change. "'Tis an universal sentiment that our present system is a bad one," he said. "A convention would revive the hopes of the people and give a new direction to their passions."

Hamilton hoped to be the one to provide that new direction. Timing and presentation would make all the difference. "Men are governed by opinion; this opinion is as much influenced by appearances as by realities," he said. Fortune favored the bold. "If a government appears to be confident of its own powers, it is the surest way to inspire the same confidence in others."

## 2

HAMILTON'S RECOMMENDATIONS were for Duane's eyes only at this point. Hamilton's position on Washington's staff kept him from speaking more openly. Washington agreed with many of Hamilton's complaints against Congress but felt obliged to play the hand he'd been dealt.

Things changed for Hamilton in the spring of 1781 when he resigned from Washington's staff. Chafing at being a glorified secretary to the great man, Hamilton exaggerated a modest chiding by Washington into an aspersion on his character and quit in a huff. He transferred to an artillery corps; meanwhile he went public, albeit anonymously, with his agitation for a change of government. An essay titled "The Continentalist No. 1" appeared in the *New-York Packet* in July 1781. "It would be the extreme of vanity in us not to be sensible that we began this revolution with very vague and confined notions of the practical business of government," Hamilton declared. "To the greater part of us it was a novelty. Of those who under the former constitution had had opportunities of acquiring experience, a large proportion adhered to the opposite side"—these were the Loyalists—"and the remainder can only be supposed to have possessed ideas adapted to the narrow colonial sphere in which they had been accustomed to move, not of that enlarged kind suited to the government of an INDEPENDENT NATION."

Under the circumstances, said Hamilton, the wonder was that the government of this new nation had performed as well as it had. Five years after independence, the United States survived, despite the terrible trials of the continuing war against Britain. Yet it could have done better. "There have been many false steps, many chimerical projects and utopian speculations, in the management of our civil as well as of our military affairs." Some of these were the natural outgrowth of the revolutionary spirit of the times. "An extreme jealousy of power is the attendant on all popular revolutions and has seldom been without its evils," Hamilton said. "It is to this source we are to trace many of the fatal mistakes which have so deeply endangered the common cause, particularly that defect which will be the object of these remarks: A WANT OF POWER IN CONGRESS."

Hamilton observed that he wasn't alone in believing Congress lacked powers the country required. Members of Congress themselves were comparing notes on what additional powers it required. Yet there was little agreement on what these powers should be, and in any case the states resisted ceding authority to Congress.

The failure of reform could be tolerated no longer. "We have now had sufficient time for reflection and experience, as ample as unfortunate, to rectify our errors," Hamilton said. "To persist in them becomes disgraceful and even criminal." The experience of other nations and peoples boded ill for a continuance of America's present course. "History is full of examples where, in contests for liberty, a jealousy of power has either defeated the attempts to recover or preserve it in the first instance, or has afterwards subverted it by clogging government with too great precautions for its felicity, or by leaving too wide a door for sedition and popular licentiousness."

In the first phase of any revolution, liberty was the priority, Hamilton asserted. But order must soon complement liberty, lest the revolution run astray. "As too much power leads to despotism, too little leads to anarchy, and both eventually to the ruin of the people." Hamilton granted that the states, taken separately, still balanced liberty and order. "But this is not the case with respect to the FEDERAL GOVERNMENT." Indeed, the very success of the states boded ill for their commitment to the common cause. "The ambition and local interests of the respective members will be constantly undermining and usurping upon its prerogatives till it comes to a dissolution, if a partial combination of some of the more powerful ones does not bring it to a more SPEEDY and VIOLENT END."

Hamilton developed his arguments in subsequent "Continentalist" essays published in the same New York paper. He parried concerns that a stronger central government would pose a danger to the states and their citizens. He conceded that fear of despotism was warranted in unitary republics, where a sovereign might indeed become too powerful for his constituents, but not in confederations. "In federal governments, where different states are represented in a general council, the danger is on the other side—that the members will be an overmatch for the common head, or in other words, that it will not have sufficient influence and authority to secure the obedience of the several parts of the confederacy."

In a federal system, the institutions of the central government were offset by the institutions of the individual members, Hamilton said. "Each member has a distinct sovereignty, makes and executes laws, imposes taxes, distributes justice, and exercises every other function of government. It has always within itself the means of revenue, and on an emergency can levy forces. If the common sovereign should meditate or attempt anything unfavourable to the general liberty, each member, having all the proper organs of power, can prepare for defence with celerity and vigour. Each can immediately sound the alarm to the others and enter into leagues for mutual protection."

Where other republican theorists looked to civic virtue to sustain the republic, Hamilton relied on self-interest. And the self-interests of the member states would keep the central government from overstepping. "From the plainest principles of human nature, two inferences are to be drawn, one, that each member of a political confederacy will be more disposed to advance its own authority upon the ruins of that of the confederacy than to make any improper concessions in its favour or support it in unreasonable pretensions; the other, that the subjects of each member will be more devoted in their attachments and obedience to their own particular governments than to that of the union."

This was a problem when common action was required. "The selfishness of every part will dispose each to believe that the public burthens are unequally apportioned and that itself is the victim," Hamilton said. But it was also a safeguard against overstepping by the central government. "These, and other circumstances, will promote a disposition for abridging the authority of the federal government; and the ambition of men in office in each state will make them glad to encourage it."

Indeed, the greater danger lay in central weakness. Unchecked by federal authority, the ambitions of member states would surely produce trouble. "Political societies in close neighbourhood must either be strongly united under one government or there will infallibly exist emulations"—rivalries—"and quarrels," Hamilton said. "This is in human nature, and we have no reason to think ourselves wiser or better than other men. Some of the larger states a small number of years hence will be in themselves populous, rich and powerful in all those circumstances calculated to inspire ambition and nourish ideas of separation and independence." Although their true interest would be to preserve the union, they wouldn't see it that way. "Their vanity and self-importance will be very likely to overpower that motive and make them seek to place themselves at the head of particular confederacies independent of the general one." Disaster likely would follow. "A schism once introduced, competitions of boundary and rivalships of commerce will easily afford pretexts for war."

Already the jostling among states was occurring, the more telling for the context in which it took place. "In the midst of a war for our existence as a nation, in the midst of dangers too serious to be trifled with, some of the states have evaded or refused compliance with the demands of Congress in points of the greatest moment to the common safety," Hamilton said. "If they act such a part at this perilous juncture, what are we to expect in a time of peace and security?"

Hamilton specified six areas in which the powers of the central government should be expanded. It should have a monopoly on trade regulation, including the collection of import duties. It should be able to levy a tax on land, the principal form of property in America. It should be empowered to establish a capitation tax—also called a head tax or poll tax—on male citizens over the age of fifteen. It should receive title to unclaimed land in the states, for the purpose of sale or rent. It should be awarded a portion of the production from mines in the country. These five measures would contribute to the federal coffers. The sixth measure—the power of appointment of military and naval officers— would attach the ambitions of those officers to the central government.

"The three first articles are of immediate necessity," Hamilton said by way of explanation. "The three last would be of great present but of much greater future utility; the whole combined would give solidity and permanency to the union." Money—revenue—was always essential. "The great defect of the confederation is that it gives the United States no property, or, in other words, no revenue," Hamilton said. "And power without revenue in political society is a name."

Revenue made possible government credit, which was crucial to Hamilton's schemes. Energetic governments borrowed against their future to fund activities in the present. "Credit supposes specific and permanent funds for the punctual payment of interest, with a moral certainty of a final redemption of the principal," he wrote. Credit tied the wealthy to the government, creating the marriage of interests essential to the survival of any republic.

EVENTS INTRUDED on the elaboration of Hamilton's argument. The most important of these was the victory of American and French forces over British forces at Yorktown in October 1781. Hamilton took an active part in the battle, commanding troops who seized an important British redoubt. The victory for the American side didn't end the war, but it sufficiently discouraged the British that they suspended major operations in favor of peace talks. After several months of inaction, Hamilton resigned his military commission to prepare for the next chapter of his career. He crammed a legal education into six months of study and was admitted to the New York bar in the summer of 1782. At about the same time he was chosen as one of New York's delegates to Congress, for the term to start in November of that year.

He continued to publish his "Continentalist" essays. He focused on the need for Congress to regulate the trade of the states. Already the states were competing with each in trade, often favoring the enterprises of their own citizens over those of other states, thereby amplifying the animosities among the states. State control of trade deprived the national government of such duties as might be levied on imports from foreign countries. This latter point wasn't a huge issue yet, in that the war had suppressed imports, but Hamilton hoped duties would become a mainstay of the American government.

"The vesting Congress with the power of regulating trade ought to have been a principal object of the confederation for a variety of reasons," he declared. "It is as necessary for the purposes of commerce as of revenue." Some writers on government—David Hume, Adam Smith—contended that trade would regulate itself. "Such persons will imagine that there is no need of a common directing power," Hamilton said. He wasn't impressed by the Scotsmen's argument for free trade. "It must be rejected by every man acquainted with commercial history. Commerce, like other things, has its fixed principles, according to which it must be regulated."

Hamilton adhered to the mercantilism against which Hume and Smith contended. "To preserve the balance of trade in favour of a nation ought to be a leading aim of its policy," he said, stating the mercantilist case succinctly. A favorable balance of trade occurred when nations sold more to other nations than they purchased in return. In the process the favored nations accumulated stores of gold and silver, the mercantilists' measure of trade policy.

Trade was what fostered national power, in the view of Hamilton and the mercantilists. The British empire had been built on trade; even more so the Dutch empire, which lacked the great army and navy of Britain but competed successfully with Britain on trade. The French experience was particularly instructive for a new nation like the United States. "France was much later in commercial improvements, nor would her trade have been at this time in so prosperous a condition had it not been for the abilities and indefatigable endeavours of the great Colbert," Hamilton said. "He laid the foundation of the French commerce and taught the way to his successors to enlarge and improve it. The establishment of the woolen manufacture in a kingdom where nature seemed to have denied the means is one among many proofs how much may be effected in favour of commerce by the attention and patronage of a wise administration. The number of useful edicts passed by Louis the 14th, and since his time, in spite of frequent interruptions from the jealous enmity of Great Britain, has advanced that of France to a degree which has excited the envy and astonishment of its neighbours."

Perhaps Hamilton already imagined himself an American Colbert. In any case, he thought *someone* should play that role, and it wouldn't be an official of one of the states. "If the states had distinct interests, were unconnected with each other, their own governments would then be the proper and could be the only depositaries of such a power," Hamilton said of the control of trade. "But as they are parts of a whole with a common interest in trade, as in other things, there ought to be a common direction in that as in all other matters."

As for the revenue prospects of trade, Hamilton deemed these crucial. "No mode can be so convenient as a source of revenue to the United States," he said. Import taxes fell upon those most able to pay, namely the people wealthy enough to afford the imports. "It is therefore that mode which may be exercised by the federal government with least exception or disgust."

Managed well, trade policy would unite Americans, Hamilton said. Managed poorly, it would divide them, even destroy them as a single people. In this regard, trade reflected the broader issues at work in the politics of the nation. "It is too much characteristic of our national temper to be ingenious in finding out and magnifying the minutest disadvantages and to reject measures of evident utility," he said. "Unless we can overcome this narrow disposition and learn to estimate measures by their general tendency, we shall never be a great or a happy people, if we remain a people at all."

THE FINAL NUMBER of the "Continentalist" essays appeared on the sixth anniversary of the Declaration of Independence. By now it was clear that Britain would indeed recognize American independence, although details of the peace treaty remained to be determined. Hamilton was looking beyond the war, to a time when the centrifugal forces within the confederation would no longer be countered by the centripetal forces of the war.

The latter forces must be replaced by bonds of abiding self-interest, Hamilton said. "We may preach till we are tired of the theme the necessity of disinterestedness in republics without making a single proselyte," he said. Not virtue but interest was the driver of history, and it would be the driver of American history. Practical patriots must acknowledge this fact.

Hamilton's argument from interest now caused him to urge the creation of a class of federal officeholders spread among the several states. "The reason of allowing Congress to appoint its own officers of the customs, collectors of taxes, and military officers of every rank is to create in the interior of each state a mass of influence in favour of the federal government," he said. The American union conceivably could be held together by force, over the wishes of some of the states. But force was blunt and off-putting. "It will be wise to obviate the necessity of it by interesting such a number of individuals in each state in support of the federal government as will be counterpoised to the ambition of others, and will make it difficult for them to unite the people in opposition to the just and necessary measures of the union."

Hamilton's argument from interest didn't lend itself naturally to an uplifting vision of human betterment. But its very practicality had a transcendence of its own. "There is something noble and magnificent in the perspective of a great federal republic closely linked in the pursuit of a common interest, tranquil and prosperous at home, respectable abroad," he declared. And it was certainly better than the alternative. "There is something proportionably diminutive and contemptible in the prospect of a number of petty states with the appearance only of union, jarring, jealous and perverse, without any determined direction, fluctuating and unhappy at home, weak and insignificant by their dissentions in the eyes of other nations."

Americans faced a stark choice, Hamilton concluded. "Happy America! if those to whom thou hast entrusted the guardianship of thy infancy know how to provide for thy future repose; but miserable and undone if their negligence or ignorance permits the spirit of discord to erect her banners on the ruins of thy tranquility!"

3

T HE SPIRIT OF DISCORD was rife among the soldiers of the
Continental Army. Dissatisfaction in the ranks had already produced one spectacular mutiny, when more than a thousand soldiers
from Pennsylvania in early 1781 revolted against their lack of pay and in
the belief of some three-year men that their term of service had ended.
British commander Henry Clinton tried to exploit the insurrection by
offering full pay and pardons if they came over to the British side.
George Washington was relieved when the Pennsylvanians scorned the
offer, but he worried when they marched toward Philadelphia to compel redress of their grievances. The president of Pennsylvania, Joseph
Reed, consented to meet them and discuss their complaints, even as
their immediate commander, Anthony Wayne, tried to talk them down.
A compromise was reached; some of the men were discharged while
others were granted furloughs and paid a bonus to reenlist.

This quelled the Pennsylvania outbreak, but the mutiny virus spread.
Comparably aggrieved troops from New Jersey followed the Pennsylvania example and staged a revolt of their own. Washington was ready
for this. He found loyal troops to throw against the new mutineers, and
he executed their ringleaders.

Even so, the larger problem persisted. Most of the soldiers were sincere patriots, but they had families to feed and futures to consider. For
many, their pay was their families' support, and though they themselves
weren't going hungry anymore, their wives and children sometimes
were. The argument of the mutineers—that if the government wasn't

going to let them support their families while under arms, they would have to put down arms and find some other way—was irrefutable on moral grounds, whatever it boded for army discipline.

The complaint of the soldier-creditors took another form in the spring of 1783. Washington had made his headquarters at Newburgh, New York, from which he could keep an eye on British forces in New York City while awaiting the news from Paris. Obviously the war was winding down, and the officers in Washington's army feared they would be mustered out without having received the pay Congress had promised them. They worried that once scattered, they would never be paid.

HAMILTON HEARD the rumblings of discontent and sought to exploit them. As a member of Congress he presumed to offer guidance to Washington, his former superior. "I take the liberty to suggest to you my ideas on some matters of delicacy and importance," Hamilton wrote. "I view the present juncture as a very interesting"—worrisome—"one. I need not observe how far the temper and situation of the army make it so." The financial condition of the government was dire. "There has scarcely been a period of the revolution which called more for wisdom and decision in Congress," Hamilton said. But Congress was as hapless as ever. "We are a body not governed by reason or foresight."

Far from discouraging the army's pressure on Congress, Hamilton seemed to welcome it. "If the war continues it would seem that the army must in June subsist itself *to defend the country;* if peace should take place it *will* subsist itself to *procure justice to itself,*" he told Washington. "It appears to be a prevailing opinion in the army that the disposition to recompence their services will cease with the necessity for them, and that if they once lay down their arms, they will part with the means of obtaining justice. It is to be lamented that appearances afford too much ground for their distrust."

Others were advising Washington to smash the rebellion. Not Hamilton. "It becomes a serious inquiry what will be the true line of policy," he said. "The claims of the army urged with moderation but with firmness may operate on those weak minds"—in the country—"which are influenced by their apprehensions more than their judgments, so as to produce a concurrence in the measures which the exigencies of affairs demand."

This would be no easy task. "The difficulty will be to keep a *complaining* and *suffering army* within the bounds of moderation," Hamilton said. He counseled Washington on how to find the balance. "It will be advisable not to discountenance their endeavours to procure redress, but rather by the intervention of confidential and prudent persons, *to take the direction of them.*" In other words, Washington should lead the mutiny, without showing his hand. "This will enable you in case of extremity to guide the torrent, and bring order, perhaps even good, out of confusion."

Hamilton was looking beyond the army and the impending mutiny to the broader issue of government reform, and he urged Washington to do the same. "The great *desideratum* at present is the establishment of general funds which alone can do justice to the creditors of the United States (of whom the army forms the most meritorious class), restore public credit and supply the future wants of government. This is the object of all men of sense; in this the influence of the army, properly directed, may cooperate."

WASHINGTON HAD a high opinion of Hamilton's talents but not of all his suggestions. The general had no desire to meddle in political affairs. "I shall pursue the same steady line of conduct which has governed me hitherto," he replied. Hamilton and his colleagues in Congress, and their counterparts in the states, should do likewise. "The just claims of the army ought, and it is to be hoped will, have their weight with every sensible legislature in the Union."

Washington proceeded to shame the potential insurgents out of any thoughts of interfering in political affairs. "I was among the first who embarked in the cause of our common country," he told a meeting of his officers. "I have never left your side one moment, but when called from you on public duty." He had shared their trials and their triumphs; the army was always in his thoughts. "My heart has ever expanded with joy when I have heard its praises, and my indignation has arisen when the mouth of detraction has been opened against it." The officers must not throw away the stellar reputation they had won, and in doing so imperil all they had fought for. "Let me conjure you, in the name of our common country, as you value your own sacred honor, as you respect the rights of humanity, and as you regard the military and national character of America, to express your utmost horror and detestation of the man who wishes, under any specious pretenses, to overturn the liberties of our country, and who wickedly attempts to open the flood gates of civil discord and deluge our rising empire in blood."

Hamilton, likewise chastened, beat a quick retreat. He assured Washington that an actual coup had been the farthest thing from his mind. "As to any combination of *force*, it would only be productive of the horrors of a civil war, might end in the ruin of the country and would certainly end in the ruin of the army," he said.

Yet the problems of the government remained. The issue of finance—in particular of debts owed to various creditors, including the troops—hung over everything else, and until this issue was resolved, nothing else could be resolved either. Hamilton tried to make Washington understand what had moved him to conspire in mutiny. "The question was not merely how to do justice to the creditors, but how to restore public credit," he wrote. The creditors were demanding satisfaction, and Congress lacked the means to pay and the incentive to find the means. Hamilton hoped to enhance the incentive. "The necessity and discontents of the army presented themselves as a powerful engine." He had been wrong to try to use the army to reform the government, he now acknowledged.

Yet the government still needed reforming.

# PART II

## Blessing or Curse?

# 4

James madison had been a charter member of Virginia's state legislature, elected to the general assembly in its first session following the Declaration of Independence. He advanced to the Continental Congress in 1780, as the war against Britain was approaching a climax, and he soon came to agree with the bad things Hamilton was saying about that body. "Among the various conjunctures of alarm and distress which have arisen in the course of the revolution, it is with pain I affirm to you, sir, that no one can be singled out more truly critical than the present," Madison wrote from Philadelphia to Thomas Jefferson in March 1780. Jefferson was Madison's neighbor in Virginia, with the former's home, Monticello, lying less than thirty miles from the latter's Montpelier. Jefferson was also a mentor to Madison, who had just turned twenty-nine. And Jefferson was governor of Virginia, elected the previous year. Jefferson felt the demands of the war as they manifested themselves to the states; Madison reported how things looked at the center.

He listed the evils afflicting the government and hence the country. "Our army threatened with an immediate alternative of disbanding or living on free quarter," he said. "The public treasury empty. Public credit exhausted, nay the private credit of purchasing agents employed, I am told, as far as it will bear. Congress complaining of the extortion of the people; the people of the improvidence of Congress, and the army of both." Congress made decisions only with great difficulty, and those decisions were usually wrong. The states bickered with one another and with the central government. The collapse of credit caused a stagnation in trade.

"These are the outlines of the true picture of our public situation," Madison told Jefferson. "I leave it to your own imagination to fill them up. Believe me, sir, as things now stand, if the states do not vigorously proceed in collecting the old money and establishing funds for the credit of the new, that we are undone." He hesitated to commit such a dire report to conveyance by post lest it fall into the hands of the British and cause them to press their advantage harder. "But I know of no better at present," he told Jefferson, "and I conceive it to be absolutely necessary to be known to those who are most able and zealous to contribute to the public relief."

PART OF THE PROBLEM with Congress was that for the first five years of its existence as a legislature of an independent country, it existed in a kind of netherworld. The states had written and ratified constitutions, giving their governments concrete republican form. But there was no constitution for the United States as a whole. The Articles of Confederation were approved by Congress in 1777 but not ratified until March 1781. During that time Congress made up powers and precedents as it went along. When individual states disapproved of decisions made by Congress, they ignored the decisions as unauthorized by any agreed-upon law.

Madison and others hoped ratification of the Articles would eliminate or reduce the ambiguity about the powers of Congress. And so it did, but in the wrong direction. Before ratification, Congress was like the British Parliament, guided not by a written constitution but by norms and precedents. Creative lawmakers could construe those precedents as they chose. Ratification of the Articles reduced this scope for maneuver, by specifying the powers of Congress. And the first of the substantive articles strictly forbade overstepping. "Each State retains its sovereignty, freedom, and independence, and every power, jurisdiction, and right, which is not by this confederation, expressly delegated to the United States, in Congress assembled," the article declared.

The seventh article described how money was to be raised. "All charges of war, and all other expenses that shall be incurred for the common defense or general welfare, and allowed by the United States in Congress assembled, shall be defrayed out of a common treasury, which shall be supplied by the several States in proportion to the value of all land within each State," the article said. "The taxes for paying that proportion shall be laid and levied by the authority and direction of the legislatures of the several States." Thus Congress would determine how much in taxes each state should pay, and then the states would collect the taxes and remit them to the central government.

Except that the states did *not* collect the taxes so determined. And the Articles provided no mechanism to make them do so.

Madison sought to repair this deficiency. He proposed employing force against deadbeat states. There was no other option, he told Jefferson. "The necessity of arming Congress with coercive powers arises from the shameful deficiency of some of the states which are most capable of yielding their apportioned supplies, and the military exactions to which others already exhausted by the enemy and our own troops are in consequence exposed," Madison said. "Without such powers too in the general government, the whole confederacy may be insulted and the most salutary measures frustrated by the most inconsiderable state in the Union." He cited an example: "At a time when all the other states were submitting to the loss and inconveniency of an embargo on their exports, Delaware absolutely declined coming into the measure, and not only defeated the general object of it, but enriched herself at the expence of those who did their duty."

What mode should the compulsion take? Nothing less than military force would suffice, Madison said. Tactically, troops would be easy to use. "As long as there is a regular army on foot, a small detachment from it, acting under civil authority, would at any time render a voluntary contribution of supplies due from a state an eligible alternative." And warships might blockade the coast. "The situation of most of the states is such that two or three vessels of force employed against their trade will make it their interest to yield prompt obedience to all just requisitions on them."

Moreover, a navy accustomed to enforcing revenue collection could be employed as a general peacekeeping force. "If a naval armament was considered as the proper instrument of general government, it would be both preserved in a respectable state in time of peace, and it would be an object to man it with citizens taken in due proportions from every state. A navy so formed and under the orders of the general council of the states would not only be a guard against aggression and insults from abroad, but without it what is to protect the southern states for many years to come against the insults and aggressions of their northern brethren?"

Madison proceeded to draft an amendment to the Articles of Confederation embodying his recommendation. His point of departure was the thirteenth and final article, which declared "Every State shall abide by the determination of the United States, in Congress assembled, on all questions which by this confederation are submitted to them. And the articles of this confederation shall be inviolably observed by every State." After a long whereas paragraph drawing attention to this injunction, Madison's amendment proposed that in the event any state or states failed to meet their obligations, "the said United States in Congress assembled are fully authorised to employ the force of the United States as well by sea as by land to compel such State or States to fulfill their federal engagements."

MADISON'S AMENDMENT fell dead from his pen. The thirteenth article required that any "alteration" in the Articles receive the consent of all the states, and there was no chance that states already resisting the requisition authority of Congress would give that body the power to coerce them by military means. Madison's timing was particularly bad. The fighting against the British was approaching a climax; at a moment when all ships and troops were required for that struggle, it was impossible to imagine any being diverted to operations against any of the *states*. And supposing the war ended in victory, the last thing Americans wanted to consider was the use of military force among themselves.

Not only did Congress not agree to Madison's amendment, it failed to agree to almost anything during this period. The Articles of Confederation were the stepchild of American politics, conceived in haste and nearly forgotten during the four years required for ratification. State politics were more important in most Americans' thinking. Often Congress had difficulty even gathering a quorum. The problem grew after the victory at Yorktown, which relieved the pressure on the states to act together in the common war effort.

The ambiguous language of the Articles contributed to the paralysis.

The ninth article specified that bills on big issues could not be approved "unless nine States assent to the same." This was straightforward: on important matters, a supermajority was required. The article went on to say "Nor shall a question on any other point, excepting for adjourning from day to day, be determined unless by a majority of the United States in Congress assembled." Did this mean a majority of the United States, namely seven states? Or did it mean a majority of those states present— "in Congress assembled"? If the former, then in those cases where some state delegations did not show up, the seven-state requirement became a supermajority requirement. And this could seriously hamper the business of Congress.

Which is indeed what happened. "As it is a rule observed since the Confederation was completed that seven votes are requisite in every question," Madison reported to Jefferson in November 1781, "and there are seldom more than 7, 8, 9 or 10 states present, even the opinion of a majority of Congress is a very different thing from a constitutional vote."

## 5

ALTHOUGH ALEXANDER HAMILTON was willing to forget about the army as a driver of reform of Congress, the army wasn't ready to forget about Hamilton and Congress. The legislature, seeing no reason to subsist soldiers who weren't fighting, debated whether to discharge them or furlough them. A discharge would be more definitive, but it might come to seem hasty if an eleventh-hour snag prevented approval of the final peace treaty and hostilities resumed. So Congress voted for furloughs, during which the troops would feed and house themselves, presumably at their homes.

But not all the troops *wanted* to be furloughed. In straits themselves, they liked being fed and housed by the government. And they suspected that Congress reasoned that once furloughed and dispersed, they would be less likely to renew pressure on Congress to be paid their arrears.

A band of soldiers stationed at Lancaster, Pennsylvania, sixty miles west of Philadelphia, took matters into their own hands. "A detachment of about eighty mutineers are on their way from Lancaster to this place," Hamilton wrote to William Jackson in June 1783. Hamilton was on the committee of Congress tasked with the issue of army pay, and Jackson was the assistant secretary of war. "You will please to proceed to meet them and to endeavour by every prudent method to engage them to return to the post they have left," Hamilton directed Jackson.

While Jackson was pondering where prudence lay in the matter, the mutineers approached Philadelphia in numbers swelling as they went. Congress grew alarmed and called for protection to the government of Pennsylvania, whose quarters—the Pennsylvania statehouse—it shared. James Madison was on the same committee as Hamilton, and he described the events. "The mutinous soldiers presented themselves, drawn up in the street before the State House where Congress had first assembled," Madison recorded. "The Executive Council of the State, sitting under the same roof, was called on for the proper interposition. President Dickinson"—John Dickinson, a drafter of the Articles of Confederation, now chief executive of Pennsylvania—"came in and explained the difficulty under actual circumstances of bringing out the militia of the place for the suppression of the mutiny. He thought that without some outrages on persons or property the temper of the militia could not be relied on." The Pennsylvania militia sympathized with the mutineers; Dickinson worried that if ordered to suppress the mutiny, the militiamen might join it instead.

Hamilton, Madison and the other members of Congress concluded that Continental Army soldiers would be needed to put down the rebellion. "General St. Clair"—Arthur St. Clair, who had served with Washington in the victory at Yorktown—"then in Philadelphia, was sent for, and desired to use his interposition in order to prevail on the troops to return to the barracks," Madison wrote. "His report gave no encouragement." St. Clair explained that there weren't sufficient numbers of loyal army troops nearby.

"In this posture of things it was proposed by Mr. Izard"—Ralph Izard, member of Congress from South Carolina—"that Congress should adjourn," Madison wrote. Izard didn't want Congress to become hostage to the mutineers.

Hamilton objected. "It was proposed by Mr. Hamilton that General St. Clair in concert with the Executive Council of State should take order for terminating the mutiny," Madison recorded. Hamilton's motion, like Izard's, failed to produce a consensus.

"It was finally agreed that Congress should remain till the usual hour of adjournment, but without taking any step in relation to the alleged grievances of the soldiers," Madison wrote. "In the meantime the soldiers remained in their position, without offering any violence, individuals only occasionally uttering offensive words and wantonly pointing their muskets to the windows of the hall of Congress." A tense calm ensued. "No danger from premeditated violence was apprehended," said Madison.

But the mood gradually changed. "It was observed that spirituous drink from the tippling houses adjoining began to be liberally served out to the soldiers, and might lead to hasty excesses," Madison observed. Madison and the others kept watch through the windows for such excesses. "None were committed, however, and about 3 o'clock, the usual hour, Congress adjourned; the soldiers, though in some instances offering a mock obstruction, permitting the members to pass through their ranks." The soldiers then left too.

After they were gone, the members of Congress reassembled in an emergency session. They authorized another attempt to get the Pennsylvania government to call out its militia to suppress the rebels. This yielded nothing new. "The conference with the Executive produced nothing but a repetition of doubts concerning the disposition of the militia to act, unless some actual outrage were offered to persons or property," Madison explained. "It was even doubted whether a repetition of the insult to Congress would be a sufficient provocation."

The mutineers got wind of the discussions at the statehouse. "Reports from the barracks were in constant vibration," Madison wrote. "At one moment the mutineers were penitent and preparing submissions; the next they were meditating more violent measures. Sometimes the bank"—where government funds were held—"was their object; then the seizure of the members of Congress with whom they imagined an indemnity for their offence might be stipulated."

Concluding that discretion was the better part of valor, Congress decided to flee. The members disbanded and left Philadelphia, to reconvene in friendlier New Jersey at Princeton.

The mutiny thereupon dissolved. Some of the leaders fled the country; others were court-martialed but later pardoned. Hamilton and Madison interpreted the incident as further evidence that Congress was woefully underpowered, that it might be intimidated and compelled to flee by the government's own soldiers. Hamilton excoriated the behavior of the Pennsylvania authorities, on whom Congress had been compelled to rely for security against the rebels. "The conduct of the executive of this state was to the last degree weak and disgusting," he wrote to New York's George Clinton. "They pretended it was out of their power to bring out the militia, without making the experiment. This feebleness on their part determined the removal of Congress from a place where they could receive no support, and I believe they will not easily be induced to return." With Congress looking for a new home, Hamilton hoped New York might make a bid. "I need not urge the advantages that will accrue to a state from being the residence of Congress," he told Clinton.

Madison agreed that the Pennsylvanians had acted poorly, but he didn't want to see Congress wind up in New York, or any place farther from Virginia than Philadelphia. "Congress remain at Princeton," he wrote to Edmund Randolph, a Virginia friend and ally, in early July. "Their removal from that place will soon become an interesting question." Princeton was too small and unimportant to serve as a permanent home for the government. Moreover, the alarm that had caused the members to flee had diminished. "Not a few maintain strenuously the policy of returning to this city"—Madison was writing from Philadelphia—"in order to obviate suspicions abroad of any disaffection in the mass of so important a state"—Pennsylvania—"to the federal government." Madison detected a change in sentiment among Philadelphians. "The citizens here in general regret the departure of Congress, disavow the idea that they were unwilling to take arms in defence of Congress, and will probably enter into some declaration tending to invite their return."

## 6

WHEREVER THE GOVERNMENT might finally land, Hamilton worked to ensure it would be a different institution when it got there. He took the embarrassment of the mutiny as occasion to draft a call for a convention to revise the Articles of Confederation. "The confederation of the United States is defective in the following essential points," he wrote:

"In confining the power of the federal government within too narrow limits. . . .

"In confounding legislative and executive powers in a single body. . . .

"In the want of a federal judicature having cognizance of all matters of general concern in the last resort. . . .

"In vesting the United States in Congress assembled with the *power of general taxation* . . . and yet rendering that power, so essential to the existence of the union, nugatory, by withholding from them all control over either the imposition or the collection of the taxes for raising the sums required. . . .

"In not making proper or competent provision for interior or exterior defence. . . .

"In not vesting in the United States a general superintendence of trade, equally necessary in the view of revenue and regulation. . . .

"In requiring the assent of *nine* states to matters of principal importance and of seven to all others."

Hamilton's indictment of the Articles of Confederation was in fact a great deal longer than these listed failings, and all were elaborated in excruciating detail. Several lengthy "whereas" paragraphs followed, culminating in the resolution "That it be earnestly recommended to the several states to appoint a convention to meet at ___ on the ___ day of ___ with full powers to revise the confederation and to adopt and propose such alterations as to them shall appear necessary to be finally approved or rejected by the states respectively."

Perhaps it was the length that put off his colleagues. Perhaps it was the comprehensiveness of Hamilton's condemnation, which suggested something more dramatic than mere "alteration" of the Articles. Likely, other delegates wanted to give the Articles a chance to operate in peacetime before junking them.

Whatever their reasons, the other members failed to rally, or even respond, to Hamilton's plan. "Resolution intended to be submitted to Congress at Princeton in 1783; but abandoned for want of support," he wrote on the copy of the draft.

AMID THE MUTINY in Pennsylvania, George Washington in New York was taking his farewell from the Continental Army and, he thought, his public career. "The great object for which I had the honor to hold an appointment in the service of my country being accomplished," the general wrote in a circular letter to the states, "I am now preparing to resign it into the hands of Congress and to return to that domestic retirement which it is well known I left with the greatest reluctance, a retirement for which I have never ceased to sigh through a long and painful absence, and in which, remote from the noise and trouble of the world, I meditate to pass the remainder of life in a state of undisturbed repose."

But before leaving, he had words for his countrymen. Americans should be proud of the independence they had won, and they should cherish the opportunity independence had given them to set an example to the world. "They are from this period to be considered as the actors on a most conspicuous theatre, which seems to be peculiarly designated by Providence for the display of human greatness and felicity," he said. "Here they are not only surrounded with everything which can contribute to the completion of private and domestic enjoyment, but

Heaven has crowned all its other blessings by giving a fairer opportunity for political happiness than any other nation has ever been favored with."

America's timing could not have been better. "The foundation of our empire was not laid in the gloomy age of ignorance and superstition, but at an epocha when the rights of mankind were better understood and more clearly defined than at any former period," Washington said. "The free cultivation of letters, the unbounded extension of commerce, the progressive refinement of manners, the growing liberality of sentiment, and, above all, the pure and benign light of revelation, have had a meliorating influence on mankind and increased the blessings of society. At this auspicious period the United States came into existence as a nation, and if their citizens should not be completely free and happy, the fault will be entirely their own."

The outcome of the Americans' experiment was still pending. "It is in their choice and depends upon their conduct whether they will be respectable and prosperous or contemptible and miserable as a nation," Washington said. "This is the time of their political probation; this is the moment when the eyes of the whole world are turned upon them. This is the moment to establish or ruin their national character forever." Together Americans had won the war; divided they might lose the peace. "This is the favorable moment to give such a tone to our federal government as will enable it to answer the ends of its institution; or this may be the ill-fated moment for relaxing the powers of the Union, annihilating the cement of the Confederation and exposing us to become the sport of European politics, which may play one state against another." The war was won, but the meaning of the revolution remained to be determined. "According to the system of policy the states shall adopt at this moment, they will stand or fall, and by their confirmation or lapse, it is yet to be decided whether the revolution must ultimately be considered as a blessing or a curse."

## 7

DANIEL SHAYS HAD some thoughts on the meaning of the revolution, and these days he was as inclined to account it a curse as a blessing. The son of Irish immigrants to Massachusetts, Shays had been part of the Massachusetts militia that mustered in response to the first fighting in the American Revolution, at Lexington and Concord. He took part in the battle of Bunker Hill and later helped capture Ticonderoga from the British. He rose to the rank of captain. Yet like many other soldiers he didn't get paid what he had been promised, in his case by the state government of Massachusetts. Where many of his comrades in similar circumstances mutinied or threatened to, Shays simply resigned, hoping he could support his family better as a farmer than he had been able to do as a soldier.

He discovered he couldn't. The war and its outcome unsettled the economy of western Massachusetts, where Shays lived. The farmers of the western part of the state had long felt put upon by the merchants and city folk of Boston; Boston was the capital of the state, and the merchants were the dominant interest group in state politics. The merchants themselves suffered from the war and peace, as their principal connections had been to Britain and the British West Indies. The war sundered this trade, and the peace treaty failed to restore it. Yet the treaty had not relieved the merchants of their debts to British creditors, despite effectively depriving them of the means to repay those debts. The merchants might simply have refused to pay the British, but they continued to hope for a resumption of their British trade and tried to act like model trading partners. At a loss for ways to balance their books, they squeezed their own debtors, including the western farmers. And they prevailed upon the state to keep the western debtors from delaying or blocking their efforts to collect.

The westerners grew increasingly frustrated. Starting in 1782 they threatened government agents with the sort of violence inflicted on the British officials who had tried to collect the taxes imposed by the Stamp Act, the infamous measure that lit the fuse for the Revolutionary War. In 1783 they forcibly prevented the sale-for-debt of properties of defaulting farmers. Many of the protesters were veterans of the war and familiar with arms, which they brandished menacingly. Governor John Hancock, the lead signer of the Declaration of Independence, was reluctant to use force against the protesters, but the merchants and most law-abiding citizens of Massachusetts demanded he do something to see that state laws were enforced. Hancock chose instead to resign in early 1785, leaving the problem to his successor, James Bowdoin.

By this time Daniel Shays was being cited as the leader of the rebellion, though he modestly shared the honor—and presumably the liability—with his comrades. And the rebels' numbers, while hard to pin down, mounted to the thousands. Bowdoin felt obliged to answer force with force, and raised an army of his own, of three thousand, commanded by General Benjamin Lincoln, a Revolutionary War veteran.

George Washington had commanded Lincoln, and the two had remained in touch after the war. The troubles in Massachusetts distressed Washington greatly. "Are your people getting mad?" he wrote to Lincoln, meaning insane. "Are we to have the goodly fabric that eight years were spent in rearing, pulled over our heads? What is the cause of all these commotions? When and how is it to end?"

Lincoln was delayed in answering Washington's letter by the very commotion he was tasked with ending. His response, drafted at free moments in the campaign against the rebels, made a sobering read for Washington. The question whether the people of Massachusetts were going mad deserved a direct reply. "Many of them appear to be absolutely so, if an attempt to annihilate our present constitution and dissolve the present government can be considered as evidences of insanity," Lincoln wrote. Was the fabric of government being pulled over the heads of the law-abiding? "There is great danger that it will be so," he said. "For there doth not appear to be virtue enough among the people to preserve a perfect republican government."

What had caused the commotions? "The causes are too many and too various for me to pretend to trace and point them out," Lincoln told Washington. But he would describe the most important. "Among those I may rank the ease with which property was acquired, with which credit was obtained, and debts were discharged in the time of the war. Hence people were diverted from their usual industry and economy. A luxuriant mode of living crept into vogue, and soon that income by which the expences of all should as much as possible be limited was no longer considered as having anything to do with the question at what expence families ought to live, or rather which they ought not to have exceeded." In other words, people had begun to live beyond their means. But they couldn't do so forever. "The day arrived when all discovered that things were fast returning back into their original channels, that the industrious were to reap the fruits of their industry, and that the indolent and improvident would soon experience the evils of their idleness and sloth. Very many startled at the idea, and instead of attempting to subject themselves to such a line of conduct which duty to the public and a regard to their own happiness evidently pointed out, they contemplated how they should evade the necessity of reforming their system and of changing their present mode of life."

They implored the government to rescue them, Lincoln told Washington. "County conventions were formed and the cry for paper money, subject to depreciation, as was declared by some of their public resolves, was the clamour of the day." They appealed to the Massachusetts legislature, called the General Court, for a tax holiday and a moratorium on foreclosures. The General Court refused. "Failing of their point, the disaffected in the first place attempted, and in many instances succeeded, to stop the courts of law and to suspend the operations of government," Lincoln wrote. "This they hoped to do until they could by force sap the foundations of our constitution and bring into the legislature creatures of their own, by which they could mold a government at pleasure and make it subservient to all their purposes."

Washington doubtless read Lincoln's version as reflecting the views of someone unsympathetic to the insurgents. But since he shared Lincoln's outlook, he saw no reason to dispute it.

He was at least as interested in Lincoln's account of the military campaign against the rebels. "We commenced our march in the morning of the 20th"—of January 1787—"for Worcester, where the court of common pleas, and court of the general session of the peace were to set on the 23d, which courts we were ordered to protect," Lincoln wrote. The government army arrived in time; the courts opened on schedule and completed their business without incident.

Yet Shays remained at large. "Shays did not point his force to any object until the 24th," Lincoln said. "Then he took a post from which he could suddenly strike the public magazine"—the arsenal at Springfield—"which seemed to be his object." Lincoln anticipated him and blocked the route. "He came on in open column, was repeatedly warned of his danger by General Shepard"—William Shepard, a Revolutionary War veteran who was now Lincoln's second in command— "and finally if he progressed in any degree farther he would fire upon him. He moved, and the general fired over him, hoping to deter him from proceeding, but to no effect." Shepard then fired two artillery pieces into the rebel column. "By these shots three men were killed and a number wounded," Lincoln said. "His people were thrown into the utmost confusion, and dispersed for a time, but soon collected as they were not followed by General Shepard, who could have destroyed a great proportion of them had he been disposed to do it." Lincoln wanted Washington to know that he had treated the rebels with as much forbearance as their misconduct allowed.

The dispersal of the rebels was far from a defeat. They soon regrouped. "Part of them were on the east and part on the west side of the Connecticut River," Lincoln told Washington. Shays commanded the contingent on the east bank; Luke Day, another veteran of the Revolutionary War, commanded the west bank. "Shays had placed his guards on the east bank of the river so that they had cut off all communication to the town of Springfield from the north and the west in the common routes. It was with the greatest difficulty that new ones could be formed as the snow was very deep." Yet the winter opened another route. "I moved up the river on the ice," Lincoln explained. Lincoln's army prevented a joining of the Shays and Day wings of the rebel force, leaving Lincoln in a dominant position.

He thereupon sent Shays a surrender demand under a flag of truce. "Whether you are convinced or not of your error in flying to arms, I am fully persuaded that before this hour you have the fullest conviction on your own mind that you are not able to execute your original purposes," Lincoln declared to Shays, referring to the attempt to seize the arsenal. "Your resources are few, your force is inconsiderable and hourly decreasing from the disaffection of your men. You are in a post where you have neither cover nor supplies, and in a situation in which you can neither give aid to your friends nor discomfort to the supporters of good order and government. Under these circumstances, you cannot hesitate a moment to disband your deluded followers." The alternative would be swift and decisive. "If you should not, I must approach and apprehend the most influential characters among you. Should you attempt to fire upon the troops of government, the consequences might be fatal to many of your men."

Shays played for time. "We are sensible of the embarrassments the people are under," he replied, employing "people" as a synonym for his popular army. The "embarrassments" were the military disadvantages Lincoln had alluded to. "But that virtue which truly characterises the citizens of a republican government hath hitherto marked our paths with a degree of innocence, and we wish and trust it will still be the case."

He made a counteroffer. "The people are willing to lay down their arms on the condition of a general pardon, and return to their respective homes, as they are unwilling to stain the land which we in the late war purchased at so dear a rate with the blood of our brethren and neighbours," Shays said. "Therefore we pray that hostilities may cease on your part until our united prayers may be presented to the General Court and we receive an answer." A messenger had already been sent to Boston for this purpose. "If this request may be complied with, government shall meet with no interruption from the people. But let each army occupy the posts where they now are."

Lincoln answered curtly: "Your request is totally inadmissible, as no powers are delegated to me which would justify a delay of my operations." The rebels must disband at once. Otherwise Lincoln would attack.

Awaiting Shays's response to this renewed demand, Lincoln informed Governor Bowdoin of the exchange and warned that the situation would grow worse if he—Lincoln—failed to press his current advantage. "He is receiving daily supplies of provisions and some few recruits," Lincoln said of Shays. "Shays and his abettors must be treated as open enemies," he said. "The sooner it is done, the better, for if we drive him from one strong post, he flies to another. In these movements he could not be supported if he was not comforted by the many disaffected in the counties."

Shays refused Lincoln's demand once more. Instead he silently led his army away from Springfield in the direction of Petersham. Lincoln learned of the movement on the evening of February 3, and he ordered his men to follow at once. "The first part of the night was pleasant, and the weather clement," he reported to Washington. "But between two and three o'clock in the morning, the wind shifting to the westward, it became very cold and squally, with considerable snow." The marching grew harder as the snow deepened. Lincoln would have let the men seek shelter, but there was none in the vicinity. "Under these circumstances they were obliged to continue their march. We reached Petersham about 9 o'clock in the morning exceedingly fatigued with a march of thirty miles, part of it in a deep snow and in a most violent storm. When this abated, the cold increased and a great proportion of our men were frozen in some part or other."

Yet the swiftness of the march paid off. "We approached nearly the centre of the town, where Shays had covered his men, and had we not been prevented from the steepness of a large hill at our entrance and the depth of the snow from throwing our men rapidly into it we should have arrested very probably one half this force," Lincoln told Washington. "They were so surprised as it was that they had not time to call in their out-parties or even their guards. About 150 fell into our hands, and none escaped but by the most precipitate flight in different directions."

Lincoln was pleased to report that this stroke had broken the back of the insurgency. "The spirit of rebellion is now nearly crushed in this state, and the opposition to government is hourly decreasing," he told Washington. Henceforth it would be up to the courts to deal with the leaders of the rebellion, could they be found, and for the legislature to take measures to make sure it didn't happen again.

WASHINGTON WAS DELIGHTED to hear of the outcome of the campaign. "The suppression of those tumults and insurrections with so little bloodshed is an event as happy as it was unexpected," he replied to Lincoln.

Yet he was shaken by the whole affair. "Good God!" he wrote to Henry Knox, currently the war secretary for the Confederation government. "Who besides a tory could have foreseen or a Briton predicted them! Were these people wiser than others, or did they judge of us from the corruption and depravity of their own hearts?"

Washington was profoundly disappointed in his compatriots, that their actions and omissions had brought the country to such a pass. "If three years ago, any person had told me that at this day I should see such a formidable rebellion against the laws and constitutions of our own making as now appears, I should have thought him a bedlamite—a fit subject for a madhouse," he told Knox while the outcome in Massachusetts still pended. Washington wondered if everything he and other Americans had fought for was being lost. "Our affairs, generally, seem really to be approaching to some awful crisis. God only knows what the result will be."

8

WHAT WASHINGTON DEEMED an awful crisis, Alexander Hamilton accounted an opportunity. Some of the difference was temperamental. Washington preferred calm, while Hamilton thrived on uproar, to the extent of creating his own when circumstances didn't provide enough. But some reflected the different arcs of their careers. Washington expected that his days of great accomplishment were over; he currently enjoyed all the esteem his ego desired. Hamilton's career had hardly started, his egotism was far from sated, and every crack in the status quo afforded an avenue he might exploit to advance himself.

The Massachusetts troubles had just started when Hamilton retired from Congress to pursue his legal career. His 1780 marriage to Elizabeth Schuyler, of the wealthy and distinguished Schuyler family of New York state, afforded Hamilton entrée to the circles of power in New York; it shortly made him responsible for a growing family. As much as he relished politics, he required money, and the practice of law promised to provide it. He took from his time in public office a knowledge of his gifts in that area and the wishes of his admirers that he one day return. "The homilies you delivered in Congress are still recollected with pleasure," wrote James McHenry of Maryland. "The impressions they made are in favor of your integrity, and no one but believes you a man of honor and republican principles. Were you ten years older and twenty thousand pounds richer, there is no doubt but that you might obtain the suffrages of Congress for the highest office in their gift."

This was heady stuff for the kid from the Caribbean, and while Hamilton couldn't make the years turn faster, he began working on the twenty thousand pounds. He helped clients collect debts owed them from the war and in the process collected substantial fees. Some of the clients had ties to Britain, being Loyalists or British merchants, and hence were unpopular with many New Yorkers. But Hamilton took the position that a debt was a debt and must be repaid. He went deeper into finance by organizing a group that created the Bank of New York, the second bank in America and the first outside Philadelphia. He kept in touch with comrades from the war through the Society of the Cincinnati, an organization of officer veterans who relived the old days even as they sparked suspicions among the democratically minded about exclusive societies and the role of the military in a republic.

And when the troubles in Massachusetts caused alarmed observers in several states to consider more seriously a stronger central government, Hamilton reentered the political arena. In Massachusetts the Shays rebellion suggested that the states needed help in maintaining law and order; elsewhere matters of commerce—of trade disputes between states, and between America and Britain—pressed to the fore. Virginia and Maryland in 1785 sent delegates to a meeting at Washington's Mount Vernon to resolve disputes over the Potomac River and the Chesapeake Bay; the modest success of this meeting prompted the Virginia legislature to propose a convention of all the states to talk about trade and related issues. Other states sent approving responses, and the meeting was scheduled for Annapolis in September 1786. Hamilton accepted appointment as one of New York's delegates.

JAMES MADISON WASN'T particularly optimistic about the Annapolis meeting. He had rejoined the Virginia General Assembly after leaving Congress in 1783 and devoted himself to the affairs of his home state. His greatest contribution was his support for a bill, drafted by Thomas Jefferson, to guarantee religious freedom for Virginians.

Madison kept up on efforts to reform the national government, and he agreed to be part of Virginia's delegation to the Annapolis meeting. But the failure of previous attempts, including his own, to reform the national government had left him disillusioned. "I am far from entertaining sanguine expectations from it," he said of the Annapolis convention. Yet he was willing to make another try. "I cannot disapprove of the experiment." The turmoil in Massachusetts made clear that something had to be done. "And if anything can be done, it seems as likely to result from the proposed convention, and more likely to result from the present crisis, than from any other mode or time."

HE WAS RIGHT to be pessimistic. The Annapolis convention proved a bust. Four states wanted nothing to do with it. Four states appointed delegates who failed to reach Annapolis. The remaining five states—Virginia, New York, Pennsylvania, New Jersey and Delaware—were represented by a total of twelve delegates.

Hamilton and Madison renewed the acquaintance they had made in Congress, and they and the other ten required little time to conclude that anything of substance proposed by this gathering would make a laughingstock of them and the idea of reform.

They quickly pivoted, treating the current meeting as merely organizational for a larger meeting to follow. Hamilton drafted a statement of impressive length embellishing the Annapolis proceeding as being, by the mere fact of its occurrence, an important first step toward reform, and inviting the thirteen states to send delegates to a convention in Philadelphia the following May "to take into consideration the situation of the United States, to devise such further provisions as shall appear to them necessary to render the constitution of the Federal Government adequate to the exigencies of the Union, and to report such an act for that purpose to the United States in Congress assembled as when agreed to by them, and afterwards confirmed by the legislatures of every state, will effectually provide for the same."

PART III

Conspiracy at Philadelphia

## 9

T HE APPOINTMENTS FOR the convention go on auspiciously," Madison wrote to Thomas Jefferson in Paris in March 1787. Jefferson was the American minister to France. "Since my last, Georgia, South Carolina, New York, Massachusetts and New Hampshire have come into the measure." Somewhat to Madison's surprise, the dismal showing at Annapolis hadn't discredited the movement for reform; the pivot appeared to have succeeded. The states were falling into line; even Congress, which hadn't agreed on much lately, gave its approval to the Philadelphia convention, albeit with the understanding that the convention was being held "for the sole and express purpose of revising the Articles of Confederation."

Gathering the states and their delegations was just the start. "What may be the result of this political experiment cannot be foreseen," Madison continued. "The difficulties which present themselves are on one side almost sufficient to dismay the most sanguine, whilst on the other side the most timid are compelled to encounter them by the mortal diseases of the existing constitution." Jefferson had read the papers and reports from America; Madison saw no need to recite the maladies in detail. "Suffice it to say that they are at present marked by symptoms which are truly alarming, which have tainted the faith of the most orthodox republicans, and which challenge from the votaries of liberty every concession in favor of stable government not infringing fundamental principles, as the only security against an opposite extreme of our present situation." In other words, things had gotten so bad that there was finally a chance to make them better.

Madison sketched the changes he desired. "It will be expedient in the first place to lay the foundation of the new system in such a ratification by the people themselves of the several states as will render it clearly paramount to their legislative authorities." Madison intended to usurp the authority of state legislatures; in the enterprise he planned he couldn't expect the legislatures' cooperation. But he *could* hope for the support of the people of the states, who would be asked to ratify the new charter the Philadelphia convention would produce.

As to what that charter would entail, Madison began with a definitive assertion of national supremacy. "Over and above the positive power of regulating trade and sundry other matters in which uniformity is proper," he said, referring to the announced agenda of the convention, he added an objective that was decidedly *not* on the agenda: "to arm the federal head with a negative in all cases whatsoever on the local legislatures." Madison's "negative" was a veto akin to what the British Crown had exercised over laws passed by American provincial assemblies. Just as the royal governors had disallowed provincial laws thought to infringe on the prerogatives of the empire, so Madison's national government would disallow state laws that jeopardized the national interest.

By this one provision, state sovereignty would be destroyed. The states would become the creatures of the national government. Madison justified his audacity as made necessary by the peril the country faced. "Without this defensive power, experience and reflection have satisfied me that however ample the federal powers may be made, or however clearly their boundaries may be delineated on paper, they will be easily and continually baffled by the legislative sovereignties of the states." Madison's priority was the national good, yet he thought the states would come to thank him. "The effects of this provision would be not only to guard the national rights and interests against invasion but also to restrain the states from thwarting and molesting each other, and even from oppressing the minority within themselves by paper money and other unrighteous measures which favor the interest of the majority."

Stealing sovereignty from the state legislatures would undercut the justification for the one-state, one-vote principle of the Articles of Confederation and would allow—even compel—a shift to proportional representation in the new government. The big states would gain power while the small states would lose it. This change was only right, Madison judged; otherwise Delaware would continue to wield as much power as his and Jefferson's Virginia. The change was also practicable. "A majority of the states conceive that they will be gainers by it. It is recommended to the eastern states by the actual superiority of their populousness, and to the southern by their expected superiority. And if a majority of the larger states concur, the fewer and smaller states must finally bend to them."

TO EDMUND RANDOLPH, now the Virginia governor, who would join him on the state's delegation, Madison was more explicit. "I am glad to find that you are turning your thoughts towards the business of May next," he wrote to Randolph in April. "My despair of your finding the necessary leisure as signified in one of your letters, with the probability that some leading propositions at least would be expected from Virginia, had engaged me in a closer attention to the subject than I should otherwise have given. I will just hint the ideas which have occurred, leaving explanations for our interview."

Randolph had shown himself to be more conservative than Madison, and so Madison approached him conservatively. "I think with you that it will be well to retain as much as possible of the old Confederation," he said, before adding "though I doubt whether it may not be best to work the valuable articles into the new system, instead of engrafting the latter on the former." Madison thought the approach of merely amending the Articles would defeat itself. "An explanatory address must of necessity accompany the result of the convention on the main object. I am not sure that it will be practicable to present the several parts of the reform in so detached a manner to the states as that a partial adoption will be binding. Particular states may view the different articles as conditions of each other, and would only ratify them as such. Others might ratify them as independent propositions. The consequence would be that the ratification of both would go for nothing." Madison said he needed to think the matter through more thoroughly. But he was already convinced that a whole new charter was needed; amendments would never suffice. "My ideas of a reform strike so deeply at the old Confederation, and lead to such a systematic change, that they scarcely admit of the expedient."

To wit: "I hold it for a fundamental point that an individual independence of the states is utterly irreconcilable with the idea of an aggregate sovereignty." Yet the states couldn't and shouldn't be made to disappear, Madison said. "A consolidation of the states into one simple republic is not less unattainable than it would be inexpedient." Attachments to the states were too stubborn, and America was too large. "Let it be tried then whether any middle ground can be taken which will at once support a due supremacy of the national authority, and leave in force the local authorities so far as they can be subordinately useful."

Under a system of aggregate—or national—sovereignty, proportional representation would be essential, Madison said. "According to the present form of the Union, an equality of suffrage, if not just towards the larger members of it, is at least safe to them, as the liberty they exercise of rejecting or executing the acts of Congress, is uncontrollable by the nominal sovereignty of Congress." That is, the big states could simply ignore Congress when they felt their interests slighted. Not so in the new system Madison envisioned. "Under a system which would operate without the intervention of the states, the case would be materially altered. A vote from Delaware would have the same effect as one from Massachusetts or Virginia." This in contrast to conditions under the Articles, where each Delaware voter had much greater influence than each Virginian.

Madison was even more emphatic than before that the national legislature must possess the right to disallow state laws. "Let it have a negative in all cases whatsoever on the legislative acts of the states as the king of Great Britain heretofore had," he told Randolph. "This I conceive to be essential." Nothing less would do. "Without such a defensive power, every positive power that can be given on paper will be unavailing."

Madison would bolster the legislative supremacy of the national government with a judiciary independent of the states. "Let this national supremacy be extended also to the judiciary department," he said. "If the judges in the last resort depend on the states and are bound by their oaths to them and not to the Union, the intention of the law and the interests of the nation may be defeated by the obsequiousness of the tribunals to the policy or prejudices of the states."

Madison revealed to Randolph how far he had thought through his ideal scheme. "A government formed of such extensive powers ought to be well organized," he wrote. "The legislative department may be divided into two branches: One of them to be chosen every ___ years by the legislatures or the people at large, the other to consist of a more select number, holding their appointments for a longer term and going out in rotation. Perhaps the negative on the state laws may be most conveniently lodged in this branch."

"A national executive will also be necessary," Madison continued. He had no fixed opinions on the executive; he would defer to the convention.

"An article ought to be inserted expressly guarantying the tranquility of the states against internal as well as external dangers," he said. This was perhaps his boldest assertion so far, granting the national government a police power over the states even in their simply domestic affairs.

Ratification, as Madison had said to Jefferson, ought to circumvent the state legislatures, which would never agree to their own demise. "To give the new system its proper energy it will be desirable to have it ratified by the authority of the people," he told Randolph.

Madison admitted he was thinking big. "I am afraid you will think this project, if not extravagant, absolutely unattainable and unworthy of being attempted," he wrote. Yet he couldn't in conscience ask less—"conceiving it myself to go no further than is essential." Madison acknowledged the practical difficulties of getting the convention to agree to his scheme, even as he minimized those difficulties. "They may be less formidable on trial than in contemplation. The change in the principle of representation will be relished by a majority of the states, and those too of most influence." He reiterated his argument that large states would find proportional representation immediately appealing, while the growing states would find it prospectively so. And the stagnant small states would have no choice but to go along.

As Madison read the portents, public opinion was moving in the direction the country needed to go. Time was of the essence. "Unless the Union be organized efficiently on republican principles, innovations of a much more objectionable form may be obtruded," he said to Randolph. "Or in the most favorable event, the partition of the empire"—the United States—"into rival and hostile confederacies will ensue."

.    .    .

GEORGE WASHINGTON HAD to be courted by different means. The retired general had not committed to attending the Philadelphia convention, but he seemed interested. Madison recognized that Washington's participation would add irreplaceable legitimacy to the undertaking, and he did everything he could to bring him aboard.

"Dear sir," Madison wrote to Washington in mid-April. "I have been honoured with your letter of the 31 of March, and find with much pleasure that your views of the reform which ought to be pursued by the convention give a sanction to those which I have entertained." Madison knew how Washington had bridled under state meddling during the Revolutionary War, and so he stressed the need for national supremacy in a new government. "A negative *in all cases whatsoever* on the legislative acts of the states, as heretofore exercised by the kingly prerogative, appears to me to be absolutely necessary, and to be the least possible encroachment on the state jurisdictions," Madison said. "Without this defensive power, every positive power that can be given on paper will be evaded and defeated. The states will continue to invade the national jurisdiction, to violate treaties and the law of nations, and to harass each other with rival and spiteful measures dictated by mistaken views of interest."

Madison appreciated that Washington was skeptical of democracy—of the ability of the people to make good laws without the firm guidance of their betters. "Another happy effect of this prerogative would be its control on the internal vicissitudes of state policy and the aggressions of interested majorities on the rights of minorities and of individuals," Madison wrote of the national veto on state laws. "The great desideratum which has not yet been found for republican governments seems to be some disinterested and dispassionate umpire in disputes between different passions and interests in the state." The new national government would be that umpire.

Madison knew Washington wasn't averse to the employment of force when appropriate. "The right of coercion should be expressly declared," Madison wrote. "With the resources of commerce in hand, the national administration might always find means of exerting it either by sea or land."

Yet Madison understood that Washington wasn't trigger-happy. The national negative of state laws could make the resort to force rare, he assured the general.

## 10

M R. MADISON IS a character who has long been in public life," wrote William Pierce after encountering Madison in Philadelphia. Pierce was a Virginian by birth and a veteran of the Revolutionary War. Following the war he moved to Georgia, where his new neighbors selected him to represent them at the Philadelphia convention. "And what is very remarkable, every person seems to acknowledge his greatness," Pierce continued regarding Madison. "He blends together the profound politician with the scholar. In the management of every great question he evidently took the lead in the convention, and though he cannot be called an orator, he is a most agreeable, eloquent and convincing speaker. From a spirit of industry and application which he possesses in a most eminent degree, he always comes forward the best-informed man of any point in debate. The affairs of the United States, he perhaps has the most correct knowledge of, of any man in the Union. He has been twice a member of Congress, and was always thought one of the ablest members that ever sat in that council. Mr. Madison is about 37 years of age, a gentleman of great modesty, with a remarkable sweet temper. He is easy and unreserved among his acquaintance, and has a most agreeable style of conversation."

Madison's agreeableness was put to the test at the outset of the convention. He arrived in Philadelphia comfortably ahead of the announced start, planning to greet the other delegates as they appeared. But they did not appear, at least not in sufficient numbers to launch the meeting on time. "Monday last was the day for the meeting of the convention," Madison wrote to Jefferson on Tuesday, May 15. "The number as yet assembled is but small." Rainy weather had muddied the roads in the north and slowed travel to Philadelphia; Madison hoped this was the cause of the delay and not last-minute cold feet. He didn't think his project could stand another Annapolis-style flop.

He took heart from those who *had* appeared. "Among the few is General Washington, who arrived on Sunday evening amidst the accla-mations of the people, as well as more sober marks of the affection and veneration which continues to be felt for his character," Madison told Jefferson. Washington's participation eased Madison's mind enor-mously. Had the great man held aloof, the project would have been crippled from the start. Others of the Virginia delegation had arrived too or were expected shortly. "The governor"—Randolph—"Messrs. Wythe and Blair, and Dr. McClurg are also here. Col. Mason is to be here in a day or two." Madison was guardedly hopeful. "There is a prospect of a pretty full meeting on the whole, though there is less punctuality in the outset than was to be wished."

Madison employed the delay to his advantage. He gathered with the Virginia delegation and some friendly Pennsylvanians to coordinate the campaign of the large states in favor of the plan he had devised. They agreed that Randolph should present the plan to the convention at first opportunity, to seize the initiative and set the tone of the debate.

Their efforts didn't pass unnoticed. Delaware, as the smallest of the states and the one with the most to lose, sent five delegates, a number exceeded only by Virginia and Pennsylvania. George Read was one of the Delaware men, and he kept his eyes and ears open against whatever might harm his state. "I am in possession of a copied draft of a fed-eral system intended to be proposed, if something nearly similar shall not precede it," he wrote to John Dickinson, who likewise represented Delaware and was one of those delayed in the mud. What most caught his attention was the reconfiguration of the legislature, to be chosen according to population. This would have a devastating effect on Dela-ware's ability to defend its interests. "By this plan our state may have a representation in the house of delegates of one member in eighty"—as opposed to the current one in thirteen. The small states must stick together, Read said. "Their deputies should keep a strict watch upon the movements and propositions from the larger states, who will prob-ably combine to swallow up the smaller ones by addition, division, or impoverishment." And Dickinson had better hurry. "If you have any wish to assist in guarding against such attempts, you will be speedy in your attendance."

WHILE MADISON AND the Virginians plotted their offensive, and Read and the small-state delegates prepared their defenses, Benjamin Franklin played host. After Washington, Franklin was the celebrity of the convention, but age—eighty-one—and infirmity precluded a leading role for him in the deliberations. Yet Franklin's newly built home was only a few blocks from the Pennsylvania statehouse, where the convention was held, and he took the opportunity of the delay to throw a dinner party for the delegates who had arrived. A friend had sent Franklin a cask of porter; Franklin replied with thanks and a description of how he had put the cask to use. "We have here at present what the French call *une assemblée des notables*—a convention composed of some of the principal people from the several states of our confederation. They did me the honor of dining with me last Wednesday, when the cask was broached, and its contents met with the most cordial reception and universal approbation. In short, the company agreed unanimously, that it was the best porter they had ever tasted."

Washington enjoyed the porter with everyone else, but he found the waiting irksome. When he was a young man trying to impress the world, Washington had learned punctuality, and ever afterward he accounted tardiness a character flaw. "I have yielded to what appeared to be the wishes of many of my friends, and am now here as a delegate to the convention," Washington wrote to Arthur Lee, a fellow Virginian and a diplomat during the Revolutionary War, on May 20. "Not more than four states were represented yesterday. If any have come in since, it is unknown to me. These delays greatly impede public measures, and serve to sour the temper of the punctual members, who do not like to idle away their time."

FINALLY ON MAY 25, eleven days late, a quorum was achieved and the convention commenced. Washington was nominated for presiding officer, and the nomination was immediately seconded. "General Washington was accordingly unanimously elected by ballot and conducted to the chair," Madison wrote in a journal he began keeping. "In a very emphatic manner he thanked the convention for the honor they had conferred on him, reminded them of the novelty of the scene of business in which he was to act, lamented his want of better qualifications, and claimed the indulgence of the house towards the involuntary errors which his inexperience might occasion."

The delegates were introduced and their credentials read. Robert Yates of New York, who kept a journal of his own, added a note regarding the credentials of the delegates from the smallest state: "Delaware restrained its delegates from assenting to an abolition of the fifth article of the confederation, by which it is declared that each state shall have one vote." George Read and his colleagues thereby launched a preemptive counterattack against Virginia.

It didn't work. "Governor Randolph opened the business of the convention," James McHenry, a Maryland delegate, recorded the next day. "He observed that the confederation fulfilled none of the objects for which it was framed. 1st. It does not provide against foreign invasions. 2dly. It does not secure harmony to the states. 3d. It is incapable of producing certain blessings to the states. 4th. It cannot defend itself against encroachments. 5th. It is not superior to state constitutions."

Randolph elaborated on these deficiencies in the terms Madison had outlined earlier. The governor then offered an alternative to the Articles of Confederation; this too followed Madison's plan. The points that attracted the immediate attention of all the delegates specified a bicameral legislature, with the numbers in each house proportioned to either the free populations of the various states or their quotas of contribution to the national treasury. The latter was understood to be a proxy for the wealth of the states. The members of the first house would be elected directly by the people of the states; the members of the second house would be chosen by the first house. The national legislature would have the authority to veto state laws and to employ military force against defiant states. The national executive would be chosen by the legislature. The national judiciary would likewise be chosen by the legislature.

To the delegates unaware of what Madison and the Virginians had been plotting, Randolph's proposal came as a jolt. The governor admitted the sweep of the plan. "He candidly confessed that they were not intended for a federal government," Robert Yates paraphrased. "He meant a strong consolidated union, in which the idea of states should be nearly annihilated."

Shocking though the Virginia plan was, it provided the basis of debate for the first weeks of the convention. This was precisely as Madison intended. The day after the delegates heard the plan, they voted to reconfigure the convention into a committee of the whole, a procedure that loosened parliamentary rules and fostered freer discussion. Each day George Washington would call the convention to order and then would relinquish his seat to Nathaniel Gorham of Massachusetts, the chairman of the committee.

Yet Washington relinquished nothing of his authority. At the outset the convention agreed that their deliberations would be kept secret from those on the outside. Like the shift to the committee of the whole, the ban on airing the proceedings would promote franker debate. Madison especially endorsed the ban; he didn't want the opponents of his intended overthrow of the existing government to set a backfire in the country at large before the new constitution was completed. Washington agreed and became the enforcer of the ban.

William Pierce explained how this played out. "When the convention first opened at Philadelphia, there were a number of propositions brought forward as great leading principles for the new government to be established for the United States," Pierce recalled of the introduction of the Virginia plan. "A copy of these propositions was given to each member with the injunction to keep everything a profound secret. One morning, by accident, one of the members dropt his copy of the propositions, which being luckily picked up by General Mifflin was presented to General Washington, our president, who put it in his pocket. After the debates of the day were over, and the question for adjournment was called for, the general"—Washington—"arose from his seat, and previous to his putting the question addressed the convention in the following manner: 'Gentlemen, I am sorry to find that some one member of this body has been so neglectful of the secrets of the convention as to drop in the statehouse a copy of their proceedings, which by accident was picked up and delivered to me this morning. I must entreat gentlemen to be more careful, lest our transactions get into the newspapers and disturb the public repose by premature speculations. I know not whose paper it is, but there it is' (throwing it down on the table). 'Let him who owns it take it.'"

"At the same time he bowed, picked up his hat, and quitted the room with a dignity so severe that every person seemed alarmed," Pierce wrote. "For my part I was extremely so, for putting my hand in my pocket I missed my copy of the same paper. But advancing up to the table my fears soon dissipated. I found it to be the hand writing of another person. When I went to my lodgings at the Indian Queen"—an inn where many of the delegates stayed during the convention—"I found my copy in a coat pocket which I had pulled off that morning. It is something remarkable that no person ever owned the paper."

## II

THE DEBATE OVER the Virginia plan laid bare the issue at the heart of the convention. Were the delegates trying to reform the existing government, or did they intend to destroy that government and replace it with a new one?

South Carolinians liked Charles Pinckney so much they sent two of him to represent their state in Philadelphia. The elder Charles (Cotesworth) Pinckney was forty-one and an officer veteran of the Revolutionary War; the convention delegates referred to him as General Pinckney. The younger Charles Pinckney was twenty-nine and a cousin of the general; he was Mr. Pinckney.

The two challenged Edmund Randolph regarding the Virginia plan. "Mr. Charles Pinckney wished to know of Mr. Randolph whether he meant to abolish the state governments altogether," recorded Madison. After Randolph dodged the question, the elder Pinckney took the floor. "General Pinckney expressed a doubt whether the act of Congress recommending the convention, or the commissions of the deputies to it, could authorize a discussion of a system founded on different principles from the federal constitution."

Gouverneur Morris was a New Yorker by birth and a Pennsylvanian by adoption; like Franklin he was one of the few delegates who could commute to the convention from home. An able lawyer, he was also a bon vivant—the antithesis, it seemed, of the austere Washington. A story attributed to Hamilton related an exchange between Morris and Washington: "When the convention to form a Constitution was sitting in Philadelphia in 1787, of which General Washington was president, he had stated evenings to receive the calls of his friends. At an interview between Hamilton, the Morrises, and others, the former remarked that Washington was reserved and aristocratic even to his intimate friends, and allowed no one to be familiar with him. Gouverneur Morris said that was a mere fancy, and he could be as familiar with Washington as with any of his other friends. Hamilton replied, 'If you will, at the next reception evenings, gently slap him on the shoulder and say, 'My dear General, how happy I am to see you look so well!' a supper and wine shall be provided for you and a dozen of your friends.' The challenge was accepted. On the evening appointed, a large number attended; and at an early hour Gouverneur Morris entered, bowed, shook hands, laid his left hand on Washington's shoulder, and said, 'My dear General, I am very happy to see you look so well!' Washington withdrew his hand, stepped suddenly back, fixed his eye on Morris for several minutes with an angry frown, until the latter retreated abashed, and sought refuge in the crowd. The company looked on in silence. At the supper, which was provided by Hamilton, Morris said, 'I have won the bet but paid dearly for it, and nothing could induce me to repeat it.'"

Morris, in response to the comments by the Pinckneys, reminded the delegates of the difference between a federal system and a national government—"the former being a mere compact resting on the good faith of the parties, the latter having a complete and compulsive operation." Morris added, "In all communities there must be one supreme power, and one only." Under the Articles, supreme power rested with the states, and from this flowed the problems with the current confederation.

George Mason agreed. Mason was a Virginia colleague of Madison and Randolph, besides being the author of the Virginia declaration of rights, which provided inspiration to both Jefferson's Declaration of Independence and, later, the federal Bill of Rights. "Mr. Mason observed that the present confederation was not only deficient in not providing for coercion and punishment against delinquent states, but argued very cogently that punishment could not in the nature of things be executed on the states collectively, and therefore that such a government was necessary as could directly operate on individuals," Madison recorded.

Despite the doubts of the Pinckneys, the strictures on the delegates from Delaware, and the limiting injunction of Congress—not to mention a general feeling that they were pushing the limits of their states' authorizations and even of their own integrity—the convention's members took a vote on the central proposition put forward by Randolph: "that a national government ought to be established, consisting of a supreme legislative, executive and judiciary."

The key words here were *national, established* and *supreme.* This would be a government of the nation and not of the states. It would be a newly established government, not a renovation of the existing government. And it, rather than the states, would be supreme.

Of the eight delegations present and voting, six—Massachusetts, Pennsylvania, Delaware, Virginia, North Carolina and South Carolina—gave their approval. Connecticut was opposed, and New York was divided. The motion passed.

WITH THIS VOTE the convention crossed a Rubicon. But the delegates didn't burn the bridge that carried them over, for the vote came in the committee of the whole and therefore didn't bind the convention itself. The Delawareans hadn't technically exceeded their credentials; they and the South Carolinians presumably were awaiting a more propitious moment to employ the veto they thought they still possessed.

Yet the vote was significant enough that the skeptics felt obliged to put forward an alternative plan. New Jersey's William Paterson bucked the tide of the convention in the first of his plan's resolutions: "That the Articles of Confederation ought to be so revised, corrected and enlarged as to render the federal constitution adequate to the exigences of government and the preservation of the Union." The Articles would still form the basis of government; there would be no coup against them.

The enlarged powers Paterson envisioned included the regulation of trade by Congress and the collection of tariffs on imports. These powers were the stated objective of the abortive Annapolis conference; Paterson was trying to roll back the calendar to the time of that meeting. He would let stand the one-state, one-vote rule on decisions in Congress, which would remain unicameral. The small states could breathe easily if the New Jersey plan passed.

Paterson defended the plan with vigor. "He preferred it because it accorded, first, with the powers of the convention and, second, with the sentiments of the people," Madison recorded. "If the confederacy was radically wrong, let us return to our states and obtain larger powers, not assume them of ourselves. I came here not to speak my own sentiments but the sentiments of those who sent me. Our object is not such a government as may be best in itself, but such a one as our constituents have authorized us to prepare and as they will approve."

The equality of states was inviolable under the Articles, Paterson said. And the Articles remained in force. "He read the fifth article of Confederation giving each state a vote, and the thirteenth declaring that no alteration shall be made without unanimous consent," Madison noted. "This is the nature of all treaties. What is unanimously done, must be unanimously undone." Paterson stated the matter as emphatically as he could: "We have no power to vary the idea of equal sovereignty."

THE VIRGINIA PLAN thus failed at the threshold, Paterson said. But it had other faults as well. "It is urged that two branches in the legislature are necessary. Why? For the purpose of a check. But the reason of the precaution is not applicable to this case. Within a particular state, when party heats prevail, such a check may be necessary. In such a body as Congress it is less necessary, and, besides, the delegations of the different states are checks on each other. Do the people at large complain of Congress?"—that is, of excessive power in Congress? "No. What they wish is that Congress may have more power."

"The plan of Mr. Randolph will also be enormously expensive," Paterson said. "Allowing Georgia and Delaware two representatives each in the popular branch, the aggregate number of that branch will be 180. Add to it half as many for the other branch and you have 270 members coming once at least a year from the most distant parts as well as the most central parts of the republic. In the present deranged state of our finances can so expensive a system be seriously thought of?" It could not, said Paterson. He believed the people concurred.

## 12

Colonel hamilton is deservedly celebrated for his talents," wrote William Pierce, who made a habit of characterizing his fellow delegates. "He is a practitioner of the law, and reputed to be a finished scholar. To a clear and strong judgment he unites the ornaments of fancy, and whilst he is able, convincing, and engaging in his eloquence, the heart and head sympathize in approving him. Yet there is something too feeble in his voice to be equal to the strains of oratory. It is my opinion that he is rather a convincing speaker, than a blazing orator. Col. Hamilton requires time to think. He enquires into every part of his subject with the searchings of philosophy, and when he comes forward, he comes highly charged with interesting matter. There is no skimming over the surface of a subject with him; he must sink to the bottom to see what foundation it rests on. His language is not always equal, sometimes didactic like Bolingbroke's, at others light and tripping like Stern's. His eloquence is not so diffusive as to trifle with the senses, but he rambles just enough to strike and keep up the attention. He is about 33 years old, of small stature, and lean. His manners are tinctured with stiffness, and sometimes with a degree of vanity that is highly disagreeable."

Madison characterized Hamilton somewhat differently. "Mr. Hamilton had been hitherto silent on the business before the convention," Madison wrote on June 18, "partly from respect to others whose superior abilities, age and experience rendered him unwilling to bring forward ideas dissimilar to theirs, and partly from his delicate situation with respect to his own state, to whose sentiments as expressed by his colleagues he could by no means accede."

But Hamilton could be silent no longer. Too much was at stake for the public welfare, indeed for the fate of American republicanism. "He was obliged therefore to declare himself unfriendly to both plans," Madison wrote of Hamilton. The New Jersey plan was the weaker of the two, in that it left the Articles of Confederation intact and sovereignty in the hands of the states. Hamilton thought the delegates were being too timid in hewing to the letter of the instructions from their states to merely amend the Articles of Confederation. "We owed it to our country to do on this emergency whatever we should deem essential to its happiness," Madison paraphrased. "The states sent us here to provide for the exigences of the Union. To rely on and propose any plan not adequate to these exigences, merely because it was not clearly within our powers, would be to sacrifice the means to the end."

"The great question is, what provision shall we make for the happiness of our country?" continued Hamilton. He adduced a series of principles and properties he thought essential to the success of any government. First, the people must have "an active and constant interest in supporting it." At present, the people had such an interest in supporting their state governments but not the national government. In fact, the states' interests actively obstructed the national government—for example, in matters of taxes, trade and debts.

Hamilton's second principle was "the love of power." He put the matter starkly: "Men love power." When they had it, they wanted more. When they lost it, they wanted it back. "The states have constantly shewn a disposition rather to regain the powers delegated by them than to part with more, or to give effect to what they had parted with." The loudest voices in the states railed against the national government. "The ambition of their demagogues is known to hate the control of the general government." The people of the states exhibited a milder form of this trait. "The citizens have not that anxiety to prevent a dissolution of the general government as of the particular governments," Hamilton said. These existing priorities were what the delegates had to change.

Which brought him to his third property of a successful government: "an habitual attachment of the people." This was similar to his first property but operated at the level of emotion rather than material interest. And it, too, currently favored the states over the general government. "The whole force of this tie is on the side of the state governments," Hamilton said. "Its sovereignty is immediately before the eyes of the people: its protection is immediately enjoyed by them. From its hand distributive justice and all those acts which familiarize and endear government to a people are dispensed to them."

Hamilton's fourth property was "force, by which may be understood a coercion of laws or coercion of arms." The states possessed a near monopoly of force. The Articles, as generally interpreted, withheld permission to employ force against the states or their people. The Shays rebellion had caused some people in Massachusetts to look to the national government for protective force, but this exception set no usable precedent. "How can this force be exerted on the states collectively?" asked Hamilton rhetorically. "It is impossible. It amounts to a war between the parties. Foreign powers also will not be idle spectators. They will interpose, the confusion will increase, and a dissolution of the Union will ensue."

Hamilton's fifth essential property of successful government was "influence." Madison summarized Hamilton's explanation: "He did not mean corruption but a dispensation of those regular honors and emoluments which produce an attachment to the government. Almost all the weight of these is on the side of the states, and must continue so as long as the states continue to exist. All the passions we see, of avarice, ambition, interest which govern most individuals and all public bodies fall into the current of the states and do not flow in the stream of the general government. The former therefore will generally be an overmatch for the general government and render any confederacy in its very nature precarious."

HAMILTON IDENTIFIED FAILED federations in history and showed how they had lacked one or more of his five prerequisites. How could America avoid a similar fate? he asked. "Only by such a complete sovereignty in the general government as will turn all the strong principles and passions above mentioned on its side."

The New Jersey plan fell particularly short in this regard. The scheme of equal representation for the states appealed to the small states, but it offered nothing to encourage the large states to yield anything to the central government. "It is not in human nature that Virginia and the large states should consent to it, or if they did, that they should long abide by it," Hamilton said. "It shocks too much the ideas of justice and every human feeling." As an axiom of politics, he added: "Bad principles in a government, though slow, are sure in their operation and will gradually destroy it."

Yet he couldn't say the Virginia plan was much better, for it too divided sovereignty between the states and the central government. This was an impossibility, Hamilton said. "Two sovereignties cannot coexist within the same limits." One or the other must give way.

"What then is to be done?" he asked. He confessed he didn't have a good answer—at least not one the convention was likely to embrace. "The extent of the country to be governed discouraged him," Madison paraphrased. "The expence of a general government was also formidable unless there were such a diminution of expence on the side of the state governments as the case would admit." Hamilton had a solution here, a drastic one. "If they"—the state governments—"were extinguished, he was persuaded that great economy might be obtained by substituting a general government."

Hamilton said he did not intend to shock the delegates by proposing the extinction of the states. "On the other hand he saw no *other* necessity"—than the shock to conventional wisdom—"for declining it. They are not necessary for any of the great purposes of commerce, revenue or agriculture. Subordinate authorities he was aware would be necessary. There must be district tribunals: corporations for local purposes. But cui bono"—for whose benefit?—"the vast & expensive apparatus now appertaining to the states?"

Beyond the resistance of those with a vested personal interest in state offices, Hamilton thought the problems with an all-powerful national government were quite manageable. "The only difficulty of a serious nature which occurred to him was that of drawing representatives from the extremes to the center of the community," Madison recorded. Hamilton thought good salaries for members of Congress would suffice. These would have to be higher than had been discussed so far. "The moderate wages for the first branch would only be a bait to little demagogues," he said.

He knew this would not go down well with a majority of the delegates or of the people in the states. "This view of the subject almost led him to despair that a republican government could be established over so great an extent," Madison wrote. "He was sensible at the same time that it would be unwise to propose one of any other form." He wished he could. "In his private opinion he had no scruple in declaring, supported as he was by the opinions of so many of the wise and good, that the British government was the best in the world, and that he doubted much whether anything short of it would do in America."

He acknowledged that this would be another shock to a people who had fought a bloody war to free themselves from the British government. "He hoped gentlemen of different opinions would bear with him in this and begged them to recollect the change of opinion on this subject which had taken place and was still going on. It was once thought that the power of Congress was amply sufficient to secure the end of their institution. The error was now seen by everyone. The members most tenacious of republicanism, he observed, were as loud as any in declaiming against the vices of democracy. This progress of the public mind led him to anticipate the time when others as well as himself would join in the praise bestowed by Mr. Neckar"—Jacques Necker, finance minister for Louis XVI of France—"on the British Constitution, namely that it is the only government in the world 'which unites public strength with individual security.'"

The genius of the British government was its balance. "In every community where industry is encouraged, there will be a division of it into the few and the many," Hamilton said. "Hence separate interests will arise. There will be debtors and creditors etc. Give all power to the many, they will oppress the few. Give all power to the few, they will oppress the many. Both therefore ought to have power, that each may defend itself against the other. To the want of this check we owe our paper money, instalment laws etc."—measures Hamilton deemed a blight on the country. "To the proper adjustment of it the British owe the excellence of their constitution."

He elaborated: "Their House of Lords is a most noble institution. Having nothing to hope for by a change, and a sufficient interest by means of their property in being faithful to the national interest, they form a permanent barrier against every pernicious innovation, whether attempted on the part of the Crown or of the Commons."

Some of the delegates in the convention had likened the proposed senate to the House of Lords. Their proposal didn't go far enough, Hamilton said. "No temporary senate"—one whose members served

fixed terms—"will have the firmness enough to answer the purpose."
Not even the seven-year terms suggested by some would do. "Gentlemen differ in their opinions concerning the necessary checks from the
different estimates they form of the human passions. They suppose
seven years a sufficient period to give the senate an adequate firmness, from not duly considering the amazing violence and turbulence
of the democratic spirit. When a great object of government is pursued, which seizes the popular passions, they spread like wild fire, and
become irresistible."

For the executive and its powers, Hamilton likewise looked to Britain. "As to the executive, it seemed to be admitted that no good one
could be established on republican principles," he said. But an executive was necessary. "Can there be a good government without a good
executive?" He thought not. Honesty compelled the conclusion: "The
English model was the only good one on this subject." Hamilton
explained, "The hereditary interest of the king was so interwoven with
that of the nation and his personal emoluments so great that he was
placed above the danger of being corrupted from abroad, and at the
same time was both sufficiently independent and sufficiently controlled
to answer the purpose of the institution at home." By contrast, republican executives stood no such proof against tampering. "Men of little
character acquiring great power become easily the tools of intermed-
dling neighbours."

"What is the inference from all these observations?" asked Hamilton. He didn't think America would adopt the British model completely.
But insightful Americans should draw a lesson. "We ought to go as far
in order to attain stability and permanency as republican principles will
admit," he said. "Let one branch of the legislature"—the senate—"hold
their places for life, or at least during good behaviour. Let the executive
also be for life." This would keep the executive and the senators from
chasing after votes, from pandering to the baser interests of the people.

"Is this a republican government?" asked Hamilton. "Yes, if all the
magistrates are appointed and vacancies are filled by the people, or a
process of election originating with the people." So long as the people,
or their representatives, chose the official of the national government in
the first place, they didn't have to do so again for their government to
qualify as republican. A life term would be especially important for the

executive, to preserve him from temptation in the service of prolonging a fixed term. "An executive for life has not this motive for forgetting his fidelity and will therefore be a safer depository of power."

Hamilton knew how this sounded. "It will be objected probably that such an executive will be an *elective monarch*." He didn't deny it, but he did qualify it. "*Monarch* is an indefinite term. It marks not either the degree or duration of power." And the elective version he described would lack the most obnoxiously anti-republican feature of most monarchies: their hereditary character.

HAMILTON HAD SPOKEN a long time. He was nearing the end. He sketched his own scheme of government in lieu of the Virginia and New Jersey plans. His legislature would have two houses. The members of the first house would be elected by the people for three-year terms. The members of the second house would be chosen by electors chosen by the people and would serve for life during good behavior— that is, as long as they avoided egregious scandal. The executive would be chosen by electors chosen by the electors chosen by the people, or alternatively by electors chosen by the state legislatures; the executive would serve for life during good behavior. The executive would possess veto power over all legislation. All state laws contrary to the national constitution or national laws would be null and void. This negative power would be enforced by the governors of the states, who would be appointed by the national government.

By this means Hamilton proposed to render the states clearly subordinate to the national government. "He was aware that it went beyond the ideas of most members," Madison paraphrased. "But will such a plan be adopted out of doors?"—meaning beyond the convention. Hamilton turned the question on its head. Would the people adopt the other plans before the convention? "At present they will adopt neither. But he sees the Union dissolving or already dissolved. He sees evils operating in the states which must soon cure the people of their fondness for democracies. He sees that a great progress has been already made and is still going on in the public mind. He thinks therefore that the people will in time be unshackled from their prejudices, and whenever that happens they will themselves not be satisfied at stopping where the plan of Mr. Randolph"—the Virginia plan—"would place them but be ready to go as far at least as he"—Hamilton—"proposes."

And why should they not? "What even is the Virginia plan," said Hamilton, lapsing into colloquialism, "but pork still, with a little change of the sauce?"

## 13

MADISON LET the shock waves from Hamilton's assault on the convention's work settle overnight. Perhaps he thought the jolt would do the delegates good. By staking out a far more centralizing scheme than anything yet proposed, Hamilton might have made a reform along the lines of the Virginia plan appear moderate by comparison.

Whatever Madison's thinking, when he rose the next day he ignored most of what Hamilton had said and leveled his own attack on the New Jersey plan. The responsibility of the convention was twofold, Madison declared: "First, to preserve the Union. Second, to provide a government that will remedy the evils felt by the states both in their united and individual capacities." He posed a series of questions about the New Jersey plan by way of showing where it fell short.

"Will it prevent those violations of the law of nations and of treaties which if not prevented must involve us in the calamities of foreign wars?" he asked. Such wars had not yet occurred, Madison conceded, but only by the indulgence of other countries, for various of the states had given foreigners cause for grievance. Their patience would not last forever, and the weakness of the individual states and of the Confederation would tempt the foreigners beyond endurance. This must not be permitted. "A rupture with other powers is among the greatest of national calamities," Madison said. "It ought therefore to be effectually provided that no part of a nation shall have it in its power to bring them on the whole. The existing Confederacy does not sufficiently provide against this evil." Neither would the New Jersey plan. "It does not supply the omission. It leaves the will of the states as uncontrolled as ever."

"Will it prevent encroachments on the federal authority?" asked Madison. Again, such encroachments were already common. "By the federal articles, transactions with the Indians appertain to Congress, yet in several instances the states have entered into treaties and wars with them. In like manner no two or more states can form among themselves any treaties etc. without the consent of Congress, yet Virginia and Maryland in one instance and Pennsylvania and New Jersey in another have entered into compacts without previous application or subsequent apology." The Articles forbade the states from raising troops without the consent of the other states, yet Massachusetts had already done so in response to the Shays rebellion. "Is she not now augmenting them without having even deigned to apprize Congress of her intention?" The New Jersey plan did nothing to prevent further trampling upon the authority of Congress.

"Will it prevent trespasses of the states on each other?" Such trespasses were manifold, Madison said. The states regularly gave preference to their own citizens over those of other states in matters of law. States issued paper money in order to defraud creditors in other states. "We have seen retaliating acts on this subject which threatened danger not to the harmony only but the tranquility of the Union," Madison declared. "The plan of Mr. Patterson, not giving even a negative on the acts of the states, leaves them as much at liberty as ever to execute their unrighteous projects against each other.

"Will it secure the internal tranquility of the states themselves?" Not in the slightest, said Madison. "The insurrections in Massachusetts admonished all the states of the danger to which they were exposed. Yet the plan of Mr. Patterson contained no provisions for supplying the defect of the Confederation on this point."

"Will it secure a good internal legislation and administration to the particular states?" Events had shown that bad laws and maladministration spilled across state lines, said Madison. He listed four categories of the mischief done by inept or corrupt state governments: "First, the multiplicity of the laws passed by the several states. Second, the mutability of their laws. Third, the injustice of them. Fourth, the impotence of them." Once more the New Jersey plan fell fatally short.

"Will it secure the Union against the influence of foreign powers over its members?" Madison considered foreign meddling inevitable. He cited cases from Greek, Roman and more recent European history to show that confederacies were chronically vulnerable to being picked apart by enemies. "The plan of Mr. Patterson, not giving to the general councils any negative on the will of the particular states, left the door open for the like pernicious machinations among ourselves."

Madison recognized that the smaller states were most attracted to the New Jersey plan. He suspected that some of them might use that plan as a device to block the more thorough reforms the current crisis demanded. He warned them against any such thinking. The most likely consequence would not be a maintenance of the status quo but a dissolution of the Union. Madison hesitated even to raise this dire prospect, but he could not in good conscience refrain from doing so. "Let the Union of the states be dissolved, and one of two consequences must happen," he said. "Either the states must remain individually independent and sovereign, or two or more confederacies must be formed among them." In either case the small states would suffer. Independence would leave them naked to the world; new confederacies would be formed on terms that favored the stronger states.

Summarizing, Madison distilled the deficiencies of the New Jersey plan—and the status quo—into a central flaw. "The great difficulty lies in the affair of representation," he said. "If this could be adjusted, all others would be surmountable." Virginians had concluded that it was simply unfair that each Delawarean counted for sixteen of them. Residents of the other big states had come to similar conclusions. They would stand it no longer. Representation must be proportional to population, or else the Union would fall to pieces.

Making a point few others had raised, Madison noted that prospective states were forming in the West. Their presence made proportional representation all the more crucial. "If they should come into the Union at all, they would come when they contained but few inhabitants. If they should be entitled to vote according to their proportions of inhabitants, all would be right and safe. Let them have an equal vote"—one state, one vote—"and a more objectionable minority than ever might give law to the whole."

. . .

MADISON'S ATTACK HELPED stymie the New Jersey plan, but it didn't dispel the astonishment produced by Hamilton's assault. James Wilson of Pennsylvania, among many others, thought Hamilton went entirely too far, especially in calling for the states to be abolished.

Hamilton clarified. "He had not been understood," he told the delegates, in Madison's phrasing. "By an abolition of the states, he meant that no boundary could be drawn between the national and state legislatures; that the former must therefore have indefinite authority. If it were limited at all, the rivalship of the states would gradually subvert it. Even as corporations"—non-governmental bodies—"the extent of some of them, as Virginia, Massachusetts etc., would be formidable." The states could continue to exist as administrative districts of the national government, Hamilton said. But they must be no more than that. "As *states,* he thought they ought to be abolished."

This hardly calmed the critics. Neither did Hamilton's subsequent remarks on the fundamental deficiencies of republicanism. "He concurred with Mr. Madison in thinking we were now to decide forever the fate of republican government," Hamilton said, in Madison's paraphrase. "And that if we did not give to that form due stability and wisdom, it would be disgraced and lost among ourselves, disgraced and lost to mankind forever." Personally, Hamilton would not mourn the loss. "He acknowledged himself not to think favorably of republican government." But he knew that most of the delegates did, and he now urged them to make the best republican government possible.

## 14

MANASSEH CUTLER WAS a New England clergyman and part-time scientist who in the summer of 1787 had business with Congress, which was then meeting in New York. While waiting for his chance to lobby the legislature regarding the future of Ohio, where he had land interests, he traveled to Philadelphia to see that city and meet some of its residents. In early July he engaged a room at an inn recommended to him by friends. "This tavern (Indian Queen) is situated in Third Street, between Market Street and Chestnut Street, and is not far from the center of the city," he wrote in his journal. "It is kept in an elegant style and consists of a large pile of buildings, with many spacious halls and numerous small apartments appropriated for lodging rooms. As soon as I had inquired of the bar-keeper, when I arrived last evening, if I could be furnished with lodgings, a livery servant was ordered immediately to attend me, who received my baggage from the hostler and conducted me to the apartment assigned by the bar-keeper, which was a rather small but a very handsome chamber (No. 9), furnished with a rich field bed, bureau, table with drawers, a large looking-glass, neat chairs, and other furniture. Its front was east and, being in the third story, afforded a fine prospect toward the river and the Jersey shore."

The Indian Queen treated its guests with style. "The servant that attended me was a young, sprightly, well-built black fellow, neatly dressed—blue coat, sleeves and cape red, and buff waistcoat and breeches, the bosom of his shirt ruffled, and hair powdered. After he had brought up my baggage and properly deposited it in the chamber, he brought two of the latest London magazines and laid them on the table. I ordered him to call a barber, furnish me with a bowl of water for washing, and to have tea on the table by the time I was dressed."

Cutler wound up taking his tea elsewhere, which turned out to be a good thing. "Being told, while I was at tea, that a number of the members of the Continental Convention, now convened in this city for the purpose of forming a federal constitution, lodged in this house, and that two of them were from Massachusetts, immediately after tea, I sent into their hall (for they live by themselves) to Mr. Strong and requested to speak with him. We had never been personally acquainted, nor had I any letter to him, but we had both of us an hearsay knowledge of each other, and Mr. Gerry had lately mentioned to Mr. Strong that he daily expected me, in consequence of a letter he had received from Governor Bowdoin. Mr. Strong very politely introduced me to Mr. Gorham of Charlestown, Mass; Mr. Madison and Mr. Mason and his son, of Virginia; Governor Martin, Hon. Hugh Williamson, of North Carolina; the Hon. John Rutledge and Mr. Pinckney, of South Carolina; Mr. Hamilton, of New York, who were lodgers in the house, and to several other gentlemen who were spending the evening with them."

Cutler was a convivial sort who brought out the best in those he met. "I spent the evening with these gentlemen very agreeably. Mr. Strong and Mr. Gorham insisted on my sitting a while with them, after the other gentlemen retired, that they might inquire with more freedom and more minutely into state affairs in Massachusetts. We sat until half after one. They both of them very politely offered to wait on me to any part of the city, and to introduce me to any gentleman of their acquaintance I should wish to see."

Cutler thanked them for the offer but said his business with Congress required that he be ready to return to New York at a moment's notice. Yet Caleb Strong insisted on taking Cutler to meet Elbridge Gerry, who had brought his wife and young child to Philadelphia and had rented a house. Cutler made certain to rise early the next morning. "Mr. Strong was up as early as myself, and we took a walk to Mr. Gerry's, in Spruce Street, where we breakfasted," Cutler recorded. "Few old bachelors, I believe, have been more fortunate in matrimony than Mr. Gerry. His lady is young, very handsome and exceedingly amiable.

She appears to be possessed of fine accomplishments. I should suppose her not more than 17, and believe he must be turned of 55. They have been married about eighteen months, and have a fine son about two months old, of which they appear both to be extravagantly fond."

Cutler was struck by the difference between Philadelphia and Boston. "I was surprised to find how early ladies in Philadelphia can rise in the morning, and to see them at breakfast at half after five, when in Boston they can hardly see a breakfast table at nine without falling into hysterics," he wrote. "I observed to Mrs. Gerry that it seemed to be an early hour for ladies to breakfast. She said she always rose early, and found it conducive to her health. She was inured to it from her childhood in New York, and that it was the practice of the best families in Philadelphia."

Elbridge Gerry told Cutler he'd received a letter from Governor Bowdoin asking him to introduce Cutler to Benjamin Franklin, a fellow Bostonian by birth. Gerry said he'd be delighted to do the honors, and that five that afternoon might be a good time.

After breakfast Strong showed Cutler around the city, including the statehouse. "This is a noble building," observed Cutler. "The architecture is in a richer and grander style than any public building I have before seen. The first story is not an open walk, as is usual in buildings of this kind. In the middle, however, is a very broad cross-aisle, and the floor above supported by two rows of pillars. From this aisle is a broad opening to a large hall, toward the west end, which opening is supported by arches and pillars. In this hall the courts are held, and, as you pass the aisle you have a full view of the court. The supreme court was now sitting. This bench consists of only three judges. Their robes are scarlet; the lawyers', black. The chief judge, Mr. McKean, was sitting with his hat on, which is the custom but struck me as being very odd, and seemed to derogate from the dignity of a judge. The hall east of the aisle is employed for public business. The chamber over it is now occupied by the Continental Convention, which is now sitting, but sentries are planted without and within—to prevent any person from approaching near—who appear to be very alert in the performance of their duty."

Sightseeing filled the day, until the late afternoon, when Gerry escorted him to Franklin's home. "Dr. Franklin lives in Market Street, between Second and Third Streets, but his house stands up a courtyard at some distance from the street," Cutler recorded. "We found him in his garden, sitting upon a grass plat under a very large mulberry, with several other gentlemen and two or three ladies."

Cutler had been looking forward to this moment. "There was no curiosity in Philadelphia which I was so anxious to see as this great man, who has been the wonder of Europe as well as the glory of America." Yet he suspected Franklin would be hard to get to know. "A man who stood first in the literary world and had spent so many years in the courts of kings, particularly in the refined court of France, I conceived would not be of very easy access, and must certainly have much of the air of grandeur and majesty about him. Common folks must expect only to gaze at him at a distance, and answer such questions as he was pleased to ask. In short, when I entered his house, I felt as if I was going to be introduced to the presence of a European monarch."

He at once discovered his mistake. "How were my ideas changed when I saw a short, fat, trunched old man in a plain Quaker dress, bald pate, and short white locks, sitting without his hat, who, as Mr. Gerry introduced me, rose from his chair, took me by the hand, expressed his joy to see me, welcomed me to the city, and begged me to seat myself close to him," Cutler wrote. "His voice was low, but his countenance open, frank and pleasing." Cutler handed Franklin his letters of introduction. "After he had read them, he took me again by the hand and, with the usual compliments, introduced me to the other gentlemen of the company, who were most of them members of the Convention."

Cutler fit right in. "We entered into a free conversation, and spent our time most agreeably until it was dark," he wrote. "The tea table was spread under the tree, and Mrs. Bache, a very gross and rather homely lady, who is the only daughter of the doctor and lives with him, served it out to the company. She had three of her children about her, over whom she seemed to have no kind of command, but who appeared to be excessively fond of their grandpapa."

Franklin was pleased to learn that Cutler was a naturalist. "The Doctor showed me a curiosity he had just received, and with which he was much pleased. It was a snake with two heads, preserved in a large vial." Franklin couldn't decide whether this was a new species or a mere freak. But it brought something to his mind. "The Doctor mentioned the situation of this snake, if it was traveling among bushes, and one head should choose to go on one side of the stem of a bush and the other head should prefer the other side, and that neither of the heads would consent to come back or give way to the other. He was then going to mention a humorous matter that had that day taken place in Convention, in consequence of his comparing the snake to America, for he seemed to forget that everything in Convention was to be kept a profound secret; but the secrecy of Convention matters was suggested to him, which stopped him, and deprived me of the story he was going to tell."

## 15

WHAT CUTLER MISSED hearing was how the convention had reached an impasse. The large states, led by Madison and the Virginians, persisted in their efforts to overthrow the Articles and replace them with a new charter that fairly reflected the greater wealth and population of the large states. The small states clung to the one-state, one-vote model of the Articles, if not to the Articles themselves. Other matters, chiefly concerning the powers of the legislature and the nature of the executive, hung fire awaiting resolution of the representation issue. Until then, the convention was like Franklin's two-headed snake, caught on the stem of the bush and unable to move forward.

The delay didn't bother Franklin, in his comfortable house and garden, surrounded by his family. But the out-of-towners had their patience tested. "It is impossible to judge how long we shall be detained here, but from present appearances I fear until July, if not later," George Mason had written to his family in late May. "I begin to grow heart-ily tired of the etiquette and nonsense so fashionable in this city. It would take me some months to make myself master of them, and that it should require months to learn what is not worth remembering as many minutes, is to me so discouraging a circumstance as determines me to give myself no manner of trouble about them." In early June Mason amended his estimate. "It is impossible to judge when the business will be finished, most probably not before August," he said. "*Festina lente*"—make haste slowly—"may very well be called our motto."

By early July he had stopped trying to guess when the convention would end.

Several delegates had to write home for more money to pay their room and board bills. Alexander Hamilton eventually grew so frustrated that he left the convention and departed Philadelphia. He traveled back to New York to attend to his law practice. George Washington wrote to Hamilton there saying that the affairs of the convention had grown more paralyzed since he left. "They are now, if possible, in a worse train than ever," Washington declared. "You will find but little ground on which the hope of a good establishment can be formed. In a word, I *almost* despair of seeing a favourable issue to the proceedings of the convention, and do therefore repent having had any agency in the business."

Madison refused to give up hope. "The convention continue to sit, and have been closely employed since the commencement of the session," he wrote to Jefferson. Madison wished he could provide details, but the code of silence forbade it. He would fill Jefferson in at a later date, whenever that might be. "It is not possible to form any judgment of the future duration of the session. I am led by sundry circumstances to guess that the residue of the work will not be very quickly despatched." Yet he would stay the course. The American people deserved no less.

FRANKLIN SUGGESTED SEEKING higher help. "Mr. President," he said to Washington in the convention chair, while in fact speaking to the delegates as a group. "The small progress we have made after four or five weeks close attendance and continual reasonings with each other, our different sentiments on almost every question, several of the last producing as many noes as ayes, is methinks a melancholy proof of the imperfection of the human understanding. We indeed seem to feel our own want of political wisdom, since we have been running about in search of it. We have gone back to ancient history for models of government, and examined the different forms of those republics which having been formed with the seeds of their own dissolution now no longer exist. And we have viewed modern states all round Europe, but find none of their constitutions suitable to our circumstances.

"In this situation of this assembly, groping as it were in the dark to find political truth, and scarce able to distinguish it when presented to us, how has it happened, sir, that we have not hitherto once thought of humbly applying to the Father of Lights to illuminate our understandings? In the beginning of the contest with Great Britain, when we were sensible of danger we had daily prayer in this room for the divine protection. Our prayers, sir, were heard, and they were graciously answered. All of us who were engaged in the struggle must have observed frequent instances of a superintending providence in our favor.

"To that kind providence we owe this happy opportunity of consulting in peace on the means of establishing our future national felicity. And have we now forgotten that powerful friend? Or do we imagine that we no longer need his assistance? I have lived, sir, a long time, and the longer I live, the more convincing proofs I see of this truth—that God governs in the affairs of men. And if a sparrow cannot fall to the ground without his notice, is it probable that an empire can rise without his aid? We have been assured, sir, in the sacred writings, that 'except the Lord build the house, they labour in vain that build it.'

"I firmly believe this. And I also believe that without his concurring aid we shall succeed in this political building no better than the builders of Babel. We shall be divided by our little partial local interests; our projects will be confounded, and we ourselves shall become a reproach and bye word down to future ages. And what is worse, mankind may hereafter from this unfortunate instance, despair of establishing governments by human wisdom and leave it to chance, war and conquest.

"I therefore beg leave to move that henceforth prayers imploring the assistance of Heaven, and its blessings on our deliberations, be held in this Assembly every morning before we proceed to business, and that one or more of the clergy of this city be requested to officiate in that service."

Franklin wasn't known for his piety, and so his motion for a morning prayer seemed incongruous to some. Others took it as a hint to the more self-assured of the delegates that they didn't know everything.

Hamilton, at this point still in attendance, was nothing if not self-assured, and he seemed to resent the hint. After Roger Sherman seconded Franklin's motion, Hamilton objected that beseeching heaven at this stage of the proceedings would betray desperation on the part of the convention. The public would take alarm.

Franklin rejoined that public alarm might do the convention good amid its impasse. Something was needed to break the deadlock.

Another objection was stated: that the convention had no funds to pay a preacher.

Franklin had made his point, and he didn't press the matter. The convention adjourned without voting on his resolution.

WITH OR WITHOUT heaven's help, the impasse finally broke when Roger Sherman and Oliver Ellsworth of Connecticut proposed a compromise that favored the large states in one house of the legislature and the small states in the other. What would be called the House of Representatives would have its members apportioned by population; the Senate would represent each of the states equally.

Ellsworth understood that the proposal wouldn't please the big-state men. "I confess that the effect of this motion is to make the general government partly federal and partly national," he told the convention. But it provided the protection they wanted. "This will secure tranquility and still make it efficient, and it will meet the objections of the larger states. In taxes they will have a proportional weight in the first branch of the general legislature." Because legislation would have to pass both houses, the small states would not be able to impose their will on the large states.

Ellsworth went on to say this was the best offer the big states would get. "If the great states refuse this plan, we will be forever separated." He hoped the big states would think carefully before refusing. "When in the hour of common danger we united as equals, shall it now be urged by some that we must depart from this principle when the danger is over? Will the world say that this is just?"

Franklin provided a homelier rationale. "The diversity of opinions turns on two points," he said. "If a proportional representation takes place, the small states contend that their liberties will be in danger. If an equality of votes is to be put in its place, the large states say their money will be in danger. When a broad table is to be made, and the edges of planks do not fit, the artist takes a little from both, and makes a good joint. In like manner here both sides must part with some of their demands, in order that they may join in some accommodating proposition."

The big-state men grumbled. The small states would not be able to impose their will on the large states, to be sure. But neither would the large states—or, rather, the people of the large states, who constituted a majority of the nation—be able to impose their will on the nation, which was what Madison and the other big-state men desired.

Madison hadn't wanted a government partly federal and partly national. He had wanted a government wholly national. But when the convention accepted the Connecticut compromise, he reconciled himself to getting half what he'd aimed for.

IN FACT, it wasn't clear he got even that. The check the Senate placed on the House of Representatives made this new government far more like the existing government under the Articles of Confederation than like the government Madison had proposed. If the convention ended on this note, he would have to account it a failure.

Fortunately for him, there was more to be said and done. As the delegates defined the powers of the new Congress, they gave it most of the attributes Madison had sought for it, save the veto on state laws. Madison had to settle for the new constitution's assertion that it and the laws made under its authority would be the "supreme law of the land." This established the principal of national sovereignty, but it left interpretation and enforcement to be determined.

The new executive was made independent of the legislature, but without the life tenure Hamilton had wanted. Instead the executive would serve a term of four years, renewable without limit. The executive would be chosen by electors appointed by the states, with each state having as many electors as it had senators and representatives together. This scheme split the difference between the proportional representation in the House of Representatives and the equal representation in the Senate. The expectation was that in some elections, perhaps most of them, no candidate would get a majority of electors, in which cases the winner would be chosen by the House of Representatives, with each state's delegation there having a single vote.

Of the substantive, as opposed to procedural, questions the delegates had to resolve, the most vexing involved the institution of slavery. In 1776 slavery had been legal in every state, but during the eleven years since then Pennsylvania and the New England states had passed emancipation laws, with New York and New Jersey expected to follow before long. During the same period when the delegates in Philadelphia were writing a new constitution, the existing Congress, meeting in New York, was writing an ordinance forbidding slavery in the territory north of the Ohio River. Indeed, part of Manasseh Cutler's urgent business with Congress was drafting the anti-slavery provision of the Northwest Ordinance.

Many Southerners hoped slavery would similarly disappear in the South. Washington, Jefferson and other slaveholders deemed the institution an affront to republicanism and a blight on America's good name. But emancipation posed greater challenges in the South than in the North. The Southern economy depended on slavery in a way the Northern economy had not, and the vastly greater number of Southern slaves raised the question of what was to be done with them once freed. Were they to be citizens? A subordinate class of some sort? With no model of a biracial republic to work from, even ardent advocates of emancipation found themselves at a loss.

The issue of slavery emerged first in the debate over representation. Many of the delegates, and Madison himself at times, judged the principal difference among the states to be a reflection of their differences in size. But on June 30 Madison put the matter otherwise. "The states were divided into different interests not by their difference of size, but by other circumstances, the most material of which resulted partly from climate, but principally from the effects of their having or not having slaves," he said. "These two causes concurred in forming the great division of interests in the United States. It did not lie between the large and small states; it lay between the Northern and Southern, and if any defensive power were necessary"—each to balance the other—"it ought to be mutually given to these two interests." Writing about himself, Madison declared, "He was so strongly impressed with this important truth that he had been casting about in his mind for some expedient that would answer the purpose. The one which had occurred was that instead of proportioning the votes of the states in both branches to their respective numbers of inhabitants, computing the slaves in the ratio of 5 to 3, they should be represented in one branch according to the number of free inhabitants only; and in the other according to the whole number, counting the slaves as if free. By this arrangement the Southern scale would have the advantage in one house, and the Northern in the other. He had been restrained from proposing this expedient by two considerations: one was his unwillingness to urge any diversity of interests on an occasion where it is but too apt to arise of itself; the other was the inequality of powers that must be vested in the two branches and which would destroy the equilibrium of interests."

The five to three ratio, or three-fifths when reversed, came from debates in the Continental Congress over tax requisitions made of the states. Congress judged that a state's wealth was a better measure of its ability to pay than its population. And in a largely agrarian economy, landed wealth was the principal form of wealth. But assessing the value of land was difficult and prone to fudging. Population was adopted as a proxy; people were relatively easy to count. Yet enslaved laborers were understood to be less productive than free labor, given the lack of incentives to slaves to work any harder than necessary to avoid the lash. After some haggling, the rule agreed upon was that the average slave was sixty percent, or three-fifths, as productive as a free laborer, and so three-fifths of the total number of slaves were counted toward the requisition. Now Madison proposed applying that ratio to representation.

Mr. Charles Pinckney of South Carolina accepted the rule, yet not without hinting at payback later. "He thought the blacks ought to stand on an equality with whites, but would agree to the ratio settled by Congress," Madison recorded.

Rufus King of Massachusetts didn't like writing slavery into the new constitution. "He thought the admission of them along with whites at all would excite great discontents among the states having no slaves," Madison wrote.

James Wilson of Pennsylvania wanted a sounder theoretical basis than Madison offered for the ratio he proposed, even as he acknowledged he might not get it. "Mr. Wilson did not well see on what principle the admission of blacks in the proportion of three fifths could be explained. Are they admitted as citizens? Then why are they not admitted on an equality with white citizens? Are they admitted as property? Then why is not other property admitted into the computation? These were difficulties however which he thought must be overruled by the necessity of compromise."

Gouverneur Morris brought up another objection. "Mr. Govr. Morris was compelled to declare himself reduced to the dilemma of doing injustice to the Southern states or to human nature, and he must therefore do it to the former," Madison paraphrased. "For he could never agree to give such encouragement to the slave trade as would be given by allowing them a representation for their negroes, and he did not believe those states would ever confederate on terms that would deprive them of that trade." Where the free states could swell their population and hence representation only by natural increase or voluntary immigration, the slave states could buy more representation by purchasing more slaves.

Morris's linking of representation to the slave trade proved the key to the solution the convention reached after considerably more debate. Luther Martin of Maryland joined Rufus King in resenting the writing of slavery into the new charter of the American republic. "It was inconsistent with the principles of the revolution and dishonorable to the American character to have such a feature in the constitution," Martin said.

John Rutledge of South Carolina gave principles the back of his hand. "Religion and humanity had nothing to do with this question," he said. "Interest alone is the governing principle with nations. The true question at present is whether the Southern states shall or shall not be parties to the Union." Rutledge, opposing limits on the slave trade, added that Southern states were not the only ones to profit from slavery. "If the Northern states consult their interest, they will not oppose the increase of slaves which will increase the commodities of which they will become the carriers."

Oliver Ellsworth of Connecticut pleaded agnosticism on the slave trade. "Let every state import what it pleases," he said. "The morality or wisdom of slavery are considerations belonging to the states themselves." He agreed with Rutledge on the shared benefits of slavery. "What enriches a part enriches the whole." He wanted to let things be. "The states are the best judges of their particular interest. The old confederation had not meddled with this point, and he did not see any greater necessity for bringing it within the policy of the new one."

Charles Pinckney seconded Rutledge's threat. "South Carolina can never receive the plan if it prohibits the slave trade," he said. "In every proposed extension of the powers of Congress, that state has expressly and watchfully excepted that of meddling with the importation of negroes." Yet Pinckney left the door slightly ajar. "If the states be all left at liberty on this subject, South Carolina may perhaps by degrees do of herself what is wished, as Virginia and Maryland have already done." Those states had terminated their participation in what Virginian George Mason called "this infernal traffic"—the Atlantic slave trade.

Oliver Ellsworth seized on the opening. "This widening of opinions has a threatening aspect," he told the delegates, in Madison's recounting. "If we do not agree on this middle and moderate ground he was afraid we should lose two states, with such others as may be disposed to stand aloof, should fly into a variety of shapes and directions, and most probably into several confederations and not without bloodshed."

The middle ground Ellsworth referred to was an emerging compromise on slavery and the slave trade—what Gouverneur Morris called "a bargain among the Northern and Southern states." Roger Sherman seconded Ellsworth's opinion on the need for such a bargain. "It was better to let the Southern states import slaves than to part with them"— the Southern states—"if they made it a sine qua non," Sherman said.

The bargain, as it finally emerged, was that the slave trade could continue for another twenty years, and three-fifths of the slave population would be counted toward representation. Slavery itself was left to the states to keep or abolish within their borders. Yet all the states were required to assist in the return of escaped slaves to their masters.

Strikingly, this grand bargain was accomplished without letting the words *slave* or *slavery* appear in the final product. Madison was one of those slave owners who hoped his state and the country would outgrow slavery, and he did not want to burden the new constitution with anachronistic—and anti-republican—labels. "Mr. Madison thought it wrong to admit in the constitution that there could be property in men," he wrote of himself. And so euphemisms—"person held to service" and "other persons"—were employed instead.

"MR. PRESIDENT," said Benjamin Franklin to George Washington on September 17, when the last of the compromises had been made. "I confess that there are several parts of this constitution which I do not at present approve, but I am not sure I shall never approve them; for having lived long, I have experienced many instances of being obliged by better information or fuller consideration to change opinions even on important subjects which I once thought right but found to be otherwise. It is therefore that the older I grow, the more apt I am to doubt my own judgment and to pay more respect to the judgment of others.

"Most men, indeed, as well as most sects in religion think themselves in possession of all truth, and that wherever others differ from them it is so far error. Steele, a Protestant in a dedication tells the pope that the only difference between our churches in their opinions of the certainty of their doctrines is the Church of Rome is infallible and the Church of England is never in the wrong. But though many private persons think almost as highly of their own infallibility as of that of their sect, few express it so naturally as a certain French lady who in a dispute with her sister said 'I don't know how it happens, Sister, but I meet with nobody but myself that's always in the right—*Il n'y a que moi qui a toujours raison.*'

"In these sentiments, sir, I agree to this constitution with all its faults, if they are such, because I think a general government necessary for us, and there is no form of government but what may be a blessing to the people if well administered, and believe farther that this is likely to be well administered for a course of years, and can only end in despotism, as other forms have done before it, when the people shall become so corrupted as to need despotic government, being incapable of any other.

"I doubt too whether any other convention we can obtain may be able to make a better constitution. For when you assemble a number of men to have the advantage of their joint wisdom, you inevitably assemble with those men all their prejudices, their passions, their errors of opinion, their local interests and their selfish views. From such an assembly can a perfect production be expected? It therefore astonishes me, sir, to find this system approaching so near to perfection as it does; and I think it will astonish our enemies, who are waiting with confidence to hear that our councils are confounded like those of the builders of Babel, and that our states are on the point of separation, only to meet hereafter for the purpose of cutting one another's throats.

"Thus I consent, sir, to this constitution because I expect no better, and because I am not sure that it is not the best. The opinions I have had of its errors, I sacrifice to the public good. I have never whispered a syllable of them abroad. Within these walls they were born, and here they shall die.

"If every one of us in returning to our constituents were to report the objections he has had to it, and endeavor to gain partisans in support of them, we might prevent its being generally received, and thereby lose all the salutary effects and great advantages resulting naturally in our favor among foreign nations as well as among ourselves from our real or apparent unanimity. Much of the strength and efficiency of any government in procuring and securing happiness to the people depends on opinion, on the general opinion of the goodness of the government, as well as of the wisdom and integrity of its governors. I hope therefore that for our own sakes as a part of the people, and for the sake of posterity, we shall act heartily and unanimously in recommending this constitution (if approved by Congress and confirmed by the conventions) wherever our influence may extend, and turn our future thoughts and endeavors to the means of having it well administered.

"On the whole, sir, I cannot help expressing a wish that every member of the convention who may still have objections to it would, with me, on this occasion doubt a little of his own infallibility and, to make manifest our unanimity, put his name to this instrument."

Franklin allowed a few moments for his words to sink in. Then, on the chance that not quite everyone was persuaded, he closed by offering a formula that would hide the holdouts. "Done in Convention, by the unanimous consent of the States present the 17th. of September etc. In witness whereof we have hereunto subscribed our names."

PART IV

*Patrick Henry Smells a Rat*

## 16

ONE OF THE SECRETS of George Washington's success was his knowledge of his strengths and his limitations. He was a good soldier and commander, and in any situation calling for courage and military leadership he did not hesitate to act boldly and decisively. But he was not an orator or a debater, and his grasp of political history and theory was slight compared to many of his contemporaries. And so he was content, during the Philadelphia convention, to preside over the debates rather than to engage in them. As a result, while nearly everyone else was bruised and diminished during the summer's sparring over the fate of the nation, Washington emerged untouched, his prestige as great as ever.

He put that prestige to use when the convention closed. The delegates accepted Franklin's proposal to vote as states, and the decision of the states was unanimous, excepting Rhode Island, which had never sent delegates. Three individual delegates—George Mason, Edmund Randolph and Elbridge Gerry—withheld their signatures.

In his final act as president, Washington sent the constitution to Congress with a letter of transmittal. He had some explaining to do, for this letter was the first official notice of how greatly the convention had exceeded its authority. "We have now the honor to submit to the consideration of the United States in Congress assembled that Constitution which has appeared to us the most advisable," Washington wrote. This opening sentence gave the game away. The delegates had been authorized to propose amendments to the Articles, not to write a new constitution.

Washington continued, "The friends of our country have long seen and desired that the power of making war, peace and treaties, that of levying money and regulating commerce and the correspondent executive and judicial authorities should be fully and effectually vested in the general government of the Union." Putting the matter this way cast the opponents of such a sweeping transfer of power from the states to the central government as enemies of America. "But the impropriety of delegating such extensive trust to one body of men is evident," said Washington to that very body of men, namely Congress. "Hence results the necessity of a different organization"—which consigned the Congress of the Confederation to the ash heap.

Washington wasn't usually this artful in his correspondence. In truth, the letter had been drafted by Gouverneur Morris, who had also produced the final draft of the constitution. But Washington signed the letter, and he never signed anything he didn't believe. "It is obviously impracticable in the federal government of these states to secure all rights of independent sovereignty to each and yet provide for the interest and safety of all," he continued. "Individuals entering into society must give up a share of liberty to preserve the rest."

Washington expected complaints about the proposed constitution. "That it will meet the full and entire approbation of every state is not perhaps to be expected." Political life demanded sacrifice. "Each will doubtless consider that had her interests been alone consulted the consequences might have been particularly disagreeable or injurious to others."

Washington assured the members of Congress that the delegates had done the best they could. In this belief they presented the new constitution to their fellow Americans. "That it may promote the lasting welfare of that country so dear to us all and secure her freedom and happiness is our most ardent wish."


JAMES MADISON HOPED the critics of the constitution would be forgiving. Early signs were favorable but not conclusive. "What reception this new system will generally meet with cannot yet be pronounced," he wrote to his father. "For obvious reasons opposition is as likely to arise in Virginia as anywhere. The city of Philadelphia has warmly espoused it. Both parties there, it is said, have united on the occasion. It may happen nevertheless that a country party may spring up and give a preponderancy to the opposite scale. In this city"—Madison was writing from New York—"the general voice coincides with that of Philadelphia but there is less apparent unanimity, and it is pretty certain that the party in power will be active in defeating the new system. In Boston the reception given to it is extremely favorable we are told, but more will depend on the country than the town. The echo from Connecticut and New Jersey, as far as it has reached us, denotes a favorable disposition in those states."

Madison himself had mixed feelings about the constitution. Though it succeeded in toppling the Articles—or *would* succeed, if ratified—it fell short of what Madison had envisioned. It left the states with too much power against the national government, and the small states with too much power against the large states.

Madison detailed his disappointments to Jefferson in a post-convention postmortem. "It appeared to be the sincere and unanimous wish of the convention to cherish and preserve the Union of the states," he began. "It was generally agreed that the objects of the Union could not be secured by any system founded on the principle of a confederation of sovereign states." Thus the need for a new government.

This judgment winning general approval, the convention had turned to implementing it. But the delegates soon fell to bickering. Madison described the clash over the executive as "peculiarly embarrassing." Delegates deadlocked for weeks on the mode of election and the term of office. "A few would have preferred a tenure during good behaviour"—that is, for life. "A considerable number would have done so in case an easy and effectual removal by impeachment could be settled." But no one was sure whether impeachment would actually work. Once the convention decided on fixed-length terms, they squabbled over what the length should be. "It was much agitated whether a long term, seven years for example, with a subsequent and perpetual ineligibility, or a short term with a capacity to be re-elected, should be fixed," Madison said. Those favoring a single long term distrusted incumbents not to rig reelections. Those wanting a renewable short term said the best men would resent having to campaign repeatedly and would therefore shun the office. The eventual decision—for renewable terms of four years—split the difference, satisfying no one.

Madison's major disappointment was the Senate—"the great anchor of the government," as he described the upper chamber to Jefferson. The equality of states in the Senate, and the requirement for its concurrence in legislation, violated the cardinal tenet of republicanism: that people should govern themselves on the basis of civic equality. It left the Union in large part a confederation of the states rather than a republic of the people. The fight over the Senate "created more embarrassment, and a greater alarm for the issue of the convention than all the rest put together," Madison told Jefferson. "It ended in the compromise which you will see, but very much to the dissatisfaction of several members from the large states"—including Madison himself.

The final draft of the constitution was nothing like what Madison had hoped for. Without a veto of state laws, the central government would find itself constantly fighting encroachments by the states. Without truly proportional representation, the small states retained inordinate influence over national affairs. Without a clear demarcation between national and state authority, the country would lurch from crisis to crisis.

But Madison agreed with Franklin that it was the best that could be done in present circumstances. The wonder was that the delegates had been able to agree on anything at all. "It is impossible to consider the degree of concord which ultimately prevailed as less than a miracle," Madison told Jefferson.

## 17

THREE DAYS AFTER Madison wrote to Jefferson, a letter appeared in the *Independent Journal* of New York. "To the People of New York," it began: "After an unequivocal experience of the inefficacy of the subsisting federal government, you are called upon to deliberate on a new Constitution for the United States of America."

The author of the letter identified himself only as "Publius," whom classically educated readers would have identified with Publius Valerius Publicola, a founder of the Roman republic. In actuality the author was Alexander Hamilton. During the month since the signing of the constitution in Philadelphia, the document had been read by Congress and sent to the states for their consideration. This sending wasn't a foregone conclusion. If enough members had been sufficiently outraged by the coup in Philadelphia against the Articles and themselves, they might have refused to collaborate in their official demise. But the thinking in Congress tracked the thinking in Philadelphia. The big states were eager for almost any change that broke the stranglehold of the small states on national action, and the small states feared being left out of a new republic fashioned by the big states. One by one the states summoned conventions of their own to review the proposed constitution.

In New York the balance was close between those in favor of the constitution, who called themselves Federalists, and those opposed, who became Antifederalists. Though the constitution wasn't nearly as strong as Hamilton had wished, he judged it far better than the Articles, and he threw his weight behind it, beginning with the letter to the *Independent Journal*. "The subject speaks its own importance," Hamilton said, "comprehending in its consequences nothing less than the existence of the Union, the safety and welfare of the parts of which it is composed, the fate of an empire in many respects the most interesting in the world." On the outcome of the decision hinged the fate not of America alone. "It seems to have been reserved to the people of this country, by their conduct and example, to decide the important question whether societies of men are really capable or not of establishing good government from reflection and choice, or whether they are forever destined to depend for their political constitutions on accident and force."

Hamilton warned his readers against the wiles of the Antifederalists. "Among the most formidable of the obstacles which the new Constitution will have to encounter may readily be distinguished the obvious interest of a certain class of men in every state to resist all changes which may hazard a diminution of the power, emolument, and consequence of the offices they hold under the state establishments; and the perverted ambition of another class of men, who will either hope to aggrandize themselves by the confusions of their country or will flatter themselves with fairer prospects of elevation from the subdivision of the empire into several partial confederacies than from its union under one government."

The fight would be ugly. "A torrent of angry and malignant passions will be let loose," Hamilton wrote. The battle lines were already hardening and the strategy coming clear. "They will mutually hope to evince the justness of their opinions and to increase the number of their converts by the loudness of their declamations and the bitterness of their invectives."

Hamilton stated his stance on the constitution as frankly as anonymity allowed. "It is your interest to adopt it," he declared to the readers of the *Journal*. "I am convinced that this is the safest course for your liberty, your dignity, and your happiness." His reasons would become clear in letters to follow, he promised.

"THE UNDERTAKING WAS proposed by Alexander Hamilton to James Madison with a request to join him and Mr. Jay in carrying it into effect," Madison wrote years later. Hamilton had suggested that the three compose a written defense of the new constitution, to be published serially in New York papers. Madison and John Jay agreed. Hamilton also approached Gouverneur Morris and William Duer. Morris declined; Duer wrote a couple of pieces before dropping out.

Jay devoted the next four Publius numbers to explaining the foreign peril to which a weak government exposed Americans. Jay claimed that the dangers from foreign armies, foreign diplomats and foreign agents were greater than Americans realized. He spoke from his experience as American envoy to Spain during the Revolutionary War, peace commissioner in Paris at the end of the war, and foreign secretary of the Confederation after the war. Jay's exposure to the world of the great powers had made a hard-eyed realist of him. "It is too true, however disgraceful it may be to human nature, that nations in general will make war whenever they have a prospect of getting anything by it," he said. Britain and France would try to shut America out of the Atlantic fishery. Spain would close the Mississippi to Americans if it could, and Britain the St. Lawrence. Those countries would respect American interests and rights only to the degree America could defend them. And America could defend them only with the energetic government the constitution would provide.

Hamilton returned as Publius to describe the dangers to America from disputes among the states. Americans were no more angels than Europeans. "Men are ambitious, vindictive and rapacious," Hamilton declared. To expect harmony among independent American states "would be to disregard the uniform course of human events and to set at defiance the accumulated experience of ages."

American optimists looked to republican virtue to tame the devil in men's hearts. The optimists would be disappointed, Hamilton said. "Have republics in practice been less addicted to war than monarchies?" No, they had not. Why should they be? "Are not the former administered by *men* as well as the latter? Are there not aversions, predilections, rivalships, and desires of unjust acquisitions that affect nations as well as kings? Are not popular assemblies frequently subject to the impulses of rage, resentment, jealousy, avarice, and of other irregular and violent propensities?" Yes, they were, and always would be.

Skeptics of Hamilton's view asked what inducements would cause the states to war on each other. "Precisely the same inducements which have, at different times, deluged in blood all the nations in the world," he answered. Territorial disputes would arise over existing boundaries and over western lands. Commercial disputes, already occurring, would grow worse. New Jersey and Connecticut currently complained of the tax they paid New York for the right to sell produce there; this tax would increase, as taxes always did. The national debt from the war divided the thrifty states from the profligate and would trigger a beggar-thy-neighbor scramble to evade future payments. State courts sheltered their own citizens from creditors in other states; allowed to continue, such practice would escalate to outright repudiation, and violence. "A war not of parchment but of the sword would chastise such atrocious breaches of moral obligation and social justice," Hamilton said.

Wars between the American states would be more sanguinary and demoralizing than the wars of Europe. There the nations had learned over time to defend themselves and had developed rules of warfare; in America no such preparations or norms existed. "The want of fortifications, leaving the frontiers of one state open to another, would facilitate inroads," Hamilton said. "The populous states would with little difficulty overrun their less populous neighbors. Conquests would be as easy to be made as difficult to be retained. War therefore would be desultory and predatory. Plunder and devastation ever march in the train of irregulars."

A robust national union not only would prevent such wars, said Hamilton, but would protect states against insurrections within their own borders. Insurgents in a state might overawe the government of that state, but they could not withstand the power of the national government. Had Daniel Shays known he would face the army of the United States rather than the militia of Massachusetts, he never would have raised the banner of rebellion.

MADISON TOOK UP the pen at the tenth number of Hamilton's project. He observed that conventional wisdom had long held that republics had to be small to survive. Self-government could be effective only where the selves in question knew one another. Madison challenged this view. Indeed he turned it upside down, asserting that a large republic, such as the constitution would create, would be more durable than small ones.

The key was controlling faction, Madison said. The concept was important enough to warrant a definition: "By a faction, I understand a number of citizens, whether amounting to a majority or a minority of the whole, who are united and actuated by some common impulse of passion, or of interest, adversed to the rights of other citizens, or to the permanent and aggregate interests of the community." Because a faction—by Madison's definition—was opposed to the general welfare, it had to be restrained or neutralized lest it damage that welfare.

Madison proceeded by logical steps. "There are two methods of curing the mischiefs of faction: the one, by removing its causes; the other, by controlling its effects," he said. "There are again two methods of removing the causes of faction: the one, by destroying the liberty which is essential to its existence; the other, by giving to every citizen the same opinions, the same passions, and the same interests."

The first remedy for faction's cause—destroying liberty—was worse than the disease. The second remedy—giving everyone the same opinions—was impossible in a free society. Therefore, statesmen must focus on controlling faction's effects.

Madison explained how this would work under the proposed constitution. "If a faction consists of less than a majority, relief is supplied by the republican principle, which enables the majority to defeat its sinister views by regular vote," he said. The faction might annoy but it could not destroy. "It may clog the administration, it may convulse the society; but it will be unable to execute and mask its violence under the forms of the constitution."

Majority factions posed greater problems. They could legally take office and legislate their agendas, to the detriment of the rights of the minority and the interest of the nation. Madison declined here to explain how the interest of the nation was to be determined separate from the views of the majority faction. But for the sake of his argument he assumed that such separation was possible.

He moved on. "To secure the public good and private rights against the danger of such a faction, and at the same time to preserve the spirit and the form of popular government, is then the great object to which our inquiries are directed." By what means could this object be attained? By one of two methods: "Either the existence of the same passion or interest in a majority at the same time must be prevented, or the majority, having such coexistent passion or interest, must be rendered, by their number and local situation, unable to concert and carry into effect schemes of oppression." Madison had already dismissed the first alternative as impractical. The second was all that remained.

Which brought him to his main point: that the new constitution provided just such a neutralizing mechanism. The salient features here were that the government the constitution provided was republican rather than democratic, and that it was extensive.

With the other Federalists, Madison considered democracy dangerous and doomed. "A pure democracy, by which I mean a society consisting of a small number of citizens who assemble and administer the government in person, can admit of no cure for the mischiefs of faction," he said. "A common passion or interest will, in almost every case, be felt by a majority of the whole." This passion would seize the government and assail the minority, provoking the latter to violence. "Hence it is that such democracies have ever been spectacles of turbulence and contention; have ever been found incompatible with personal security or the rights of property; and have in general been as short in their lives as they have been violent in their deaths."

A republic behaved differently. "A republic, by which I mean a government in which the scheme of representation takes place, opens a different prospect and promises the cure for which we are seeking," Madison wrote. "The two great points of difference between a democracy and a republic are: first, the delegation of the government, in the latter, to a small number of citizens elected by the rest; secondly, the greater number of citizens and greater sphere of country over which the latter may be extended."

Delegation refined public views by submitting them to the scrutiny of individuals with the time and training to sift passion from true public interest. "The public voice pronounced by the representatives of the people will be more consonant to the public good than if pronounced by the people themselves," Madison said. This was his answer to the question of how the national interest would be determined.

But how to ensure that the representatives were wiser than the people? Madison finally reached his essential innovation: "The question resulting is, whether small or extensive republics are more favorable to the election of proper guardians of the public weal; and it is clearly decided in favor of the latter."

The first reason was that large republics comprised large populations, from which a better class of representatives would be chosen. Demagogues might sway a small number of people, but they would never delude a large number, especially when spread over an extensive geography.

The second and more important reason was that factions would have a harder time forming in a republic spread over a large area. "Extend the sphere, and you take in a greater variety of parties and interests," Madison said. "You make it less probable that a majority of the whole will have a common motive to invade the rights of other citizens; or if such a common motive exists, it will be more difficult for all who feel it to discover their own strength and to act in unison with each other."

The effect would be even more pronounced in a federal republic of several states. "The influence of factious leaders may kindle a flame within their particular states but will be unable to spread a general conflagration through the other states. A religious sect may degenerate into a political faction in a part of the confederacy, but the variety of sects dispersed over the entire face of it must secure the national councils against any danger from that source. A rage for paper money, for an abolition of debts, for an equal division of property, or for any other improper or wicked project, will be less apt to pervade the whole body of the Union than a particular member of it."

Madison's QED was succinct: "In the extent and proper structure of the Union, therefore, we behold a republican remedy for the diseases most incident to republican government."

MADISON'S ESSAY, later called Federalist Number 10, would be the foremost contribution to political theory of the entire set of essays, which eventually ran to eighty-five articles. But other numbers made marks as well, albeit sometimes more in the interpretation of the constitution after its ratification than in the ratification debate itself.

In Federalist 51 Madison expanded his theory of competing factions to a justification of the system of checks and balances written into the constitution. "If men were angels, no government would be necessary," Madison wrote. "If angels were to govern men, neither external nor internal controls on government would be necessary." But men were not angels, nor did angels govern men. "In framing a government which is to be administered by men over men," Madison continued, "the great difficulty lies in this: you must first enable the government to control the governed, and in the next place oblige it to control itself." In the system specified by the proposed constitution, the legislative branch would hold the initiative, but within the legislature, the Senate and the House of Representatives would each check the other. The executive would check the legislature by the veto accorded the president. Yet the veto was not absolute; it permitted the legislature to check the president by an override. The judiciary could check both other branches but was itself restrained by the executive, which nominated federal judges, and by the legislature, whose Senate had to confirm them. Beyond this, the division of authority between the federal government and the states allowed an additional layer of checks. "Ambition must be made to counteract ambition," Madison asserted as a general principle of government. That principle was built into the constitution.

In Federalist 70 Hamilton defended the invigorated presidency projected by the constitution. "Energy in the executive is a leading character in the definition of good government," he wrote. "It is essential to the protection of the community against foreign attacks; it is not less essential to the steady administration of the laws, to the protection of property against those irregular and high-handed combinations which sometimes interrupt the ordinary course of justice, to the security of liberty against the enterprises and assaults of ambition, of faction, and of anarchy." Hamilton reminded his readers how the Romans in times of peril handed power to a dictator; this practice had saved the Roman republic on many occasions. America under the Articles of Confederation suffered from a weak executive, elected by and beholden to the legislature. The new constitution corrected this error.

In Federalist 84 Hamilton rebutted the contention that the constitution ought to include a bill of rights. The English bill of rights had the purpose of reining in the monarch; America had no monarch and no such need. Yet Hamilton didn't leave the matter there. "I go further and affirm that bills of rights, in the sense and to the extent in which they are contended for, are not only unnecessary in the proposed constitution but would even be dangerous," he said. The constitution was a limited charter, granting specific powers to the federal government. Bills of rights would blur this crucial point. "They would contain various exceptions to powers not granted; and, on this very account, would afford a colorable pretext to claim more than were granted. For why declare that things shall not be done which there is no power to do? Why, for instance, should it be said that the liberty of the press shall not be restrained, when no power is given by which restrictions may be imposed?" Not all rights could be listed; any left off the list might be presumed fair game for government trespass.

## 18

Hamilton, madison and Jay did not have the field to themselves. "Brutus" parried Publius blow for blow in the papers of New York. "When the public is called to investigate and decide upon a question in which not only the present members of the community are deeply interested, but upon which the happiness and misery of generations yet unborn is in great measure suspended, the benevolent mind cannot help feeling itself peculiarly interested in the result," Brutus declared in his opening statement.

Brutus never identified himself. He might have been Robert Yates, but the evidence is circumstantial. Yates, of the New York delegation at Philadelphia, had grown increasingly concerned at the centralizing direction of the discussions there and had finally departed in protest. If Publius was supposed to bring to mind a founder of the Roman republic, Brutus recalled the patriot who saved the republic by slaying the tyrant Caesar.

No less a threat faced the American republic from this new constitution, said Brutus. "The most important question that was ever proposed to your decision, or to the decision of any people under heaven, is before you," he told his readers. "You are to decide upon it by men of your own election, chosen specially for this purpose." If the constitution were a good one, it would produce blessings for generations to come. "But if, on the other hand, this form of government contains principles that will lead to the subversion of liberty, if it tends to establish a despotism, or, what is worse, a tyrannic aristocracy; then, if you adopt it, this only remaining asylum for liberty will be shut up, and posterity will execrate your memory."

Sadly, the constitution contained those very subversive principles. Some had suggested the flaws could be remedied by amendments after ratification. "If it has its defects, it is said, they can be best amended when they are experienced," Brutus wrote. "But remember, when the people once part with power, they can seldom or never resume it again but by force. Many instances can be produced in which the people have voluntarily increased the powers of their rulers; but few, if any, in which rulers have willingly abridged their authority." The people must not relinquish their liberty on mere promises.

The essential question, said Brutus, was whether the United States should have a consolidated government, with all authority centralized, or remain a confederation, with the thirteen sovereign states united solely for a few specified purposes. "This enquiry is important, because, although the government reported by the convention does not go to a perfect and entire consolidation, yet it approaches so near to it that it must, if executed, certainly and infallibly terminate in it. This government is to possess absolute and uncontrollable power, legislative, executive and judicial, with respect to every object to which it extends."

Brutus rejected the Federalist argument that the careful listing, or enumeration, of powers would protect the rights of the people. Enumeration was no restraint, he said, for the "common defense" and "general welfare" clauses made it a sham. The national legislators would do whatever they liked with those clauses. "They are the sole judges of what is necessary to provide for the common defence, and they only are to determine what is for the general welfare; this power therefore is neither more nor less than a power to lay and collect taxes, imposts, and excises, at their pleasure."

Brutus decried that the new government could act on the people directly, rather than through the states. "The idea of confederation is totally lost, and that of one entire republic is embraced," Brutus said. The government's intrusive power extended to taxes, which was appallingly ironic given that taxes had been the first cause of the revolution. The people were being asked to surrender to the new government what they had defended at great cost from King George. "The authority to lay and collect taxes is the most important of any power that can be granted; it connects with it almost all other powers, or at least will in process of time draw all other after it; it is the great mean of protection, security, and defence, in a good government, and the great engine of oppression and tyranny in a bad one."

Brutus did not impugn the integrity of the framers and supporters of the constitution. But their work would have evil consequences all the same. "It is a truth confirmed by the unerring experience of ages that every man, and every body of men, invested with power are ever disposed to increase it and to acquire a superiority over everything that stands in their way."

Brutus had much more to say in this essay and the fifteen that followed. The essence of his argument was that the proposed constitution was an unwise and unjustified usurpation of the powers of the states. The collection was as cogent as the Publius essays and was often better written, perhaps from being the work of a single writer rather than a trio. If the fate of the constitution had been decided in a court of law, Brutus might well have carried the day.

BUT THE COURT of politics was not a court of law, and it was the court of politics that would render the verdict on the constitution. And in that court the Federalists seemed to be winning. Delaware's convention voted to ratify in December 1787. Pennsylvania and New Jersey followed before the year's end, with Georgia and Connecticut joining in early January 1788.

But then Luther Martin tore the curtain from the Philadelphia convention by revealing its secrets to the Maryland House of Delegates. Martin had been a Maryland delegate to the convention but, like Robert Yates, left early in protest of the direction things were going. Luther's testimony to the Maryland house was long and for that reason ill-suited as a cudgel against the Federalists; he spiced it up in a series of newspaper pieces quickly reprinted as a pamphlet, and especially in a cover letter to the American people that accompanied the pamphlet.

In the letter Martin conveyed his shock at discovering that Madison and Hamilton had summoned the convention under the false pretense of amending the Articles, when they actually aimed to destroy the Articles. What was worse, most of the other delegates acquiesced or cooperated in the destruction. "Could there possibly be a greater indignity and insult offered to the majesty of the free states and the free citizens of America than for the very men who were entrusted with powers for the preservation and security of their rights, and for the establishment of a permanent system to promote their happiness, to make use of that power to destroy both the one and the other?" demanded Martin. The Philadelphia conspirators should have been ashamed of themselves. "Such a conduct in any other country, or even in this, at any other time, would have drawn down upon them the indignation and resentment of those who were thus attempted to be abused and enslaved," Martin said.

Martin's revelations and assertions thrilled the Antifederalists, who cited his words as proof of a dark design by the Federalists against the rights of the people. The resulting furor slowed the rush toward ratification. The Massachusetts convention voted in favor but called for amendments; the New Hampshire convention adjourned without a decision; Rhode Island rebuffed the constitution via referendum.

Three more states were required to reach the constitution's self-declared threshold of nine. Maryland and South Carolina were leaning toward ratification. New Hampshire and North Carolina could go either way.

But the big prizes, the ones that could make or break the constitution, were Virginia and New York. Without the former, the largest of the states, and the latter, the bridge between New England and the rest of the country, the project of Madison and Hamilton might fail even with nine states ratifying.

## 19

V IRGINIA HAD BEEN contested territory since the Philadelphia convention adjourned. Richard Henry Lee, a stalwart of
independence—indeed, the member of the Continental Congress who
had introduced the resolution to declare independence in June 1776—
fired a shot across the Federalists' bow with an open letter to Edmund
Randolph in October. Lee wanted to prevent a quick decision, which
he feared would result in ratification. Already there was talk of amending the handiwork of the Philadelphia convention, but the Federalists countered by saying ratification must come first, to stem incipient
chaos, and then amendment.

Lee thought this put things just backwards. "The establishment of
the new plan of government, in its present form, is a question that
involves such immense consequences to the present times and to posterity that it calls for the deepest attention of the best and wisest friends
of their country and of mankind," he wrote. "If it be found good after
mature deliberation, adopt it; if wrong, amend it at all events, for to
say (as many do) that a bad government must be established for fear of
anarchy, is really saying that we must kill ourselves for fear of dying."
The Federalists asserted that a new convention would take too long
to summon. Nonsense, said Lee. "Experience and the actual state of
things shew that there is no difficulty in procuring a general convention, the late one being collected without any obstruction." Not only
*could* a new convention be called; it *must* be called. "Good government
is not the work of a short time, or of sudden thought."

Lee disliked the arrangement that made the president and the Senate conspirators against the people. "In the new constitution, the president and senate have all the executive and two thirds of the legislative power," he said. "In some weighty instances (as making all kinds of treaties which are to be the laws of the land) they have the whole legislative and executive powers. They jointly appoint all officers civil and military, and they (the senate) try all impeachments either of their own members or of the officers appointed by themselves. Is there not a most formidable combination of power thus created in a few?" The combination would grow more formidable with time. "Either a monarchy or aristocracy will be generated," Lee said. "This new constitution is, in its first principles, highly and dangerously oligarchic; and it is a point agreed that a government of the few, is of all governments the worst."

He complained of the lack of a bill of rights. Appeals to the virtue of officeholders wouldn't restrain them. "It is not to be expected from human nature that the few should always be attentive to the good of the many," Lee wrote. He thought trade laws ought to require more than a simple majority, lest the more numerous northern states outmaneuver the southern. Again he dismissed appeals to virtue, this time of northern merchants. "How feeble, sir, is policy when opposed to interest among trading people."

Lee didn't deny some of the merits of the new constitution. These made it all the more important to remedy the deficiencies. "As this constitution abounds with useful regulations at the same time that it is liable to strong and fundamental objections, the plan for us to pursue will be to propose the necessary amendments and express our willingness to adopt it with the amendments, and to suggest the calling of a new convention for the purpose of considering them. To this I see no well-founded objection, but great safety and much good to be the probable result."


GEORGE MASON, unlike Lee, had been at Philadelphia, although he departed in a huff after refusing to sign the constitution. "Colonel Mason left Philadelphia in an exceeding ill humour," Madison wrote to Jefferson. "A number of little circumstances arising in part from the impatience which prevailed towards the close of the business conspired to whet his acrimony." Mason felt that his appeals for last-minute

changes had been slighted. "He returned to Virginia with a fixed disposition to prevent the adoption of the plan if possible."

Mason's campaign commenced with a letter to George Washington
laying out the deficiencies of the constitution. "There is no declaration of rights," said Mason. "And the laws of the general government
being paramount to the laws and constitutions of the several states, the
declarations of rights in the separate states are no security. Nor are the
people secured even in the enjoyment of the benefits of the common-
law"—the English common law—"which stands here upon no other
foundation than its having been adopted by the respective acts forming
the constitutions of the several states."

The dominant role accorded the Senate made Congress unrepre-
sentative of the people, Mason said. The unelected character of the
senators, their apportionment by states, and their connection with the
executive in making appointments and treaties and in trying impeachments "will destroy any balance in the government and enable them to
accomplish what usurpations they please upon the rights and liberties
of the people."

The federal judiciary was too powerful. It would "absorb and destroy
the judiciaries of the several states, thereby rendering law as tedious,
intricate and expensive, and justice as unattainable by a great part of
the community, as in England, and enabling the rich to oppress and
ruin the poor."

Mason considered the executive especially alarming. "The president
of the United States has no constitutional council (a thing unknown
in any safe and regular government); he will therefore be unsupported
by proper information and advice, and will generally be directed by
minions and favourites; or he will become a tool to the Senate." Even if
the executive didn't fall under the sway of the Senate, the office would
be dangerous. "The president of the United States has the unrestrained
power of granting pardons for treason, which may be sometimes exercised to screen from punishment those whom he had secretly instigated
to commit the crime, and thereby prevent a discovery of his own guilt."
If the president *did* ally with the Senate, the states could be crushed.
"By declaring all treaties supreme laws of the land, the executive and
the Senate have, in many cases, an exclusive power of legislation."

Mason distrusted Congress to employ its authority over trade fairly.
"By requiring only a majority to make all commercial and navigation

laws, the five southern states (whose produce and circumstances are totally different from that of the eight northern and eastern states) will be ruined, for such rigid and premature regulations may be made as will enable the merchants of the northern and eastern states not only to demand an exorbitant freight but to monopolize the purchase of the commodities at their own price for many years."

Nor was there reliable rein on the power of Congress generally. "Under their own construction of the general clause"—the necessary and proper clause—"at the end of the enumerated powers, the Congress may grant monopolies in trade and commerce, constitute new crimes, inflict unusual and severe punishments, and extend their power as far as they shall think proper." State laws, now subordinate to federal law, would give no protection to the people.

Mason denounced the twenty-year ban on ending slave imports. His complaint had less to do with the welfare of the enslaved than with the health of the Union. "Such importations render the United States weaker, more vulnerable, and less capable of defence," he said.

Should the proposed constitution be ratified as written, American republicanism was in grave peril. "This government will commence in a moderate aristocracy," Mason said. "It is at present impossible to foresee whether it will in its operation produce a monarchy or a corrupt oppressive aristocracy. It will most probably vibrate some years between the two, and then terminate in the one or the other."

Mason refocused his indictment of the constitution when the Virginia convention opened in June, in Richmond. He condemned the drafters for creating what they had no authority to create. "It is a national government and no longer a confederation," he said. The action of the Philadelphia convention was not simply illegal but dangerous. "The very idea of converting what was formerly a confederation to a consolidated government is totally subversive of every principle which has hitherto governed us. This power is calculated to annihilate totally the state governments." The constitution didn't avow this destructive intent, and neither did the Federalists. But annihilation was inevitable in the dual structure the constitution specified. Taxes alone would break the system. "Will the people of this great community submit to be individually taxed by two different and distinct powers? Will they suffer themselves to be doubly harassed?" asked Mason. They would not. "These two concurrent powers cannot exist long together;

the one will destroy the other. The general government being paramount to and in every respect more powerful than the state governments, the latter must give way to the former."

The American states were too far-flung to be amalgamated into a single government and that government remain republican, Mason said. "Is it to be supposed that one national government will suit so extensive a country, embracing so many climates and containing inhabitants so very different in manners, habits, and customs? It is ascertained by history that there never was a government over a very extensive country without destroying the liberties of the people." The record of the past was clear. "Monarchy may suit a large territory, and despotic governments ever so extensive a country, but popular governments can only exist in small territories."

## 20

G EORGE MASON WAS no orator. Many Virginians admired his careful reasoning, but his tepid delivery left listeners flat.

Not so with Patrick Henry, whose talents were the perfect complement to Mason's. In the culture of Virginia politics, none stood higher than Henry. Washington had eclipsed him in the esteem of the nation, but Washington's reputation was military rather than political. And Washington, though four years older than Henry, was in some ways a son of Henry, who more than any other Virginian had set the wheels of revolution in motion. Henry's speech to the 1775 Virginia convention weighing grievances against Britain was still held in awe. Many in Virginia had been calling for patience, asking for time to resolve the differences with Britain. Such time had passed, said Henry. "Let us not, I beseech you, sir, deceive ourselves longer. Sir, we have done everything that could be done to avert the storm which is now coming on. We have petitioned—we have remonstrated—we have supplicated—we have prostrated ourselves before the throne." All to no avail. "Our petitions have been slighted; our remonstrances have produced additional violence and insult; our supplications have been disregarded; and we have been spurned, with contempt, from the foot of the throne." There was no longer room for hope. "If we wish to be free," said Henry, "we must fight! I repeat it, sir, we must fight! An appeal to arms and to the God of hosts is all that is left us!"

An eyewitness to Henry's performance that day left a record. "Imagine to yourself this sentence"—the one about fighting—"delivered with all the calm dignity of Cato, of Utica—imagine to yourself the Roman senate, assembled in the capitol, when it was entered by the profane Gauls, who at first were awed by their presence, as if they had entered an assembly of the gods. Imagine that you heard Cato addressing such a senate—imagine that you saw the handwriting on the wall of Belshaz-zar's palace—imagine you heard a voice as from heaven uttering the words 'We must fight' as the doom of fate, and you may have some idea of the speaker, the assembly to whom he addressed himself, and the auditory, of which I was one."

Henry wasn't finished. Yes, he acknowledged, America was out-numbered. But numbers weren't the whole story. "Three millions of people armed in the holy cause of liberty and in such a country as that which we possess are invincible by any force which our enemy can send against us. . . . The battle, sir, is not to the strong alone; it is to the vigilant, the active, the brave." Besides, America had no choice. "If we were base enough to desire it, it is now too late to retire from the con-test. There is no retreat but in submission and slavery! Our chains are forged. Their clanking may be heard on the plains of Boston. The war is inevitable—and let it come. I repeat, sir, let it come!

"It is vain, sir, to extenuate the matter. Gentlemen may cry 'Peace, peace'; but there is no peace. The war is actually begun. The next gale that sweeps from the north will bring to our ears the clash of resound-ing arms. Our brethren are already in the field; why stand we here idle? What is it that gentlemen wish? What would they have. Is life so dear, or peace so sweet, as to be purchased at the price of chains and slavery? Forbid it, Almighty God!"

Henry gazed around the room, and then toward heaven. Raising his arms, almost like Jesus on the cross, he pronounced, "I know not what course others may take, but as for me, give me liberty or give me death!"

Henry's framing of the choice—liberty or death—became the guid-ing spirit of the revolution, propelling men like Washington to take arms. Henry's words inspired Thomas Paine and also Jefferson, who, as a law student in Williamsburg, caught Henry's performance from the wings of the hall.

Henry helped draft Virginia's declaration of rights and Virginia's state constitution. He was elected governor five times.

His crucial role in the founding of modern Virginia gave him a proprietary feeling toward its interests and prerogatives. He looked askance at anything that threatened to impinge on Virginia's freedom and autonomy. His eminence in the state's affairs made him a natural to attend the Philadelphia convention in 1787. His Virginia compatriots selected him.

But he declined the honor. A neighbor asked him why.

"I smelt a rat," said Henry.

THE RODENT WAS still reeking when Henry read the proposed constitution. Perhaps he now regretted having boycotted the Philadelphia meeting, which in his absence had produced the centralizing charter he feared. He wouldn't make the same mistake again, instead taking a seat in the Virginia convention at the head of the Antifederalist forces.

"Mr. Chairman," he declared in his opening speech: "The public mind, as well as my own, is extremely uneasy at the proposed change of government." Henry proposed to speak for the Virginia public. "I consider myself as the servant of the people of this commonwealth, as a sentinel over their rights, liberty, and happiness." Those possessions were under insidious assault. Nor was the peril to Virginia alone. "I conceive the republic to be in extreme danger."

Henry bristled at the opening words of the constitution, which revealed the coup attempted by the Philadelphia cabal. "What right had they to say, 'We, the People,'? . . . Who authorised them to speak the language of, 'We, the People,' instead of, 'We, the States'?" No one had authorized them; they had usurped the authority of the states. They had been tasked with proposing amendments to the Articles of Confederation; instead they conspired in the Articles' destruction, presuming to replace the confederation with "one great consolidated national government of the people of all the states."

The Federalists claimed the compulsion of mounting disorder. Their claims had no basis in the lives of Virginians, Henry said. "Disorders have arisen in other parts of America, but here, sir, no dangers, no insurrection or tumult, have happened. Everything has been calm and tranquil." The conspirators pushed ahead nonetheless, and in doing so they created the very disorder they claimed to be averting. "We are wandering on the great ocean of human affairs. I see no landmark to guide us. We are running we know not whither. Difference in opinion has gone to a degree of inflammatory resentment in different parts of the country, which has been occasioned by this perilous innovation."

Henry contended that the Federalists were trying to undo the nation's work of the previous decade. "Here is a revolution as radical as that which separated us from Great Britain," he said. The American Revolution had been all about expanding liberty, Henry said; the Federalist counterrevolution was about limiting it. "The rights of conscience, trial by jury, liberty of the press, all your immunities and franchises, all pretensions to human rights and privileges, are rendered insecure, if not lost, by this change." Henry professed amazement that so many others were willing to surrender without a fight. "Is this tame relinquishment of rights worthy of freemen? Is it worthy of that manly fortitude that ought to characterize republicans?" Eight states had ratified the constitution; that was on their consciences. Henry would not have Virginia join them. "I declare that if twelve states and an half had adopted it, I would with manly firmness, and in spite of an erring world, reject it."

Henry conceded he might be waging a losing battle. He was being pilloried and slandered for his opposition. He had been there before. "Twenty-three years ago was I supposed a traitor to my country. I was then said to be a bane of sedition because I supported the rights of my country." Similar charges were being leveled at him now. "I may be thought suspicious when I say our privileges and rights are in danger." But they *were* in danger.

Henry resented the opprobrium heaped upon the Confederation by those intending its downfall. "The Confederation: this same despised government, merits, in my opinion, the highest encomium. It carried us through a long and dangerous war. It rendered us victorious in that bloody conflict with a powerful nation. It has secured us a territory greater than any European monarch possesses." What more could Americans want?

The Federalists declared that any faults in the constitution could be repaired by amendment. They were being disingenuous, Henry said. The requirement that three-fourths of the states approve any amendment gave veto power to a very small minority. "One-twentieth part of the American people may prevent the removal of the most grievous inconveniencies and oppression by refusing to accede to amendments," he reckoned. "A trifling minority may reject the most salutary amendments."

Yet amendments were what the proposed constitution sorely needed. "This constitution is said to have beautiful features, but when I come to examine these features, sir, they appear to me horribly frightful. Among other deformities, it has an awful squinting; it squints towards monarchy." Entirely too much power was accorded the executive. "Your president may easily become king." Or a tyrant. "If your American chief be a man of ambition and abilities, how easy is it for him to render himself absolute! The army is in his hands, and if he be a man of address, it will be attached to him. And it will be the subject of long meditation with him to seize the first auspicious moment to accomplish his design." The legislature was equally flawed. "Your senate is so imperfectly constructed that your dearest rights may be sacrificed by what may be a small minority."

Worst of all was the lack of a bill of rights. Many others had advanced this objection by now, but none made more of it than Henry. Some delegates were proposing that the convention approve the constitution with a proviso that a bill of rights be added as soon as possible; Henry heaped scorn on the idea. Such a proviso would have no legal standing, he said; a state either ratified the constitution or it did not. Beyond this, Henry followed Alexander Hamilton in declaring that any enumeration of rights would leave other rights more imperiled than before. "What is the inference when you enumerate the rights which you are to enjoy?" Henry asked rhetorically. "That those not enumerated are relinquished." Referring to a particular version of the proviso, Henry said, "There are only three things to be retained: religion, freedom of the press, and jury trial. Will not the ratification carry everything excepting these three things? Will not all the world pronounce that we intended to give up all the rest?"

Among the rights Henry feared losing was the right to hold property in slaves. Henry did not like slavery; he lamented the day the institution entered America. "It would rejoice my very soul that every one of my fellow beings was emancipated," he said. "As we ought with gratitude to admire that decree of Heaven which has numbered us among the free, we ought to lament and deplore the necessity of holding our fellow men in bondage."

But slavery *had* entered America, and removing it surpassed current political ingenuity. The slaves must remain slaves, for the time being at least. "Is it practicable by any human means to liberate them without producing the most dreadful and ruinous consequences?" asked Henry. He thought not.

Nevertheless, northern states might decree emancipation. *They* would suffer no consequences, for they had few slaves. They could indulge their consciences at no cost to themselves.

How might the northerners mandate emancipation? The Federalists were arguing that the constitution conveyed no such authority to the national government. They lacked imagination or honesty, Henry said. He described a scenario that would end in emancipation. Suppose America went to war. "May Congress not say that every black man must fight?" The slaves would require an incentive to fight; the obvious one was emancipation. A northern majority might not be able to resist. "Have they not power to provide for the general defence and welfare?" asked Henry. "May they not think that these call for the abolition of slavery?"

Henry repeated that he wished slavery did not exist in America. But this sentiment didn't make him willing to place the fate of Virginia in irresponsible hands. "As much as I deplore slavery, I see that prudence forbids its abolition. I deny that the general government ought to set them free, because a decided majority of the states have not the ties of sympathy and fellow-feeling for those whose interest would be affected by their emancipation."

Henry drew toward his close. Advocates of the constitution claimed to perceive bright promise in the system they proposed to create; Henry saw just the opposite. "I see the awful immensity of the dangers with which it is pregnant. I see it. I feel it. I see beings of a higher order, anxious concerning our decision. When I see beyond the horizon that binds human eyes, and look at the final consummation of all human things, and see those intelligent beings which inhabit the ethereal mansions reviewing the political decisions and revolutions which in the progress of time will happen in America, and the consequent happiness or misery of mankind—I am led to believe that much of the account on one side or the other will depend on what we now decide. Our own happiness alone is not affected by the event. All nations are interested in the determination."

WHILE HENRY WAS speaking, the sky above the meeting hall grew dark with thunderclouds. Decades later, another delegate remembered Henry's peroration and the effect it produced. "The decision"—on the constitution—"was still uncertain, and every mind and every heart was filled with anxiety," the delegate said. "Mr. Henry partook most deeply of this feeling, and while engaged, as it were, in his last effort, availed himself of the strong sensation which he knew to pervade the house, and made an appeal to it which, in point of sublimity, has never been surpassed in any age or country of the world. After describing, in accents which spoke to the soul, and to which every other bosom deeply responded, the awful immensity of the question to the present and future generations, and the throbbing apprehensions with which he looked to the issue, he passed from the house and from the earth, and looking, as he said, 'beyond that horizon which binds mortal eyes,' he pointed—with a countenance and action that made the blood run back upon the aching heart—to those celestial beings, who were hovering over the scene and waiting with anxiety for a decision which involved the happiness or misery of more than half the human race. To those beings—with the same thrilling look and action—he had just addressed an invocation that made every nerve shudder with supernatural horror—when lo! a storm, at that instant arose, which shook the whole building, and the spirits whom he had called, seemed to have come at his bidding. Nor did his eloquence, or the storm, immediately cease, but availing himself of the incident, with a master's art, he seemed to mix in the fight of his ethereal auxiliaries, and, 'rising on the wings of the tempest, to seize upon the artillery of Heaven, and direct its fiercest thunders against the heads of his adversaries.' The scene became insupportable, and the house rose without the formality of adjournment, the members rushing from their seats with precipitation and confusion."

HENRY'S THEATRICS notwithstanding, it was growing apparent that the Antifederalists were falling short in Virginia. They would not be able to prevent their state's approval of the constitution. Virginians recognized that for all the constitution's faults, its closer approximation of proportional representation than the Articles provided gave a big state like Virginia more influence in the national government.

Yet the Antifederalists' efforts had not been wasted, for the convention was willing to propose amendments as a first order of business for the new national government. On June 25 the convention voted 89 to 79 to ratify; on the same day it appointed a committee to propose amendments. This committee incorporated the objections of George Mason, Patrick Henry and others into forty amendments—twenty specifying rights reserved to the people and twenty altering the structure of the new government. The proposed amendments were forwarded to Congress along with the certification of the favorable ratification vote.

Mason wasn't happy with this outcome. While others on the losing side reconciled themselves to the adoption of the constitution, Mason recommended a continuing opposition. "Mr. Mason wished to excite some confusion by a publication addressed to those who were averse to the new government," an observer of the events reported to a friend. Yet Mason bungled the presentation.

Another account suggested that he actively misled his colleagues as to what he intended. "Previous to the adjournment of the late convention, a proposition was made by Mr. Mason that the minority should meet at the public buildings and prepare an address to reconcile the minds of their constituents to the new plan of government," this account stated. Most of those invited thought reconciliation a good idea. "Accordingly a very full meeting was had, when to their surprise an address was offered for their signatures, tending to irritate rather than to quiet the public mind. A number of that respectable body immediately withdrew, others for some time either remained in silence, or, in general terms recommended temper and moderation—till at length Benjamin Harrison Esq., of Charles City, rose and in a firm and manly style opposed not only the address which had been read, but earnestly recommended an adjournment without taking any farther steps in the business. He observed they had done their duty as free and independent men in opposing the constitution, but as it had been adopted by a majority of their countrymen it became their duty to submit as good citizens until those destructive consequences to their liberty should appear which the minority apprehended, in which however he hoped they would be mistaken."

Harrison's words elicited general support, and Mason withdrew his address—and apparently destroyed it, as no copy ever surfaced.

The failed effort cast a shadow over Mason's reputation. A separate version of the events declared, "It was him who first started the idea of keeping up an opposition to the constitution after it had been fairly decided on by the people; to which, effect, a remonstrance was introduced, which wore so much of the native bitterness and austerity of the father on its countenance as to make the hearts of the most daring revolt at the sight; whence he became as solitary and contemptible with his own party in remonstrance then as he had been publicly infamous in his attacks on the other before."

Patrick Henry acquiesced in ratification more gracefully than Mason. An account from a few years later, when political parties were taking hold in America, described Henry's actions following the vote. "The birth of party spirit has been variously conjectured; the result of the Richmond convention for the adoption of the federal constitution was one of its imputed parents," the account began. "In the evening of the day of the final vote, General Meade and Mr. Cabell assembled the *discontents* in the old senate chamber, and after a partial organization of the party, a deputation was sent to Patrick Henry inviting him to take the chair. The venerated patriot accepted. Understanding that it was their purpose to concert a plan of resistance to the operations of the federal government, he addressed the meeting with his accustomed animation upon important occasions, observing, 'he had done his duty strenuously in opposing the constitution, in the *proper place,* and with all the powers he possessed. The question had been fully discussed and settled, and, that as true and faithful republicans, they had all better go home! They should cherish it and give it fair play—support it too, in order that the federal administration might be left to the untrammeled and free exercise of its functions'; reproving, moreover, the half-suppressed factious spirit which he perceived had well nigh broken out. The impressive arguments of Mr. Henry produced the gratifying effect he had hoped for."

## 21

WHILE THE RATIFICATION BATTLE was raging in Virginia, the same struggle played out in New York. Amid the furor Madison kept in close touch with Hamilton, who related that in his state the fight over the constitution had become entangled in local politics. George Clinton was the only governor independent New York had ever known, and although he had supported the plan of Hamilton and Madison to revise the Articles of Confederation, he didn't like the constitution the Philadelphia convention ended up producing. Clinton especially disliked the monopoly over trade the constitution would accord the federal government. Tariffs were the lifeblood of New York's state government—its principal revenue source and a vital instrument of political leverage. Clinton had constructed the most powerful political machine in the country, and he mobilized it against ratification.

"As Clinton is truly the leader of his party, and is inflexibly obstinate, I count little on overcoming opposition by reason," Hamilton reported to Madison in May. "Our only chances will be the previous ratification by nine states, which may shake the firmness of his followers; and a change in the sentiments of the people, which have been for some time travelling towards the constitution." Hamilton hoped to keep the sentiments moving. "We shall leave nothing undone to cultivate a favourable disposition in the citizens at large."

Madison could help by delivering Virginia. "We think here that the situation of your state is critical," Hamilton said. He proposed a sharing of intelligence as swift as horses could gallop. "I believe you meet nearly at the time we do," he said of their respective conventions. "It will be of vast importance that an exact communication should be kept up between us at that period; and the moment *any decisive* question is taken, if favourable, I request you to dispatch an express to me with pointed orders to make all possible diligence, by changing horses etc. All expences shall be thankfully and liberally paid."

Clinton and his allies landed a heavy blow against the constitution by a lopsided victory in the vote for delegates to the New York convention. "They have a majority of two thirds," Hamilton reported to Madison in early June. Yet Clinton hadn't survived a decade in New York's turbulent politics by taking unnecessary risks, and Hamilton thought the governor might play a cautious game. Rather than ratify or reject the constitution, Clinton might opt for adjournment of the convention without a decision. "This will give an opportunity to the state to *see how the government works and to act according to circumstances*," Hamilton wrote.

Their thinking was subtle, so Hamilton explained: "The leaders of the party hostile to the constitution are equally hostile to the Union. They are, however, afraid to reject the constitution at once because that step would bring matters to a crisis between this state and the states which had adopted the constitution, and between the parties in the state." New York itself might break apart. "They therefore resolve upon a long adjournment as the safest and most artful course to effect their final purpose. They suppose that when the government gets into operation it will be obliged to take some steps in respect to revenue etc. which will furnish topics of declamation to its enemies in the several states and will strengthen the minorities. If any considerable discontent should show itself they will stand ready to head the opposition. If on the contrary the thing should go on smoothly and the sentiments of our own people should change, they can then elect to come into the Union. They at all events take the chances of time and the chapter of accidents."

For himself, Hamilton judged this course irresponsibly dangerous. Too many things had to fall into place for them not to fall completely apart. "I fear an eventual disunion and civil war," he said. He again implored Madison to deliver Virginia—with higher help, if necessary. "God grant that Virginia may accede," he said. "Her example will have a vast influence on our politics."

The New York convention, held at Poughkeepsie, commenced as unfavorably for the constitution as Hamilton feared. "Our chance of success here is infinitely slender, and none at all if you go wrong," he wrote to Madison. Clinton's men were delaying, as Hamilton had predicted. Yet two sides could play that game. Hamilton and his allies drew out the debate, hoping for good news from Virginia. "We are going on very deliberately in the discussion," Hamilton told Madison.

A glimmer appeared with news from New Hampshire of that state's approval of the constitution. New Hampshire made nine; the constitution would take effect. The Articles were a dead letter; the status quo was irretrievable. New York's choice now lay between joining the new Union and going alone.

Unfortunately for Hamilton and the Federalists, going alone seemed acceptable to the New York Antifederalists. Hamilton thought he and his colleagues were making progress, yet only up to a point. "Our arguments confound, but do not convince. Some of the leaders, however, appear to me to be convinced *by circumstances* and to be desirous of a retreat. This does not apply to the Chief, who wishes to establish *Clintonism* on the basis of *Antifederalism.*"

This made Virginia's decision all the more crucial. "Our only chance of success depends on you," Hamilton told Madison.


"IT WAS AT about noon on a very hot day," a resident of Poughkeepsie later recalled of July 2, 1788, "when I saw an express rider on a powerful bay horse flecked with foam, dismount at the courthouse door, and placing his bridle-reins in the hands of a negro boy standing by, hastened to the door of the convention chamber and delivered a sealed package to Mr. Barclay, the doorkeeper. The courier was colonel William Smith Livingston, who had ridden express, changing horses several times, from New York City to Poughkeepsie, a distance of eighty-one miles, in less than ten hours. The package he brought contained a dispatch from the president of the Virginia convention at Richmond, and a letter from Madison to Hamilton announcing that Virginia had, on the 25th day of June, unconditionally ratified the constitution.

"The reading of that dispatch gave great joy to the Federalists in the convention, and they cheered loudly. Many people, out of curiosity, had gathered in front of the courthouse after the arrival of the courier, and when the nature of his errand was made known, a part of them formed a little procession and, led by the music of a fife and drum, marched around the courthouse several times. In the evening they lighted a small bonfire. Before sunset Power"—a local newspaper publisher—"had printed an 'extra' on a sheet of paper seven by ten inches in size, which contained the form of the ratification by Virginia."

The news from Virginia thrilled Federalists all over New York state. Arriving as it did just ahead of Independence Day, the report intensified patriotic celebrations of the holiday. The *New York Daily Advertiser* recounted a dinner at Dawson's Tavern in Brooklyn where Federalists cheered the good already accomplished and anticipated the good to come. "All that conviviality and harmony were displayed which the importance of the occasion demanded, and the heart-felt delight of each individual gave birth to," the paper declared. It proceeded to list the toasts presented to—

1. The United States.
2. The illustrious Washington.
3. The King and Queen of France.
4. The day we now commemorate.—May our latest posterity have cause to bless it.
5. The new Constitution—May the year, month, and day in which it was form'd, and the Illustrious members who subscribed it, be ever held in grateful remembrance by every true American.
6. The immortal memory of those heroes whose blood was nobly shed to establish our freedom.
7. The dignity of the people—May every American be a good man, and every good man a Federalist.
8. Peace, freedom, independence and happiness throughout the world.
9. May continual disappointment and never-dying remorse, pain, poverty and contempt, ever attend those Antifederalists who, thro' motives of interest, stand opposed to a government, formed for the good of their country.
10. May the Federalists of the present era enjoy uninterrupted political happiness under the new government, and may the benevolent spirit of unanimity speedily link the timid and misinformed opposers of it, in the golden chain of harmony and peace.

11. May literature grow and be encouraged, and may the importation and use of foreign superfluities rapidly give place to extensive agriculture and manufactures.

12. The American fair—May their sentiments be in favor of the Federal Government, and may they discard from their esteem the man who opposes it.

13. May the United States, cemented by the new Constitution, rise beautiful as a Phoenix from the ashes of contempt; and may commerce, in all its branches, flourish unrestricted under its auspices, as long as America has a name amongst the nations.

The festivities concluded with the performance of a song composed for the occasion, praising the Federalists as heroes and damning the Antifederalists as traitors:

> Ye well approved patriots, whose talents and worth
> Our most grateful expressions demand,
> On this awful occasion we challenge you forth,
> In defence of the Union to stand;
> Those Antis arrest, in their daring career,
> Who for gain would their country undo;
> From them we have everything evil to fear,
> And all things to hope for from you.

The New York Antifederalists weren't ready to concede defeat, though. The *New York Journal* ran a letter from Albany describing a Federalist celebration there, and the Antifederalist reaction. "When the news of the adoption of the constitution by the state of Virginia arrived here," the correspondent related, "the Federal party caused the bells to be rung, walked up to the fort in procession, had ten guns fired with three huzzas between each shot. The same evening the Antifederal party had a meeting, and concluded on walking to the fort in procession the next morning to burn the constitution, which they put into execution about eight o'clock."

This brought both sides to July 4th. They hailed the day together—at first. "About eleven both parties joined to celebrate independency, walked in procession to the fort, and had thirteen cannon fired." The two sides separated to have their own luncheons, at which the guests imbibed with the gusto appropriate to the occasion. They were still feeling the effects during the afternoon's military review. The militiamen included Federalists and Antifederalists, who ordinarily marched together but on this occasion diverged. The Antifederalists gathered outside the tavern that hosted the Antifederalist luncheon, firing guns and making other loud statements of defiance to the Federalists.

"The Federalists then began their maneuvers by walking through the city, carrying a small field piece and firing it at different parts of the town," the correspondent continued. "They turned up the lane which leads from Court to Green street, intending to go past Mr. Hilton's"—the Antifederalist tavern—"but as soon as they entered the street a violent engagement ensued. Stones, clubs and bricks were used on both sides. The light horse were beat back, and went round the block to the other end of the street, where they joined in the action. It was expected some lives would have been lost, for the artillery made use of bayonets; the Federal party being most powerful, forced into the house, and made prisoners of those who had not escaped." Some of the injuries were severe. "Mr. Graham, was the first knocked down by a stone on the head and his life was for some minutes despaired of."

In fact no lives were lost, although that didn't prevent exaggerated retellings from saying some had been. Yet the violence was real enough, and it made the stakes at Poughkeepsie appear greater than ever.


"I FELICITATE YOU sincerely on the event in Virginia," Hamilton wrote to Madison when he read of the ratification. But he didn't at all like the long list of amendments that accompanied the Virginia decision. "I fear the system will be wounded in some of its vital parts by too general a concurrence in some very injudicious recommendations."

The Virginia approach of attaching amendments to ratification complicated Hamilton's work. "Different things are thought of—*conditions precedent,* or previous amendments; conditions *subsequent,* or the proposition of amendments upon condition, that if they are not adopted within a limited time, the state shall be at liberty to *withdraw* from the Union, and lastly *recommendatory amendments.*" Less damaging would be "constructive declarations" of the sentiments of the Poughkeepsie convention. "We will go as far as we can in the lat-ter without invalidating the act"—of ratification—"and will concur in rational recommendations," Hamilton said.

Ten days' more labor moved the Antifederalists hardly at all. They were holding out for a qualified ratification. Hamilton hadn't given up. "Everything possible will yet be attempted to bring the party from that stand to an unqualified ratification," he assured Madison. Yet he didn't think he could get there. Hamilton would consider it a victory if he could keep the qualifications to a minimum, perhaps to one—albeit a drastic one. "The only qualification will be *the reservation* of a right to recede in case our amendments have not been decided upon in one of the modes pointed out in the constitution within a certain number of years, perhaps five or seven."

Hamilton hoped this would satisfy the other states. "If this can in the first instance be admitted as a ratification I do not fear any further consequences," he said. He and Madison might yet get most of what they had worked for. "Congress will I presume recommend certain amendments to render the *structure* of the government more secure. This will satisfy the more considerate and honest opposers of the con-stitution, and with the aid of time will break up the party."


MADISON TRIED TO squelch the thought of a conditional recommen-dation. "I am sorry that your situation obliges you to listen to proposi-tions of the nature you describe," he wrote to Hamilton. "My opinion is that a reservation of a right to withdraw if amendments be not decided on under the form of the constitution within a certain time is a *con-ditional* ratification, that it does not make New York a member of the new Union, and consequently that she could not be received on that plan. Compacts must be reciprocal; this principle would not in such a case be preserved."

Madison went on to make a statement that would have profound ramifications in subsequent decades but at the moment was simply his own opinion: "The constitution requires an adoption *in toto,* and *for-ever.*" Presuming to speak for other Federalists, he added, "It has been so adopted by the other states." He went on, "An adoption for a limited time would be as defective as an adoption of some of the articles only. In short any *condition* whatever must vitiate the ratification." The question had come up in Virginia and been rejected. "This idea of reserving right to withdraw was started at Richmond and considered as a conditional ratification, which was itself considered as worse than a rejection."

HAMILTON AGREED ON the merits of Madison's arguments; he hoped to persuade his fellow delegates at Poughkeepsie on the politics of them. The proceedings at the convention were recorded haphazardly, sometimes by newspapers. The pro-ratification *New York Daily Advertiser* summarized a speech of Hamilton against conditional ratification, after another delegate had proposed that course. "Mr. Hamilton then urged many forcible reasons to prove that even if it were consistent with the constitution to accept us on these terms, it was entirely improbable that the other states would submit to it," the *Advertiser* wrote. "Their interests and their pride would be opposed to it. Their pride, because the very proposal is an insult; and the animosity of some states, embittered as it is by what they deemed a kind of commercial tyranny, and a system of selfish, partial politics, would receive most pungent gratification from a diminution of our fortune and our power. Their interests would be opposed, because the misfortunes of one powerful state commonly contribute to the prosperity of its neighbors.

"Mr. Hamilton, after recapitulating his arguments in a concise and cogent manner, entreated the Convention in a pathetic"—that is, emotional—"strain to make a solemn pause, and weigh well what they were about to do, before they decided on a subject so infinitely important. The orator then closed his address, and received from every unprejudiced spectator the murmur of admiration and applause."

As for the *prejudiced* spectators: "Very different was the effect upon his opposers. They sickened at the splendor of his triumph. Inspired by jealousy and wounded by conscious disgrace, they retired with malice still more embittered, and an obstinacy more confirmed than before."

Several days later Hamilton reiterated his argument against conditional ratification. "The terms of the constitution import"—signify—"a perpetual compact between the different states; this certainly is not. Treaties and engagements with foreign nations are perpetual; this cannot be under this adoption." Conditional ratification would merely serve to alienate the other states. "States and men are averse to inequality.

They would be fully bound, we partially." The advocates of conditional ratification placed too much confidence in New York's importance to the other states. "Should we risk so much on so little?" asked Hamilton. "Is it worth the jeopardy by which it must be obtained?"

Hamilton declared that the Antifederalists had waited too long. If they really wanted leverage with the other states, they should have moved sooner on the constitution. "It is too late now as ten states have adopted it," he said.

Hamilton offered a substitute for conditional ratification. The convention should vote on the constitution as it stood, and then, if a majority favored ratification, the convention should send a circular letter to the governors of the other states recommending changes to the constitution.

Hamilton's suggestion broke the deadlock. Persuaded by his argument on the infeasibility of conditions, or perhaps spooked by the thought of being left behind as the America ship of state sailed away under the new orders of the constitution, the Antifederalist opposition softened. Seizing on Hamilton's suggestion of a circular letter, enough of them switched sides to enable a narrow—30 to 27—victory for ratification.

The circular letter, drafted in part by Hamilton, declared, "We, the members of the convention of this state have deliberately and maturely considered the constitution proposed for the United States. Several articles in it appear so exceptionable to a majority of us that nothing but the fullest confidence of obtaining a revision of them by a general convention, and an invincible reluctance to separating from our sister states, could have prevailed upon a sufficient number to ratify it without stipulating for previous amendments. We all unite in opinion that such a revision will be necessary to recommend it to the approbation and support of a numerous body of our constituents." The letter, noting that other states too were calling for amendments, urged the summoning of a new constitutional convention "to meet at a period not far remote." The letter was signed by the president of the New York convention, George Clinton.

PART V

## The Language of Republicanism

## 22

D EAR SIR," wrote John Adams to John Jay on July 18, 1788. "I am honoured with your letter of the 4th of July and thank you for your friendly congratulations on my arrival."

Adams was writing from his home in Braintree, Massachusetts, to which he had just returned after a decade of diplomatic service in Europe. He had represented the United States in Spain, France, the Netherlands and Britain. He was a dutiful diplomat rather than a gifted one, lacking the social arts and soothing disposition to win favor in foreign courts. "He is not qualified, by nature or education, to shine in courts," observed Jonathan Sewall, who knew Adams from Massachusetts and encountered him again in England. "His abilities are, undoubtedly, quite equal to the mechanical parts of his business as ambassador; but this is not enough. He cannot dance, drink, game, flatter, promise, dress, swear with the gentlemen, and talk small talk and flirt with the ladies; in short, he has none of the essential arts or ornaments which constitute a courtier. There are thousands who, with a tenth part of his understanding and without a spark of his honesty, would distance him infinitely in any court in Europe."

Adams was glad to be relieved of his diplomatic responsibilities and return to America. On landing he learned that the fate of the country's government hung on the decisions of Virginia and New York. By the time he reached Braintree, Virginia had ratified, leaving New York as the crucial undecided state. Adams had worked closely with Jay, and he was pleased to receive Jay's reports on the New York proceedings.

Adams was a devoted Federalist, although till now only from afar. "The decision of the convention at Poughkeepsie is of very great importance to this nation, perhaps to some others," he wrote to Jay. "I am extremely anxious that, as the new constitution has already proceeded so far, it should be adopted kindly and cordially by all the three"—states—"that remain." He added, "A little time I hope will reconcile all."

Yet he wasn't sure it would. On the same day, he wrote to Virginia's Arthur Lee, another comrade from the revolution. "The accession of Virginia to the new constitution is a great event," Adams said. But it was a chancy one. "What would Aristotle and Plato have said if anyone had talked to them of a federative republic of thirteen states, inhabiting a country of five hundred leagues in extent? The new government must act with caution and make itself felt by its beneficence, or we shall have a new convention for amendments. It is a severe mortification to me to find so many of my old friends in opposition. But this is no surprise to me, as I have always differed very materially from them in opinion of the best plan of government."

In fact Adams prided himself on differing from others. He had gained notoriety for defending the British soldiers charged with murder in what cousin Samuel Adams and others called the Boston Massacre. He made no secret of his impatience with Benjamin Franklin when the two served together in France. He even grumbled against Washington at times.

Yet the very stiffness of Adams's neck made him appealing to many as a candidate for office. His integrity stood out in a field not always known for that quality. Nor did it diminish his appeal that he had been away from the country and thereby had avoided the offense-giving that inevitably accompanies politics.

Adams wasn't home long before the invitations to reengage began arriving. "I am apprehensive that you may think of me for a senator, as I find that some other gentlemen have done and continue to do," he responded to one such query. He hoped his name would not be put forward. "You know very well how ungracious and odious the non-acceptance of an appointment by election is, and therefore let me beg of you not to expose me to the necessity of incurring the censure of the public and the obloquy of individuals by so unpopular a measure."

Others promoted Adams for president of Congress. The invitation was honorific, for the Congress in question was about to be dissolved in favor of the Congress of the newly ratified government. Adams spurned this too, telling his daughter, "If my future employment in public depends on a journey to New York, or on the feather of being for a week or a day president of Congress, I will never have any other than private employments while I live. I am willing to serve the public on manly conditions, but not on childish ones; on honourable principles, not mean ones."

Still others wanted to make Adams the first vice president. Washington was the consensus choice for president; no one dared to challenge him. But the Constitution declared that the vice presidency would go to the second-place finisher in the vote of electors, each of whom would cast two ballots. So technically Adams and any other candidates for vice president would be running for president, against Washington.

Adams was torn. "My mind has balanced all circumstances, and all are reducible to two articles: vanity and comfort," he wrote to his wife, Abigail. "I have the alternative in my own power. If they mortify my vanity they give me comfort. They cannot deprive me of comfort without gratifying my vanity."

Comfort was no small temptation for Adams. "The few months that have passed since I have been at home have been the happiest portion of my life," he wrote to a friend. "The agriculture, the manufactures and the commerce of this country I found in a much more flourishing condition than I expected; and the political state of it, by the acceptance and organization of the new government, manifestly improving. The late elections for the new system have gone very well, and fallen upon men of the best heads, the most experience, and the most constancy."

Yet vanity wouldn't rest, because politics wouldn't rest. Sometimes politics intruded on Adams's homestead. "We had a review of the militia upon my farm, and a battle that threw down all my fences," he wrote to an old friend and neighbor. "I wish, however, that Governor Hancock and General Lincoln would not erect their military reputations upon the ruins of my stone walls." John Hancock's name was being circulated for vice president by those who preferred him to Adams; Benjamin Lincoln was lieutenant governor and likely to ascend to governor if Hancock became vice president. "Methinks I hear you whisper, it won't be long ere they erect their civil and political characters upon some other of your ruins," Adams said. "If they do, I shall acquiesce, for the public good. Lincoln I esteem very much; the other I respect as my governor."

BUT NOT AS VICE PRESIDENT. With the presidency to be filled by Virginian Washington, the country looked north for a vice president. George Clinton thought himself a likely candidate, but his Antifederalism worked against him, as did his opponents in New York. Because Massachusetts was where the revolution had started, its leaders figured in the reckoning for vice president, and John Hancock, as Massachusetts governor, seemed a viable prospect. But Hancock, like Clinton, had made enemies, and some doubted his integrity.

Adams had no integrity issues, and he too was from Massachusetts. He was also appropriately diffident. "Our fellow citizens are in the midst of their elections for the new government," Adams wrote to Jefferson in early January 1789. Jefferson was still in Paris and was eager to know how the new system was faring. The states were choosing their delegations to Congress: members of the House of Representatives by popular vote, senators by choice of the state legislatures. The states were also choosing their presidential electors. Here the choice was not specified by the Constitution, and in its silence some states gave voters the responsibility while other states reserved it to the legislatures. The states set their own calendars in the choosing, subject only to a deadline of February 4, when the electors would meet in the state capitals to cast their ballots for president and, effectively, vice president.

Adams understood the logic of balancing South and North, Virginia and Massachusetts. He himself, as a member of the committee appointed by the Continental Congress to compose the Declaration of Independence, had insisted that Jefferson, as a Virginian, do the first drafting. Now the favor was being returned, perhaps. Adams awaited the news phlegmatically. "I have enjoyed a luxury for the last six months which I have never before tasted, for at least eight and twenty years, and have looked down upon all you statesmen with sovereign compassion," he continued in the letter to Jefferson. "The new government has my best wishes and most fervent prayers for its success and prosperity. But whether I shall have anything more to do with it, besides praying for it, depends on the future suffrages of freemen."

The freemen—via the electors—made Adams vice president. All the electors gave Washington one of their ballots, and nearly half gave their second to Adams, with the other second ballots scattered among ten additional candidates. Governors Clinton and Hancock were among the distant laggards.

Adams was prone to see the clouds in any sky, and thus he greeted the news of his election. The states and the people had chosen the new government, he observed to Jefferson, but would they allow it to work? "It may be found easier to give authority than to yield obedience." A first order of business would be the unfinished part of ratification. "Amendments to the Constitution will be expected and no doubt discussed," Adams said. He asked Jefferson for advice. "Will you be so good as to look over the code"—the Constitution—"and write me your sentiments of amendments which you think necessary or useful?" Adams had long championed the separation of powers, especially the separation of the executive from the legislature. The Constitution made a start on this, but Adams thought it could be bolstered. "Without this our government is in danger of being a continual struggle between a junto of grandees for the first chair." Other matters were scarcely less pressing. "The success of the new plan will depend in the first place upon a revenue, to defray the interest of the foreign and domestic debt. But how to get a revenue? How to render smuggling and evasion shameful?" It would be a challenge. "You must expect the first operations will be very slow," Adams told Jefferson.

Adams was a fervent republican, but he distrusted democracy. Ordinary people simply weren't up to the task of making good choices in governance, he judged. The habit of popular elections was already proving pernicious. "The constancy of the people in a course of annual elections has discarded from their confidence almost all the old staunch firm patriots who conducted the revolution in all the civil departments, and has called to the helm pilots much more selfish and much less skillful," Adams told a friend. "I cannot however lay all the blame of this upon the people. Many of my brother patriots have flattered the people by telling them they had virtue, wisdom and talents, which the people themselves have found out by experience they had not. And this has disgusted them with their flatterers." The new Constitution mitigated the democratic tendencies in American politics, but the battle never ended.

To Mercy Otis Warren, the sister of one rebel, the wife of another, and a doughty defender of American rights herself, besides being a friend of John and Abigail Adams, Adams shared his concerns about the capacity of Americans to govern themselves. "The people of our united America find it much easier to institute authority than to yield obedience," he repeated. "They have smarted severely under a total oblivion of the two first principles of liberty and of commerce: that laws are the fountain of freedom and punctuality the source of credit." The Constitution—which Mercy Warren had opposed—made a start on resolving the problem, Adams thought. But it might not be sufficient. "There is still room to fear that there is not enough of the spirit of Union to insure obedience to the laws nor enough of shame and scorn of evasion to secure that revenue on which punctuality will depend. The resources of this country are abundantly superiour to every exigency, and if they are not applied it must be owing to a want of knowledge or a want of integrity."

YET ADAMS'S DOUBTS didn't prevent him from accepting his new office with grace and dignity. He made the journey from Braintree to New York, on the way meeting well-wishers to himself and the new government. The leading men of Hartford escorted him through their city while church bells pealed a salute to triumphant Federalism. New Haven voted Adams the freedom and privileges of their town. At the New York state line Adams was saluted by the light cavalry of Westchester County, which rode beside him for several miles.

The new Congress had already gathered at Federal Hall in Manhattan; Adams greeted the members of the Senate as that body's presiding officer, commencing the sole function specified for the vice president by the Constitution. "Invited to this respectable situation by the suffrages of our fellow citizens, according to the Constitution, I have thought it my duty cheerfully and readily to accept it," he said. "Unaccustomed to refuse any public service, however dangerous to my reputation or disproportioned to my talents, it would have been inconsistent to have adopted another maxim of conduct at this time, when the prosperity of the country and the liberties of the people require, perhaps as much as ever, the attention of those who possess any share of the public confidence."

Adams recognized among the senators many heroes of the revolution—"those celebrated defenders of the liberties of this country, whom menaces could not intimidate, corruption seduce, nor flattery allure; those intrepid assertors of the rights of mankind, whose philosophy and policy have enlightened the world in twenty years more than it was ever before enlightened in many centuries by ancient schools or modern universities." He congratulated the country on having written and ratified the Constitution. He set a model for future vice presidents by lavishing praise on the president. "If we look over the catalogue of the first magistrates of nations, whether they have been denominated presidents or consuls, kings or princes, where shall we find one whose commanding talents and virtues, whose over-ruling good fortune have so completely united all hearts and voices in his favor? Who enjoyed the esteem and admiration of foreign nations and fellow citizens with equal unanimity?"

He concluded with a challenge, a charge and a benediction: "A trust of the greatest magnitude is committed to this legislature, and the eyes of the world are upon you. Your country expects, from the results of your deliberations, in concurrence with the other branches of government, consideration abroad and contentment at home—prosperity, order, justice, peace, and liberty. And may God Almighty's providence assist you to answer their just expectations."

## 23

Thomas Jefferson was pleased on the whole that the Constitution had been ratified, but he had doubts about some of its parts. "I like the organization of the government into legislative, judiciary and executive," he wrote to Madison. "I like the power given the legislature to levy taxes, and for that reason, solely, approve of the greater house being chosen by the people directly." He liked that tax bills had to originate in the House of Representatives, making the requirement for popular approval of taxes still more secure. "I am captivated by the compromise of the opposite claims of the great and little states, of the latter to equal and the former to proportional influence," he said. "I am much pleased too with the substitution of the method of voting by persons, instead of that of voting by states"—in Congress. "And I like the negative given to the executive with a third of either house."

Jefferson proceeded to the parts he did not like. "First the omission of a bill of rights providing clearly and without the aid of sophisms for freedom of religion, freedom of the press, protection against standing armies, restriction against monopolies, the eternal and unremitting force of the habeas corpus laws, and trials by jury in all matters of fact triable by the laws of the land and not by the law of nations." Jefferson had read the arguments of those who defended the absence of a bill of rights, and he found them wanting. "To say, as Mr. Wilson"—James Wilson of Pennsylvania—"does, that a bill of rights was not necessary because all is reserved in the case of the general government which is not given, while in the particular ones all is given which is not reserved, might do for the audience to whom it was addressed, but is surely a *gratis dictum,* opposed by strong inferences from the body of the instrument, as well as from the omission of the clause of our present confederation which had declared that in express terms." Jefferson proclaimed himself an absolutist on the people's rights. "A bill of rights is what the people are entitled to against every government on earth, general or particular, and what no just government should refuse or rest on inference."

"The second feature I dislike, and greatly dislike, is the abandonment in every instance of the necessity of rotation in office, and most particularly in the case of the president," Jefferson continued. "Experience concurs with reason in concluding that the first magistrate will always be reelected if the constitution permits it. He is then an officer for life." There would be no removing a determined incumbent. "If once elected and at a second or third election outvoted by one or two votes, he will pretend false votes, foul play, hold possession of the reins of government, be supported by the states voting for him," Jefferson said.

Jefferson conceded that he and Madison disagreed on some basic issues. "I own I am not a friend to a very energetic government," he said. "It is always oppressive." Jefferson thought Americans—including Madison, although Jefferson didn't cite him specifically—had overreacted to the Shays rebellion. "Calculate that one rebellion in 13 states in the course of 11 years is but one for each state in a century and a half. No country should be so long without one. Nor will any degree of power in the hands of government prevent insurrections. France, with all its despotism, and two or three hundred thousand men always in arms, has had three insurrections in the three years I have been here, in every one of which greater numbers were engaged than in Massachusetts and a great deal more blood was spilt."

Jefferson judged that Madison and the supporters of ratification ought to heed the demands for a bill of rights. From what he had read of the ratification debates, he perceived a consensus on a core of rights to be guaranteed. "It seems pretty generally understood that this should go to juries, habeas corpus, standing armies, printing, religion and monopolies," he said. The standing armies and monopolies were to be protected *against.* Doubtless some arguing was still ahead. "There may be difficulty in finding general modifications of these suited to the habits of all the states. But if such cannot be found then it is better to establish trials by jury, the right of habeas corpus, freedom of the press and freedom of religion in all cases, and to abolish standing armies, in time of peace, and monopolies, in all cases, than not to do it in any."

And always better to err on the side of liberty, Jefferson said. "The few cases wherein these things may do evil cannot be weighed against the multitude wherein the want of them will do evil." He had confidence reasonable men could reach agreement. "I hope therefore a bill of rights will be formed to guard the people against the federal government, as they are already guarded against their state governments in most instances."

## 24

J EFFERSON SEEMS TO have guessed that Madison would play a large role in drafting a bill of rights. It was an apt surmise. During the ratification fight, Madison had opposed the idea of amendments to the Constitution. They were unnecessary, he believed, for the reasons adduced by Hamilton, James Wilson and others. And by opening the handiwork of the Philadelphia convention—*his* handiwork, as he increasingly saw it—to modification so soon, they might cause the whole document to unravel.

But he couldn't ignore the demands of the various states for amendments as a condition—albeit nonbinding—of ratification. To refuse the demands would suggest bad faith and therefore be bad politics, especially as the new government was just commencing operation. Nor were Jefferson's arguments wholly lost on him.

So Madison decided that amendments should be the initial order of business of the new Congress. He won election to the House of Representatives in the first elections to that body, and he urged his colleagues to start in.

They were in no hurry. Most were Federalists, and more than a few hoped amendments would be forgotten if postponed. Besides, they had other matters to attend to. They had to organize Congress and figure out how to make it run. They needed to devise a method for funding the new government and to this end spent weeks debating tariffs. They argued over how to address the president: as "Your highness," "Your excellency," "Mr. President," or something else.

Madison took part in these debates. He argued for tariffs on rum, wine, tea, coffee, sugar and, most controversially, slaves. "The dictates of humanity, the principles of the people, the national safety and happiness, and prudent policy requires it of us," he said of a ten-dollar duty on each slave. "It is to be hoped that by expressing a national disapprobation of this trade, we may destroy it and save ourselves from reproaches, and our posterity the imbecility ever attendant on a country filled with slaves."

He had little patience with the fuss over what to call the president. Some in the House expressed alarm that a fancy title would make the president more ambitious. Madison disagreed. "I do not conceive titles to be so pregnant with danger as some gentlemen apprehend," he said. "I believe a president of the United States clothed with all the powers given in the Constitution would not be a dangerous person to the liberties of America if you were to load him with all the titles of Europe or Asia." Even so, he preferred simplicity. "I am not afraid of titles because I fear the danger of any power they could confer, but I am against them because they are not very reconcilable with the nature of our government or the genius of the people," he said. "Instead of increasing they diminish the true dignity and importance of a republic, and would in particular, on this occasion, diminish the true dignity of the first magistrate himself." America was different from Europe, and its usages should reflect that difference. "If we borrow, the servile imitation will be odious, not to say ridiculous also—we must copy from the pompous sovereigns of the East or follow the inferior potentates of Europe; in either case, the splendid tinsel or gorgeous robe would disgrace the manly shoulders of our chief. . . . The more simple, the more republican we are in our manners, the more rational dignity we acquire."

BUT AFTER TWO MONTHS of such things, Madison insisted the House turn its attention to amendments. Further delay was unacceptable, he told his colleagues. "This house is bound by every motive of prudence not to let the first session pass over without proposing to the state legislatures some things to be incorporated into the Constitution as will render it as acceptable to the whole people of the United States," he said.

To ensure acceptability, Madison wrote the amendments himself.

He explained to wary Federalists that he was giving away nothing of substance. "I will not propose a single alteration which I do not wish to see take place as intrinsically proper in itself," he pledged. His amendments emphasized the rights of the people, which the government ought not to trample in any case. The arguments of the Antifederalists had not been without effect, he acknowledged. "I do conceive that the Constitution may be amended; that is to say, if all power is subject to abuse, that then it is possible the abuse of the powers of the general government may be guarded against in a more secure manner than is now done, while no one advantage arising from the exercise of that power shall be damaged or endangered by it. We have in this way something to gain and, if we proceed with caution, nothing to lose."

Madison had read the letters from all the state conventions proposing amendments; ignoring those which required a change in the structure of the new government, he distilled from the recommendations a list of rights he thought could be prudently added to the Constitution. At this point Madison assumed the amendments would be inserted appropriately into the document itself rather than affixed as an addendum.

He drafted a prologue to the existing prologue, positing: "That all power is originally vested in, and consequently derived from the people. That government is instituted and ought to be exercised for the benefit of the people, which consists in the enjoyment of life and liberty, with the right of acquiring and using property, and generally of pursuing and obtaining happiness and safety. That the people have an indubitable, unalienable, and indefeasible right to reform or change their government, whenever it be found adverse or inadequate to the purposes of its institution."

He proposed inserting into Article I, in the discussion of restrictions on the powers of Congress, what amounted to a bill of rights:

"The civil rights of none shall be abridged on account of religious belief or worship, nor shall any national religion be established, nor shall the full and equal rights of conscience be in any manner, or on any pretext infringed.

"The people shall not be deprived or abridged of their right to speak, to write, or to publish their sentiments; and the freedom of the press, as one of the great bulwarks of liberty, shall be inviolable.

"The people shall not be restrained from peaceably assembling and consulting for their common good; nor from applying to the legislature by petitions, or remonstrances for redress of their grievances.

"The right of the people to keep and bear arms shall not be infringed; a well armed, and well regulated militia being the best security of a free country: but no person religiously scrupulous of bearing arms, shall be compelled to render military service in person.

"No soldier shall in time of peace be quartered in any house without the consent of the owner; nor at any time, but in a manner warranted by law.

"No person shall be subject, except in cases of impeachment, to more than one punishment, or one trial for the same offence; nor shall be compelled to be a witness against himself; nor be deprived of life, liberty, or property without due process of law; nor be obliged to relinquish his property, where it may be necessary for public use, without a just compensation.

"Excessive bail shall not be required, nor excessive fines imposed, nor cruel and unusual punishments inflicted.

"The rights of the people to be secured in their persons, their houses, their papers, and their other property from all unreasonable searches and seizures, shall not be violated by warrants issued without probable cause, supported by oath or affirmation, or not particularly describing the places to be searched, or the persons or things to be seized.

"In all criminal prosecutions, the accused shall enjoy the right to a speedy and public trial, to be informed of the cause and nature of the accusation, to be confronted with his accusers, and the witnesses against him; to have a compulsory process for obtaining witnesses in his favor; and to have the assistance of counsel for his defence.

"The exceptions here or elsewhere in the constitution, made in favor of particular rights, shall not be so construed as to diminish the just importance of other rights retained by the people; or as to enlarge the powers delegated by the constitution; but either as actual limitations of such powers, or as inserted merely for greater caution."

These restrictions would apply to Congress. Madison also proposed a restriction on the states: "No state shall violate the equal rights of conscience, or the freedom of the press, or the trial by jury in criminal cases."

He recommended that Article III, on the judiciary, be amended to guarantee the right to trial by jury.

He concluded by proposing to insert a new Article VII: "The powers delegated by this constitution, are appropriated to the departments to which they are respectively distributed, so that the legislative department shall never exercise the powers vested in the executive or judicial; nor the executive exercise the powers vested in the legislative or judicial; nor the judicial exercise the powers vested in the legislative or executive departments.

"The powers not delegated by this constitution, nor prohibited by it to the states, are reserved to the states respectively."

IN JUSTIFYING THESE amendments to the House, Madison reiterated that he had been a skeptic on a bill of rights. Yet he had never been among those who thought a bill of rights pernicious, he said; at worst it would be superfluous. Now, having read the objections to the Constitution without a bill of rights, he had concluded that it would be a positive addition. "I am inclined to believe, if once bills of rights are established in all the states as well as the federal Constitution, we shall find that although some of them are rather unimportant, yet upon the whole they will have a salutary tendency."

Madison had been persuaded by the Antifederalists that Congress should be more carefully restrained than the original wording of the Constitution demanded. "It is true the powers of the general government are circumscribed," he said. "They are directed to particular objects. But even if government keeps within those limits, it has certain discretionary powers with respect to the means, which may admit of abuse to a certain extent." The "necessary and proper" clause was an invitation to such abuse by unscrupulous legislators—"for it is them who are to judge of the necessity and propriety to accomplish those special purposes which they may have in contemplation, which laws in themselves are neither necessary or proper."

Madison had been less persuaded by the Antifederalist arguments regarding powers reserved to the states and the people. Yet these views were widely shared, and for that reason shouldn't be ignored. "Perhaps words which may define this more precisely than the whole of the instrument now does may be considered as superfluous," he said. "I admit they may be deemed unnecessary; but there can be no harm in making such a declaration."

This was his guiding principle overall. "I have proposed nothing that does not appear to me as proper in itself, or eligible as patronized by a respectable number of our fellow citizens," he said. "And if we can make the Constitution better in the opinion of those who are opposed to it, without weakening its frame or abridging its usefulness in the judgment of those who are attached to it, we act the part of wise and liberal men to make such alterations as shall produce that effect."

25

T HOMAS JEFFERSON'S PLEASURE at the progress of liberty in
America was accompanied by a feeling that America's example
was catching on in France. He marked the stirrings of dissatisfaction
against the regime of Louis XVI, triggered by the writings of intel-
lectuals like Rousseau and Voltaire but also by the observation of what
America had accomplished against the regime of George III. As the
author of the Declaration of Independence, Jefferson took personal
pride in hearing his assertion that "all men are created equal" rendered
into French.

By May 1789, Jefferson could write to Madison, "The revolution
of this country has advanced thus far without encountering anything
which deserves to be called a difficulty. There have been riots in a few
instances in three or four different places, in which there may have been
a dozen or twenty lives lost." But nothing inordinate or worrisome to
lovers of liberty.

The big story was the convening of the Estates General for the
first time in more than two centuries. The condition of government
finance was dire, not least from having underwritten America's revolt
against Britain. And the tax system, created for a much earlier time
and not conspicuously fair then, was in crying need of reform. Yet
before the Estates General could get to the tax code, the three estates it
comprised—clergy, nobility, people—had to establish rules for decision-
making. The clergy and nobles wanted to vote by estates, thinking they
would ally against the people. The people—the *tiers état*—wanted to

vote by numbers of delegates, chiefly because their delegates outnumbered those of the clergy and nobles. The fight resembled the one that
had taken place at the Philadelphia convention when the larger states
argued for voting by population and the smaller for voting by states.

The third estate appeared determined to have their way. "The deputies of the tiers etat seem almost to a man inflexibly determined against
the vote by orders," Jefferson told Madison. Some of the clergy and
nobles were talking of combining their orders into one, creating an
assembly not unlike the American Senate, with the people's delegates
to be a French version of the American House of Representatives.
But the third estate wasn't buying. "The tiers etat manifest no respect
for that or any other modification whatever." A deadlock had ensued.
"On this preliminary question the parties are so irreconcilable that it is
impossible to foresee what issue it will have. The tiers etat, as constituting the nation, may propose to do the business of the nation either with
or without the minorities in the houses of clergy and nobles which side
with them. In that case, if the king should agree to it, the majorities in
those two houses would secede, and might resist the tax-gatherers. This
would bring on a civil war."

Much rested with Louis, whom Jefferson viewed with guarded
optimism. "The king may incline the balance as he pleases," Jefferson
said. "Happy that he is an honest unambitious man, who desires neither
money nor power for himself, and that his most operative minister"—
Jacques Necker, minister of finance—"though he has appeared to trim
a little, is still in the main a friend to public liberty."

As a philosopher and student of government, Jefferson found the
political struggle fascinating for what it revealed of human nature and
the will to power; as the American minister to France, he deemed the
contest momentous for how it might affect the country to which the
United States remained connected by the wartime treaty of alliance.
Beggars can't be choosers, and during the war the United States had
taken help where it could be found. But a marriage between monarchical France and republican America was destined for trouble. Jefferson
could hope that the changes in France might remake that nation into a
constitutional monarchy, with power in the hands of representatives of
the people, or even into a republic. If such were to occur, the marriage
might prosper for decades.

As a devoted republican, Jefferson cheered for the reformers against the reactionary old guard. But as the American minister, he took care that his cheers be of the silent type. America mustn't meddle in the affairs of another country. And Jefferson understood that the American minister would have to deal with whatever government wound up in power after affairs sorted themselves out. To root for one side would undermine his credibility with the other, should that other side win.

Even so, he couldn't avoid involvement entirely. The Marquis de Lafayette had become Jefferson's friend after rescuing Virginia from the British during the war. Lafayette won election to the Estates General, where he found himself in a quandary. His views were decidedly reformist, but his constituents among the nobles wanted him to defend the status quo. He consulted Jefferson. "I received one day a note from the Marquis de la Fayette, informing me that he should bring a party of six or eight friends to ask a dinner of me the next day," Jefferson wrote in his memoirs. "I assured him of their welcome. When they arrived, they were La Fayette himself, Duport, Barnave, Alexander La Meth, Blacon, Mounier, Maubourg, and Dagout. These were leading patriots, of honest but differing opinions sensible of the necessity of effecting a coalition by mutual sacrifices, knowing each other, and not afraid therefore to unbosom themselves mutually." Lafayette made the introductions.

"The cloth being removed and wine set on the table, after the American manner, the Marquis introduced the objects of the conference by summarily reminding them of the state of things in the Assembly, the course which the principles of the constitution were taking, and the inevitable result, unless checked by more concord among the Patriots themselves," Jefferson recounted. "He observed that although he also had his opinion, he was ready to sacrifice it to that of his brethren of the same cause: but that a common opinion must now be formed, or the aristocracy would carry everything, and that whatever they should now agree on, he, at the head of the national force, would maintain." Lafayette commanded the army.

"The discussions began at the hour of four, and were continued till ten o'clock in the evening; during which time I was a silent witness to a coolness and candor of argument unusual in the conflicts of political opinion; to a logical reasoning, and chaste eloquence, disfigured by no gaudy tinsel of rhetoric or declamation, and truly worthy of being placed in parallel with the finest dialogues of antiquity, as handed to us by Xenophon, by Plato and Cicero," Jefferson said. "The result was an agreement that the king should have a suspensive veto on the laws, that the legislature should be composed of a single body only, that to be chosen by the people. This concordat decided the fate of the constitution. The patriots all rallied to the principles thus settled, carried every question agreeably to them, and reduced the aristocracy to insignificance and impotence."

Jefferson realized that his official impartiality had been compromised, and he tried to make matters right. "I waited on Count Montmorin"—Louis's foreign minister—"the next morning, and explained to him with truth and candor how it had happened that my house had been made the scene of conferences of such a character. He told me he already knew everything which had passed, that, so far from taking umbrage at the use made of my house on that occasion, he earnestly wished I would habitually assist at such conferences, being sure I should be useful in moderating the warmer spirits, and promoting a wholesome and practicable reformation only."

Jefferson reaffirmed his desire not to meddle inappropriately. "I told him I knew too well the duties I owed to the king, to the nation, and to my own country to take any part in councils concerning their internal government, and that I should persevere with care in the character of a neutral and passive spectator, with wishes only and very sincere ones, that those measures might prevail which would be for the greatest good of the nation," he wrote. With the advantage of hindsight, Jefferson added, "I have no doubt indeed that this conference was previously known and approved by this honest minister, who was in confidence and communication with the patriots and wished for a reasonable reform of the constitution."


ENCOURAGED IMPLICITLY by Montmorin, and explicitly by Lafayette, Jefferson waded deeper. Lafayette suggested that Jefferson, as an experienced drafter of declarations for Americans, should try his hand for the people of France. Jefferson accepted the suggestion, and produced a draft "Charter of Rights, solemnly established by the King and Nation." Jefferson's charter called for annual meetings of the Estates General, which alone would make laws and levy taxes on the French people; submission of the military to civil authority; abolition of the favored tax treatment of the aristocracy and the clergy; and guarantees of press freedom and habeas corpus.

Jefferson worked swiftly, but events moved faster. To break the deadlock over voting, the delegates of the Third Estate peremptorily declared themselves the National Assembly, representing not simply their constituents but the nation as a whole. The delegates of the other estates were invited to join the assembly but with no special standing or privileges. Louis, alarmed at this turn, evicted the delegates from the hall where they had been meeting. The delegates, following the model of the American colonies when their assemblies had been prorogued by royal governors, refused to disband. Gathering on a tennis court nearby, they swore an oath not to go home before they had given France a constitution.

Things looked grim for Louis. Jefferson described the reaction at Versailles following the assembly's assertion of authority. "When the king passed the next day through the lane they formed from the Chateau to the hotel des etats (about half a mile) there was a dead silence," Jefferson wrote in late June. "On his coming out, a feeble cry of 'Vive le roy' was raised by some children, but the people remained silent and sullen."

Louis summoned soldiers to maintain order and perhaps intimidate those who were seizing power from him. The tactic failed. The sullenness became turmoil, which affected the soldiers no less than the people. "It began in the French guards, extended to those of every other denomination (except the Swiss) and even to the body guards of the king," Jefferson wrote. "They began to quit their barracks, to assemble in squads, to declare they would defend the life of the king, but would not cut the throats of their fellow citizens. They were treated and caressed by the people, carried in triumph through the streets, called themselves the soldiers of the nation, and left no doubt on which side they would be in case of a rupture."

Louis's travails were only beginning. Defections spread, and attempts to stem them sparked violence. The king summoned troops from beyond the city; these merely inflamed the people. By the morning of July 14 the popular momentum was irresistible. A crowd gathered before the Bastille, an old fortress and palace. The soldiers there took fright and fired on the people. "The people rushed against the place, and almost in an instant were in possession of a fortification, defended by 100 men, of infinite strength, which in other times had stood several regular sieges and had never been taken," Jefferson said.

The initial entry was suspiciously easy. "How they got in has as yet been impossible to discover," Jefferson wrote. "Those who pretend to have been of the party tell so many different stories as to destroy the credit of them all."

The subsequent work was harder, and bloody. "They took all the arms, discharged the prisoners and such of the garrison as were not killed in the first moment of fury, carried the Governor and Lieutenant governor to the Greve (the place of public execution), cut off their heads, and set them through the city in triumph to the Palais Royal. About the same instant, a treacherous correspondence having been discovered in Monsieur de Flesselles, prevot des marchands, they seized him in the hotel de ville, where he was in the exercise of his office, and cut off his head."

Moderates like Lafayette tried to calm the crowd. But the mob had a mind of its own. "The demolition of the Bastille was now ordered, and begun," Jefferson recorded. At this point some of the king's crack troops defected. This spread panic to Versailles, where Louis and his court resided. "They believed that the aristocrats of Paris were under pillage and carnage, that 150,000 men were in arms coming to Versailles to massacre the royal family, the court, the ministers and all connected with them, their practices and principles. The aristocrats of the nobles and clergy in the Estates General vied with each other in declaring how sincerely they were converted to the justice of voting by persons, and how determined to go with the nation all its lengths." Louis's ministers resigned en masse.

The violence eased—but only momentarily, Jefferson thought. "We cannot suppose this paroxysm confined to Paris alone. The whole country must pass successively through it, and happy if they get through it as soon and as well as Paris has done." Rumors were rampant. "I went yesterday to Versailles to satisfy myself what had passed there, for nothing can be believed but what one sees, or has from an eye witness. They believe there still that 3000 people have fallen victims to the tumults of Paris." This was grossly exaggerated. "Mr. Short"—William Short, Jefferson's secretary—"and myself have been every day among them in order to be sure of what was passing. We cannot find with certainty that anybody has been killed but the three beforementioned, and those who fell in the assault or defence of the Bastille. How many of the garrison were killed nobody pretends to have ever heard. Of the assailants, accounts vary from 6 to 600. The most general belief is that there fell about 30. There have been many reports of instantaneous executions by the mob, on such of their body as they caught in acts of theft or robbery. Some of these may perhaps be true. There was a severity of honesty observed of which no example has been known. Bags of money offered on various occasions, through fear or guilt, have been uniformly refused by the mobs. The churches are now occupied in singing 'De profundis' and 'Requiems for the repose of the souls of the brave and valiant citizens who have sealed with their blood the liberty of the nation.'"

Paris simmered that summer, and occasionally boiled over. "The spirit of tumult seemed to have subsided, when yesterday it was excited again by a particular incident," Jefferson wrote to John Jay in late July. "Monsieur Foullon, one of the obnoxious ministry, who, as well as his brethren, had absconded, was taken in the country, and as is said by his own tenants, and brought to Paris. Great efforts were exerted, by popular characters, to save him. He was at length forced out of the hands of the Garde Bourgeoise, hung immediately, his head cut off, and his body drawn through the principal streets of the city." Other officials ran for their lives. "The Intendant of Paris, Monsieur de Chauvigny, accused of having entered into the designs of the same ministry, has been taken at Compiegne, and a body of 200 men on horseback are gone for him. If he be brought here, it will be difficult to save him. Indeed it is hard to say at what distance of time the presence of one of those ministers, or of any of the most obnoxious of the fugitive courtiers, will not rekindle the same bloodthirsty spirit." Before Jefferson could send this letter, he added a postscript: "I just now learn that Bertier de Chauvigny was brought to town in the night last night and massacred immediately."

Calm returned slowly and uncertainly. "The city is as yet not entirely quieted," Jefferson wrote in August. "Every now and then summary execution is done on individuals, by individuals, and nobody is in condition to ask for what or by whom." The city militia was still mustering, and its authority was far from complete. Outside the city, things were worse. "The details from the country are as distressing as I had apprehended they would be. Most of them are doubtless false, but many must still be true. Abundance of chateaux are certainly burnt and burning and not a few lives sacrificed. The worst is probably over in this city; but I do not know whether it is so in the country."

AMID THE TUMULT, Jefferson took satisfaction from being consulted by those struggling to chart a republican path for France. The reformers, almost to a man, looked to America for inspiration. "It is impossible to desire better dispositions towards us than prevail in this assembly," Jefferson wrote to Madison. "Our proceedings have been viewed as a model for them on every occasion; and though in the heat of debate men are generally disposed to contradict every authority urged by their opponents, ours has been treated like that of the bible, open to explanation but not to question."

The French experience confirmed, to Jefferson's satisfaction, conclusions he had reached previously. "Never was there a country where the practice of governing too much had taken deeper root and done more mischief," he said of the old regime in France. Americans should keep this in mind as they inaugurated their own new government. Less government was almost always better than more. Excessive centralization drove people to violence.

Jefferson noted a sentiment in some of his compatriots that Britain, rather than France, was America's most promising partner in foreign affairs. John Adams held this view, as did Alexander Hamilton. Jefferson thought they couldn't be more wrong. "When of two nations, the one has engaged herself in a ruinous war for us, has spent her blood and money to save us, has opened her bosom to us in peace, and received us almost on the footing of her own citizens; while the other has moved heaven, earth and hell to exterminate us in war, has insulted us in all her councils in peace, shut her doors to us in every part where her interests would admit it, libeled us in foreign nations, endeavored to poison them against the reception of our most precious commodities; to place these two nations on a footing, is to give a great deal more to one than to the other if the maxim be true that to make unequal quantities equal you must add more to the one than to the other," Jefferson wrote.

Hamilton and the others argued that they were simply being realistic, that affairs of state were not the same as affairs between individuals. Jefferson rejected this proposition. "To say in excuse that gratitude is never to enter into the motives of national conduct is to revive a principle which has been buried for centuries with its kindred principles of the lawfulness of assassination, poison, perjury, etc. All of these were legitimate principles in the dark ages which intervened between ancient and modern civilization, but exploded and held in just horror in the 18th century. I know but one code of morality for men whether acting singly or collectively. He who says I will be a rogue when I act in company with a hundred others but an honest man when I act alone will be believed in the former assertion, but not in the latter."

Jefferson reflected on what could be expected of popular governments. A French friend had inquired about the attachment of the English and the Americans to trial by jury. Jefferson replied, "We think in America that it is necessary to introduce the people into every department of government as far as they are capable of exercising it; and that this is the only way to ensure a long continued and honest administration of its powers." Jefferson made a series of assertions about the people. "1. They are not qualified to exercise themselves the executive department, but they are qualified to name the person who shall exercise it. With us therefore they choose this officer every four years. 2. They are not qualified to legislate. With us therefore they only choose the legislators. 3. They are not qualified to judge questions of *law*, but they are very capable of judging questions of *fact*. In the form of juries therefore they determine all matters of fact, leaving to the permanent judges to decide the law resulting from those facts."

With France struggling toward a first constitution, and America relaunching under its second, Jefferson mused on the durability of constitutions. In particular, how long could a given constitution be expected to serve the interests of the people? Ought constitution-makers write for the ages, or for the moment?

"The question whether one generation of men has a right to bind another seems never to have been started either on this or our side of the water," Jefferson observed to Madison. "Yet it is a question of such consequences as not only to merit decision, but place, also, among the fundamental principles of every government." Jefferson had concluded in the negative. "No such obligation can be transmitted," he said. "The earth belongs in usufruct to the living," he said, employing the legal term for right of use. "The dead have neither powers nor rights over it."

The consequence for lawmakers was clear: "No society can make a perpetual constitution, or even a perpetual law. The earth belongs always to the living generation." If the living generations chose to extend existing law, that was their prerogative. But they were under no obligation to do so. Reckoning a generation as lasting nineteen years, Jefferson asserted, "Every constitution, then, and every law, naturally expires at the end of nineteen years. If it be enforced longer, it is an act of force and not of right."

## 26

THE CONSTITUTION IMPLIED the existence of a cabinet in stating that on matters of policy the president should seek the advice of "the principal officer in each of the executive departments." George Washington chose for his first cabinet Thomas Jefferson as secretary of state, Alexander Hamilton as secretary of the treasury, Henry Knox as secretary of war, and Edmund Randolph as attorney general. Vice President John Adams hovered outside the president's official family, being connected by the Constitution more closely to the legislative branch, as presiding officer of the Senate.

At this time the difference in philosophies of the men near Washington seemed unremarkable. All favored the new Constitution, even Randolph, who had come around to supporting what he had refused to sign at Philadelphia. Jefferson and Hamilton were the farthest apart on the central question of the optimal scope and ambition of the national government, but this difference seemed nothing more than the sort of difference expected among intelligent, forceful individuals weighing important policy choices. Washington had chosen his cabinet secretaries partly for geographic balance—Jefferson and Randolph were from Virginia, Hamilton was from New York and Knox from Massachusetts—but also because he valued their range of views. Washington's cabinet was small in number but capacious enough for both Jefferson's faith in republican virtue and Hamilton's suspicion of republican vice.

·  ·  ·

HAMILTON'S PHILOSOPHY of government surfaced to the general public just months after he took office. Congress, at his prompting, requested an account of America's national debt and a plan for funding it. In January 1790 Hamilton delivered the report he had, in effect, requested of himself. He commenced with a statement of his theory of finance, what he called "these plain and undeniable truths: That exigencies are to be expected to occur in the affairs of nations in which there will be a necessity for borrowing. That loans in times of public danger, especially from foreign war, are found an indispensable resource even to the wealthiest of them. And that in a country which, like this, is possessed of little active wealth, or in other words, little monied capital, the necessity for that resource must, in such emergencies, be proportionably urgent." Many Americans had hoped to pay off the debt and render themselves as taxpayers debt-free. In a few dozen words, Hamilton exploded such hopes. Debt would be the country's constant companion.

Having established this principle, or at least asserted it, Hamilton proceeded to the corollary: "To be able to borrow upon good terms, it is essential that the credit of a nation should be well established." Why? "When the credit of a country is in any degree questionable, it never fails to give an extravagant premium, in one shape or another, upon all the loans it has occasion to make." Good credit was simply good business.

How was good credit to be established? "By good faith, by a punctual performance of contracts," said Hamilton. "States, like individuals, who observe their engagements, are respected and trusted, while the reverse is the fate of those who pursue an opposite conduct."

The bulk of the outstanding debt of the United States had been incurred during the war against Britain. "It was the price of liberty," Hamilton said. For this reason, its treatment was especially significant. "The faith of America has been repeatedly pledged for it, and with solemnities that give peculiar force to the obligation." That the debt remained outstanding was the fault of the inept government under the Articles of Confederation. The Constitution made possible a new start.

The hopes of America's creditors had risen on mere ratification. Hamilton noted that the market value of government bonds had nearly doubled since then. The creditors' hopes were a bellwether of other good things to follow. "To justify and preserve their confidence, to promote the increasing respectability of the American name, to answer the calls of justice, to restore landed property to its due value, to furnish new resources both to agriculture and commerce, to cement more closely the union of the states, to add to their security against foreign attack, to establish public order on the basis of an upright and liberal policy—these are the great and invaluable ends to be secured by a proper and adequate provision at the present period for the support of public credit."

Hamilton adduced another reason for putting public credit on a solid footing. "It is a well known fact that in countries in which the national debt is properly funded, and an object of established confidence, it answers most of the purposes of money," he explained. Money had been a constant problem in the colonies, with the insufficiency of coin driving several colonial governments to issue paper money. The government of the United States and the governments of the individual states had been forced to the same expedient during the war. But paper money was prone to devaluation, as the issuers printed ever more of it. The result was economic turbulence and prospective paralysis.

Hamilton had bigger plans for a monetary system, but for now he preached the merits of reliable government debt. Under a regime of confidence that government would pay its debts punctually and at face value, government notes would be almost as good as gold and better than other forms of paper. "The benefits of this are various and obvious," Hamilton said. "First, trade is extended by it, because there is a larger capital to carry it on. . . . Secondly, agriculture and manufactures are also promoted by it, for the like reason. . . . Thirdly, the interest of money will be lowered by it, for this is always in a ratio to the quantity of money and to the quickness of circulation. This circumstance will enable both the public and individuals to borrow on easier and cheaper terms." The benefits would spread throughout the economy. "From the combination of these effects, additional aids will be furnished to labour, to industry, and to arts of every kind."

How, then, to create this regime of confidence? Simply, said Hamilton, by pledging the new government to the complete repayment of all outstanding government debt.

To the holders of the debt, this statement sounded like obvious moral truth. Lenders deserved to receive back what they had lent plus the interest they had been promised.

Yet the statement provoked immediate controversy. By this time a large portion of the debt was no longer in the hands of those who had loaned the money to the government, often as an act of patriotism amid the war. Instead it rested with speculators who had purchased notes from the original owners, often for dimes on the dollar, and who since had hectored government officials, including Hamilton, to see that they were paid back in dollars for their dimes. Which was precisely what Hamilton—after "mature reflection," he said—proposed to do.

He devoted considerable effort to justifying this course. To do otherwise would be unfair to the speculators, he said, although he called them "purchasers." They had bought the bonds in the expectation that the government would redeem them at face value. Hamilton wasn't immune to the complaints of those who had sold the bonds, often under duress of poverty. "That the case of those who parted with their securities from necessity is a hard one cannot be denied," he said. But they had made a reasoned decision that money in the hand was worth more than an uncertain bond, and they had no legitimate complaint against those who had relieved their need, at considerable financial risk.

Besides, for the government to try to sort the worthy from the unworthy among the bondholders would be impractical and presumptuous. It would reverse the recent rise in the market value of government bonds and undo the good effects of that rise, including the emerging possibility that bonds would circulate in lieu of money. And it would contravene Article VI of the Constitution, which dictated that "all debts contracted and engagements entered into before the adoption of this Constitution shall be as valid against the United States under this Constitution as under the Confederation."

For all these reasons, Hamilton said, the national debt must be paid in full.

YET THERE WAS a second form of government debt: the debts of the states. The Constitution said nothing about paying off those. And most people, speculators and original holders alike, supposed those debts would remain the responsibility of the states that had issued them.

Hamilton thought otherwise. He proposed that the federal government assume the debts of the states and repay them at face value out of federal revenues. He supported this part of his proposal on grounds of justice and efficiency. In depriving the states of the right to levy tariffs, he said, the Constitution deprived them of revenues by which they would have paid their debts. Moreover, most of the state debt, like most of the federal debt, had been incurred in the common effort to defeat the British. As Hamilton had said about the federal debt, it was the price of American liberty, and thus it was America's responsibility. Federal assumption of state debts would not raise or lower the total debt, but would reduce "collision and confusion" among states as they dealt with creditors state by state.

Hamilton offered another reason for federal assumption of state debts, one that would become clearer in subsequent proposals. Assumption was a first step, after the Constitution itself, in Hamilton's program of nation-building. Governments needed money, and they needed the support of the people who possessed it. Hamilton wanted those people to look to the federal government rather than to the states. Nothing would make them look to the federal government more readily than the knowledge that the federal government was the one that would be repaying them, or not. "If all the public creditors receive their dues from one source, distributed with an equal hand, their interest will be the same," said Hamilton. "And having the same interests, they will unite in the support of the fiscal arrangements of the government." If the creditors had to deal with the individual states, their attention would be diffused. "There will be distinct interests, drawing different ways. That union and concert of views among the creditors which in every government is of great importance to their security and to that of public credit will not only not exist, but will be likely to give place to mutual jealousy and opposition."

## 27

Hamilton's argument for paying the federal debt at full value won favor with a majority in Congress, but his proposal that the federal government assume the state debts sparked stiff opposition, not least from James Madison. Madison had valued Hamilton's help in overthrowing the old regime, but he was having second thoughts about where the New Yorker was taking the new regime.

Madison rose in the House to rebut Hamilton. "We have been told, sir, not only that the assumption of the state debts by the United States is a matter of right on the part of the states, and a matter of obligation on the part of the United States, but likewise that it is equitable; nay, that it is a matter of necessity," he said. Yet the supporters of assumption had utterly failed to prove anything like either equity or necessity. On the contrary, equity lay in acknowledging and honoring the efforts of states like Virginia to pay their debts, not to penalize them by making them pay the debts of other states.

As for necessity: "A gentleman from Massachusetts"—Fisher Ames—"has said that the people of Massachusetts never would submit to a rejection of the measure; that it will create a spirit of opposition to the government; in short, that it will endanger the union itself," Madison observed. Madison said he didn't take such warnings lightly. "These are consequences that would be dreadful to me—if I could suppose they would really take place, and that evils of greater magnitude would not ensue from an adoption of the measure." In truth it was those other evils Madison worried more about. "Sir, if we could ascertain the opinions of our constituents individually, I believe we should find four-fifths of the citizens of the United States against the assumption." Madison heard no cry for assumption from the state legislatures. The New Hampshire legislature had been lately in session. "Have they asked for this assumption? No." Massachusetts had been in session. "There has been no declaration from them."

Cutting to the heart of the Hamilton project, Madison rejected the unwarranted expansion of federal power entailed by assumption. "It has been asserted that it would be politic to assume the state debts because it would add strength to the national government," he said. "There is no man more anxious for the success of the government than I am, and no one who will join more heartily in curing its defects. But I wish these defects to be remedied by additional constitutional powers, if they should be found necessary. This is the only proper, effectual and permanent remedy."

The Constitution, as written and ratified, authorized no such action as assumption. Some cited discussions in the Philadelphia convention as supporting assumption. Madison denied this, as one who had been there and taken closer notes than anyone else. No such provision had been proposed, let alone approved. Nor was there any prior feeling, in the old Congress, that the state debts were the responsibility of the national government. "Was it ever supposed that they were to be thrown into one common mass, and that the states should be called on collectively to provide for them?" No, emphatically not. "If such a proposition had been made in the old Congress it never would have found a second."

Madison especially resented the implication from Hamilton and the other supporters of assumption that they were the true nationalists, the defenders of the Union. Madison didn't remind the House, since the members didn't need the reminder, that he was the chief architect of the new government. Mildly but firmly, he said, "I would recommend to them no longer to assume a preeminence over us in the nationality of their motives; and that they would forbear those frequent assertions that if the state debts are not provided for, the federal debts shall also go unprovided for; nay, that if the state debts are not assumed, the union will be endangered. Sir, I am persuaded that if the gentlemen knew the motives that govern us, they would blush at such intemperate as well as inconsistent language."

· · ·

BEFORE THE ASSUMPTION question could be resolved, it became entangled with a second question, of less immediate but more lasting importance: where to locate the national capital. The experience of Hamilton and Madison in being run out of Philadelphia by mutinous soldiers made them appreciate the need for a secure site for the government. Following that flight, Congress had sojourned in Annapolis and Trenton before settling on New York, where it remained through the final years of the Articles of Confederation. The new government under the Constitution commenced operations in New York. The city at the mouth of the Hudson suited New Englanders and New Yorkers, but lawmakers from the southern states found the journey inconvenient. The southerners marshaled sufficient votes to return the seat of government to Philadelphia but only until a decision on a permanent home was made.

"The question of assumption still occupies Congress," Jefferson wrote in the spring of 1790 to Henry Lee, a fellow Virginian and a noted cavalry officer from the war. Light-Horse Harry Lee, he was called, and he would have a son, Robert, who would grow up to be Virginia's second-most celebrated soldier, after only Washington. "The partisans of both sides of it are nearly equally divided, and both extremely eager to carry their point," Jefferson told Lee. Jefferson opposed assumption on the principle of not wishing to aggrandize the federal government, but he hadn't dug in his heels. "It will probably be sometime before it is ultimately decided. In the mean while the voice of the nation will perhaps be heard. Unluckily it is one of those cases wherein the voice will be all on one side"—the monied classes—"and therefore likely to induce a false opinion of the real wish of the public."

Jefferson explained to James Monroe, a young Virginian who had unsuccessfully run against Madison for Congress but appeared destined for greater things, how assumption and the seat of government had become connected. "Congress has been long embarrassed by two of the most irritating questions that ever can be raised among them: 1. the funding the public debt, and 2. the fixing on a more central residence," Jefferson wrote to Monroe. "After exhausting their arguments and patience on these subjects, they have for some time been resting on their oars, unable to get along as to these businesses, and indisposed to attend to anything else till they are settled. And in fine it has become probable that unless they can be reconciled by some plan of compromise, there will be no funding bill agreed to, our credit (raised by late prospects to be the first on the exchange at Amsterdam, where our paper is above par) will burst and vanish, and the states separate to take care every one of itself. This prospect appears probable to some well informed and well-disposed minds."

The prospect of a breakup, hardly a year after the new government had begun operation, focused the minds of those who wished the Union well. "Endeavours are therefore using to bring about a disposition to some mutual sacrifices," Jefferson continued. He was preaching the need for compromise, even while he acknowledged the affinity he felt for the non-assumptionists. "I have been and still am of their opinion that Congress should always prefer letting the states raise money in their own way where it can be done," he told Monroe. "But in the present instance I see the necessity of yielding for this time to the cries of the creditors in certain parts of the union, for the sake of union, and to save us from the greatest of all calamities, the total extinction of our credit in Europe."

The subject of the location of the capital was equally vexing. "It is proposed to pass an act fixing the temporary residence of 12 or 15 years at Philadelphia, and that at the end of that time it shall stand *ipso facto* without further declaration transferred to Georgetown," Jefferson explained, referring to the Maryland town below the falls of the Potomac. "In this way, there will be something to displease and something to soothe every part of the Union but New York, which must be contented with what she has had. If this plan of compromise does not take place, I fear one infinitely worse, an unqualified assumption, the perpetual residence on the Delaware"—at Philadelphia. Jefferson was pleased to observe that at least some of the interested members were behaving well. "The Pennsylvania and Virginia delegations have conducted themselves honorably and unexceptionally on the question of residence. Without descending to talk about bargains, they have seen that their true interests lay in not listening to insidious propositions made to divide and defect them, and we have seen them at times voting against their respective wishes rather than separate."

JEFFERSON DIDN'T PROPOSE to descend to bargaining, yet he wasn't above facilitating compromise on matters that might otherwise wreck the new government. A few years later he recalled his role in breaking the deadlock over assumption and the location of the capital. "The assumption of the state debts in 1790 was a supplementary measure in Hamilton's fiscal system," Jefferson wrote. "When attempted in the House of Representatives it failed. This threw Hamilton himself and a number of members into deep dismay. Going to the president's one day I met Hamilton as I approached the door. His look was somber, haggard and dejected beyond description, even his dress uncouth and neglected. He asked to speak with me. We stood in the street near the door. He opened the subject of the assumption of the state debts, the necessity of it in the general fiscal arrangement, and its indispensable necessity towards a preservation of the union, and particularly of the New England states, who had made great expenditures during the war on expeditions which though of their own undertaking were for the common cause; that they considered the assumption of these by the Union so just, and its denial so probably injurious, that they would make it a *sine qua non* of a continuance of the Union. That as to his own part, if he had not credit enough to carry such a measure as that he could be of no use and was determined to resign."

Hamilton remarked that although he and Jefferson headed different departments in the government, the success of the administration was their common concern, and they should make common cause. "He added his wish that I would interest my friends from the South, who were those most opposed to it," Jefferson recounted. "I answered that I had been so long absent from my country that I had lost a familiarity with its affairs, and being but lately returned had not yet got into the train of them, that the fiscal system being out of my department I had not yet undertaken to consider and understand it, that the assumption had struck me in an unfavorable light, but still not having considered it sufficiently I had not concerned in it, but that I would revolve what he had urged in my mind." From the vantage of his recalling, Jefferson added, "It was a real fact that the eastern and southern members (South Carolina however was with the former) had got into the most extreme ill-humor with one another. This broke out on every question with the most alarming heat, the bitterest animosities seemed to be engendered, and though they met every day, little or nothing could be done from mutual distrust and antipathy."

Jefferson resumed his narrative: "On considering the situation of things, I thought the first step towards some conciliation of views would be to bring Mr. Madison and Col. Hamilton to a friendly discussion of the subject. I immediately wrote to each to come and dine with me the next day, mentioning that we should be alone, that the object was to find some temperament for the present fever, and that I was persuaded that men of sound heads and honest views needed nothing more than explanation and mutual understanding to enable them to unite in some measures which might enable us to get along. They came, I opened the subject to them, acknowledged that my situation had not permitted me to understand it sufficiently but encouraged them to consider the thing together. They did so; it ended in Mr. Madison's acquiescence in a proposition that the question should be again brought before the House by way of amendment from the Senate, that though he would not vote for it, nor entirely withdraw his opposition, yet he should not be strenuous, but leave it to its fate."

Fate needed a nudge. "It was observed, I forget by which of them, that as the pill would be a bitter one to the southern states, something should be done to soothe them; that the removal of the seat of government to the Potomac was a just measure, and would probably be a popular one with them and would be a proper one to follow the assumption. It was agreed to speak to Mr. White"—Alexander White of Virginia—"and Mr. Lee, whose districts lay on the Potomac and to refer to them to consider how far the interests of their particular districts might be a sufficient inducement in them to yield to the assumption. This was done. Lee came into it without hesitation; Mr. White had some qualms but finally agreed. The measure came down by way of amendment from the Senate and was finally carried by the change of White's and Lee's votes."

An additional sweetener sealed the deal. "The removal to Potomac could not be carried unless Pennsylvania could be engaged in it," Jefferson said. "This Hamilton took on himself, and chiefly, as I understood, through the agency of Robert Morris"—former finance minister of the Confederation government, currently a senator from Pennsylvania—"obtained a vote of that state, on agreeing to an intermediate residence at Philadelphia."

## 28

Buoyed by his success on the debt question, Hamilton turned to the second part of his grand design for the economy. He had been thinking about a national bank for years, intending it as another device to wed the wealthy to the national government. At the end of 1790 he revealed his plan to Congress.

"A national bank is an institution of primary importance to the prosperous administration of the finances and would be of the greatest utility in the operations connected with the support of the public credit," Hamilton said. National banks were common in the most advanced countries of Europe, where centuries of experience with them by merchants and government officials had proven the value of the concept. "Theorists and men of business unite in the acknowledgment of it."

This being so, Hamilton said, one might have expected unanimity of support behind a national bank for the United States. Sadly, this was not the case. "Doubts have been entertained, jealousies and prejudices have circulated, and though the experiment is every day dissipating them within the spheres in which effects are best known, yet there are still persons by whom they have not been entirely renounced."

Accordingly Hamilton felt obliged to school the members of Congress on the virtues of a national bank. These fell under several headings. First was the augmentation of the productive capital of the country blessed with a national bank. Gold and silver were inert in the hands of merchants, but they came alive in the hands of bankers,

Hamilton said. "The money which a merchant keeps in his chest waiting for a favorable opportunity to employ it produces nothing till that opportunity arrives. But if instead of locking it up in this manner, he either deposits it in a bank or invests it in the stock of a bank, it yields a profit during the interval." Bankers used the gold and silver as backing for loans amounting to two or three times the value of the precious metal. These loans were, in effect, new money.

The second virtue of the establishment of a national bank was the increase it provided to the financial power of the national government. "The reason is obvious," Hamilton said. "The capitals of a great number of individuals are, by this operation, collected to a point and placed under one direction." The benefit of this linkage, what Hamilton called the "intimate connection of interest between the government and the bank of a nation," was especially great during time of war, but it persisted into peace as well.

The third great virtue of a national bank was the convenience it provided in the collecting of taxes. Under the best of circumstances, collecting federal taxes in thirteen states was a challenge. Doing so through different banks in every state made things worse. "This is attended with trouble, delay, expense and risk," Hamilton said. A single national bank would expedite the process, making the money collected more quickly available. A virtuous circle would take shape, benefiting both the government and the economy at large. "Whatever enhances the quantity of circulating money adds to the ease with which every industrious member of the community may acquire that portion of it, of which he stands in need, and enables him the better to pay his taxes as well as to supply his other wants."

Hamilton acknowledged the criticisms that had been leveled against national banks: that they promoted usury, crowded out other lending, encouraged speculation, invited corruption, and drove gold and silver out of circulation. He rebutted these one by one. Far from promoting usury—the charging of excessive interest rates—a national bank would bring interest rates down, Hamilton said. A critical factor in determining interest rates was the uncertainty of payment. A national bank would tend to stabilize the economy, thereby reducing uncertainty and interest rates. Again, rather than crowding out other lending, a national bank would increase such lending, by improving the overall performance of the economy and making more money available for all manner of purposes, including lending. Under the regime of a national bank there would be less rather than more speculation and corruption, since both those evils thrived in fractured, opaque markets, which were just the opposite of the unified, transparent market the national bank would provide.

As for driving out gold and silver, the rebuttal to this charge was slightly more complicated. Hamilton pointed out that nations that did not possess gold and silver mines, as the United States did not then, could acquire such precious metals only through trade with other countries. In particular, America had to sell more in exports than it purchased in imports; the difference in this positive balance of trade would appear as a net gain of gold and silver. A national bank would improve the efficiency of export production. By this means it would actually draw in, rather than drive out, gold and silver.

Hamilton sketched the national bank he had in mind. It would be chartered by the federal government and be capitalized at ten million dollars, with twenty-five thousand shares being sold for four hundred dollars each. Payment for each share would be in one hundred dollars of gold or silver coin and three hundred dollars in bonds created under the plan to fund the federal debt. Two million dollars of the ten million in stock would be reserved for purchase by the federal government. The bank would be managed by twenty-five directors, of which one would be named president, who would make regular reports on the bank's operation to the secretary of the treasury.

The bank would be established and run on sound business principles, Hamilton said, but its first obligation would be to the American people. "Public utility is more truly the object of public banks than private profit," he said. "And it is the business of government to constitute them on such principles that while the latter will result in a sufficient degree to afford competent motives to engage in them, the former be not made subservient to it." Restating the case for a national bank a bit differently, Hamilton concluded, "Such a bank is not a mere matter of private property, but a political machine of the greatest importance to the state."

JEFFERSON WASN'T BUYING Hamilton's argument for a minute. Jefferson didn't like banks, which were still a novelty in America; he believed they undermined the agrarian values that must underpin American republicanism. He saw how banks transferred power from the laboring classes to the speculative classes. Jefferson likened finance to a gamble, and financiers to gamblers. *These* gamblers, moreover, sought to rig the game in their favor, with the assistance of Hamilton and his allies.

Besides being pernicious, Hamilton's bank was unconstitutional, Jefferson judged. "I consider the foundation of the Constitution as laid on this ground: That 'all powers not delegated to the United States, by the Constitution, nor prohibited by it to the States, are reserved to the States or to the people,'" he wrote. This was a slightly edited version of the last of the amendments Madison had proposed to Congress, which had fashioned them into twelve for submission to the states. Ten of the twelve would soon be ratified as the Bill of Rights; Jefferson was referring to what would be the Tenth Amendment.

It pinned down an argument the Federalists had made from the start: that the Constitution allowed the national government only those powers specifically delegated by the charter itself. Jefferson continued: "To take a single step beyond the boundaries thus specially drawn around the powers of Congress is to take possession of a boundless field of power, no longer susceptible of any definition. The incorporation of a bank, and the powers assumed by this bill, have not, in my opinion, been delegated to the United States by the Constitution."

Jefferson examined the Constitution clause by clause in search of the powers Hamilton sought for the bank. He failed to find them. "They are not among the powers specially enumerated: for these are: 1st. A power to lay taxes for the purpose of paying the debts of the United States; but no debt is paid by this bill, nor any tax laid. Were it a bill to raise money, its origination in the Senate would condemn it by the Constitution." Money bills had to originate in the House. "2d. 'To borrow money.' But this bill neither borrows money nor ensures the borrowing it. The proprietors of the bank will be just as free as any other money holders to lend or not to lend their money to the public." The government didn't need the bank in order to borrow the money required for government operations. "3. To 'regulate commerce with foreign nations, and among the states, and with the Indian tribes.' To erect a bank, and to regulate commerce, are very different acts. He who erects a bank creates a subject of commerce in its bills; so does he who makes a bushel of wheat or digs a dollar out of the mines; yet neither of these persons regulates commerce thereby. To make a thing which may be bought and sold is not to prescribe regulations for buying and selling."

The backers of the bank appealed as well to the more general— "necessary and proper"—powers granted by the Constitution to the national government. Their argument didn't stand scrutiny here either, Jefferson said. The enumerated powers didn't require a bank. "They can all be carried into execution without a bank. A bank therefore is not *necessary,* and consequently not authorized by this phrase." The bank's advocates asserted that a bank would facilitate the collection of taxes. "Suppose this were true," Jefferson rejoined. "Yet the Constitution allows only the means which are '*necessary,*' not those which are merely 'convenient' for effecting the enumerated powers. If such a latitude of construction be allowed to this phrase as to give any non-enumerated power, it will go to every one, for there is not one which ingenuity may not torture into a *convenience* in some instance *or other,* to *some one* of so long a list of enumerated powers. It would swallow up all the delegated powers, and reduce the whole to one power." Clearly the framers of the Constitution didn't intend this, or they wouldn't have inserted the word *necessary.* "Therefore it was that the Constitution restrained them to the *necessary* means, that is to say, to those means without which the grant of power would be nugatory."


MADISON SIDED WITH Jefferson against Hamilton and the bank. In a speech to the House, Madison noted the same constitutional objections as Jefferson, and added other objections that were political or economic. Hamilton had asked for a charter of twenty years for the bank; this was too long, said Madison. "A period of twenty years is to this country as a period of a century in the history of other countries." No one could know what would happen during that time. Moreover, Madison distrusted that a grant of powers such as Hamilton proposed for the bank could ever be withdrawn. "Granting the powers on any principle is granting them in *perpetuum,*" he said. A fundamental feature of politics was that power found ways to defend and extend itself.

Madison mocked certain advocates of the bank for the somersaults they had turned. Elbridge Gerry of Massachusetts, for one, had changed his tune since 1787 in Philadelphia. "He said the powers of the Constitution were then dark, inexplicable and dangerous, but now, perhaps as the result of experience, they are clear and luminous!"

Madison complained that the terms of sale of the bank shares would favor insiders and discriminate against ordinary people. Moreover, the charter would be of tremendous value to these favored few, yet Hamilton proposed simply to give it away. "The public ought to derive greater advantages from the institution than those proposed," Madison said. "The profits will be so great that the government ought to receive a very considerable sum for granting the charter."

Madison ended at the same place as Jefferson. "The constructions of the Constitution which have been maintained on this occasion go to the subversion of every power whatever in the several states," he said. If Congress were allowed to define the scope of its own powers, there would be no restraining the federal government and no preserving the powers of the states.

Madison looked to the American people for guidance on what the government should be allowed to do. Hamilton's bank would serve the interests of a small number of financial insiders; until the treasury secretary provided a stronger case that it would also serve the people at large, Madison would withhold his support. "The enlightened opinion and affection of the people are the only solid basis for the support of this government," he said.

Madison distilled the arguments against the bank into a pair of messages for Washington to use in case the bank bill passed and the president decided to veto it. Madison had become an adviser to the president, offering Washington a window on Congress as well as access to Madison's long ruminations on the nature of government. The first message stuck to the constitutional case against it. "I object to the bill because it is an essential principle of the government that powers not delegated by the Constitution cannot be rightfully exercised; because the power proposed by the bill to be received is not expressly delegated; and because I cannot satisfy myself that it results from any express power by fair and safe rules of implication," Madison wrote for Washington to sign.

The second version of the message might be appended to the first, or it could stand alone. It stressed the unfairness of Hamilton's scheme to the ordinary people of America. "I object to the bill because it appears to be unequal between the public and the institution in favor of the institution, imposing no conditions on the latter equivalent to the stipulations assumed by the former," Madison offered for Washington. "I object to the bill because it is in all cases the duty of the government to dispense its benefits to individuals with as impartial a hand as the public interest will permit; and the bill is in this respect unequal to individuals holding different denominations of public stock and willing to become subscribers."

WASHINGTON HADN'T VETOED anything so far, and he wasn't eager to begin. Yet he might have to.

Hamilton astutely guided the bank bill through Congress, where it passed the Senate on a voice vote—indicating a majority so large no tally need be taken—and the House by 39 to 20. The measure went to Washington for his approval or veto.

"The constitutionality of the national bank was a question on which his mind was greatly perplexed," Madison recalled. "His belief in the utility of the establishment and his disposition to favor a liberal construction of the national powers formed a bias on one side. On the other, he had witnessed what passed in the convention which framed the Constitution, and he knew the tenor of the reasonings and explanations under which it had been ratified by the state conventions. His perplexity was increased by the opposite arguments and opinions of his official advisers Mr. Jefferson and Mr. Hamilton. He held several free conversations with me on the subject, in which he listened favorably, as I thought, to my views of it, but certainly without committing himself in any manner whatever. Not long before the expiration of the ten days allowed for his decision, he desired me to reduce into form the objections to the bill, that he might be prepared in case he should return it without his signature." This would signify a veto.

Madison was encouraged that his objections to the bank had taken root with Washington. "From this circumstance, with the manner in which the paper had been requested and received, I had inferred that he would not sign the bill." Others drew the same conclusion. "The delay had begotten strong suspicions in the zealous friends of the bill that it would be rejected," Madison said.

Yet others drew hope from the president's indecisiveness. One of the bank's backers had put Washington on the clock. "He had been making an exact computation of the time elapsed," Madison recounted. This man thought Washington would miss the deadline for returning the bill to Congress, and it would become law without his signature.

He obviously didn't know Washington, who was never not punctual. But neither did Madison, in this case. Safely before the deadline, Washington signed the bill and summoned the Bank of the United States into existence.

## 29

T HE MEASURES OF CONGRESS have given a great spring to trade," declared the *Gazette of the United States* in March 1791. This twice-weekly Philadelphia paper was summarizing the work of Congress as that body concluded its first two-year term under the Constitution. "The states have been eased of their debts, which would have crushed some of them by their weight. But the revenue of the whole country, under one system of management, will enable the United States to provide for them, almost without feeling the burden." The Bank of the United States was certain to be a tremendous success. "The bank is an institution which our extensive and wealthy country ought not to be without. It will assist us to extend our intercourse from North to South, and we shall like one another better, as we know one another more." The Federalist majority in Congress had performed brilliantly, and the country as a whole was the beneficiary. "America, which was in the shade before, seems now to stand in the sunshine. Its prospects are the brightest that any nation on Earth enjoys."

Readers familiar with the history of the *Gazette* and its management weren't surprised that its judgment on Congress was so positive. John Fenno had been an ardent Federalist when he founded the *Gazette* in New York in 1789, and he remained one. The Constitution made no provision for publishing the proceedings of Congress, and Fenno hoped to fill the need—to the benefit of the country, the Federalist cause and his own pocketbook. When the government moved to Philadelphia in 1790, Fenno and the *Gazette* did too. He received encouragement from Hamilton and other Federalist leaders, in the form of loans and indications that the administration would throw business his way. He captured much of the market on political reporting and commentary in the capital, excerpting from congressional debates and running editorials applauding the fine work of the Washington administration.

THE PAPER'S TILT WASN'T lost on Jefferson and Madison, who determined to counter it with a journal relating their side of the story. Jefferson read enough of the *Gazette* to conclude that it was "a paper of pure Toryism, disseminating the doctrines of monarchy, aristocracy and the exclusion of the influence of the people," as he told his son-in-law. He went on: "We have been trying to get another weekly or half-weekly paper set up—excluding advertisements, so that it might go through the states—and furnish a Whig vehicle of intelligence." Jefferson chose his labels carefully: Tory was the name applied to the pro-British Loyalists of the American Revolution, and Whig to the pro-independence Patriots.

With subsidies of their own, to obviate advertisements, which would have made the paper more expensive to mail, Jefferson, Madison and their allies enlisted Philip Freneau to launch the *National Gazette*. To offset the government work Hamilton channeled to Fenno, Jefferson hired Freneau as a translator for the State Department. Freneau's qualifications for the job were modest, but so were the demands. He understood he would be judged on the quality not of his translations but of his defense of the positions Jefferson called Whig.

Freneau introduced the paper in the autumn of 1791. "The *National Gazette* shall be published on the Monday and Thursday mornings of every week, in the city of Philadelphia, and sent to the more distant subscribers by the most ready and regular modes of conveyance," he said. "Such persons resident in the city of Philadelphia, as inclined to become subscribers, shall be supplied early on the mornings of publication, at their own houses. The price will be $3 a year." Coverage would be broad. "The paper shall contain, among other interesting particulars, the most important foreign intelligence, collected not only from the British, French and Dutch newspapers (a constant and punctual supply of which has been engaged) but also from original communications, letters and other papers to which the editor may have an opportunity of recurring for the most authentic information relative to the affairs of Europe. The department for domestic news will be rendered as complete and satisfactory as possible by inserting a judicious detail of such occurrences as shall appear worthy the notice of the public. The most respectful attention shall be paid to all decent productions of entertainment in prose or verse that may be sent for insertion, as well as to such political essays as have a tendency to promote the general interest of the Union. There will also be inserted, during the sessions of Congress, a brief history of the debates and proceedings of the supreme legislature of the United States, executed, it is hoped, in such a manner as to answer the expectations and gratify the curiosity of every reader."

Freneau was pleased to open his columns to writers of Whiggish bent. One who contributed frequently, and anonymously, was James Madison. For a man who had argued at Philadelphia for elevating the national government far above the states, Madison now advocated a surprisingly balanced position between the two. "Here then is a proper object presented both to those who are most jealously attached to the separate authority reserved to the states, and to those who may be more inclined to contemplate the people of America in the light of one nation," Madison wrote. "Let the former continue to watch against every encroachment which might lead to a gradual consolidation of the states into one government. Let the latter employ their utmost zeal, by eradicating local prejudices and mistaken rivalships, to consolidate the affairs of the states into one harmonious interest."

Madison shifted his position on other aspects of governance too. In Federalist 10 he had argued that republicanism would fare better in a large country than in a small one; in the *National Gazette* he said something nearly the opposite. "Public opinion sets bounds to every government, and is the real sovereign in every free one," he began. "As there are cases where the public opinion must be obeyed by the government, so there are cases where, not being fixed, it may be influenced by the government." The latter cases allowed for encroachments on liberty, and they happened most frequently in big countries. "The larger a country the less easy for its real opinion to be ascertained, and the less difficult to be counterfeited. When ascertained or presumed, the more respectable it is in the eyes of individuals. This is favorable to the authority of government. For the same reason, the more extensive a country, the more insignificant is each individual in his own eyes. This may be unfavorable to liberty."

The way to combat the encroachment on liberty was to amplify public opinion so that it couldn't be counterfeited by government, Madison said. Not coincidentally, amplifying public opinion was what the *National Gazette* and its supporters were doing. "Whatever facilitates a general intercourse of sentiments, as good roads, domestic commerce, a free press, and particularly a *circulation of newspapers through the entire body of the people*, and representatives going from and returning among every part of them, is equivalent to a contraction of territorial limits, and is favorable to liberty."

In another essay Madison characterized the three common kinds of government: monarchies, aristocracies and republics. Monarchies were most common in large states, even though they were least fit to govern there. "In monarchies there is a two-fold danger—1st, That the eyes of a good prince cannot see all that he ought to know—2d, That the hands of a bad one will not be tied by the fear of combinations against him. Both these evils increase with the extent of dominion." Aristocracies typically appeared in smaller states. "The smaller the state, the less intolerable is this form of government, its rigors being tempered by the facility and the fear of combinations among the people," Madison said.

The republic was Madison's ideal form of government. "A republic involves the idea of popular rights," he said. "A representative republic *chooses* the wisdom of which hereditary aristocracy has the *chance;* whilst it excludes the oppression of that form. And a confederated republic attains the force of monarchy whilst it equally avoids the ignorance of a good prince and the oppression of a bad one." But republics, especially confederated ones, required constant attention. "To secure all the advantages of such a system, every good citizen will be at once a sentinel over the rights of the people, over the authorities of the confederal government, and over both the rights and the authorities of the intermediate governments."

Madison's warnings about the threats to liberty were intended as criticism of the Washington administration and the Federalists in Congress, and they were understood as such. Likewise his assessment of empires and their dependent territories, of which Britain and its colonies were the foremost example. Already critics of the administration complained that Hamilton's economic policies, with their tilt toward the commercial classes, tended to re-subordinate America to Britain, the great commercial power of the age; Madison explained where this would lead. "All dependent countries are to the superior state not in the relation of children and parent, according to the common phrase, but in that of slave and master, and have a like influence on character. By rendering the labour of the one the property of the other, they cherish pride, luxury, and vanity on one side; on the other, vice and servility, or hatred and revolt."

AND THEN HE WROTE something really remarkable—remarkably prescient and remarkably discouraging. "In every political society, parties are unavoidable," Madison said.

He might as well have announced that the republican dream of the founders was a fraud. From the first intimations of trouble with Britain, a tenet of Americans' political faith was that they were different from the British: that they cherished liberty with greater devotion, that they clung to their rights more stubbornly, and especially that they were more virtuous in their political dealings with one another. Politics in Britain had grown jaded and corrupt; self-interest and dishonesty pervaded Parliament and tarnished the Crown.

The declaration of American independence—the proclamation of an American republic—reflected the same desire that had driven the first colonists from England to New England: the desire to separate themselves from the corruption of the mother country. Just as the Pilgrims of the early seventeenth century had sailed the Atlantic to save their immortal souls, so the patriots of the late eighteenth century had made a moat of the Atlantic to save their political souls.

And nothing so signaled republican virtue—nothing so demonstrated the difference between the old world of Britain and the new world of America—as the banishing of parties. Parties stood between citizens and their government, placing party interest above the interests of the people. The founders of the American republic had hoped and expected that parties would never take root in America.

Yet now, in January 1792, Madison acknowledged that parties were unavoidable, even in republics. Formerly he and others had spoken of factions, groups of individuals with similar interests. Factions posed a problem for republics in that they could hinder pursuit of the general interest. But they were not an existential threat, for they lacked the permanence of parties. Factions were the equivalent of the common cold: discomforting but temporary. Parties were akin to consumption, as tuberculosis was then called: chronic and often deadly.

But parties were inevitable, said Madison now. Presumably they would afflict America forever. "The great object should be to combat the evil," he continued. Several strategies presented themselves: "1. By establishing a political equality among all. 2. By withholding *unnecessary* opportunities from a few to increase the inequality of property by an immoderate, and especially an unmerited, accumulation of riches. 3. By the silent operation of laws which, without violating the rights of property, reduce extreme wealth towards a state of mediocrity and raise extreme indigence towards a state of comfort. 4. By abstaining from measures which operate differently on different interests, and particularly such as favor one interest at the expense of another. 5. By making one party a check on the other, so far as the existence of parties cannot be prevented nor their views accommodated." In what amounted to a retreat from the Enlightenment language of the Declaration of Independence, Madison observed, "If this is not the language of reason, it is that of republicanism."

Madison distinguished between natural parties and artificial ones. "In all political societies, different interests and parties arise out of the nature of things," he said. "The great art of politicians lies in making them checks and balances to each other." Some politicians—Madison here declined to name the Federalists, but readers of the *National Gazette* would make their own connections—drew from this inarguable premise a pernicious corollary: "Let us then increase these *natural distinctions* by favoring an inequality of property; and let us add to them *artificial distinctions,* by establishing *kings,* and *nobles,* and *plebeians.* We shall then have the more checks to oppose to each other; we shall then have the more scales and the more weights to perfect and maintain the equilibrium."

This was inane, Madison said. "From the expediency in politics of making natural parties mutual checks on each other, to infer the propriety of creating artificial parties in order to form them into mutual checks, is not less absurd than it would be in ethics to say that new vices ought to be promoted where they would counteract each other, because this use may be made of existing vices."

HAVING DISTINGUISHED between natural and artificial parties, Madison took care to claim the mantle of nature for his own side in the contest with the Federalists. While Hamilton served countinghouse and city, Madison and Jefferson looked to farm and country. And they did so in belief in the virtue farm and country sustained. "The life of the husbandman is preeminently suited to the comfort and happiness of the individual," Madison said. "*Health,* the first of blessings, is an appurtenance of his property and his employment. *Virtue,* the health of the soul, is another part of his patrimony, and no less favored by his situation. *Intelligence* may be cultivated in this as well as in any other walk of life. If the mind be less susceptible of polish in retirement than in a crowd, it is more capable of profound and comprehensive efforts. Is it more ignorant of some things? It has a compensation in its ignorance of others. *Competency* is more universally the lot of those who dwell in the country, when liberty is at the same time their lot. The extremes both of want and of waste have other abodes. 'Tis not the country that peoples either the Bridewells or the Bedlams." Bridewell was a London prison and Bedlam the insane asylum. "These mansions of wretchedness are tenanted from the distresses and vices of overgrown cities."

Some manufactures were necessary, but they didn't require cities and factories. "It is fortunate in general, and particularly for this country, that so much of the ordinary and most essential consumption, takes place in fabrics which can be prepared in every family, and which constitute indeed the natural ally of agriculture," Madison said. "The former is the work within doors, as the latter is without; and each being done by hands or at times that can be spared from the other, the most is made of everything."

Ordinary men and women were the salt of the American earth and the foundation of republicanism. "The class of citizens who provide at once their own food and their own raiment may be viewed as the most truly independent and happy. They are more: they are the best basis of public liberty and the strongest bulwark of public safety. It follows that the greater the proportion of this class to the whole society, the more free, the more independent and the more happy must be the society itself."

In another essay, Madison asked pointedly, "The Union: who are its real friends?" He answered negatively at first, pointing in accusation at the Federalists: "Not those who favor measures which, by pampering the spirit of speculation within and without the government, disgust the best friends of the Union. Not those who promote unnecessary accumulations of the debt of the Union instead of the best means of discharging it as fast as possible; thereby increasing the causes of corruption in the government, and the pretexts for new taxes under its authority, the former undermining the confidence, the latter alienating the affection of the people. Not those who study by arbitrary interpretations and insidious precedents to pervert the limited government of the Union into a government of unlimited discretion, contrary to the will and subversive of the authority of the people. Not those who avow or betray principles of monarchy and aristocracy in opposition to the republican principles of the Union and the republican spirit of the people."

Having identified the Union's enemies, Madison moved on to its friends. "The real friends to the Union are those: Who are friends to the authority of the people, the sole foundation on which the Union rests. Who are friends to liberty, the great end for which the Union was formed. Who are friends to the limited and republican system of government, the means provided by that authority, for the attainment of that end. Who are enemies to every public measure that might smooth the way to hereditary government; for resisting the tyrannies of which the Union was first planned, and for more effectually excluding which, it was put into its present form. Who considering a public debt as injurious to the interests of the people and baneful to the virtue of the government, are enemies to every contrivance for *unnecessarily* increasing its amount, or protracting its duration, or extending its influence. In a word, those are the real friends to the Union who are friends to that republican policy throughout, which is the only cement for the Union of a republican people; in opposition to a spirit of usurpation and monarchy."

THE CHARGE OF MONARCHISM was a potent one, for it rekindled the spirit of the revolution. At every opportunity, Madison and Jefferson deployed it against Hamilton and the Federalists. Hamilton's support at the Philadelphia convention for a lifetime presidency lent credence to the charge. So did the activities of the Society of the Cincinnati, which some members hoped would become hereditary. When Hamilton and Washington took part in Cincinnati doings, opponents of the administration bewailed encroaching monarchism.

Something as innocent as a birthday party could set off the howlers. "It appears by the conduct of some men that we are only republicans in name and not in principle," one "Valerius" twitted in the *National Gazette* after a celebration of Washington's birthday. "For surely the customs and manners emanating from, and congenial with, monarchy must be incongruous in a republic. Who will deny that the celebrating of birthdays is not a striking feature of royalty? We hear of no such thing during the republic of Rome. Even Cincinnatus, now consigned to immortal fame, received no adulation of this kind." Valerius disavowed any aspersions on the character of Washington himself, who was indeed a great man. "But surely the office he enjoys is a sufficient testimony of the people's favor, without worshiping him likewise." Valerius supposed Washington merely tolerated the fuss made over him. "I believe I may venture to say that such fulsome adulation does not accord with his feelings."

A birthday fete wasn't a crime in itself. "But when I consider it a forerunner of other monarchical vices, and holding up an improper example in this country, and an example of precedent, I cannot but execrate the measure," Valerius said. "I am well aware that courtiers and all the sycophantic tribe will endeavor to take off the force of these remarks, and others of a similar nature that have been lately made by some republican writers, by bawling out faction, sedition etc." Honest men would not be fooled by such baseless allegations. "I appeal then to the good sense of my countrymen, whether by placing one man above all equality and heaping honors upon him, it does not, in the same proportion, lessen the consequence of every other person. And whether this is not sowing the seeds of distinctions and inequality which will indubitably produce a change in our government."

## 30

J OHN ADAMS HAD TROUBLE keeping busy as vice president. His role as presiding officer of the Senate was part-time at best, given the decisive Federalist majority there, which minimized chances of tie votes a vice president might break. Nor was Adams a parliamentarian per se, being too impatient with protocol and form.

With time heavy on his hands, Adams grew even grouchier than was his custom. He saw enemies everywhere, from wartime Loyalists to his Paris partner Franklin, who had died in 1790. After complaining to a friend about criticism from the Loyalists, Adams declared, "I have long expected that my memory would be blackened by a thousand lies from that quarter, but there is another region from which volumes of obloquy will be found in dastardly secret letters concerning me. I mean from the fools and slaves of Franklin in France, England, Holland and elsewhere. I expect more lies and slanders from that quarter than from the Tories." Franklin had been behind it all, Adams said. "Never did the little passions of envy, jealousy and rivalry operate with more malignity on any human heart than they did in that of that old dotard against me."

Adams's constant fear was that history would overlook his contribution to the establishment of the American republic. He thought his pamphlet of 1776, *Thoughts on Government,* contained more insight than Thomas Paine's celebrated *Common Sense* of the same year. He judged his 1787 *Defence of the Constitutions of Government of the United States of America* more profound than the *Federalist Papers* of that year and the

next. But no one seemed to agree. "Gratitude is a delicacy too exqui-
site for one ever to receive or hope for," Adams grumbled to a friend.
"Instead of gratitude I have received nothing but abuse and insolence
for this work"—the *Defence*—from the ignorant and profligate, and the
wise and virtuous look on and are silent at least, if they do not smile and
applaud. In short, my dear sir, a man who is concerned in a revolution is
greatly to be pitied; he must surrender his judgement and his integrity
into the hands of a mob, or he must run the gauntlet."

Adams at times thought the country was out to get him. "It has
appeared to be the desire both of North and South to annihilate me
and my office," he told another friend. He was too Federalist for the
South and too honest for the North. While in Paris he had antagonized
French officials, who were now plotting to depose him from the vice
presidency by promoting a rival at the next election. "There is a French
intrigue at work to this purpose as deep as it is wicked," Adams said.
And it would probably work. "My countrymen with all their sagacity
and with all their vigilance are not enough acquainted with the world,
nor with the history of their own revolution to be upon their guard
against political inventions concealed with infinite art, urged with
unwearied diligence, multiplied and varied with fruitful ingenuity, and
pursued with long perseverance."

Adams conceived himself surrounded by fools. "The populace are
made the dupes of their own feelings; aristocrats are bloated with their
own pride," he said. Yet such was his lot in life, and he wouldn't change
his course. "To me these things are familiar. I have been a suffering
witness and have a good memory. But my misfortune is that no man
knows them all but myself. . . . I shall go on, however, as long as independent spirit and principles will support me."


IN THE SUMMER OF 1791 Adams received a letter from Jefferson.
The two men had first met as delegates to the Continental Congress,
where their partnership had been productive—of the Declaration of
Independence, most notably—and cordial. Each professed himself an
admirer and friend of the other. It probably aided the relationship that
they spent little actual time together. Sooner or later Adams found fault
with most of those he associated with, as indeed he did with Jefferson
after they became associates in Washington's administration. Jefferson

was aware of Adams's sensitivity, which gave him pause in communicating with him. "I have a dozen times taken up my pen to write to you and as often laid it down again, suspended between opposing considerations," Jefferson began his letter to Adams. "I determine however to write from a conviction that truth between candid minds can never do harm."

Jefferson explained that he had written a private letter recommending the reprinting of Thomas Paine's *Rights of Man,* a collection of essays defending the principle of revolution. "I thought so little of this note that I did not even keep a copy of it, nor ever heard a tittle more of it till, the week following, I was thunderstruck with seeing it come out at the head of the pamphlet," he told Adams. "I hoped however it would not attract notice. But I found on my return from a journey of a month that a writer came forward under the signature of Publicola, attacking not only the author and principles of the pamphlet but myself as its sponsor, by name. Soon after came hosts of other writers defending the pamphlet and attacking you by name as the writer of Publicola.

"Thus were our names thrown on the public stage as public antagonists," Jefferson continued. "That you and I differ in our ideas of the best form of government is well known to us both, but we have differed as friends should do, respecting the purity of each other's motives and confining our difference of opinion to private conversation. And I can declare with truth in the presence of the almighty that nothing was further from my intention or expectation than to have had either my own or your name brought before the public on this occasion. The friendship and confidence which has so long existed between us required this explanation from me, and I know you too well to fear any misconstruction of the motives of it."

Jefferson closed by assuring Adams that he himself had never written under a pseudonym. "Some people here who would wish me to be, or to be thought, guilty of improprieties have suggested that I was Agricola, that I was Brutus etc. etc. I never did in my life, either by myself or by any other, have a sentence of mine inserted in a newspaper without putting my name to it. And I believe I never shall."

Adams responded testily, albeit only indirectly at Jefferson. "I give full credit to your relation of the manner in which your note was written and prefixed to the Philadelphia edition of Mr. Paine's pamphlet on the rights of man," Adams wrote to Jefferson. "But the misconduct of the person who committed this breach of your confidence, by making it public, whatever were his intentions, has sown the seeds of more evils than he can ever atone for. The pamphlet, with your name to so striking a recommendation of it, was not only industriously propagated in New York and Boston, but, that the recommendation might be known to everyone, was reprinted with great care in the newspapers and was generally considered as a direct and open personal attack upon me by countenancing the false interpretation of my writings as favouring the introduction of hereditary monarchy and aristocracy into this country."

The slander then spread, Adams declared. "Emboldened by these murmurs, soon after appeared the paragraphs of an unprincipled libeler in the New Haven Gazette, carefully reprinted in the papers of New York, Boston and Philadelphia, holding up the vice president"— Adams—"to the ridicule of the world for his meanness, and to their detestation for wishing to subjugate the people to a few nobles. These were soon followed by a formal speech of the lieutenant governor of Massachusetts very solemnly holding up the idea of hereditary powers and cautioning the public against them, as if they were at that moment in the most imminent danger of them."

Adams perceived a conspiracy in Boston and Philadelphia against him. "These things were all accompanied with the most marked neglect both of the governor and lieutenant governor of this state towards me, and altogether operated as an hue and cry to all my enemies and rivals, to the old constitutional faction of Pennsylvania in concert with the late insurgents of Massachusetts, both of whom consider my writings as the cause of their overthrow, to hunt me down like a hare, if they could."

Adams accepted Jefferson's claim never to have written anything anonymous for a newspaper. "And I with equal frankness declare that I never did, either by myself or by any other, have a sentence of mine inserted in any newspaper since I left Philadelphia," he said. This was a much narrower disclaimer, covering merely the period since the most recent adjournment of Congress. In fact Adams had previously written a long series of unsigned essays for the *National Gazette* under the title "Discourses on Davila."

He explicitly denied writing the essays attacking Jefferson. "I neither wrote nor corrected Publicola," he said. "The writer in the composition of his pieces followed his own judgment, information and discretions without any assistance from me."

Adams expressed surprise at another part of Jefferson's letter. "You observe 'That you and I differ in our ideas of the form of government is well known to us both.' But, my dear sir, you will give me leave to say that I do not know this. I know not what your idea is of the best form of government. You and I have never had a serious conversation together that I can recollect concerning the nature of government. The very transient hints that have ever passed between us have been jocular and superficial, without ever coming to any explanation."

Adams feared that Jefferson had been heeding Adams's enemies. "If you suppose that I have or ever had a design or desire of attempting to introduce a government of king, lords and commons—in other words, an hereditary executive or an hereditary senate—either into the government of the United States or that of any individual state, in this charge you are wholly mistaken," he said. "There is not such a thought expressed or intimated in any public writing or private letter of mine, and I may safely challenge all mankind to produce such a passage and quote the chapter and verse. If you have ever put such a construction on anything of mine, I beg you would mention it to me, and I will undertake to convince you that it has no such meaning."

Adams was proud of the positive effects of his written works, though he believed he hadn't been given sufficient credit. Indeed, his candid opinions had brought down upon him further abuse. "My unpolished writings, although they have been read by a sufficient number of persons to have assisted in crushing the insurrection of the Massachusetts"—the Shays rebellion—"the formation of the new constitutions of Pennsylvania, Georgia and South Carolina, and in procuring the assent of all the states to the new national constitution, yet they have not been read by great numbers," he told Jefferson. "Of the few who have taken the pains to read them, some have misunderstood them and others have willfully misrepresented them, and these misunderstandings and misrepresentations have been made the pretense for overwhelming me with floods and whirlwinds of tempestuous abuse, unexampled in the history of this country."

Adams suspected that John Hancock was striving to replace him as vice president, with Samuel Adams to take Hancock's spot as Massachusetts governor. "Many of the detesters of the present national government will undoubtedly aid them," Adams said to Jefferson. "Many people think too that no small share of a foreign influence, in revenge for certain untractable conduct at the treaty of peace, is and will be intermingled." Adams was referring to the French, presumably upset at him for not falling for their wiles in Paris, as Franklin had done.

Adams thought the country was on the brink of dissolution. "I must own to you that the daring traits of ambition and intrigue, and those unbridled rivalries which have already appeared, are the most melancholy and alarming symptoms that I have ever seen in this country," he told Jefferson.

ADAMS'S RESPONSE TO Jefferson was true as far as it went, but it might have gone further. Adams was not Publicola, but his son John Quincy Adams *was*. Adams must have known this, and have understood that the younger Adams was using the nom de plume to defend his father while enabling his father to deny having done so himself.

As for Adams's never having wished hereditary office upon the United States, Jefferson heard a functionally different version from Alexander Hamilton. Shortly after receiving Adams's letter, Jefferson had a conversation with Hamilton and took notes. Hamilton condemned Adams's writings, in particular his Davila essays, as "having a tendency to weaken the present government," in Jefferson's paraphrase. Hamilton continued in his own voice: "The present government is not that which will answer the ends of society by giving stability and protection to its rights. . . . It will probably be found expedient to go into the British form." Yet Hamilton was willing to let things play out. "Since we have undertaken the experiment, I am for giving it a fair course, whatever my expectations may be. The success indeed so far is greater than I had expected, and therefore at present success seems more possible than it had done heretofore, and there are still other and other stages of improvement which, if the present does not succeed, may be tried and ought to be tried before we give up the republican form altogether." Returning to Adams, Hamilton said, "For that mind must be really depraved which would not prefer the equality of political rights which is the foundation of pure republicanism, if it can be obtained consistently with order. Therefore whoever by his writings disturbs the present order of things is really blamable, however pure his intentions may be. And he was sure Mr. Adams's were pure."

## 31

J EFFERSON AND ADAMS WERE willing to let the matter drop for the time being, although this exchange seems to have raised doubts in each man's mind about the candor of the other. Both turned their attention to the approaching election of 1792. Adams hoped to retain his position as vice president, although he regularly professed indifference to the matter. "The winter is very mild; politics dull," Adams wrote to John Jay in January. "Speculation brisk. As we have little interest in these things we shall have a freer scope for friendship." When politics wasn't dull, Adams pronounced it distasteful. "If intrigues and maneuvers in elections have not been practised, and are not now practising, I have been misinformed," he wrote in March. "And if the people are not every day deceived by artifice and falsehood, I have no understanding. The share that has been assigned to me in public affairs, the circumstances of my fortune and family, as well as my age, make me very willing to resign to any other who may possess more of the popular favor or national confidence. The hosannas of blind enthusiasts I never coveted."

Jefferson meanwhile worked to ensure that Washington retain *his* office. The question wasn't whether the great man could be elected again, but whether he would *run* again. Jefferson's and Madison's defeat by Hamilton in the battle of the bank had left Jefferson discouraged about the direction the country was heading in. He still judged the bank unconstitutional, but at this early moment there was no generally accepted way to challenge its constitutionality in court. He disliked what the ascendancy of the financial class—as demonstrated by

Hamilton's victory on assumption and now the bank—augured for the country. "We are ruined, sir," Jefferson wrote to James Monroe, "if we do not overrule the principles that 'the more we owe, the more prosperous we shall be,' 'that a public debt furnishes the means of enterprise,' 'that if ours should be once paid off, we should incur another by any means however extravagant.'"

After the bank commenced operations, Jefferson's critique grew more pointed. "The bank filled and overflowed in the moment it was opened," he told Monroe. The bank sucked in money that should have been put to better use. "Thus it is that we shall be paying 13 per cent per annum for 8 millions of paper money instead of having that circulation of gold and silver for nothing." The money men had conjured a means of taxing the common people of America for their own selfish gain. "It is impossible to say where the appetite for gambling will stop," Jefferson said.

When the summer of 1791 revealed a broad malaise in the economy, Jefferson blamed the frenzy surrounding the start of the bank. "Ships are lying idle at the wharfs," he wrote to a friend. "Buildings are stopped, capitals withdrawn from commerce, manufactures, arts and agriculture, to be employed in gambling, and the tide of public prosperity, almost unparalleled in any country, is arrested in its course and suppressed by the rage of getting rich in a day. No mortal can tell where this will stop, for the spirit of gaming, when once it has seized a subject, is incurable. The tailor who has made thousands in one day, though he has lost them the next, can never again be content with the slow and moderate earnings of his needle."

The turmoil continued. "It is computed there is a dead loss at New York of about 5 millions of dollars, which is reckoned the value of all the buildings of the city; so that if the whole town had been burnt to the ground it would have been just the measure of the present calamity, supposing goods to have been saved," Jefferson wrote during the spring of 1792. "In Boston the dead loss is about a million of dollars." Philadelphia and its environs were equally ravaged. "Buildings and other improvements are suspended. Workmen turned adrift. Country produce not to be sold at any price: because even substantial merchants, who never meddled with paper, cannot tell how many of their debtors have meddled and may fail; consequently they are afraid to make any new money arrangements till they shall know how they stand."

Jefferson feared for the republic. "The rage of gambling in the stocks of various descriptions is such, and the profits *sometimes* made, and therefore *always* hoped, in that line are so far beyond any interest which an individual can give, that all their money and credit is centered in their own views," he wrote. "The bank has just now notified its proprietors that they may call for a dividend of 10 per cent on their capital for the last 6 months. This makes a profit of 20 per cent per annum. Agriculture, commerce, and everything *useful* must be neglected when the *useless* employment of money is so much more lucrative."

Jefferson thought—and certainly hoped—that the speculators would meet their comeuppance. "This nefarious business is becoming more and more the public detestation, and cannot fail, when the knowledge of it shall be sufficiently extended, to tumble its authors headlong from their heights," he declared in March 1792. "Money is leaving the remoter parts of the Union, and flowing to this place"—Philadelphia—"to purchase paper; and here a paper medium supplying its place; it is shipped off in exchange for luxuries. The value of property is necessarily falling in the places left bare of money. In Virginia, for instance, property has fallen 25 per cent in the last twelve months."

Yet the demise of the speculators might wreck the country. "I learn with real concern the calamities which are fallen on New York and which must fall on this place also," Jefferson wrote in April. "No man of reflection who had ever attended to the South Sea bubble in England, or that of Law in France"—two infamous speculations—"and who applied the lessons of the past to the present time, could fail to foresee the issue." Prudent men might learn from collapse, but the cycle would surely be repeated. "Such is the public cullability"—gullibility—"in the hands of cunning and unprincipled men that it is doomed by nature to receive these lessons once in an age at least."

JEFFERSON EXPECTED no help from Hamilton in saving the country. Hamilton's policies were the cause of the speculative frenzy. Only Washington offered hope, which was why the president must serve another term.

Washington had accepted the presidency in 1789 with some reluctance; he subsequently confided to Jefferson, Hamilton and others that he looked toward 1793 as the moment he might relinquish the office and its burdens. Jefferson told Washington why he mustn't retire. "When you first mentioned to me your purpose of retiring from the government, though I felt all the magnitude of the event, I was in a considerable degree silent," Jefferson wrote in May 1792. "I knew that to such a mind as yours, persuasion was idle and impertinent; that before forming your decision, you had weighed all the reasons for and against the measure, had made up your mind on full view of them, and that there could be little hope of changing the result." Jefferson had realized that the republic could not claim Washington's services forever. "I knew we were some day to try to walk alone; and if the essay should be made while you should be alive and looking on, we should derive confidence from that circumstance, and resource if it failed. The public mind too was calm and confident, and therefore in a favorable state for making the experiment."

But things had changed. "The public mind is no longer confident and serene," Jefferson said. The money mongers had set the country on a path to ruin, and they had undermined the government in doing so. "This corrupt squadron, deciding the voice of the legislature, have manifested their dispositions to get rid of the limitations imposed by the constitution on the general legislature, limitations, on the faith of which, the states acceded to that instrument." Nor were they finished. "The ultimate object of all this is to prepare the way for a change from the present republican form of government to that of a monarchy, of which the English constitution is to be the model." The signs had been evident for years. "That this was contemplated in the Convention is no secret, because its partisans have made none of it. To effect it then was impracticable, but they are still eager after their object, and are predisposing everything for its ultimate attainment. So many of them have got into the legislature that, aided by the corrupt squadron of paper dealers, who are at their devotion, they make a majority in both houses."

The defenders of the country and the Constitution were overmatched at present. "The republican party, who wish to preserve the government in its present form, are fewer in number," Jefferson told Washington, in one of his first references to the republicans as a party. "They are fewer even when joined by the two, three or half dozen antifederalists who, though they dare not avow it, are still opposed to any

general government, but being less so to a republican than a monarchical one, they naturally join those whom they think pursuing the lesser
evil."

Jefferson didn't want to sound alarmist, but he was deeply worried. "Of all the mischiefs objected to the system of measures before
mentioned, none is so afflicting and fatal to every honest hope as the
corruption of the legislature," he said. "As it was the earliest of these
measures, it became the instrument for producing the rest, and will be
the instrument for producing in future a king, lords and commons, or
whatever else those who direct it may choose. Withdrawn such a distance from the eye of their constituents, and these so dispersed as to be
inaccessible to public information, and particularly to that of the conduct of their own representatives, they will form the most corrupt government on earth, if the means of their corruption be not prevented."

Jefferson sought to counter the corruptionists' influence by rallying
the republicans. "The only hope of safety hangs now on the numerous representation which is to come forward the ensuing year"—as a
result of elections to Congress. "Some of the new members will probably be either in principle or interest with the present majority, but it
is expected that the great mass will form an accession to the republican
party." They wouldn't be able to undo all the damage the corruptionists
had effected, yet they could make a start. "Some parts of the system
may be rightfully reformed, a liberation from the rest unremittingly
pursued as fast as right will permit, and the door shut in future against
similar commitments of the nation." Such an outcome would be the
best for the country, Jefferson said. "This is the alternative least likely
to produce convulsion."

Yet it was hardly inevitable. "Should the majority of the new members be still in the same principles with the present, and shew that we
have nothing to expect but a continuance of the same practices, it is
not easy to conjecture what would be the result, nor what means would
be resorted to for correction of the evil," Jefferson told Washington.
"True wisdom would direct that they should be temperate and peaceable, but the division of sentiment and interest happens unfortunately
to be so geographical that no mortal can say that what is most wise and
temperate would prevail against what is most easy and obvious." The
North held the debt that was owed by the South, leading Jefferson to

fear a rupture along sectional lines. "I can scarcely contemplate a more incalculable evil than the breaking of the union into two or more parts," he said.

Which was why the president must remain in office. "I consider your continuance at the head of affairs as of the last importance. The confidence of the whole union is centered in you. Your being at the helm will be more than an answer to every argument which can be used to alarm and lead the people in any quarter into violence or secession. North and South will hang together if they have you to hang on."

## 32

HAMILTON AGREED WITH Jefferson on less and less these days, but he concurred that Washington was essential to the country. Hamilton made his own argument as to why Washington must accept another term. "I have lost no opportunity of sounding the opinions of persons whose opinions were worth knowing on these two points— 1st. the effect of your declining upon the public affairs, and upon your own reputation—2dly. the effect of your continuing in reference to the declarations you have made of your disinclination to public life," Hamilton said. Washington fretted that having long said he sought no political position, he would seem a hypocrite if he remained in office.

"And I can truly say that I have not found the least difference of sentiment on either point," Hamilton continued. "The impression is uniform—that your declining would be to be deplored as the greatest evil that could befall the country at the present juncture, and as critically hazardous to your own reputation—that your continuance will be justified in the mind of every friend to his country by the evident necessity for it. 'Tis clear, says everyone with whom I have conversed, that the affairs of the national government are not yet firmly established— that its enemies, generally speaking, are as inveterate as ever—that their enmity has been sharpened by its success and by all the resentments which flow from disappointed predictions and mortified vanity—that a general and strenuous effort is making in every state to place the administration of it in the hands of its enemies as if they were its safest guardians—that the period of the next House of Representatives is

likely to prove the crisis of its permanent character—that if you continue in office nothing materially mischievous is to be apprehended—if
you quit much is to be dreaded—that the same motives which induced
you to accept originally ought to decide you to continue till matters have
assumed a more determinate aspect—that indeed it would have been
better, as it regards your own character, that you had never consented to
come forward than now to leave the business unfinished and in danger
of being undone—that in the event of storms arising there would be
an imputation either of want of foresight or want of firmness—and, in
fine, that on public and personal accounts, on patriotic and prudential
considerations, the clear path to be pursued by you will be again to obey
the voice of your country, which it is not doubted will be as earnest and
as unanimous as ever."

Speaking in his own voice, Hamilton concluded, "I trust, sir, and I
pray God that you will determine to make a further sacrifice of your
tranquility and happiness to the public good."


WASHINGTON WAS WILLING to be persuaded, but he had some
things to say first. He chided his cabinet secretaries for the political
quarrels they allowed into his administration. In a letter to Jefferson,
Washington reflected on the challenges America was facing with other
countries, then declared, "How unfortunate and how much is it to
be regretted, then, that whilst we are encompassed on all sides with
avowed enemies and insidious friends, that internal dissentions should
be harrowing and tearing our vitals. The last, to me, is the most serious,
the most alarming, and the most afflicting of the two."

Washington asked for more tolerance and less certitude among
his advisers. "Without more charity for the opinions and acts of one
another in governmental matters, or some more infallible criterion by
which the truth of speculative opinions, before they have undergone
the test of experience, are to be forejudged than has yet fallen to the lot
of fallibility, I believe it will be difficult if not impracticable to manage
the reins of government or to keep the parts of it together," he told
Jefferson. "For if, instead of laying our shoulders to the machine after
measures are decided on, one pulls this way and another that before the
utility of the thing is fairly tried, it must, inevitably, be torn asunder.

And, in my opinion, the fairest prospect of happiness and prosperity that ever was presented to man will be lost—perhaps forever!"

"My earnest wish and my fondest hope, therefore, is that instead of wounding suspicions and irritable charges there may be liberal allowances, mutual forbearances, and temporising yieldings on *all sides,*" Washington said. "Under the exercise of these, matters will go on smoothly and, if possible, more prosperously. Without them everything must rub, the wheels of government will clog, our enemies will triumph, and by throwing their weight into the disaffected scale may accomplish the ruin of the goodly fabric we have been erecting."

Washington wrote to Hamilton in the same vein and in some of the same words. "Differences in political opinions are as unavoidable as, to a certain point, they may perhaps be necessary," he said. "But it is to be regretted exceedingly that subjects cannot be discussed with temper, on the one hand, or decisions submitted to without having the motives which led to them improperly implicated on the other. And this regret borders on chagrin when we find that men of abilities— zealous patriots—having the same *general* objects in view, and the same upright intentions to prosecute them, will not exercise more charity in deciding on the opinions and actions of one another."

Washington expected better from his closest advisers. "I would fain hope that liberal allowances will be made for the political opinions of one another, and instead of those wounding suspicions and irritating charges with which some of our gazettes are so strongly impregnated and cannot fail, if persevered in, of pushing matters to extremity and thereby tear the machine asunder, that there might be mutual forbearances and temporising yieldings *on all sides.* . . . My earnest wish is that balsam may be poured into *all* the wounds which have been given, to prevent them from gangrening, and from those fatal consequences which the community may sustain if it is withheld."

PART VI

---

*Monarchists and Jacobins*

## 33

Washington's chiding had no effect on Jefferson or Hamilton. Each man replied at length reiterating that the other was to blame for the rift within the administration. Yet both were willing to suffer Washington's displeasure if such was the cost of getting him to agree to serve another term. He did agree, and the contest for president was a formality, as nearly everyone else in America was as eager as Jefferson and Hamilton that Washington remain in office.

The other races in 1792 were more vigorously contested. The season shaped up as a test of strength between Jefferson's Republicans—as they were calling themselves, although often in lowercase—and Hamilton's Federalists. Elections for Congress were key, and Jefferson took pride and hope from the results. "The elections for Congress have produced a decided majority in favor of the republican interest," he reported to Thomas Pinckney of South Carolina in early December. "I think we may consider the tide of this government as now at the fullest, and that it will, from the commencement of the next session of Congress, retire and subside into the true principles of the Constitution." John Adams faced a stiff challenge to retain the vice presidency, Jefferson noted. "There will be a strong vote against Mr. Adams." But Adams would probably survive. "The strength of his personal worth and his services will, I think, prevail over the demerit of his political creed."

Events proved Jefferson correct. Adams defeated George Clinton of New York and returned as vice president. The Republicans in Congress asserted their views more successfully. Hamilton's influence diminished, although he remained a formidable presence, in part because he found a new issue with which to tax Jefferson's Republicans.

THE REVOLUTION IN FRANCE had never been an affair of the meek, but it recently had grown more violent. The assembly created under France's first constitution moved too swiftly for the king and his remaining conservative supporters, and too slowly for the radicals who rejected the idea of a constitutional monarchy as inadequate to the needs of the French people. The assembly broke into factions corresponding to the conservatives and the radicals and lurched from crisis to crisis. The troubles metastasized after the then-ruling faction in the assembly declared war on Austria, whose emperor openly sympathized with Louis. Prussia and Britain joined the war against France, putting still greater strain on the government in Paris. The invasion of French territory by Austrian and Prussian forces triggered riots in the capital that escalated into the bloody murder of some thousand persons accused of conspiring with the enemies of France and the revolution. Power swung to the radicals known as Jacobins and the violence escalated further, culminating for the moment in the execution of Louis for treason.

Hamilton and his Federalist allies seized on the sanguinary turn in France to criticize Jefferson and the Republicans. The Federalists declared that into such chaos would America descend if the democratic tendencies of Jefferson and the Republicans weren't quickly checked.

The violence in France took Jefferson by surprise, but he defended the French revolution as vital to the advance of liberty. Blame for the bloody turn it had taken lay with the unreconstructed monarchists who sought to reestablish the old order, he said. "In the struggle which was necessary, many guilty persons fell without the forms of trial, and with them some innocent. These I deplore as much as anybody, and shall deplore some of them to the day of my death. But I deplore them as I should have done had they fallen in battle. It was necessary to use the arm of the people, a machine not quite so blind as balls and bombs, but blind to a certain degree." Yet all would turn out well. "Time and truth will rescue and embalm their memories, while their posterity will be enjoying that very liberty for which they would never have hesitated to offer up their lives."

Amid the trials of the American Revolution, Alexander Hamilton concluded that the Continental Congress was woefully inadequate to the needs of a great country. He shared his views with others and promoted plans for a new government.

James Madison reached the same conclusion during the same period. Even after the Articles of Confederation were ratified, Madison judged that the national government required much broader powers.

By the *Preſident* and the *Supreme Executive Council* of the Commonwealth of *Pennſylvania,*

## A PROCLAMATION.

WHEREAS the General Aſſembly of this Commonwealth, by a law entitled 'An act for co-operating with " the ſtate of Maſſachuſetts bay, agreeable to the articles of " confederation, in the apprehending of the proclaimed rebels " DANIEL SHAYS, LUKE DAY, ADAM WHEELER " and ELI PARSONS," have enacted, " that rewards ad" ditional to thoſe offered and promiſed to be paid by the ſtate " of Maſſachuſetts Bay, for the apprehending the aforeſaid' " rebels, be offered by this ſtate ;" WE do hereby offer the following rewards to any perſon or perſons who ſhall, within the limits of this ſtate, apprehend the rebels aforeſaid, and ſecure them in the gaol of the city and county of Philadelphia, ——— viz For the apprehending of the ſaid Daniel Shays, and ſecuring him as aforeſaid, the reward of *One hundred and Fifty Pounds* lawful money of the ſtate of Maſſachuſetts Bay, and *One Hundred Pounds* lawful money of this ſtate ; and for the apprehending the ſaid Luke Day, Adam Wheeler and Eli Parſons, and ſecuring them as aforeſaid, the reward (reſpectively) of *One Hundred Pounds* lawful money of Maſſachuſetts Bay and *Fifty Pounds* lawful money of this ſtate : And all judges, juſtices, ſheriffs and conſtables are hereby ſtrictly enjoined and required to make diligent ſearch and enquiry after, and to uſe their utmoſt endeavours to apprehend and ſecure the ſaid Daniel Shays, Luke Day, Adam Wheeler and Eli Parſons, their aiders, abettors and comforters, and every of them, ſo that they may be dealt with according to law.

    GIVEN in Council, under the hand of the Preſident, and the Seal of the State, at Philadelphia, this tenth day of March, in the year of our Lord one thouſand ſeven hundred and eighty-ſeven.

                          BENJAMIN FRANKLIN.

ATTEST
   JOHN ARMSTRONG, jun. Secretary.

An armed rebellion in western Massachusetts headed by Revolutionary War veteran Daniel Shays caused many in America to fear that self-government would lead to dissolution unless drastic measures were taken. Here, Pennsylvania offers a reward for the rebels' capture.

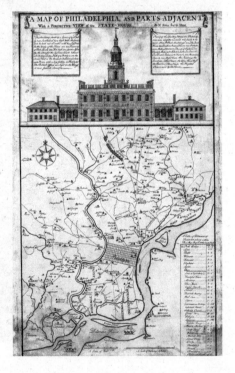

After a failed first try in Annapolis in 1786, Madison and Hamilton succeeded in gathering delegates to a convention in Philadelphia in 1787.

George Washington presided over the Philadelphia convention. When the delegates couldn't decide what powers to give the president under their new scheme, they took comfort from assuming Washington would be the first president and would figure things out as he went along.

Declining health kept Benjamin Franklin from engaging consistently in the debates at the convention, but his timely comments helped cool passions and pointed the way to compromise.

Once approved by the convention, the new Constitution was sent to the states for ratification. Hamilton and Madison were the strongest voices for the Federalists, as the supporters of ratification were called. Patrick Henry of Virginia, the great orator of American independence, spoke powerfully for the Antifederalist cause.

After an acrimonious contest, the Constitution was ratified. Washington was elected president, as expected, and was inaugurated at Federal Hall in New York, where the new government commenced operations.

The founders of the new government had hoped America would be spared the kind of political parties that, to their way of thinking, had corrupted government in Britain and other European countries. Yet parties soon emerged over such controversial issues such as the Bank of the United States.

To Americans inclined to favor a stronger central government, a rebellion among whiskey distillers in western Pennsylvania seemed proof of the peril awaiting weakness. To Americans still skeptical of power at the center, Washington's military response appeared the greater danger.

Two terms as president produced more partisan sniping than Washington could finally stand, and he retired. John Adams, after serving fretfully as Washington's vice president, let his friends put his name forward to be Washington's successor.

Abigail Adams had gotten used to living apart from her husband during much of his public life, but after he was elected president she joined him in Philadelphia, America's capital in the late 1790s. She offered sage advice and unvarnished views of the many people she disagreed with.

Political parties, once latent, burst into the open during Adams's term. Adams and Hamilton headed the Federalists, Thomas Jefferson and Madison the Republicans. As Adams's vice president, Jefferson felt compelled to cloak his opposition in secrecy.

By the election of 1800, the parties were in full roar. A scandal over sex and blackmail contributed to a rift among the Federalists, and Hamilton broke with Adams. Meanwhile Jefferson enlisted Aaron Burr to boost the Republicans' chances in New York.

The Republicans trounced the Federalists, but a tie in electors pushed the contest to the House of Representatives, where Hamilton helped tip the balance to Jefferson, who took his oath of office in the unfinished Capitol in the new city of Washington. Jefferson declared, "We are all Republicans; we are all Federalists," but no one took him seriously.

America's fate was entangled with that of France, Jefferson said. The French were fighting for the same freedoms America had vindicated a decade earlier. "The liberty of the whole earth was depending on the issue of the contest; and was ever such a prize won with so little innocent blood?" Jefferson thought not. "My own affections have been deeply wounded by some of the martyrs to this cause, but rather than it should have failed, I would have seen half the earth desolated. Were there but an Adam and an Eve left in every country, and left free, it would be better than as it now is."

The Federalists had chafed at the continuing American alliance with France, and they disliked the debt America owed the French. They took the overthrow of the monarchy as cause for dissolving the alliance and disavowing the debt. The alliance and the debt had been contracted with a government that no longer existed, they said; therefore the alliance and the debt no longer existed.

Jefferson rejected the argument as contradicting the fundamental principles of republicanism. "We surely cannot deny to any nation that right whereon our own government is founded, that every one may govern itself according to whatever form it pleases, and change these forms at its own will, and that it may transact its business with foreign nations through whatever organ it thinks proper, whether king, convention, assembly, committee, president or anything else it may choose," he wrote to Gouverneur Morris, the new minister to France. "The will of the nation is the only thing essential to be regarded." The French people, acting through their national assembly and then the convention, had revealed their will, and the United States had the obligation to respect it. The United States also had an *interest* in respecting it, Jefferson told Morris. "Mutual good offices, mutual affection and similar principles of government seem to destine the two nations for the most intimate communion; and I cannot too much press it on you to improve every opportunity which may occur in the changeable scenes which are passing, and to seize them as they occur, for placing our commerce with that nation and its dependencies on the freest and most encouraging footing possible."

HAMILTON AND THE FEDERALISTS denounced Jefferson's interpretation of the events in France as dangerously naïve, and they thought his tolerance for the violence there revealed an alarming undercurrent in the democratic philosophy he espoused.

Hamilton proclaimed himself a friend of the initial reforms in France, and he asserted the same for all Americans. "In the early periods of the French revolution, a warm zeal for its success was in this country a sentiment truly universal," he said. "The love of liberty is here the ruling passion of the citizens of the United States, pervading every class, animating every bosom. As long therefore as the revolution of France bore the marks of being the cause of liberty, it united all hearts concentered all opinions."

But things had changed in France, and with them had changed attitudes in America. "The excesses which have constantly multiplied with greater and greater aggravations have successively though slowly detached reflecting men from their partiality for an object which has appeared less and less to merit their regard," Hamilton said. Yet some in America clung to their initial beliefs. "They were willing to overlook many faults, to apologise for some enormities, to hope that better justifications existed than were seen, to look forward to more calm and greater moderation after the first shocks of the political earthquake had subsided."

They had been disappointed. "Instead of this, they have been witnesses to one volcano succeeding another, the last still more dreadful than the former, spreading ruin and devastation far and wide; subverting the foundations of right, security and property; of order, morality and religion; sparing neither sex nor age; confounding innocence with guilt; involving the old and the young, the sage and the madman, the long tried friend of virtue and his country and the upstart pretender to purity and patriotism; the bold projector of new treasons with the obscure in indiscriminate and profuse destruction."

The self-declared friends of France had been compelled to choose, Hamilton said. "They have found themselves driven to the painful alternative of renouncing an object dear to their wishes or of becoming by the continuance of their affection for it accomplices with vice, anarchy, despotism and impiety."

Amazingly, many chose the latter. "Though an afflicting experience has materially lessened the number of the admirers of the French revolution among us and has served to chill the ardor of many more who profess still to retain their attachment to it from what they suppose to be its ultimate tendency, yet the effect of experience has been thus far much less than could reasonably have been expected," Hamilton said. "The predilection for it still continues extensive and ardent."

The willful blindness of Jefferson and his Francophile friends boded ill for America's future. "This partiality is the most inauspicious circumstance that has appeared in the affairs of this country," Hamilton said. "It leads involuntarily and irresistibly to apprehensions concerning the soundness of our principles and the stability of our welfare. It is natural to fear that the transition may not be difficult from the approbation of bad things to the imitation of them."

Well-wishers to America must hope for a change in these misguided attitudes—indeed, they must actively combat them. "We cannot consider the public happiness as out of the reach of danger so long as our principles continue to be exposed to the debauching influence of admiration for an example which, it will not be too strong to say, presents the caricature of human depravity," Hamilton said. "If there be any thing solid in virtue, the time must come when it will have been a disgrace to have advocated the revolution of France in its late stages."

The battle would be lonely. "This is a language to which the ears of the people of this country have not been accustomed. Everything has hitherto conspired to confirm the pernicious fascination by which they are enchained." Jefferson and his ilk had done their insidious work well, Hamilton said. "There has been a positive and a negative conspiracy against the truth which has served to shut out its enlightening ray." Public figures and journalists had conspired to pervert the truth about what was actually happening in France. Many of the common people of America had been beguiled by this false version of reality. "Hence the voice of reason has been stifled and the nation has been left unadmonished to travel on in one of the most degrading delusions that ever disparaged the understandings of an enlightened people."

Though lonely and hard, the battle must be fought. For the sake of America, the American people must be brought back to their senses. "To recall them from this dangerous error, to engage them to dismiss their prejudices and consult dispassionately their own good sense, to lead them to an appeal from their own enthusiasm to their reason and humanity, would be the most important service that could be rendered to the United States at the present juncture," Hamilton declared. "The error entertained is not on a mere speculative question. The French revolution is a political convulsion that in a great or less degree shakes the whole civilized world. And it is of real consequence to the principles and of course to the happiness of a nation"—America—"to estimate it rightly."

## 34

THE FRENCH QUESTION in American politics became more immediate as the European war intensified. The French government, now in republican guise, demanded that its republican ally America come to its aid. France had rescued America during the Americans' war against reactionary monarchy a decade before; the time had come for America to return the favor.

Jefferson remained sympathetic toward France, but he balked at going to war on France's behalf. And he knew most Americans did, too. "No country perhaps was ever so thoroughly against war as ours," he wrote to Gouverneur Morris for relay to the French government. "These dispositions pervade every description of its citizens, whether in or out of office." France could still count on America's moral support, just not its military support. Speaking as America's chief diplomat, Jefferson told the French that the United States would observe a "fair neutrality" between the European belligerents. He pointed out that this would still serve France well. "Indeed we shall be more useful as neutrals than as parties by the protection which our flag will give to supplies of provision."

The other members of Washington's cabinet, and the president himself, were even less inclined than Jefferson to join France at war. On the question of neutrality, the administration enjoyed a rare consensus. A relieved Washington announced to the world that "the duty and interest of the United States require that they should with sincerity and good faith adopt and pursue a conduct friendly and impartial toward the belligerent powers."

THE CONSENSUS WITHIN the administration on the neutrality decision didn't keep it from becoming a new bone of contention between the Federalists and the Republicans. Some of the latter, without disputing the decision itself, protested the process by which it was made. To wit, by proclaiming neutrality on his own authority, Washington usurped a central prerogative of Congress, the Republicans said. And in doing so, he revealed the monarchist bent of the Federalist philosophy.

Hamilton entered the lists in defense of the president, authoring a series of essays that appeared in the *Gazette of the United States* over the pseudonym Pacificus. Hamilton commenced with an attack on the patriotism of the administration's critics. "As attempts are making very dangerous to the peace, and it is to be feared not very friendly to the Constitution of the United States," he wrote, "it becomes the duty of those who wish well to both to endeavour to prevent their success." He elaborated his allegation: "The objections which have been raised against the proclamation of neutrality lately issued by the president have been urged in a spirit of acrimony and invective which demonstrates that more was in view than merely a free discussion of an important public measure; that the discussion covers a design of weakening the confidence of the people in the author of the measure"—Washington—"in order to remove or lessen a powerful obstacle to the success of an opposition to the government." In other words, the Republicans were imperiling America in order to advance themselves.

Hamilton rebutted the Republican complaints against the neutrality proclamation in three ways, according to the challenges they made to it. As strict constructionists of the Constitution, the Republicans had asserted that the president lacked the authority to proclaim neutrality. No clause of the Constitution accorded him that power, they said. And any reasonable interpretation of the Constitution put that authority in the hands of Congress. The Constitution explicitly reserved to Congress the power to declare war; implicit in that was the power to declare not-war, namely neutrality. Yet Washington had not asked Congress for a neutrality declaration; indeed he had not even consulted Congress on the issue. In doing so he had usurped the authority of Congress.

Hamilton rejected the Republican line with a neat bit of sophistry. "If the legislature have a right to make war on the one hand, it is on the other the duty of the executive to preserve peace till war is declared," he said. "In this distribution of powers the wisdom of our Constitution is manifested. It is the province and duty of the executive to preserve to the nation the blessings of peace. The legislature alone can interrupt those blessings, by placing the nation in a state of war."

The second complaint of the Republicans was that neutrality, by constituting a refusal to side with France against Britain, contravened America's treaty of alliance with France. Hamilton exaggerated the number of Republicans making this argument; the complaint of most of the Republicans was not with neutrality per se but with the executive aggrandizement involved in its proclamation. Hamilton assailed the straw man he had created. "The alliance between the United States and France is a defensive alliance," he said. "In the caption of it, it is denominated a 'Treaty of Alliance Eventual and Defensive.' In the body of it (Article the 2d), it is again called a defensive alliance. The words of that article are as follow: 'The essential and direct end of the present defensive alliance is to maintain effectually the liberty, sovereignty and independence, absolute and unlimited, of the United States, as well in matters of government as of commerce.'"

In a defensive alliance, the parties were required to assist each other only if one or the other were attacked. But the present war had begun at the initiative of the French. The Republicans pleaded extenuating circumstances: that the other European powers were preparing to attack France. This didn't matter, said Hamilton. "No position is better established than that the power which first declares or actually begins a war, whatever may have been the causes leading to it, is that which makes an offensive war. Nor is there any doubt that France first declared and began the war against Austria, Prussia, Savoy, Holland, England and Spain."

Hamilton might have rested his case here. But he proceeded to his strongest argument for abstaining from France's war: American self-interest. "All contracts are to receive a reasonable construction," he said, speaking as a lawyer. "Self-preservation is the first duty of a nation," he continued, speaking as a statesman. The United States had no interest in France's fight with its European neighbors, nor did it have the capacity to intervene effectively. "We are wholly destitute of naval force," he pointed out. Absent that, America could do nothing for France even if it wanted to. Declaring war on Britain would open America to British blockade and to attack from Canada. War against Spain would endanger America's southern and western borders.

The Republican advocates of war on France's behalf—again, a far smaller number than Hamilton implied—foolishly conflated personal morality with the morality of nations, he said. The Republicans proclaimed a debt of gratitude that America owed to France for her help during America's time of trouble. "It is at this shrine"—gratitude—"we are continually invited to sacrifice the true interests of the country, as if 'All for love and the world well lost' were a fundamental maxim in politics," he declared derisively. The code among nations was a stern one. "An individual may on numerous occasions meritoriously indulge the emotions of generosity and benevolence not only without an eye to, but even at the expence of his own interest. But a nation can rarely be justified in pursuing a similar course, and when it does so ought to confine itself within much stricter bounds." Self-interest came first, benevolence second if at all.

Such calculation had inspired French support for America in the Revolutionary War, Hamilton said. It wasn't love of liberty but hatred of Britain that had caused King Louis to cast his country's lot with the United States. Any who thought otherwise were willfully blind or criminally disingenuous. Hamilton favored the latter explanation as he delivered another slap against "those who love France more than the United States."

This was the fundamental problem with the Republicans' approach to foreign policy, he said. In their fatuous appeal to norms that didn't apply to the affairs of nations, they put the interest of another country ahead of that of the United States. The ongoing upheaval in France itself should serve as a cautionary example. "It ought to teach us not to overrate foreign friendships, to be upon our guard against foreign attachments," Hamilton said. "The former will generally be found hollow and delusive; the latter will have a natural tendency to lead us aside from our own true interest and to make us the dupes of foreign influence." Hamilton reiterated, in what would become a theme of Federalist thought: "Foreign influence is truly the Grecian horse"—Trojan horse—"to a republic. We cannot be too careful to exclude its entrance."

JEFFERSON GROANED as he read the Pacificus pieces. He wrote in haste to Madison: "For god's sake, my dear sir, take up your pen, select the most striking heresies, and cut him to pieces in the face of the public. There is nobody else who can and will enter the lists with him." Jefferson knew that what he called "heresies" would be persuasive if unrebutted. "Nobody answers him, and his doctrine will therefore be taken for confessed."

Jefferson might have taken up the pen himself but for two constraints. The first was his recognition that he wasn't adept at hand-to-hand partisan combat. He could write as elegantly from first principles as anyone in America, but he lacked the biting wit required of those engaged in the cut-and-thrust at close quarters. He would be the general of the Republican political army, devising overall strategy; the actual fighting would be accomplished better by others.

The second reason for his diffidence was that he was secretary of state. Jefferson didn't know for certain who Pacificus was, but he might have guessed it was Hamilton or someone Hamilton had enlisted for the purpose of defending the administration's neutrality policy. There was no dishonor in that—in defending the administration of which one was a part. For Jefferson to *attack* the administration was another matter entirely. It would be interpreted by many as being dishonorable and disloyal. Jefferson wasn't willing to risk that. So Jefferson enlisted Madison to do the dirty work.

Madison wasn't thrilled about the assignment. "I have forced myself into the task," he told Jefferson after drafting part of his response. "I can truly say I find it the most grating one I ever experienced." Madison recognized he wasn't a match for Hamilton either, in the genre of dueling essays. He lacked the zest for battle, and, more crucially, hadn't spent the time Hamilton had studying the neutrality issue. "I feel at every step I take the want of counsel on some points of delicacy as well as of information as to sundry matters of fact." Besides, Madison realized there would be no end to this battle. "One thing that particularly vexes me is that I foreknow from the prolixity and pertinacity of the writer that the business will not be terminated by a single fire, and of course that I must return to the charge in order to prevent a triumph without a victory."

But he went ahead, corresponding with Jefferson about the project and employing encryption lest Federalist-appointed postmasters open their letters. This created problems of its own. "I am extremely morti-fied in looking for the key to the cypher, to find that I left it in Phila-delphia," he wrote to Jefferson from his home in Virginia.

Eventually he sorted things out and began his rebuttal. "Several pieces with the signature of Pacificus were lately published which have been read with singular pleasure and applause by the foreigners and degenerate citizens among us who hate our republican government and the French revolution," Madison said, slandering a large part of the American population. Writing as Helvidius, he characterized the Paci-ficus essays as a clever bit of misdirection. "They offer themselves to the reader in the dress of an elaborate dissertation; they are mingled with a few truths that may serve them as a passport to credulity; and they are introduced with professions of anxiety for the preservation of peace, for the welfare of the government, and for the respect due to the present head of the executive, that may prove a snare to patriotism." Their real purpose was quite different. "Under colour of vindicating an important public act of a chief magistrate who enjoys the confidence and love of his country, principles are advanced which strike at the vitals of its Constitution, as well as at its honor and true interest."

Madison derided Hamilton's first argument even as he mischarac-terized it. "The basis of the reasoning is, we perceive, the extraordinary doctrine that the powers of making war and treaties are in their nature executive and therefore comprehended in the general grant of execu-tive power." Hamilton—that is, Pacificus—had not claimed for the president the right to make war and treaties, only to declare neutrality. Madison ignored the distinction to assert a larger, sounder point. "The natural province of the executive magistrate is to execute laws, as that of the legislature is to make laws. All his acts therefore, properly executive, must pre-suppose the existence of the laws to be executed."

This clearly applied to the declaration of war. "A declaration that there shall be war is not an execution of laws," said Madison. "It does not suppose pre-existing laws to be executed; it is not in any respect an act merely executive. It is, on the contrary, one of the most deliberative acts that can be performed." The Constitution expressly reserved that deliberation to Congress. To say that a declaration of neutrality was different from a declaration of war was disingenuous, Madison said. A declaration of neutrality preempted the deliberations of Congress, declaring a result before the deliberations began.

Hamilton was consciously blurring the line between the legislative branch and the executive, Madison contended. Hamilton's aim became apparent in his assertion that the executive had the power to make treaties. Again, Hamilton hadn't said that, but Madison had a punch line he wanted to deliver: "In theory, this is an absurdity—in practice a tyranny."

Tyranny was indeed the tendency, if not the outright intent, of the administration's power grab, he continued. "The power of the legislature to declare war and judge of the causes for declaring it is one of the most express and explicit parts of the Constitution. To endeavor to abridge or affect it by strained inferences and by hypothetical or singular occurrences naturally warns the reader of some lurking fallacy." The lurking fallacy was that the president should take on attributes of monarchs, who did indeed declare war and judge of their causes.

The Federalists' disregard of the Constitution betrayed nothing so much as their insatiable lust for power, Madison argued. They would deny any such thing, but true republicans—as opposed to the Federalist fakes—must reject their denials. "We are to regard it as morally certain that in proportion as the doctrines make their way into the creed of the government and the acquiescence of the public, every power that can be deduced from them will be deduced and exercised sooner or later by those who may have an interest in so doing," he said. "The character of human nature gives this salutary warning to every sober and reflecting mind. And the history of government, in all its forms and in every period of time, ratifies the danger. A people, therefore, who are so happy as to possess the inestimable blessing of a free and defined Constitution cannot be too watchful against the introduction, nor too critical in tracing the consequences, of new principles and new constructions that may remove the landmarks of power."

It was particularly appalling that the Federalists were making their attack where they were. "In no part of the Constitution is more wisdom to be found than in the clause which confides the question of war or peace to the legislature and not to the executive department," Madison said. "Beside the objection to such a mixture of heterogeneous pow-

ers, the trust and the temptation would be too great for any one man."
Washington wouldn't succumb; he was too honest for that. But the
lesser men who would succeed him certainly would. "War is in fact the
true nurse of executive aggrandizement. In war a physical force is to
be created, and it is the executive will which is to direct it. In war the
public treasures are to be unlocked, and it is the executive hand which is
to dispense them. In war the honors and emoluments of office are to be
multiplied, and it is the executive patronage under which they are to be
enjoyed. It is in war, finally, that laurels are to be gathered, and it is the
executive brow they are to encircle. The strongest passions and most
dangerous weaknesses of the human breast—ambition, avarice, vanity,
the honorable or venal love of fame—are all in conspiracy against the
desire and duty of peace."

Washington would not make himself king, but America might yet
have a monarch, Madison warned. "It is a plain consequence that every
addition that may be made to the sole agency and influence of the
executive in the intercourse of the nation with foreign nations is an
increase of the dangerous temptation to which an *elective and temporary* magistrate is exposed, and an *argument* and *advance* towards the
security afforded by the personal interests of an *hereditary* magistrate."

## 35

WHILE LEAVING the Republican arguing to Madison, Jefferson directed the diplomacy of the neutrality policy. The European war raised demand for American produce, especially foodstuffs; American farmers and merchants responded by sending cargoes across the Atlantic. The British and the French each sought to deny American commerce to the other, and their navies seized American ships. The British compounded the injury by the impressment of American sailors: the forcible seizure of seamen the British claimed were deserters from the British navy.

Jefferson had expected no better of the British. Even before the current war with France, they had been obstructing and harassing American trade, as indeed they had done since the Revolutionary War. "Great Britain is still endeavoring to plunder us of our carrying business," he wrote to James Monroe during Washington's first term. "The parliament have a bill before them to admit wheat brought in *British* bottoms to be warehoused rent free, so that the merchants are already giving a preference to British bottoms for that commodity. Should we lose the transportation of our own wheat, it will put down a great proportion of our shipping, already pushed by British vessels out of some of the best branches of business."

What made the British depredations the more irksome to Jefferson was the complicity of Hamilton and the Federalists in the injuries. "Our treasury still thinks that these new encroachments of Great Britain on our carrying trade must be met by passive obedience and nonresistance, lest any misunderstanding with them should *affect our credit, or the prices of our public paper,*" he told Monroe. As always, the Federalists placed the interests of speculators ahead of those of honest working people.

The new British seizures made the de facto British-Federalist alliance all the more dangerous to American liberties. In his role as secretary of state, Jefferson protested the seizures to London as a violation of America's rights—specifically, the right of a neutral to trade freely during wartime. International law hardly existed at this time, and international norms were violated in the breach as much as the observance. Yet Jefferson cited precedent from as far back as classical times to contend that "free bottoms make free goods." Ships and their cargoes were treated as having the nationality of their owners; to seize the ships and cargoes was to seize the property of parties not at war. Just as British or French marines could not legitimately land on American shores and carry away corn or wheat, so British naval officers and seamen could not board American ships and commandeer the craft and their cargoes.

Jefferson's protest picked apart a British order declaring ships bound for France to be liable to search and seizure. One article of the order made contraband of such innocuous and previously protected items as corn and flour. "This article is so manifestly contrary to the law of nations that nothing more would seem necessary than to observe that it is so," Jefferson wrote to Thomas Pinckney, the American minister in London, for relay to the British government. "Reason and usage have established that when two nations go to war, those who choose to live in peace retain their natural right to pursue their agriculture, manufactures, and other ordinary vocations; to carry the produce of their industry for exchange to all nations, belligerent or neutral, as usual; to go and come freely, without injury or molestation; and, in short, that the war among others shall be, for them, as if it did not exist."

Jefferson acknowledged exemptions for implements of war. These were not at issue here. "Corn, flour, and meal are not of the class of contraband, and consequently remain articles of free commerce," he said. Britain had no right to interfere with trade in them. Doing so deprived American citizens of the fruits of their labors—indeed of their ability to make a living.

The American government could not submit to the British policy, and it would not, Jefferson said. "No nation can subscribe to such pretensions; no nation can agree, at the mere will or interest of another, to have its peaceable industry suspended and its citizens reduced to idleness and want." Nor were exports the only goods threatened; imports were imperiled too. "Our ships do not go to France to return empty; they go to exchange the surplus of our produce, which we can spare, for surpluses of other kinds, which they can spare, and we want; which they can furnish on better terms, and more to our mind, than Great Britain or her friends." America would not be dictated to by Britain on trade or anything else. "We have a right to judge for ourselves what market best suits us, and they have none to forbid to us the enjoyment of the necessaries and comforts which we may obtain from any other independent country."

JEFFERSON'S ARGUMENT FOR neutral rights would underpin American foreign policy for more than a century. His reasoning would be repeated by secretaries of state and presidents down to the twentieth century. Yet the British found Jefferson's logic unpersuasive. Their seizure order stood, and the takings continued.

Jefferson wasn't surprised. He already judged the British arrogant scoundrels, and their seizure policy confirmed the judgment.

He *was* surprised, though, and more than a little discomfited by the French violations of American rights. Jefferson had thought America and France held similar views on liberty; France's actions indicated otherwise. "The French have been guilty of great errors in their conduct towards other nations," Jefferson told Thomas Randolph, his son-in-law. America was among the aggrieved. "The war between them and England embarrasses our government daily and immensely."

The embarrassments over shipping were just the start. The new government in Paris sent as minister to America a novice diplomat named Edmond-Charles Genêt. Thirty years old, Genêt was the son of a functionary of the old regime; perhaps to prove his bona fides to the new one, he committed one outrage after another against American neutrality. He recruited soldiers and sailors to fight for France against its enemies; he arranged construction and provision of ships to be employed on France's behalf. He openly criticized America's neutrality policy and demanded its revision.

Jefferson tried to be tolerant. He perceived Genêt as a fellow lover of liberty, and he admired Genêt's passion. When he chastised the French minister, he did so gently and in private. In a letter intended to be confidential, Jefferson told Genêt that he had consulted with President Washington about Genêt's activities, and the president had determined that the arming and outfitting of vessels to cruise against nations with which the United States was at peace was "incompatible with the territorial sovereignty of the United States." Speaking with Washington's authority, Jefferson delineated the principle: "It is the *right* of every nation to prohibit acts of sovereignty from being exercised by any other within its limits; and the *duty* of a neutral nation to prohibit such as would injure one of the warring powers." As for Genêt's recruiting activities: "The granting military commissions within the United States by any other authority than their own is an infringement on their sovereignty, and particularly so when granted to their own citizens to lead them to commit acts contrary to the duties they owe their own country."

Genêt refused to accept Jefferson or even Washington as the arbiter of American policy. Fresh from France, where governments were overturned in the street, he appealed to the American people. "Genet has thrown down the gauntlet to the president by the publication of his letter and my answer, and is himself forcing that appeal to the public, and risking that disgust which I had so much wished should have been avoided," Jefferson related to James Madison.

Jefferson lost patience. In another letter to Madison he characterized Genêt as "hot-headed, all imagination, no judgment, passionate, disrespectful and even indecent towards the president in his written as well as verbal communications." Jefferson was particularly exasperated by the position in which Genêt placed the American friends of France. "If ever it should be necessary to lay his communications before Congress or the public, they will excite universal indignation. He renders my position immensely difficult. He does me justice personally, and, giving him time to vent himself and then cool, I am on a footing to advise him freely, and he respects it, but he breaks out again on the very first occasion, so as to show that he is incapable of correcting himself."

Genêt thought he was serving France, Jefferson said, but in reality he was doing the opposite. His reckless course was risking America's alienation. "His conduct is indefensible by the most furious Jacobin. I only wish our countrymen may distinguish between him and his nation, and if the case should ever be laid before them, may not suffer their affection to the nation to be diminished."

WHAT RENDERED Genêt's behavior still more infuriating to Jefferson was that it made Hamilton and the Federalists more insufferable than ever. Hamilton cited with relish a passage from a highly regarded treatise, *The Law of Nations,* first published in Paris by the distinguished jurist Emmerich de Vattel, condemning the very activities Genêt was engaged in. "As the right of levying soldiers belongs solely to the nation, so no person is to enlist soldiers in a foreign country without the permission of the sovereign," Hamilton quoted Vattel. "They who undertake to enlist soldiers in a foreign country, without the sovereign's permission, and, in general, *whoever alienates the subjects of another* violates one of *the most sacred rights* both of the prince and the state. Foreign recruiters *are hanged immediately* and very justly."

Hearing that Republicans in Philadelphia were planning a celebration for Genêt upon the French minister's arrival in the capital city, Hamilton drafted a message warning them off. "The good sense and prudence of the citizens of Philadelphia, it is hoped, will guard them against being led into so unadvised a step," Hamilton wrote. "Every discreet man must perceive at once that it is highly the interest of this country to remain at peace and as a mean to this to observe a strict neutrality in the present quarrel between the European powers. Public manifestations even of strong wishes in our citizens in favour of any of the contending parties might interfere with this object, in tending to induce a belief that we may finally take a side."This was especially true in the national capital, as manifestations there might be interpreted as having the approval of the government.

Hamilton reminded the Philadelphia Republicans of the blood on the hands of the government Genêt represented. "If we feel kind dispositions towards France for the assistance afforded us in our revolution, it will not do us honor to forget that Louis the XVI was then the sovereign of the country—that the succour afforded depended on his pleasure," Hamilton said. "*Of this we are sure.* There is no ambiguity. Whether he has suffered justly the melancholy fate which he has recently experienced is *at least a question.* No satisfactory evidence of the affirmative has yet appeared in this country. We have seen strong assertions but no proof. To the last awful moment, he persevered in declaring his innocence." This being so, the Philadelphians should definitely reconsider all demonstrations of support for Genêt. "Any extraordinary honors to the representative of those who consigned him to so affecting a doom would be as little consonant with decorum and humanity as with true policy."

Hamilton's warning was never published. But neither did the grand celebration take place. The Philadelphia Republicans apparently conducted their own review of affairs, possibly aided by sentiments like those articulated by Hamilton. A more modest reception was made to suffice.

How much more modest was difficult to tell, for the competing papers of the Republicans and Federalists reported the reception differently. But at least one group of Philadelphians staged a counterdemonstration *against* Genêt and in favor of the Washington administration's neutrality policy. "A committee of the commercial and trading interests, consisting of about one hundred gentlemen, waited on the President of the United States at his house," recounted the *Gazette of the United States*. The committee presented an address to Washington endorsing the "wisdom and goodness" of the neutrality policy and pledging not only to support it by their own actions but "to discountenance in the most pointed manner any contrary disposition in others."

JEFFERSON CONCLUDED that the Genêt problem had to be resolved. He urged Washington to order Genêt's recall to France. Washington was pleased to oblige. Jefferson wrote to Gouverneur Morris in Paris directing him to tell the French government of the "painful necessity" that prompted the president's decision. Washington and Jefferson wanted Genêt's removal to do as little damage as possible to American relations with France. Morris should tell French authorities that the Genêt question reflected not at all on the larger Franco-American partnership. "The president would, indeed, think it greatly unfortunate were they to take it in any other light, and therefore charges you very particularly with the care of presenting this proceeding in the most soothing view, and as the result of an unavoidable necessity on his part," Jefferson wrote.

.  .  .

MORE THAN A CENTURY later Americans would again obsess that alien ideas were undermining American self-government. But where the communism that sparked the red scares after World War I and World War II occupied but one end of the political spectrum and served the interests of one political party chiefly, the obsessions of the 1790s occupied both ends of the spectrum and brought out the worst in both political parties. The specter of Jacobinism haunted the Federalists, while the nightmare of monarchism spoiled the sleep of Republicans.

To be sure, the breathlessness of the public debate—between Hamilton and Madison in their dueling essays, for example—reflected political interest as well as conviction. Hamilton wanted to injure the Republicans, Madison to weaken the Federalists.

But interest rarely excludes sincerity, and it didn't at this time. Jefferson in particular was more vehement in private than in public. "While you are exterminating the monster aristocracy and pulling out the teeth and fangs of its associate, monarchy, a contrary tendency is discovered in some here," he wrote to Lafayette. "A sect has shewn itself among us who declare they espoused our new constitution not as a good and sufficient thing itself, but only as a step to an English constitution, the only thing good and sufficient in itself, in their eye." The sect was largely sectional, Jefferson said. "It is from the eastward chiefly that these champions for a king, lords and commons come. They get some important associates from New York, and are puffed off by a tribe of Agioteurs"—speculators—"which have been hatched in a bed of corruption made up after the model of their beloved England. Too many of these stock jobbers and king-jobbers have come into our legislature, or rather too many of our legislature have become stock jobbers and king-jobbers."

To another French friend, Jefferson wrote, "The zealous apostles of English despotism here will increase the number of its disciples." Indeed, the process had begun. "A germ of corruption indeed has been transferred from our dear mother country and has already borne fruit." To Thomas Paine, recently author of *Rights of Man*, Jefferson marveled, "Would you believe it possible that in this country there should be high and important characters who need your lessons in republicanism, and who do not heed them? It is but too true that we have a sect preaching up and pouting after an English constitution of king, lords, and commons, and whose heads are itching for crowns, coronets and mitres."

The result was the partisanship that was splitting America. "Parties seem to have taken a very well defined form," Jefferson wrote to James Monroe. "The old tories, joined by our merchants who trade on British capital, paper dealers, and the idle rich of the great commercial towns, are with the kings. All other descriptions with the French. The war has kindled and brought forward the two parties with an ardour which our own interests, merely, could never excite."

## 36

B ENJAMIN RUSH KNEW everyone who was anyone in American politics. He had served in the Continental Congress with Washington, Franklin, Jefferson and Adams and had put his signature to the Declaration of Independence beside theirs. Thomas Paine asked Rush's opinion about the arguments that went into *Common Sense.* Rush became a friend to Hamilton and a link between Hamilton and Federalists in Pennsylvania, Rush's state, during the ratification fight. Madison consulted with Rush on how to deprive Adams of reelection to the vice presidency. "I sincerely regret on several accounts that the present incumbent"—Adams—"is to undergo the mortification that awaits him," Madison wrote to Rush from Virginia; "for if he should not be thrown out, the number of adverse votes will have that effect on his sensibility. But his political sins are held unpardonable by the republican zeal of this quarter." Adams meanwhile confided his political envies to Rush. "The history of our Revolution will be one continued lie from one end to the other," Adams wrote to Rush. "The essence of the whole will be *that Dr. Franklin's electrical rod smote the earth and out sprung General Washington. That Franklin electrified him with his rod—and thenceforward these two conducted all the policy, negotiations, legislation and war.*"

In 1793 Rush played a different role than confidant and sounding board. Rush was a physician, one of the most distinguished in America. And he stood at the center of the first public health crisis of the new republic, which unfolded that summer in Philadelphia. The crisis originated with the arrival of refugees from Saint-Domingue, the French colony in the West Indies that would become Haiti, following an uprising against French rule there. Philadelphia's founding as a Quaker city had given it a reputation as a haven for those in need, and the refugees sought it out.

The ships that carried the refugees also carried mosquitoes infected with the virus that causes yellow fever. No one understood the role played by the mosquitoes, but the outbreak of disease not long after the refugees' arrival seemed suspicious, as did the fact that the cases first clustered around the Delaware River wharf and spread inland from there.

Rush had been surgeon general of the Continental Army and he was a professor at America's first medical school, at the University of Pennsylvania. Even as he treated patients afflicted with the disease, he kept a record for posterity. The symptoms were quite varied, he noted. "The precursors, or premonitory signs, were costiveness"—constipation; "a dull pain in the right side; defect of appetite; flatulency; giddiness or pain in the head; a dull, watery, brilliant yellow or red eye; dim and imperfect vision; a hoarseness or slight sore throat; low spirits or unusual vivacity; a moisture on the hands; a disposition to sweat at nights or after moderate exercise, or a sudden suppression of night sweats."

But some people had no premonitory signs. "Many went to bed in good health and awoke in the night with a chilly fit," Rush remarked. "Many rose in the morning after regular and natural sleep and were seized at their work or after a walk with a sudden and unexpected attack of the fever."

The jaundice that gave the disease its name was a sure sign of trouble, Rush said. "Its early appearance always denoted great danger." After the first symptoms, the progress of the disease could be dramatic. "The vomiting, which came on about the fourth or fifth day, was accompanied with a burning pain in the region of the stomach," Rush wrote. "It produced great anxiety and tossing of the body from one part of the bed to another." The sickroom was no place for the faint of heart once the vomiting began. "The contents of the stomach were sometimes thrown up with a convulsive motion that propelled them in a stream to a great distance, and in some cases all over the clothes of the bystanders."

The fever spread to the brain and nervous system. "In the nervous system the symptoms of the fever were different according as it affected the brain, the muscles, the nerves or the mind," Rush noted. "The sudden and violent action of the contagion induced apoplexy in several people. In some, it brought on syncope"—fainting—"and in others, convulsions in every part of the body. The apoplectic cases generally proved fatal, for they fell chiefly upon hard drinkers. Persons affected by syncope or convulsions sometimes fell down in the streets."

Mental symptoms were striking. "The mind suffered with the morbid states of the brain and nerves," Rush wrote. "A delirium was a common symptom. It alternated in some cases with the exacerbations and remissions of the fever. In some, it continued without a remission until a few hours before death." Patients could grow manic. "Such was the degree of this mania in one man that he stripped off his shirt, left his bed, and ran through the streets with no other covering than a napkin on his head, at 8 o'clock at night, to the great terror of all who met him. The symptoms of mania occurred most frequently towards the close of the disease, and sometimes continued for many days, and weeks, after all the febrile symptoms had disappeared."

The sufferers were not themselves in other obvious ways. "The *senses* and *appetites* exhibited several marks of the universal ravages of this fever upon the body," Rush explained. "A deafness attended in many cases. . . . Many were affected with temporary blindness. . . . There was in many persons a soreness to the touch, which extended all over the body."

Some patients became extremely thirsty, to the point of drinking themselves to death with water. "One of my patients who suffered by an excessive draught of cold water declared just before he died that 'he could drink up the Delaware,'" Rush said. "It was always an alarming symptom when this thirst came on in this extravagant degree in the last stage of the disorder."

The appetite for food diminished at first, as it did with other fevers. "But it returned much sooner than is common, after the patient began to recover," Rush said. "So keen was the appetite for solid, and more especially for animal food, after the solution of the fever, that many suffered from eating aliment"—food—"that was improper from its quality or quantity. There was a general disrelish for wine, but malt liquors were frequently grateful to the appetite."

Sexual desire was depressed in the early stages, but it too rebounded. "The convalescence from this disorder was marked in some instances by a sudden revival of the venereal appetite. Several weddings took place in the city between persons who had recovered from the fever. Twelve took place among the convalescents in the hospital at Bush-hill. I wish I could add that the passion of the sexes for each other, among those subjects of public charity, was always gratified only in a lawful way." It was not. "Delicacy forbids a detail of the scenes of debauchery which were practiced near the hospital in some of the tents which had been appropriated for the reception of convalescents."

In part because no one knew how the disease was spread, Philadelphia reacted slowly to the outbreak. "The first reports of the existence of this fever were treated with neglect or contempt," Rush said. "A strange apathy pervaded all classes of people." Rush's warnings did no good. "I bore my share of reproach for 'terrifying our citizens with imaginary danger.' I answered it by lamenting 'that they were not terrified enough.'"

In time they were. "Fear or terror now sat upon every countenance," Rush said. "The disease appeared in many parts of the town remote from the spot where it originated (although in every instance it was easily traced to it). This set the city in motion. The streets and roads leading from the city were crowded with families flying in every direction for safety to the country. Business began to languish. Water-street between Market and Race-streets became a desert."

The poor suffered worst, as the poor generally do. But no class escaped. "The contagion, after the second week in September, spared no rank of citizens. Whole families were confined by it. There was a deficiency of nurses for the sick, and many of those who were employed were unqualified for their business. There was likewise a great deficiency of physicians from the desertion of some and the sickness and death of others. At one time, there were only three physicians who were able to do business out of their houses, and at this time, there were probably not less than 6,000 persons ill with the fever."

Rush was one of those three, and he never forgot the experience. "During the first three or four weeks of the prevalence of the disorder, I seldom went into a house the first time without meeting the parents or children of the sick in tears. Many wept aloud in my entry, or parlour, who came to ask for advice for their relations. Grief after a while descended below weeping, and I was much struck in observing that many persons submitted to the loss of relations and friends without shedding a tear or manifesting any other of the common signs of grief."

Rush almost forgot what it was like to be happy. "A cheerful countenance was scarcely to be seen in the city for six weeks. I recollect once in entering the house of a poor man, to have met a child of two years old that smiled in my face. I was strangely affected with this sight (so discordant to my feelings and the state of the city) before I recollected the age and ignorance of the child. I was confined the next day by an attack of the fever, and was sorry to hear upon my recovery that the father and mother of this little creature died a few days after my last visit to them."

America's capital city was desolated. "The streets everywhere discovered marks of the distress that pervaded the city. More than one half the houses were shut up, although not more than one third of the inhabitants had fled into the country. In walking for many hundred yards, few persons were met except such as were in quest of a physician, a nurse, a bleeder, or the men who buried the dead. The hearse alone kept up the remembrance of the noise of carriages or carts in the streets. Funeral processions were laid aside. A black man leading or driving a horse with a corpse on a pair of chair wheels, with now and then half a dozen relations or friends following at a distance from it, met the eye in most of the streets of the city at every hour of the day, while the noise of the same wheels passing slowly over the pavements kept alive anguish and fear in the sick and well every hour of the night."

CONGRESS WAS NOT in session when the fever hit, so Madison and most of the other lawmakers learned about it secondhand. Members of the executive branch, including Washington, Adams, Hamilton and Jefferson got away as soon as they credibly could. Washington, Adams and Jefferson evaded the virus; Hamilton did not. "I have myself been attacked with the reigning putrid fever, and with violence," he wrote in mid-September to the faculty of the Pennsylvania medical college. He was pleased to report a full recovery. "This I am to attribute, under

God, to the skill and care of my friend Doctor Stevens, a gentleman lately from the island of St. Croix, one to whose talents I can attest from an intimate acquaintance begun in early youth, whose medical opportunities have been of the best, and who has had the advantage of much experience both in Europe (having been in Edinburgh some years since, when the same fever raged there) and in the West-Indies, where it is frequent."

Hamilton departed for Albany, to wait out the epidemic. He wasn't welcomed at first. To prove he posed no threat, he submitted to a health examination. "This is to certify that we have visited Col. Hamilton and his lady at Greenbush, this evening, and that they are apparently in perfect health; and from every circumstance we do not conceive there can be the least danger of their conveying the infection of the pestilential fever at present prevalent in Philadelphia to any of their fellow citizens," the examining doctors declared.

Jefferson's comparative slowness to leave Philadelphia alarmed Madison. "I have long been uneasy for your health amidst the vapors of the Schuylkill," Madison wrote to Jefferson. "The new and more alarming danger has made me particularly anxious that you were out of the sphere of it. I cannot altogether condemn your unwillingness to retire from your post under the circumstances you describe"—Jefferson had said he couldn't simply drop the work of American diplomacy—"but if your stay be as unessential as I conceive it to be rendered by the absence of the President and the fever does not abate, I pray you not to sacrifice too much to motives which others do not feel." Jefferson eventually heeded the advice and joined the exodus.

One who didn't get away in time was John Todd, a Philadelphia lawyer who contracted the fever and died, leaving a young widow, Dolley Payne Todd, who would marry James Madison the following year.

The epidemic lasted until the cold weather of late autumn suppressed the activity of the mosquitoes that transmitted the disease. By then some five thousand people had died, of Philadelphia's population of around fifty thousand. This death rate—of ten percent—made it perhaps the most lethal epidemic in American history, apart from those that ravaged Indian tribes.

Public life in Philadelphia slowly resumed, though private sorrow persisted. "It afforded a subject of equal surprise and joy to behold the suddenness with which the city recovered its former habits of business," Benjamin Rush remarked. "In the course of six weeks after the disease had ceased, nothing but fresh graves and the black dresses of many of the citizens afforded a public trace of the distress which had so lately prevailed in the city."

## 37

THE PROSPECTS OF this country are gloomy," John Adams wrote in January 1794. Adams acknowledged that things were worse elsewhere. "The situation of all Europe is calamitous beyond all former examples." But this should give Americans no comfort, not even by comparison, for Europe's calamities inevitably intruded on America. "At what time and in what manner and by what means the disasters which are come and seem to be coming on mankind may be averted, I know not." And Americans, by their impulsive and bitter partisanship, made the imported afflictions worse. "Our own people have been imprudent, as I think, and are now smarting under the effects of their indiscretion."

France was the center of the troubles. "The news of this evening is that the queen of France is no more," Adams wrote to Abigail. Marie Antoinette had been executed. "When will savages be satiated with blood?" Not soon, Adams feared. "No prospect of peace in Europe, and therefore none of internal harmony in America."

Adams did see one positive sign. "Jefferson went off yesterday, and a good riddance of bad ware," he told Abigail. Jefferson had retired as secretary of state, in fulfillment of a long-standing wish to retreat from public life.

He hadn't shared his reasons with Adams. "The motives to Mr. Jefferson's resignation are not assigned, and are left open to the conjectures of a speculating world," Adams remarked to his son John Quincy Adams. "I also am a speculator in the principles and motives of men's actions and may guess as well as others 1. Mr. Jefferson has an habit as well as a disposition to expensive living, and as his salary was not adequate to his luxury, he could not subdue his pride and vanity as I have done, and proportion his style of life to his revenue. 2. Mr. Jefferson is in debt, as I have heard, to an amount of seven thousand pounds before the war, so that I suppose he cannot afford to spend his private income in the public service." Both of these observations were substantially true.

"3. Mr. Jefferson has been obliged to lower his note in politics," Adams continued. "Paine's principles"—of democracy—"when adopted by Genet were not found so convenient for a secretary of state. 4. He could not rule the roost in the ministry"—the Washington administration. "He was often in a minority."

Adams's final reason was the clincher, in his mind: "5. Ambition is the subtlest beast of the intellectual and moral field. It is wonderfully adroit in concealing itself from its owner, I had almost said from itself. Jefferson thinks he shall by this step get a reputation of an humble, modest, meek man, wholly without ambition or vanity. He may even have deceived himself into this belief. But if a prospect opens, the world will see and he will feel that he is as ambitious as Oliver Cromwell, though no soldier."

Yet Adams was ambivalent about Jefferson's departure. "He might have worn off his sharp points and become a wiser minister than he has been sometimes," Adams wrote to Charles Adams, another son. "His abilities are good; his pen is very good; and for what I know the other ministers"—members of the administration—"might be the better for being watched by him." Adams felt a personal stake in Jefferson's exit. "I don't dislike a precedent of resignation, for I sometimes feel as if it would one day be my own case, and I should be glad to have an example to quote."

Adams continued to feel himself a man without a purpose. "My country has in its wisdom contrived for me the most insignificant office that ever the invention of man contrived or his imagination conceived," he wrote to Abigail. "And as I can do neither good nor evil, I must be borne away by others and meet the common fate."

Yet he couldn't bring himself to resign. Although he might support himself by the practice of law, he had become too invested in the future of the country to leave it to others. He had started down the path of public affairs, and he must continue. "We shall soon see whether we have any government or not in this country," he said.

Adams looked to Washington for leadership, but Washington's prospects weren't what they had been. "Although he stands at present as high in the admiration and confidence of the people as ever he did, I expect he will find many bitter and desperate enemies arise in consequence of his just judgment against Genet," Adams told Abigail. "Besides that a party spirit will convert white into black and right into wrong." Not even Washington's reputation could survive the incessant assaults on the truth.

Adams had never been one to think the best of his fellow humans, but these days he often thought the worst. "We have I fear very corrupt individuals in this country," he said.

The departure of Jefferson left Hamilton more influential with Washington than ever. The treasury secretary had always defined his portfolio broadly, but now he annexed foreign policy to it. Ignoring Edmund Randolph, who replaced Jefferson as secretary of state, Hamilton pitched to Washington a strategy for dealing with the European belligerents. He didn't apologize for usurping Randolph's prerogatives, but he did explain, after his own fashion. "The present is beyond question a great, a difficult and a perilous crisis in the affairs of this country," Hamilton declared. "In such a crisis it is the duty of every man, according to situation, to contribute all in his power towards preventing evil and producing good. This consideration will I trust be a sufficient apology for the liberty I am about to take of submitting without an official call the ideas which occupy my mind concerning the actual posture of our public affairs."

Hamilton asserted that certain groups in America seemed bent on war against Britain. He didn't identify them as Republicans, because he knew Washington disliked party labels. Yet he didn't have to employ labels for the president to understand. "They unite from habitual feeling in an implacable hatred to Great Britain and in a warm attachment to France," Hamilton wrote. "Their sympathy with the latter is increased by the idea of her being engaged in defending the cause of liberty against a combination of despots who meditate nothing less than the destruction of it throughout the world. In hostility with Britain they seek the gratification of revenge upon a detested enemy with that of serving a favourite friend and in this the cause of liberty." Some of the Republicans wanted a war against Britain, to complete America's alienation from that country and America's permanent attachment to France. Even those who didn't *want* a war were willing to risk it in order to perpetuate the Franco-American alliance.

The Republicans presumed to speak for the American people, but they did not speak for all the people, Hamilton said. In some states they were a distinct minority. "The great mass of opinion in the eastern states and in the state of New York is against war if it can be avoided without absolute dishonor or the ultimate sacrifice of essential rights and interests," Hamilton told Washington. "And I verily believe that the same sentiment is the radical"—fundamental—"one throughout the United States, *some* of the towns perhaps excepted." Hamilton wanted the administration to speak for those who wished to avoid war.

He proposed approaching Britain to resolve the differences between the two countries. The president should appoint a special envoy. "Mr. Jay is the only man in whose qualifications for success there would be thorough confidence and him whom alone it would be advisable to send," Hamilton said of his *Federalist* coauthor and now the chief justice. "I think the business would have the best chance possible in his hands. And I flatter myself that his mission would issue in a manner that would produce the most important good to the nation."

After Washington took Hamilton's recommendation on Jay, the treasury secretary wrote instructions to guide Jay in his negotiations with Britain. Jay should seek indemnification for seizures of vessels and cargoes already committed, and a reasonable reinterpretation of the British naval orders for the future. Distinction should be made between actual contraband—articles of war—and foodstuffs and other ordinary provisions.

Jay should also address leftovers from the existing treaty between the United States and Britain. The United States should be indemnified for the value of slaves carried away by British ships at the end of the war, and the British should surrender forts and trading posts in the Northwest Territory they had promised to relinquish in the treaty. For its part, the United States should indemnify Britain for the hindrances states had thrown up against the collection of prewar debts owed by Americans to British creditors.

Finally, a treaty of commerce should be signed between the United States and Britain guaranteeing American rights to trade with the

British West Indies, and to trade with Britain on the same terms as other nations already trading with Britain. In exchange for this, the United States would eliminate special tariffs on British imports and allow British merchants to trade with America on terms equal to merchants of other nations.

EDMUND RANDOLPH OWED it to the dignity of his office as secretary of state to recast Hamilton's instructions in his own words, but Hamilton's recommendations became the basis for Jay's mission to Britain. To these Hamilton added details in separate letters to Jay. Hamilton knew he and Jay shared a belief that improved relations with Britain were essential to American prosperity and security—which was why Hamilton had recommended Jay for the envoy job. "We are both impressed equally strongly with the great importance of a right adjustment of all matters of past controversy and future good understanding with Great Britain," Hamilton said. Yet Jay should bargain tenaciously. "Important as this object is, it will be better to do nothing than to do anything which will not stand the test of the severest scrutiny and especially which may be construed into the relinquishment of a substantial right or interest."

Jay should negotiate as from a position of American strength. "I see not how it can be disputed with you that this country in a commercial sense is more important to Great Britain than any other," Hamilton said. "The articles she takes from us are certainly precious to her, important perhaps essential to the ordinary subsistence of her islands, not unimportant to her own subsistence *occasionally,* always very important to her manufactures, and of real consequence to her revenue." British exports to America were no less important to Britain. "We now consume of her exports from a million to a million and a half sterling more in value than any other foreign country, and while the consumption of other countries from obvious causes is likely to be stationary, that of this country is increasing and for a long, long series of years, will increase rapidly." Britain's self-interest should dictate ensuring the stability of trade relations with America.

Singularities of American geography required special attention. "The navigation of the Mississippi is to us an object of immense consequence," Hamilton reminded Jay. "Besides other considerations connected with it, if the government of the United States can procure and secure the enjoyment of it to our western country, it will be an infinitely strong link of Union between that country and the Atlantic States." Hamilton, with Jefferson and others, worried about the trans-Appalachian territories spinning away from the eastern states. Spain currently controlled the lower Mississippi and only sporadically permitted Americans free navigation. "If anything could be done with Great Britain to increase our chances for the speedy enjoyment of this right, it would be in my judgment a very valuable ingredient in any arrangement you could make," Hamilton said. "Nor is Britain without a great interest in the question, if the arrangement shall give to her a participation in that navigation and a treaty of commerce shall admit her advantageously into this large field of commercial adventure."

## 38

H UGH BRACKENRIDGE WAS a Scot by birth but a Pennsylvanian
by upbringing, his family having come to America when he was
five. He met James Madison at the College of New Jersey, which would
change its name to Princeton, the town where it was located. There
he also met Philip Freneau, with whom he embarked on a venture in
journalism. He served under George Washington in the Revolutionary
War and afterward studied law. He was admitted to the Pennsylvania
bar in Philadelphia, but judging that city too crowded with lawyers, he
headed west to Pittsburgh, the town that was emerging at the Forks of
the Ohio River in the far west of the state.

As a charter Federalist, Brackenridge supported ratification of
the Constitution. But in western Pennsylvania he found himself surrounded by farmers who despised the policies of Alexander Hamilton.
They especially loathed an excise tax on distilled spirits Hamilton got
Congress to enact to fund the debt he persuaded the government to
assume. The spirit favored in the western districts was whiskey, and the
excise became known as the whiskey tax. The westerners judged the
tax discriminatory, in that it was regressive, hitting small distillers like
themselves harder than larger producers, who were typically located in
the more populated eastern districts. In this discrimination they perceived corruption and malign intent. The westerners also judged the
tax a peculiar hardship in a region where cash, required to pay the tax,
was often scarce, in part as a result of Hamilton's city-centered financial
policies. And they simply didn't like taxes, especially new ones levied on

an essential of life. They were utterly unpersuaded by Hamilton's argument that the tax discouraged the vice of excessive drinking. Such logic
might appeal to eastern wine sippers, but not to the whiskey-swigging
men of the west.

Many of the westerners refused to pay. They ignored federal orders
to register their stills; when federal inspectors came calling, the inspectors were harassed and sometimes assaulted. One tax collector was
tarred and feathered, after the fashion of Stamp Act protests a generation before. Indeed, many of the whiskey tax resisters drew a straight
line from those protests to their own, wrapping their stills in the mantle
of the American Revolution. Others made a connection to the Shays
rebellion, although that one hadn't turned out so well.

While the Washington administration considered its alternatives,
the whiskey protesters gathered in conventions. These meetings lacked
the geographic breadth of the Continental Congress, but the parallels
seemed ominous. Emigrants to the west like Hugh Brackenridge often
felt they were moving to a new country when they crossed the Alle-
gheny Mountains, for the streams there flowed away from the Atlantic.
Gravity pulled the westerners and their commerce down the Ohio and
toward the Mississippi. It occurred to more than a few of them that a
western republic might suit their interests better than the existing eastern one, especially if the easterners insisted on imposing punitive taxes.

Things reached a crisis in the summer of 1794. The federal government intensified its efforts to collect the whiskey tax, and the resisters
stiffened their opposition. "On the evening of the 14th of July, David
Lenox, marshal of the district of Pennsylvania, was introduced to me
at my house," Hugh Brackenridge recounted later. "I had heard that
he had been on his way, serving process on delinquent distillers in the
intermediate counties from Philadelphia to the western country, and in
the western country itself." The marshal's arrival signaled an escalation
by the government; unlike the tax collectors, a marshal could arrest
people and initiate criminal proceedings.

The next day the marshal accompanied the local revenue inspector,
who identified the distillers who hadn't paid. The marshal served one
writ after another. "He had served the last writ he had to serve in that
quarter, and had just quitted the house of a distiller, of the name of
Miller, when a number of men were observed to be in pursuit of them,
and a gun was discharged," related Brackenridge, who got the story

from Lenox. "The marshal, conceiving it not to be with a view to injure but intimidate, turned and expostulated. But observing a sullenness of countenance, and advised by the inspector, who knew their disposition better, he thought proper to ride off, and escape from them." Lenox spent the night in Pittsburgh, while the inspector slept at his home several miles outside the town.

"The next morning after day-break, the inspector, having just got out of bed and opened the door, discovered a number of armed men about the house; and demanding of them who they were, and whence they came, the answer was such as induced him to consider their intention to be hostile; and on their refusing to disperse, he fired on them," Brackenridge wrote. "The fire was returned, and a contest ensued." Several of the tax resisters were wounded, one mortally.

They regrouped under James McFarlane, a Revolutionary War veteran, while the authorities pondered how the insurgents could be disarmed and pacified. They stationed a small number of soldiers at the home of the inspector, which the insurgents proceeded to surround. Under a flag of truce the insurgents demanded that the inspector surrender his commission papers and abandon his office. They were informed that the inspector was not there. He had fled.

"A second flag was sent, and a demand made that six persons should be admitted into the house to search for his papers and take them," Brackenridge recalled. "This was refused, and notice was then given, by a third flag, for the lady of the inspector and any other female part of the family to withdraw. They did withdraw, and the attack commenced. About fifteen minutes after the commencement, a flag was presented, or was thought to be presented, from the house; upon which, McFarlane, stepping from a tree behind which he stood and commanding a cessation of the firing, received a ball in the inside of his thigh, near the groin, and instantly expired."

The killing of their leader inflamed the insurgents. "The firing then continued," Brackenridge wrote. "And a message was sent to the committee"—an informal directorate of the insurgency—"who were sitting at some distance, to know whether the house should not be stormed. But in the meantime, fire had been set to a barn and to other buildings adjoining the mansion house. And in a short time the intenseness of the heat and the evident communicability of the flame to the house had struck those in the house with a sense of immediate danger of life, and they began to call for quarter. On which the firing ceased, and they were desired to come out and surrender themselves."

The soldiers did so, including three who had been wounded. The insurgents allowed them to pass. But not so their leader, a man named Kirkpatrick. "Major Kirkpatrick himself had nearly passed through when he was distinguished from the soldiers and arrested, and ordered to deliver his musket," Brackenridge wrote. "This he refused. When one presenting a gun to his breast was about to fire, he dropped upon his knee and asked quarter. The man took the major's hat from his head and put it on the muzzle of his gun."

THE INSURGENCY SWELLED. "The whole country was one inflammable mass," Brackenridge said of the western counties of Pennsylvania. "It required but the least touch of fire to inflame it. I had seen the spirit which prevailed at the time of the Stamp Act and at the commencement of the revolution from the government of Great Britain, but it was by no means so general and so vigorous amongst the common people as the spirit which now existed in this country."

The rebels gathered by hundreds and then thousands outside Pittsburgh at the meadow where General Edward Braddock had led his British force to a disastrous defeat during the French and Indian War. The rebels made no secret of their intentions. "The common language of the county at the time was they were coming to take Pittsburgh," Brackenridge wrote. "Some would talk of plundering it, others of burning it. It was an expression that Sodom had been burnt by fire from heaven, but this second Sodom should be burned with fire from earth. I believe plunder was an object with many. The shopkeepers were told at their counters, by persons cheapening their goods"—demanding lower prices—"that they would get them at a less price in a few days. The very women coming in from the country would say, 'That fine lady lives in a fine house, but her pride will be humbled by and by.' Persons were coming to the blacksmiths with old guns that had laid by a long time, to have them repaired. Others were buying up flints and powder from the stores."

The leaders and property owners of the town considered frantically how to avert the destruction. They decided to send a delegation to Braddock's Field to reason with the rebels. Brackenridge was one of

the delegates. "Advancing to the field, my reflections were not pleasant," Brackenridge recalled. "I was far from thinking myself secure from
personal danger." He enjoyed a good reputation around Pittsburgh, and
in fact had commenced a campaign for Congress. But beyond the town
his Federalist views were held against him. In any event, the insurgents
seemed to have lost all sense of morality and respectability. "The idea of
the people at the time was that law was dissolved, and that the people
themselves, in their collective capacity, were the only tribunal. There
could be no idea, therefore, that the putting a man to death who was
obnoxious to the people would be any offence."

The peril to Pittsburgh seemed greater than ever. Writing afterward, Brackenridge reflected, "The fears entertained on this occasion
may appear unreasonable, but not to anyone who has seen a large and
enraged body of men under the command of one"—a man named
Bradford, at this point—"as mad as themselves, or under no command
at all. In the first case, they will execute what the one dictates; in the
other, what any one suggests. In the present instance, I knew Bradford would have great influence, but the people themselves would have
more, and there was reason to fear both. As to burning the town, it was
doubtless more talked of than intended individually; but the talking of
it would produce the doing it, contrary to the wish of many who did
talk of it. Such is the history of the human mind in a state of anarchy."

The demeanor and apparel of the rebels inspired little confidence.
"They were dressed in what we call hunting shirts, many of them, with
handkerchiefs upon their heads. It is in this dress they equip themselves
against the Indians. They were amusing themselves with shooting with
balls at marks, and firing in the air at random, with powder only. There
was a continual discharge of guns and constant smoke in the woods and
along the bank of the river. There appeared a great wantonness of mind,
and disposition to do anything extravagant." Another group appeared
downright sinister. "Fifteen men had painted themselves black, as the
warriors amongst the Indians do when they go to war."

The rebel force grew by the hour. "People were coming in from
every quarter all that day, generally armed but some without arms,"
Brackenridge said. The spirit of revolution was in the air, and at this
point it wasn't the American Revolution. "The great bulk of the people
were certainly in earnest, and the revolutionary language and the ideas

of the French people had become familiar. It was not tarring and feathering, as at the commencement of the revolution from Great Britain, but guillotining—that is, putting to death, by any way that offered. I am persuaded that if even Bradford himself that day had ventured to check the violence of the people in any way that was not agreeable to them, and had betrayed the least partiality for the excise law, or perhaps even a remission of his zeal against it, he would have sunk in an instant from his power, and they would have hung him on the first tree."

Brackenridge was no revolutionary; the thought of guillotines gave him shivers. Yet he made a tactical decision to appear sympathetic to the grievances of the gathered horde. His own chances of survival would improve and so, he imagined, would Pittsburgh's.

He overheard a conversation about attacking the military garrison in the town. "The query everywhere was, Were we to take the garrison? I answered always that we were," he recounted. "The query then was, Could we take it? It was answered, No doubt of it. But at a great loss? Not at all, not above a thousand killed and five hundred mortally wounded."

His words had the desired sobering effect. "This loss, to the more thinking part, appeared very serious."

Discussion turned to *how* the garrison should be taken. Some urged a frontal charge; others proposed sniping at the soldiers atop the walls. Brackenridge's view was solicited. "I suggested the undermining and blowing up the bastion."

But then he offered a caveat: "They would fire upon the diggers. Besides, it would waste powder"—of which the insurgents had little. He offered a new plan: "I proposed starving out the garrison." His listeners responded that they themselves lacked provisions and would starve first.

Brackenridge didn't give up. "I had a great deal of conversation on this subject, in the bushes and at the sides of fences, laying our heads together and whispering." His counsel kept to a single theme: "I was for the most desperate measures but admitted that much blood must be lost."

Brackenridge detected a waning of enthusiasm for attacking the town. He quietly smiled to himself. But then he met a man who remained as determined as ever. "What do you think of that damned fellow, James Ross?" the man demanded, referring to one of Brackenridge's fellow envoys from Pittsburgh. "He has been here and all through camp persuading the people not to go to Pittsburgh."

Brackenridge quickly recalculated. "I saw now that it was in vain to oppose the going, and it was better to acquiesce and say they should go," he recalled. "In that case there would be more management of them than if they came in spite of opposition. I saw this and took my part decidedly. Damn the fellow, said I, what business has he with Pittsburgh? The people of Pittsburgh wish to see the army, and you must go through it and let the damned garrison see that we could take it, if we would. It will convince the government that we are no mob but a regular army and can preserve discipline and pass through a town, like the French and American armies in the course of last war, without doing the least injury to persons or property."

His stratagem seemed to work. "There was a general acclamation, and all professed a determination to molest no one."

The rebel army indeed marched through Pittsburgh. Brackenridge quietly sent word to the soldiers of the garrison that no attack was coming, lest they fire on the insurgents and ruin everything. And he hastened the rebels' progress by persuading townsmen to position whiskey and other refreshments in a field on the other side of the town, and then letting the rebels know of the reward that awaited them after their march.

PITTSBURGH WAS SPARED, but the cause of the trouble remained. While Brackenridge was lowering the temperature among the rebels, Alexander Hamilton was throwing fuel on the fire in the rest of the country. Writing as "Tully" to "the People of the United States," Hamilton warned that the turmoil in western Pennsylvania would spread if not dealt with sternly and at once. "It has from the first establishment of your present Constitution been predicted that every occasion of serious embarrassment which should occur in the affairs of the government, every misfortune which it should experience, whether produced from its own faults or mistakes or from other causes, would be the signal of an attempt to overthrow it," he said. The enemies of American liberty never slept; they merely awaited their chance to destroy the republic. "The disturbances which have recently broken out in the western counties of Pennsylvania furnish an occasion of this sort."

The whiskey tax was but the pretext, Hamilton said. The real aim was the end of the government. Of course the rebels would dissimulate, to lull the defenders of the Constitution to sleep. Hamilton wasn't lulled, and he sounded the warning: "Virtuous and enlightened citizens of a now happy country! Ye could not be the dupes of artifices so detestable, of a scheme so fatal; ye cannot be insensible to the destructive consequences with which it would be pregnant; ye cannot but remember that the government is *your own* work—that those who administer it are but your temporary agents; that *you* are called upon not to support their power, *but your own power.*"

In subsequent installments, Tully—Hamilton—waxed more strident. The challenge in Pennsylvania reduced to a central question: "Shall the majority govern or be governed?" Hamilton reworded for emphasis: "Shall the nation rule or be ruled? Shall the general will prevail or the will of a faction? Shall there be government or no government?" The opposition to the whiskey law was not the venial offense the apologists for the protesters made it out to be, but the most grievous of crimes. "Such a resistance is treason against society, against liberty, against everything that ought to be dear to a free, enlightened and prudent people." There was no middle ground in this struggle. "To tolerate were to abandon your most precious interests. Not to subdue it, were to tolerate it." Hamilton distinguished "true republicans"—Americans who insisted that the government enforce its laws—from the pretenders who cloaked their malignity with the name Republican and took the side of the rebels. "Those who openly or covertly dissuade you from exertions adequate to the occasion are your worst enemies," he wrote. "They treat you either as fools or cowards, too weak to perceive your interest and your duty, or too dastardly to pursue them. They therefore merit and will no doubt meet your contempt."

By the final Tully installment, Hamilton was beside himself. "Fellow Citizens—You are told that it will be intemperate to urge the execution of the laws which are resisted. What? Will it be indeed intemperate in your Chief Magistrate"—Washington—"sworn to maintain the Constitution, charged faithfully to execute the laws, and authorized to employ for that purpose force when the ordinary means fail—will it be intemperate in him to exert that force when the Constitution and the laws are opposed by force? Can he answer it to his conscience, to you, not to exert it?"

But the use of force might provoke a civil war, the apologists said, in Hamilton's retelling. He didn't deny it. "Fellow Citizens—Civil war is undoubtedly a great evil. It is one that every good man would wish to avoid, and will deplore if inevitable. But it is incomparably a less evil than the destruction of Government. The first brings with it serious but temporary and partial ills; the last undermines the foundations of our security and happiness."

Hamilton asked his readers to consider what would follow a failure to employ force. "Where should we be if it were once to grow into a maxim that force is not to be used against the seditious combinations of parts of the community to resist the laws? This would be to give a *carte blanche* to ambition, to licentiousness, to foreign intrigue, to make you the prey of the gold of other nations, the sport of the passions and vices of individuals among yourselves. The Hydra Anarchy would rear its head in every quarter. The goodly fabric you have established would be rent asunder and precipitated into the dust."

What, truly, had the American Revolution been but a civil war? "You knew how to encounter civil war rather than surrender your liberty to foreign domination," Hamilton said. "You will not hesitate now to brave it rather than surrender your sovereignty to the tyranny of a faction. You will be as deaf to the apostles of anarchy now as you were to the emissaries of despotism then. Your love of liberty will guide you now as it did then. You know that the *Power* of the majority and *Liberty* are inseparable. Destroy that, and this perishes."


HAMILTON'S ARGUMENTS didn't persuade everybody, but they moved the one who mattered most: George Washington. The president agreed with his former aide-de-camp that the insurrection signaled a danger to American liberty and must be met with armed force. In early August, Washington issued a proclamation condemning the violence of the insurgents and announcing his intention to send an army against them. "The essential interests of the Union demand it," he said. "The very existence of government and the fundamental principles of social order are materially involved in the issue." He gave the rebels a month to disperse and go home; after that their force would be met with much greater force.

The rebels did not go home. The violence eased, but the rebels didn't disperse.

"The moment is now come," Washington proclaimed after his deadline passed. "Government is set at defiance, the contest being whether a small portion of the United States shall dictate to the whole Union." Militias from Pennsylvania, Maryland, Virginia and New Jersey were already converging on the scene of the violence. Washington reminded Americans that he had sworn to see the laws faithfully executed. He was doing no more than that now; he could never do less.

HAMILTON TOOK PAINS to ensure the expedition's success. "You will forward as speedily as may be to Winchester two marquees, 1000 pair shoes, and two medicine chests; to Carlisle 1000 blankets, 1000 shoes, 200 rifles, 800 muskets with accoutrements proportioned, and pistol and musket flints—also two medicine chests," he wrote to Samuel Hodgdon, the quartermaster general. In another order, equally intrusive on the domain of Henry Knox, the secretary of war, Hamilton wrote, "For the Virginia and Maryland militia six six-pounders, three three-pounders and two howitzers. For the Pennsylvania militia six six-pounders, four three-pounders and three howitzers. For the Jersey militia three six-pounders, three three-pounders and one howitzer."

After weeks of such orders, sent from an office he had established in the War Department, Hamilton sent Hodgdon a personal note: "Mr. Hamilton requests Mr. Hodgdon to be so obliging as to inform him whether he has in his power or eye any horse which would be proper as a riding horse for Mr. Hamilton—easy-gaited of some blood and capable of rendering service. Mr. Hamilton would mean to purchase him."

Perhaps from the beginning, Hamilton had intended to accompany the army into the field against the insurgents. The presence of George Washington wasn't a foregone conclusion; in fact Washington would be the only president ever to lead troops in the field. But he *was* the commander in chief, and having grown tired of politics, he was eager to reprise the simpler times when he had been a soldier. He let it be known that he would ride at the head of the column.

Hamilton's presence was more of a stretch. True, he had been at

Washington's right hand during the Revolutionary War, but now he had an important job in Philadelphia, from which he would have to take leave while playing soldier again.

Hamilton urged Washington to let him come along. "Upon full reflection I entertain an opinion that it is advisable for me, on public ground, considering the connection between the immediate ostensible cause of the insurrection in the western country and my department, to go out upon the expedition against the insurgents," he wrote. "In a government like ours, it cannot but have a good effect for the person who is understood to be the adviser or proposer of a measure which involves danger to his fellow citizens, to partake in that danger, while not to do it might have a bad effect."

Washington must have thought this silly, or at any rate a spurious precedent. Civilians of the legislative and executive branches were expected to make all sorts of decisions that could involve danger to their fellow citizens, but they were hardly expected to partake of that danger on a regular basis.

Yet Washington rarely said no to Hamilton, and he didn't say no now. When Washington set out to meet the gathering militias, Hamilton rode beside him.

Hamilton continued to make the case for the necessity of force. Washington had dispatched civilian commissioners to western Pennsylvania to talk the rebels down. Amnesty was suggested for those who abjured violence and returned to their homes. Hamilton disliked the idea and tried to quash hopes of an imminent end to the crisis. "Nothing from the western country authorises an expectation of a pacific termination of that business," he wrote to Rufus King, a Federalist senator from New York. "All the militia are going forward as fast as they can be got forward." To Thomas Lee, Federalist governor of Maryland, he acknowledged that most Pennsylvanians were law-abiding, but not all. "There is a large and violent party which can only be controlled by the application of force," Hamilton wrote. The current crisis was focused and acute, he said. "The disease, however, with which we have to contend appears more and more of a malignant nature not confined to the opposition to a particular law but proceeding from a general disorderly spirit."

Hamilton declined to criticize Washington directly, but he worried that the president would go too far in offering amnesty. "Though severity towards offenders is to be avoided as much as can consist with the safety of society, yet impunity in such cases is apt to produce too much promptitude in setting the laws at defiance," he told Thomas Lee. "Repeated instances of such impunity in Pennsylvania are perhaps the principal cause of the misfortune which now afflicts itself and through it the United States. The disturbers of the peace familiarly appeal to the past experience of unpunished offences as an encouragement to the perpetration of new ones."

The approach of the federal army to the zone of the insurrection put the rebels on good behavior. None wished to tangle frontally with Washington's large and well-equipped force. Yet what Hamilton called the "disease" of opposition persisted. It manifested itself in novel ways and was often associated with a mysterious figure known as "Tom the Tinker."

Hugh Brackenridge explained the origin of the name. "A certain John Holcroft was thought to have made the first application of it," Brackenridge said. "It was at the time of the masked attack on a certain William Cochran, who rendered himself obnoxious by an entry"— registration with the authorities—"of his still, according to law. His still was cut to pieces, and this was humorously called mending his still. And the menders, of course, must be tinkers"—itinerant fixers of pots, pans and the like—"and the name, collectively, became Tom the Tinker."

Soon Tom was everywhere. "Advertisements were now put up on trees, in the highways, or in other conspicuous places, under the signature of Tom the Tinker, threatening individuals, or admonishing, or commanding them in measures with regard to the excise law. In the march from Braddock's field, the acclamation was, 'Huzza for Tom the Tinker.' It was not now, 'Are you whig or tory?' but, 'Are you a Tom the Tinker's man?' Every man was willing to be thought so, and some had a great deal of trouble to wipe off imputations to the contrary. Advertisements appeared in the gazettes from individuals, appealing to the public and averring the falsehood of aspersions upon them as favouring the excise law."

The ubiquity and elusiveness of Tom the Tinker put the government's army on edge. And edgy soldiers, especially untrained militiamen, sometimes overreact. William Findley, a western Pennsylvanian, Republican member of Congress and opponent of both the whiskey

tax and the administration's use of military force, described the killing of two civilians, one on the route of march near Lebanon and the
other in a house at Carlisle. "The one in the road was killed by the Jersey troops," Findley recounted. "He provoked an officer by foolish and
insulting language, and on laying hold on one of the bayonets of the
guard, who were ordered to arrest him, he was run through the body.
He was evidently drunk or deranged." The incident reminded Findley
of why he opposed the deployment of such a large force. "Surely so
many men in arms could easily have secured one unarmed fool, without
killing him."

The other killing was equally unnecessary. Rebels and sympathizers
had erected "liberty poles" at Carlisle. These ancient symbols of resistance to tyranny had rallied American patriots in the struggle against
George III of Britain; the intended extrapolation to George I of America was obvious. Soldiers were detached from the main column of the
government force to track down the perpetrators of this slur against
the president. Several men were seized from a barn and put under the
guard of a light horseman.

"The young man who was killed was not only innocent but very
unwell," Findley explained. "The party left him under guard of one of
their number until they would search the barn for others. The sick boy,
declaring his innocence and that he was not able to stand, attempted
to go into the house without leave. The light horseman ordered him
to stop, on the peril of being shot, and if he could not stand, to sit or
lay down, and in the meantime cocked his pistol. When the boy was
in the posture of laying himself down, and the light horseman about to
uncock his pistol, it went off and shot the boy mortally."

FINDLEY CARRIED his anti-administration feelings, increased by the
needless civilian deaths, into a meeting with Washington and Hamilton. Findley had served under Washington during the Revolutionary War, but he was no longer a revolutionary. He sympathized with
the farmers in their complaints against the whiskey tax, yet he recognized that armed opposition to the government of the United States
would be reckless and futile. The combined militias that Washington
had gathered equaled in size the Continental Army during much of

the Revolutionary War; only in their wildest dreams could the whiskey rebels stand against that.

So Findley acted as a mediator, intending to talk with Washington about a series of resolutions the insurgents had put forward. "The president opened the conversation with a discourse on the subject of the resolutions," Findley recalled. Except that Washington hadn't come to converse but rather to admonish. "He expatiated at considerable length on the evils occasioned by the insurrection, and the injury resulting from it to the cause of liberty and the general interests of republican government in the world," Findley wrote. "He said that the outrages committed against the government and the peace of the citizens in the western counties had agitated the United States from one end to the other like an electrical shock."

Washington complained of the cost of gathering and provisioning his army. "He lamented the sacrifices that farmer and merchant were under the necessity of making, and the great expense that would be incurred to the government by the expedition," Findley recalled. "He expressed his astonishment that the people were so blind to their own interest as not to have prevented the necessity of it by giving to the commissioners such assurances of their submission to the laws as would have sheltered them from punishment and secured the restoration of order, and that we"—Washington especially faulted Findley, a member of Congress—"and other well-disposed citizens had not been more successful in persuading them to take that salutary course."

The resolutions Findley and the others had presented didn't satisfy Washington. "He appealed to our own knowledge that the preparation for an expedition was the greatest part of the expense, and observed that being thus far advanced, it would be necessary to obtain further and more ample assurances of submission before he could dismiss the army," Findley wrote. "Some atonements would be required for the infractions committed against the laws."

Findley and his associates voiced their regret at the expense to the country. But they wished the president had been more patient and slower to mobilize. Many in the region felt they were being invaded. Findley and the others pointed out that force begets force: that the arrival of Washington's army had already provoked violence that wouldn't have happened otherwise.

Washington replied that circumstances had dictated his schedule. "The time the insurrection commenced was not of his choosing and was too near the winter to enable him to afford the time he wished to have given," Findley paraphrased the president. Washington worried that the insurrection would grow. "The flame having caught in Maryland, and symptoms of it having been discovered in some other places in Pennsylvania, rendered it improper to delay the expedition till the spring lest the flame should spread further."

FINDLEY FAULTED Washington on the timing of the militia expedition, but he blamed Hamilton for making the expedition appear necessary. "Perhaps the most mysterious circumstance attending the western expedition was the character sustained by the secretary of the treasury," Findley wrote afterward. Findley admitted he lacked hard evidence of Hamilton's culpability. "Frequent inquiries have been made for me, and I have often inquired of others, what station he held to which his responsibility was attached, but without any satisfactory answers." Yet everything pointed toward Hamilton.

"That he was the responsible head of the revenue department and had the direction of the measures relative to the execution of the excise law is evident from the powers vested in him by law," Findley observed. Hamilton spoke of the law as necessary for revenue, but he also sought an excuse to flex the muscles of the young government, Findley asserted. "That a government could never be considered as established till its power was put to the test by a trial of its military force is a sentiment that has been often ascribed to him, and never that I heard of contradicted," Findley said. Hamilton had acquiesced in the lax initial enforcement of the law, as though to encourage insurrection when enforcement finally came. Findley had heard that Hamilton wished the rebels had gone further. "He even in the cabinet expressed his sorrow that the town of Pittsburgh had not been burned by those who rendezvoused at Braddock's Field, that a trial of the military force of the government might have been rendered the more necessary and justifiable."

The whiskey law was designed and enforced in a way that almost guaranteed a strong reaction from the westerners, Findley said. Hamilton made no provision for court sessions near the place where the farmers lived. If they wished to defend themselves against the government's charges, they had to travel three hundred miles to Philadelphia. Most lacked the money and all lacked the time away from their crops and herds to do so. The prosecutions coincided suspiciously with the harvest, when the hardship was greatest. "If all these circumstances happened through inattention, that inattention was highly culpable," Findley said. "If they were the result of cool design, the connection of all the parts of the plan, and its eventual success, while they afford a striking evidence of dexterity and address, represent the morality of the conductor"—Hamilton—"in a very questionable point of view."

## 39

THE REBELLION IN AMERICA possibly convinced the British government not to negotiate meaningfully with John Jay. If the American republic was collapsing under its own weight, why yield anything at all?

Or perhaps William Grenville, the British foreign secretary, had already decided to ignore Jay. Grenville recognized that the Americans had little leverage in the negotiations. Although the Republicans might fulminate at British seizures and a few even call for war, the British could count on the Federalists and most crucially Washington to oppose belligerence. Thus the only threat Jay might have wielded was taken out of his hands. Nor did he come with enticements. The American market for British exports would grow, as Hamilton said, but this was a long-term proposition. Britain's war against France was immediate. In Grenville's view, and in the view of the rest of the British government, the struggle with France trumped everything else.

Jay spent five months wrangling with Grenville; in late November they put their signatures to a treaty that left the status quo essentially in place. The British promised to evacuate the forts in the northwest, but they had promised the same thing in the treaty they signed a decade earlier. They accorded America the trading privileges they granted other nations, but these were limited and didn't include substantial access to the West Indies. They consented to arbitrate debts and confiscations. But they did *not* agree to end the seizure of American ships or the impressment of American sailors.

The best that could be said for the treaty was that it appeared to reduce the risk of war. The presumption was that two countries that had just signed a treaty wouldn't turn around and start shooting at each other. Yet the reduction was in appearance only. Washington's administration hadn't been considering war against Britain, and the British hadn't conceded anything that might reduce the risk of war.

Jay understood the thinness of his accomplishment. "My opinion of the treaty is apparent from my having signed it," he wrote to Edmund Randolph. The treaty was better than nothing, but not much. Jay had played his poor hand as well as he could. "I have no reason to believe or conjecture that one more favorable to us is attainable."

THE SIGNED BUT unratified treaty made its slow way across the winter Atlantic. By the time it reached America, Hamilton had left the Washington administration, for reasons not dissimilar to Jefferson's. Hamilton wasn't quite the debtor Jefferson was, but he lacked the capital assets—Monticello and its resources, including the enslaved workforce—Jefferson enjoyed. Hamilton returned to the practice of law.

His departure left Washington and Edmund Randolph to guide the treaty to ratification. They were in no hurry to publicize its disappointing terms. Washington wasn't even sure the terms *had* to be made public. The Constitution assigns the president authority to make treaties "with the advice and consent of the Senate." Washington hadn't asked for the Senate's advice in the making of the treaty, but he did have to win the Senate's consent—that is, the votes of two-thirds of the senators—to give the treaty the force of law. The Constitution says nothing about the president's consulting the public, and Washington chose not to. He held the treaty close.

The administration's secretiveness aroused suspicions among Republicans, who were suspicious enough already. The mere appointment of Jay as envoy had struck many of the Republicans as shady. Besides having a reputation as an Anglophile, he was the chief justice; his appointment violated the separation of powers between the executive and judicial branches. It also presaged a possible conflict of interest should interpretation of the treaty come before the Supreme Court; Jay would be required to adjudicate his own handiwork, or recuse himself and leave the court understaffed.

"We are still uninformed what is Mr. Jay's treaty," Jefferson wrote to James Monroe in May 1795. The mystery deepened by the day. But one thing wasn't mysterious at all: Britain's continuing bad behavior on the ocean. "We see that the British piracies have multiplied upon us lately more than ever," Jefferson said.

Washington eventually showed the treaty to the Senate. He had no choice, since the senators would vote on it. But he still gave no hint of publishing it. Most of the senators, being Federalists, were willing to follow the president's lead and keep the treaty's secrets. One Republican, however, Stevens Mason of Virginia, smuggled the gist of the treaty out of the Senate and had it published.

The revelation provoked an uproar. In several cities Republicans held meetings to protest the treaty. The remonstrance of the Boston meeting was typical of the genre. "Resolved as the sense of the inhabitants of this town," the Boston document declared, "that the aforesaid instrument"—the treaty—"if ratified will be highly injurious to the commercial interest of the United States, derogatory to their national honor and independence, and may be dangerous to the peace and happiness of their citizens." The Bostonians adduced nineteen deficiencies in the treaty, most of them dealing with the trade that kept Boston's economy afloat. Jay's attempt to gain greater access for American exports to the British West Indies had backfired. The British got more than they gave. "In every stipulation respecting our intercourse with the colonial possessions of Great Britain, the whole commerce of the United States in such intercourse is colonized in return." The administration's boast of reciprocity in Anglo-American trade was a sham. "That reciprocity is merely nominal, and delusive," the Bostonians said. The treaty surrendered to Britain on the seizure of American ships. "It concedes a right to the British government to search and detain our vessels in time of war between them and other nations, under frivolous and vexatious pretexts." The remonstrance concluded with a plea to the president: "We earnestly hope and confidently rely that his prudence, fortitude and wisdom, which have more than once been eminently instrumental in the salvation of his country, will be equally conspicuous on the present occasion, and that the reasons we have assigned will have their influence to induce him to withhold his signature from the ratification of this alarming instrument."

WASHINGTON WASN'T USED to defending his policies in public. He had accepted the presidency much as he had accepted command of the Continental Army: on the assumption that those who selected him trusted his judgment and would defer to it. He discovered amid the fight over the Jay treaty that the American spirit of deference was evaporating quickly.

"In every act of my administration, I have sought the happiness of my fellow citizens," he replied to the Bostonians. "My system for the attainment of this object has uniformly been to overlook all personal, local and partial considerations; to contemplate the United States as one great whole; to confide that sudden impressions, when erroneous, would yield to candid reflection; and to consult only the substantial and permanent interests of our country."

Declining to address the substance of their petition, Washington politely told the Bostonians to shut up and let him do his job. "Without a predilection for my own judgment, I have weighed with attention every argument which has at any time been brought into view," he said. "But the Constitution is the guide which I never can abandon. It has assigned to the President the power of making treaties, with the advice and consent of the Senate." The president and the Senate would seek facts and opinions, but the decisions were theirs alone. "They ought not to substitute for their own conviction the opinions of others."

Hamilton provided the rebuttal the president would not. And he did so in language Washington couldn't bring himself to use. Writing from retirement under the cover of "Camillus," Hamilton blamed the criticism of the treaty on "misconception, jealousy and unreasonable dislike." He assailed the critics as small-minded and unpatriotic. "It is only to know the vanity and vindictiveness of human nature to be convinced that while this generation lasts there will always exist among us men irreconcilable to our present national constitution, embittered in their animosity in proportion to the success of its operation and the disappointment of their inauspicious predictions." Such malcontents had always afflicted the promoters of progress. "Every country at all times is cursed by the existence of men who, actuated by an irregular ambition, scruple nothing which they imagine will contribute to their own advancement and importance. In monarchies, supple courtiers; in republics, fawning or turbulent demagogues."

PART VII

———◆———

*Aliens and Seditionists*

## 40

WHEN BENJAMIN FRANKLIN left America in the autumn of 1776 to seek an American alliance with France against Britain, he took two grandsons with him. William Temple Franklin, called Temple, was the son of Franklin's son, William; Benjamin Franklin Bache, called Benny, was the son of Franklin's daughter, Sarah. Both labored under the shadow of their grandfather's accomplishment and celebrity, but Temple carried the greater burden of his father's loyalty to Britain, interpreted by the American revolutionaries as treason against the United States. Indeed, William Franklin, royal governor of New Jersey at the outbreak of the revolution, was deposed, arrested and imprisoned for his loyalism.

Benny Bache was younger than Temple and less conflicted by the war. His mother had married an English immigrant named Richard Bache, who sided with the rebels against his native land. Thus Benny had no political lines to cross to remain in the good graces of both his country and his father and grandfather. After the Franklin party reached Paris, Benny was educated at his grandfather's expense in Paris and then Geneva, learning French and Latin and sharing lessons with the likes of John Quincy Adams.

Benjamin Franklin meanwhile groomed Temple for service in politics and diplomacy. Temple acted as Franklin's secretary, handling correspondence, meeting dignitaries and supplicants, and learning the art of tactful persuasion. After the war, Franklin sought a position for Temple with the American government. But the taint of William Franklin's treason, and perhaps some envy of Benjamin Franklin, obstructed Temple's way. At the start of the Philadelphia convention, James Wilson, a Franklin friend, nominated Temple to be secretary of the convention. Alexander Hamilton at once moved to substitute the name of William Jackson for Temple's in the nomination, and Jackson got the job.

Benny Bache, by then approaching adulthood, chose a different path, yet one still in the family orbit. His grandfather's *Pennsylvania Gazette* had been the most influential paper in the colonies before the revolution, and Franklin had been America's most important publisher before he handed daily operations to a partner. In Paris, Franklin taught Benny the printing craft, and on their return to America he brought him into the printing business. When Franklin died in 1790, he bequeathed his press and other equipment to Benny, who shortly established a paper of his own. Under the name *General Advertiser and Political, Commercial, Agricultural and Literary Journal,* the paper stumbled, but in 1794 Bache refocused the paper and relaunched it as the *Aurora General Advertiser.* The nod to the Roman goddess of the dawn might have signaled the new day for the paper, or it might have referred to the new day for the American republic under the Constitution.

As a writer Bache lacked his grandfather's deft touch with satire. Yet he recognized that the broadsword had replaced the scalpel in American political commentary. He recognized as well that objectivity sold few papers. He threw his support to the Republicans, and he spared no effort in assaulting the Federalists. He couldn't have asked for a better issue than the Jay treaty with which to harangue the administration. His was the paper that published the bootlegged synopsis of the treaty, with a cover letter. "Mr. Bache, I have been daily hoping to see in the public prints a copy of the late treaty with Britain," wrote "A Citizen." "But as such a publication has not been made, I transmit enclosed the heads of that instrument collected from memory after an attentive perusal."

Bache opened the columns of the *Aurora* to condemnations of the treaty and of Washington in particular. "Awakened from their delusive dream of gratitude, and roused to action by a general sense of feeling at the accumulated injuries which your Treaty of Amity, Commerce and Navigation with Great Britain has prepared for them, the people of the United States demand with indignant pride whence has proceeded an instrument so deeply subversive of republicanism and destructive to every principle of free representative government," one "Belisarius" fulminated in an open letter to the president. The treaty was only the most recent criminal act against the American people. Belisarius listed its predecessors:

"1st. The odious principle of a distinction between the people and their Executive servants, as manifested in the mock pageantry of monarchy and the apish mimicry of kingship.

"2d. The wicked principle of legally sanctioning the rapine and plunder committed by herds of base and unprincipled speculators on those war-worn veterans of the revolution, whose blood was the price of our independence and the purchase of your fame.

"3d. Funded debt, and its twin sister assumption, to the amount of 80 millions of dollars, perpetuated on your fellow citizens through the influence of a base and corrupt maxim of your then prime minister 'that public debt is public blessing,' producing as its natural offspring.

"4th. Irredeemability of debt.

"5th. Mortgage of public funds.

"6th. Bank of the U. States and its pernicious branches. . . .

"7th. The establishment of a monied aristocracy, whose baneful power has greatly influenced all the principal measures of the government, and begotten

"8th. Servile submission to the restrictions imposed by Great Britain on our commerce and to her palpable infraction of the treaty of peace."

The list went on, culminating in—

"17th. The unconstitutional appointment of the Chief Justice of the U.S. as envoy extraordinary to G. Britain.

"18th. The unconstitutional negotiation of a treaty with G. Britain by your authority alone, without the privity and participation of the Senate.

"19th. The present unconstitutional treaty itself, which, if permitted to take effect, totally subverts and changes the federal Constitution, and which equally endangers our domestic tranquility and the continuance of peace with the French Republic."

Belisarius warned Washington not to count on the continuing support of the American people. "Gratitude may yield a falling tear at the recollection of your military services," he said. "But gratitude, sir, is a living virtue, and the stern though unerring voice of posterity will not fail to render the just sentence of condemnation on the man who has entailed upon his country deep and incurable public evils."

JOHN ADAMS THOUGHT the protests against the treaty presumptively seditious. "As the faith and honour both of the President and Senate are clearly pledged, what but a total overthrow both of the constitution and administration can be aimed at by the opposition, I cannot conceive," he wrote to Washington.

Adams's low opinion of democracy was declining by the day. One principle espoused by the democrats—that is, the Republicans—was rotation in office: a regular turnover of public posts lest they be seen as the property of an entrenched elite. Adams judged this another instance of leveling down. After the retirement of Hamilton and a few other members of the administration, Adams wrote sourly to Jefferson, "You will see by the changes in the executive department that the feelings of officers are in a way to introduce rotations enough, which are not contemplated by the Constitution. Those Republicans who delight in rotations will be gratified in all probability, till all the ablest men in the nation are rooted out. To me these things indicate something to be amiss somewhere. If public offices are to be made punishments, will a people be well served? Not long I trow"—believe.

The leveling down hit bottom in the debate over the Jay treaty. "A battle royal I expect at its ratification, and snarling enough afterwards," Adams predicted to Abigail before the Senate vote. He railed against the "treacherous publication of the treaty," as though the public had no right to be informed of what the president and Senate were about to impose upon them. He lamented that men who should have known better subscribed to such a pernicious concept. "It is a grief to me to see some of our oldest members of Congress carried away by this gust of wind," he said. That John Jay should be criticized seemed more of what Adams himself had suffered at the hands and pens of the ignorant. "Poor Jay has gone through as fiery an ordeal as I did when I was suspected of a blasphemous doubt of Tom Paine's infallibility," he told his son John Quincy. "The people repent of these faults, but they are the sin that too easily besets them." Adams added that he himself had suffered for the treaty, by remaining in Philadelphia into the unhealthy season. "The treaty hurt me more than any one, for the journey and a dysentery were too much for me," he wrote after his arrival in Massachusetts.

John Quincy, then in Holland, reported on Dutch plans to extend greater political rights among the Dutch people. Adams wished the Dutch well even as he restated his doubts about popular government. "If those patriots can keep the people with them, they will do something memorable," he said. "But it must ever be remembered that the mob is a part of the people, and I begin to fear the most influential part. The mob has established every monarchy upon Earth. The mob has ultimately overthrown every free republic. The doctrine of universal suffrage is so manifest a courtship to the mob as to need no comment. But it never can succeed for any length of time." Ordinary people were simply too ignorant and short-sighted. "These good creatures never look forward for two days," Adams said. "Property is universally and eternally irreconcilable with universal suffrage."

Reflecting on his own career, Adams told John Quincy, "It is one of the sweetest consolations of my life that I had the constancy to resist this doctrine through every stage of our revolution. A letter of mine has been printed, written in 1776 and printed within two or three years past in Youngs Magazine at Philadelphia. This letter I prize above a statue or a monument, merely as evidence of my opinion at that time and of my courage to avow it, when many of my co-patriots and more of the courters of popularity were very much inclined to admit all Nature to an equal vote." Nothing could be more destructive of good government, Adams said. "If all are admitted to a vote, the question instantly arises between men of property and men of no property, and as the latter are always the most numerous, three to one at least, the vote is always carried by them against the others. A man of property is instantly in the case of the lamb in the custody of the wolf." The people didn't know their own good. "It is humanity to those people themselves to exclude them from a vote, for they never have it and use it but to their own disgrace, remorse and destruction," he said.

And yet these were the people the Republicans wanted to empower. "The last hope of a party seems now in a desperate attack upon the

President," Adams told John Quincy. The end of the republic seemed nigh. "A successful attack upon that man would be a demonstration that elective executives are impracticable."

History affirmed as much, Adams said. "If elections of executives and legislatives are found by experience to produce better magistrates and lawgivers than hereditary education, I should join in the warfare against all hereditaments (to use an expression of our law) as heartily as any man," he wrote to John Quincy. "But as past experience has not proved it, I must wait for future experience to decide, and further to prove that legislatives and executives wholly elective can either make or execute any laws at all."

The philosophers of the age had things wrong. "In Europe most writers at the present day confound all ideas of popular esteem, affection, gratitude and respect for particular families with the feudal aristocracy," Adams said. "But these are different things. Popular families exist among African Negroes and American Indians as well as in any of the feudal kingdoms. Nor would the cessation of all the civilization in the world and the restoration of the savage life over the whole globe prevent the hereditary descent of popularity. If all public men are elective, birth will procure more votes and have more influence than ever. A few families will more decidedly govern. This appears to me—time will show. The natural descent of popularity in governments perfectly elective will be found to be so certain and so general that it will produce an aristocratical government everywhere, an exclusive aristocratical government, until laws and regulations are introduced to prevent it, against the popular inclination."

The people would run a republic into the ground. "A government of sans culottes cannot long endure," Adams said. "The poor people find themselves starved with cold and hunger in a very short time in consequence of their own rule, and soon cry '*This will not do*. We must have somebody to give us bread and clothes as well as circuses.' Hereditary popularity, which no political institutions can prevent, and which being unlimited and unconfined will always be mad or extravagant, will be found more dangerous, pernicious and destructive than hereditary prerogatives and privileges ascertained by law and directed to the national good."

"There is heresy for you!" Adams told his son. "Enough to expose me to persecution in any country at this day: but *Nullius addictus jurare in verba magestri*"—I am not bound to swear as any master dictates. "I cannot believe what I please, much less what is dictated by every fool who pleases to think himself popular."

THE TREATY CLEARED the Senate by the slimmest of margins. Twenty senators voted aye and ten nay, giving the document exactly the two-thirds majority ratification required.

Yet this didn't end the debate. The Republicans had discovered a cudgel with which to beat the administration, and they weren't about to let it go. Because the treaty involved trade, because trade touched on tariffs, and most crucially, because the Republicans controlled the House, Madison and the Republicans in the House asserted a role for themselves in the treaty's adoption. The Federalists, following Adams, declared this an assault on the Constitution, which says nothing about the House in the section on treaties.

The Republicans cared less about the treaty than about the elections of 1796. Washington proclaimed the treaty in effect on the last day of February 1796; two days later Edward Livingston, a Republican representative from New York, moved that the House demand to see the instructions and correspondence of John Jay relative to the treaty.

Albert Gallatin, having been elected to Congress following his role in defusing the Whiskey Rebellion, made the Republican case for a House role in the ratification of treaties. He acknowledged that the Constitution did not offer clear guidance in the matter. "By one section it is declared that a treaty is the supreme law of the land, that it operates as a law; yet it is to be made by the president and Senate only," Gallatin told the House. Yet laws required approval of both the House and the Senate. "Here will be an apparent contradiction," he said. "By this construction"—the construction of the Federalists—"there would appear to be two distinct legislatures." This certainly could not be so. To admit such would be to eliminate the House as a necessary part of Congress. "The president and Senate may absorb all legislative power. The executive has then nothing to do but to substitute a foreign nation for the House of Representatives, and they may legislate to any extent." Parties aside, the House could never stand for such an interpretation. "If it is allowed that treaties may regulate appropriations and repeal existing laws, and the House, by rejecting the present resolution"—the one demanding to see Jay's instructions and correspondence—"declare that they give up all control, all right to the exercise of discretion, it is tantamount to saying that they abandon their share in legislation and that day consent the whole power should be concentrated in the other branches."

The House resolution passed by a large margin, with even a few Federalists voting in favor. But Washington refused to comply. He made plain he was not going to be dictated to by the House, especially on matters touching foreign policy. "The nature of foreign negotiations requires caution, and their success must often depend on secrecy," he declared in a reply to the House. "And even when brought to a conclusion, a full disclosure of all the measures, demands or eventual concessions which may have been proposed or contemplated would be extremely impolitic, for this might have a pernicious influence on future negotiations or produce immediate inconveniences, perhaps danger and mischief, in relation to other powers."

The Philadelphia convention had considered the question, Washington said, and its concern for secrecy had been among the reasons it confined ratifying authority to the Senate, the smaller and more select of the two houses of Congress. Lest anyone question Washington's memory of the convention, he referred to the journals of that body. "In those journals it will appear that a proposition was made 'that no treaty should be binding on the United States which was not ratified by a law,' and that the proposition was explicitly rejected," the president said.

As a more general point, Washington avowed his determination to defend the separation of powers. "It is essential to the due administration of the government that the boundaries fixed by the Constitution between the different departments should be preserved," he said. The House would not see the Jay papers.


MADISON WASN'T SURPRISED by the rejection, although he didn't appreciate its dismissive tone. Nor did he like Washington's use of the journals of the Philadelphia convention. "According to my memory and that of others, the journal of the convention was by a vote deposited with the president to be kept sacred until called for by some competent authority," Madison observed to Jefferson. "How can this be reconciled with the use he has made of it?" Besides, Washington had taken the quoted passage out of context. The proposition before the convention had been about treaties of peace, he said, not treaties of commerce. Madison shared his own convention notes with Jefferson. "You will perceive that the quotation is nothing to the purpose," he said. But Washington knew he couldn't be publicly contradicted, and so could play loose with the facts.

Madison considered himself quite as qualified as Washington to interpret the meaning of the Constitution and the sense of the Philadelphia convention. And he judged the matter important, for to yield to the arguments in the president's message would steal yet more power from the House, the part of the government closest to the people. "Under that idea I entered into a free but respectful review of the fallacy of the reasons contained in the message," Madison told Jefferson, referring to a long speech he had given in the House.

But he was fighting a losing battle. Washington's prestige carried more weight than Madison's reasoning, and when the Federalists introduced a new resolution, asserting the intention of the House to pass the laws necessary to implement the treaty, it quickly gained momentum. "The banks, the British merchants, the insurance companies were at work in influencing individuals, beating down the prices of produce, and sounding the tocsin of foreign war and domestic convulsions," Madison told Jefferson. "The people have been everywhere made to believe that the object of the House of Representatives in resisting the treaty was *War,* and have thence listened to the summons 'to follow where Washington leads.'" The House narrowly voted to implement the treaty.

## 41

JOHN ADAMS DISDAINED rumors even as he trafficked in them. "It must be kept a secret wholly to yourself," he wrote to Abigail. "One of the ministry told me today that the President was solemnly determined to serve no longer than the end of his present period." Washington himself had not said anything on the subject, yet the one closest to him had. "Mrs. W. said one thing to me lately which seemed to imply as much." Conclusions were being drawn. "Men of the first weight I find consider the event as certain."

Adams told Abigail to prepare. "You know the consequence of this, to me and to yourself. Either we must enter upon ardours more trying than any ever yet experienced, or retire to Quincy, farmers for life." He would not remain where he was. "I am at least as determined not to serve under Jefferson as W. is not to serve at all. I will not be frightened out of the public service nor will I be disgraced in it."

The future weighed on Adams's mind. The presidency beckoned, but it was a daunting prize. Two days later he wrote again to Abigail, describing Washington's troubles finding a new secretary of state following the resignation of Edmund Randolph. "Happy is the country to be rid of Randolph, but where shall be found good men and true to fill the offices of government? There seems to be a necessity of distributing the offices about the states in some proportion to their numbers, but in the southern part of the Union false politics have struck their roots so deep that it is very difficult to find gentlemen who are willing to accept of public trusts and at the same time capable of discharging them."

Adams related that Washington had offered Randolph's position to seven men who declined, one after the other. And no wonder. "The expences of living at the seat of government are so exorbitant, so far beyond all proportion to the salaries, and the sure reward of integrity in the discharge of public functions is such obloquy, contempt and insult that no man of any feeling is willing to renounce his home, forsake his property and profession, for the sake of removing to Philadelphia where he is almost sure of disgrace and ruin."

The rumor about Washington persisted. "In perfect secrecy between you and me, I must tell you that I now believe the President will retire," Adams wrote to Abigail. "The consequence to me is very serious, and I am not able as yet to see what my duty will demand of me." He was bracing himself. "I shall take my resolutions with cool deliberation. I shall watch the course of events with more critical attention than I have done for some time. And what Providence shall point out to be my duty I shall pursue with patience and decision."

He wasn't ready to leave the public sphere. "It is no light thing to resolve upon retirement," he told Abigail. "My country has claims." Yet these were not the only claims. "My children have claims, and my own character has claims upon me. But all these claims forbid me to serve the public in disgrace"—as vice president after losing to Jefferson.

Adams's refusal to serve under Jefferson was partly a matter of pride. "I love my country too well to shrink from danger in her service, provided I have a reasonable prospect of being able to serve her to her honour and advantage," he told Abigail. "But if I have reason to think that I have either a want of abilities or of public confidence to such a degree as to be unable to support the government in a higher station, I ought to decline it."

Yet Adams's aversion to serving under Jefferson also reflected his growing belief that Jefferson's ideas of government imperiled the republic. "I ought not to serve in my present place under another, especially if that other should entertain sentiments so opposite to mine as to endanger the peace of the nation," he said. "It will be a dangerous crisis in public affairs if the President and Vice President should be in opposite boxes."

A WEEK LATER the front page of Benjamin Bache's *Aurora General Advertiser* carried its usual miscellany of public notices. A company created to build a bridge across the Delaware River issued a call for construction proposals. The firm of Cohen & McDonald, scriveners and commission brokers, announced the opening of a new office on Fourth Street opposite the Indian Queen hotel. Mr. Francis, a ballet master just arrived from Baltimore, was accepting students at his studio on Eighth Street. The recently ratified French constitution, translated for the convenience of the readers of the *Aurora,* was available for sale at the paper's office. Alexander Miller offered a ten-dollar reward for the return of a runaway indentured servant. The fugitive, a young German, had absconded with various clothing beyond the blue coat and overalls he normally wore in winter. "It is probable he may change his dress." The guardians of thirteen-year-old Catherine Spence, an orphan who had been kidnapped by Michael Hevice "at the head of an armed banditti," offered two hundred dollars for the return of Miss Spence and the capture of her abductor. "There is every reason to apprehend the utmost danger to the person of the said child," her guardians declared.

Tucked inside the paper on page three (of four), was a piece of lampoonery. "Political Chess: A New Song," it was called.

> *Ye political gamblers of every degree*
> *Stock-holders, land-jobbers come listen to me*
> *Since you've played all your cards with such skill and address*
> *I'll teach you the game of Political Chess.*
>
> *Let the contest begin, come, the chessboard display*
> *Set all your* Gens noirs *up in technic array*
> *Let your Chieftain surrounded with troops of his blacks*
> *Still think himself safe from immediate attacks.*
>
> *Then let us in chorus undauntedly sing*
> *With our pawns we will certainly checkmate your king.*
>
> *Let him in the midst like a monarch preside*
> *And secure in his station our efforts deride.*

*Tho' with all the mock splendor of royalty decked*
*If he cannot be taken, he yet may be checked.*

*And we will in chorus . . .*

*Let Hamilton, sweeping the board at a stride,*
*Be placed next in rank at His Majesty's side.*
*To our pawns the most active, invet'rate foe*
*And the principal engine of mischief and woe.*

*And we . . .*

*In Pitt and Adams your castles display*
*Tho' on opposite sides, they both move the same way*
*Both advocate power at the people's expence*
*And are both to the King a strong tow'r of defence.*

*And we . . .*

*Tho' your numerous checks and your long-boasted skill*
*May save you a while, we will press on you still*
*In spite of your tricks you shall meet with your fate*
*And the pawns of Democracy give you checkmate.*

The readers of Bache's verse understood his reference to *gens noirs* and black troops, for Washington had brought slaves from Mount Vernon to tend to his needs in Philadelphia, even after Pennsylvania had passed an emancipation law. To evade the Pennsylvania rule allowing slaves of visitors to claim freedom after six months' residence, Washington rotated his servants back to Virginia before the six months were up. "I wish to have it accomplished under pretext that may deceive both them and the public," the president instructed his personal secretary.

Pitt in Bache's poem was William Pitt, the British prime minister, here treated as an ally of Washington on account of the Jay treaty. The equating of Adams to Pitt suggested that the vice president was almost an official of the British government.

Neither Washington nor Adams appreciated mockery at their expense. Washington fumed in silence; Adams complained to Abigail.

"The democrats continue to pelt as you will see by the inclosed Political Chess," he wrote to her in a letter on the day the paper came out.

He monitored the political scene as closely as he had promised.
"The southern gentry are playing at present a very artful game, which
I may develop to you in confidence hereafter, under the seal of secrecy,"
Adams wrote to Abigail a week later. "Both in conversation and in letters they are representing the Vice President"—Adams himself—"as
a man of moderation. Although rather inclined to limited monarchy
and somewhat attached to the English, he is much less so than Jay or
Hamilton. For their parts, for the sake of conciliation, they should be
very willing he should be continued as Vice President, provided the
northern gentlemen would consent that Jefferson should be President."
In his own voice, unusually satirical, Adams remarked, "I most humbly
thank you for your kind condescension, Messieurs Trans-Chesapeakes."

Adams reflected on his choice of careers. A visitor from New York
reported that Adams's second son, Charles, was doing well as a young
lawyer there. Charles was a troubled soul, afflicted by alcohol and com-
parisons with a famous father; any good news came to Adams as balm
to the paternal heart. "All this was music to my ears," Adams wrote to
Charles. He hoped Charles would continue to capitalize on his opportunities. "I have had innumerable opportunities in the course of my life
which the public circumstances of the country and the delicacy of my
engagements in them have induced me to forego," he said. "I am now
too old. But there is no reason that my children should starve themselves because I have fasted. I hope that, never departing from honour,
integrity or humanity, they will however attend more to their private
interests than I have done."

He pondered mortality. "I see daily so many affecting proofs of
the debilitating power of age that I pity an old man when he exposes
himself," Adams wrote to Abigail. One such man had visited him
yesterday—"which moved the tender feelings of my heart." Adams
shook his head at the performance of cousin Samuel Adams, currently
governor of Massachusetts, in whom age aggravated some less than
sterling qualities. "His pride and vanity are vastly more extensive than
his abilities. He always had a contracted mind, though a subtle and a
bold one. He never was over honest nor over candid. He will lie a little
for his own vanity and more for his party, and as much as a Spartan for
his notions of the public good."

Adams didn't want Abigail to worry. "I feel bold and strong myself, though my hands shake. But my age admonishes me to have a care," he wrote. He would accept what fate decreed, with one important exception. "I am unchangeably determined to serve under no other than Washington."

More and more he felt he was the last virtuous man in public life. He cited Homer: "Telemachus says to the suitors, 'I am not averse / From kingly cares if Jove appoint me such.'" To Abigail he said, "I will not resist Jupiter; I will resign to his will. If his will is that any other should be president, I know his will also is that I should be a farmer, for he has given me an understanding and a heart which ought not and cannot and will not bow under Jefferson nor Jay nor Hamilton. It would be wicked in me. It would be countenancing tyranny, corruption and villainy in the people."

The more he thought about it, the more he convinced himself that only he could save the country. "I would not distress myself to obtain the privilege of carrying an heavier load than any of my fellow labourers," he told Abigail. "But if the fates destine one to attempt it, it would be dastardly to shrink if it were in one's power." Jefferson was the greatest threat; his policies would ruin America. "I will not by any pusillanimous retreat throw this country into the arms of a foreign power, into a certain war and as certain anarchy," Adams said. Yet Americans as a group were too ignorant to know better. "If the people will do such a thing, they shall have the undivided glory of it."

Nor was politics the only reason to despair. His daughter Abigail had expressed concerns about declining morals; Adams responded, "The world, my dear child, I think with you, is running wild, and quitting the substance to seize on a shadow. It is endeavouring to shake itself loose from every divine and moral tie, every restraint of law and government, every salutary bias of genuine discipline and virtuous education. If they could succeed, they would either wholly depopulate the earth or at least restore the reign of savage and brutal barbarity." He quoted from Genesis: "Oh my soul! come not thou into their secret!"


ADAMS COULDN'T STAND to read the *Aurora*, but he couldn't stop himself. In February Bache inserted this squib: "We are happy to be informed that Mr. Jefferson, that good patriot, statesman and philosopher, is perfectly recovered from his late indisposition. May he long live, and in the moment of necessity reappear and save his country from the unhappy effects to which it is exposed."

Adams cut out the piece and sent it to Abigail. "The enclosed slip from Benjamin's paper of this morning will shew you that the electioneering campaign is opened already," he said. Adams and Abigail had known Bache from their time with Franklin in Paris; though they despised his current politics, they still referred to him by first name. "The 'good patriot, statesman and philosopher' is held up as the successor," Adams continued. He refused to be drawn in. "I am determined to be a silent spectator of the silly and the wicked game and to enjoy it as a comedy, a farce or a gymnastic exhibition," he said. "I will laugh let them say what they will, and I will laugh, let it go as it will."

The one person he still admired was fading. "The President looks to me worried and growing old faster than I could wish," Adams said. And well might he worry. "The accursed spirit which actuates a vast body of people, partly Antifederalists, partly desperate debtors and partly Frenchified tools will murder all good men among us and destroy all the wisdom and virtue of our country."

Adams read Washington's decline as a portent of his own. "The subject which you think will excite all their feelings is well known to everybody in public life, but is talked of by nobody," he wrote to Abigail. "But in confidence I could name you however as good Federalists and as good men as any who think and say that he will retire and that they would, if they were he. And who would not? I declare upon my honour I would. After twenty years of such service, with such success, and with no obligation to any one, I would retire before my constitution failed, before my memory failed, before my judgment failed, before I should grow peevish and fretful, irresolute, improvident. I would no longer put at hazard a character so dearly earned, at present so uncontaminated but liable by the weakness of age to be impaired in a moment."

Yet Adams wasn't there yet. He was still in the contest. He feared he had alarmed Abigail with his warnings about the danger to the republic upon the succession to Washington. Now he reassured her. "You need not tremble to think of the subject," he said. "In my opinion there is no more danger in the change than there would be in changing a member of the Senate, and whoever lives to see it will own me to be a prophet. If Jay or even Jefferson—and one or the other it certainly will be, if the succession should be passed over—should be the man, the government will go on as well as ever. Jefferson could not stir a step in any other system than that which is begun. Jay would not wish it."

Adams predicted that Jefferson, Jay and himself would lead the voting, in some order. "If Jefferson and Jay are President and Vice President, as is not improbable, the other"—Adams—"retires without noise or cries or tears to his farm," he told Abigail. "If this other should be President and Jefferson or Jay Vice President, four years more, if life lasts, of residence in Philadelphia will be his and your portion, after which we shall probably be desirous of imitating the example of the present pair. Or if by reason of strength and fortitude eight years should be accomplished, that is the utmost limit of time that I will ever continue in public life at any rate."

"Be of good courage, therefore, and tremble not," Adams told Abigail. "I see nothing to appall me and I feel no ill forebodings or faint misgivings. I have not the smallest dread of private life, nor of public."

Yet if not dread, he acknowledged distaste for several aspects of the presidency. "I hate to live in Philadelphia in summer," he said. "I hate speeches, messages, addresses and answers, proclamations and such affected, studied constrained things. I hate levees and drawing rooms. I hate to speak to a thousand people to whom I have nothing to say."

## 42

Jefferson had been disappointed but not discouraged by the failure of the Republicans to block the Jay treaty. "The campaign of Congress is closed," he reported to James Monroe. "The Anglomen have in the end got their treaty through, and so far have triumphed over the cause of republicanism. Yet it has been to them a dear bought victory. It has given the most radical shock to their party which it has ever received, and there is no doubt they would be glad to be replaced on the ground they possessed the instant before Jay's nomination extraordinary. They see that nothing can support them but the colossus of the President's merits with the people, and the moment he retires, that his successor, if a Monocrat"—a Jefferson synonym for Federalist—"will be overborne by the republican sense of his constituents. If a Republican he will of course give fair play to that sense, and lead things into the channel of harmony between the governors and governed. In the meantime, patience."

One thing worried him, though, or rather one man: Alexander Hamilton. Jefferson hated Hamilton's principles but acknowledged the man's gifts. He credited Hamilton with orchestrating the Jay treaty and providing the arguments that got it through the Senate and past the House. "Hamilton is really a colossus to the anti-republican party," Jefferson wrote to Henry Tazewell, one of Virginia's senators. "Without numbers, he is an host within himself." Jefferson was trying to recruit Tazewell to answer Hamilton and the Federalists. "They have got themselves into a defile where they might be finished, but too much

security on the republican part will give time to his talents and inde-
fatigableness to extricate them. We have had only middling perfor-
mances to oppose to him. In truth, when he comes forward, there is
nobody but yourself who can meet him. His adversaries having begun
the attack, he has the advantage of answering them, and remains unan-
swered himself." The Federalist victory on the Jay treaty showed the
danger they posed to republican principles. "Thus it is, that Hamilton,
Jay, etc., in the boldest act they ever ventured on to undermine the
government, have the address to screen themselves, and direct the hue
and cry against those who wish to drag them into light. A bolder party-
stroke was never struck. For it certainly is an attempt of a party, which
finds they have lost their majority in one branch of the legislature, to
make a law by the aid of the other branch and of the executive, under
color of a treaty, which shall bind up the hands of the adverse branch
from ever restraining the commerce of their patron-nation"—Britain.

Jefferson reflected on how things had come to such a pass. He
traced events of the last generation. "The people of America, before
the revolution-war, being attached to England, had taken up, without examination, the English ideas of the superiority of their constitution over everything of the kind which ever had been or ever would be
tried," he wrote. "The revolution forced them to consider the subject
for themselves, and the result was an universal conversion to republicanism. Those who did not come over to this opinion, either left us
and were called Refugees, or stayed with us under the name of Tories;
and some, preferring profit to principle, took side with us and floated
with the general tide." The break with Britain had required creation of
a new government to replace the old. "Our first federal constitution,
or confederation as it was called, was framed in the first moments of
our separation from England, in the highest point of our jealousies of
independence as to her and as to each other. It formed therefore too
weak a bond to produce an union of action as to foreign nations. This
appeared at once on the establishment of peace, when the pressure of
a common enemy which had hooped us together during the war, was
taken away. Congress was found to be quite unable to point the action
of the several states to a common object."

The inadequacies of the Articles of Confederation were broadly
felt. "A general desire therefore took place of amending the federal constitution," Jefferson recounted. "This was opposed by some of those

who wished for monarchy: to wit, the Refugees now returned, the old Tories, and the timid Whigs who prefer tranquility to freedom, hoping monarchy might be the remedy if a state of complete anarchy could be brought on. A convention however being decided on, some of the monocrats got elected, with a hope of introducing an English constitution. When they found that the great body of the delegates were strongly for adhering to republicanism, and for giving due strength to their government under that form, they then directed their efforts to the assimilation of all the parts of the new government to the English constitution as nearly as was attainable. In this they were not altogether without success, insomuch that the monarchical features of the new constitution produced a violent opposition to it from the most zealous republicans in the several states."

Yet they won the contest for ratification, and the Constitution was adopted. The strength of popular support, however, was open to question. "It is still doubted by some whether a majority of the people of the U.S. were not against adopting it," Jefferson said, citing the fact that ratification was by states rather than by cumulative vote, and noting that in the largest states the majorities were small.

The new government commenced operation. "The inconveniences of an inefficient government driving the people, as is usual, into the opposite extreme, the elections to the first Congress run very much in favor of those who were known to favor a very strong government," Jefferson said. "Hence the anti-republicans appeared a considerable majority in both houses of Congress. They pressed forward the plan therefore of strengthening all the features of the government which gave it resemblance to an English constitution, of adopting the English forms and principles of administration, and of forming like them a monied interest, by means of a funding system not calculated to pay the public debt but to render it perpetual, and to make it an engine in the hands of the executive branch of the government which, added to the great patronage it possessed in the disposal of public offices, might enable it to assume by degrees a kingly authority."

The anti-republicans had kept their aims hidden at the outset. "The biennial period of Congress being too short to betray to the people, spread over this great continent, this train of things during the first Congress, little change was made in the members to the second," Jefferson wrote. "But in the meantime two very distinct parties had formed in Congress; and before the third election, the people in general became apprised of the game which was playing for drawing over them a kind of government which they never had in contemplation. At the third election, therefore, a decided majority of Republicans were sent to the lower house of Congress; and as information spread still farther among the people after the fourth election, the anti-republicans have become a weak minority."

Yet they retained a lodgment. "The members of the Senate being changed but once in six years, the completion of that body will be much slower in its assimilation to that of the people," Jefferson explained. "This will account for the differences which may appear in the proceedings and spirit of the two houses." But the Federalists' days were numbered. "It is inevitable that the Senate will at length be formed to the republican model of the people, and the two houses of the legislature, once brought to act on the true principles of the Constitution, backed by the people, will be able to defeat the plan of sliding us into monarchy, and to keep the executive within republican bounds, notwithstanding the immense patronage it possesses in the disposal of public offices, notwithstanding it has been able to draw into this vortex the judiciary branch of the government and by their expectancy of sharing the other offices in the executive gift to make them auxiliary to the executive in all its views instead of forming a balance between that and the legislature as it was originally intended, and notwithstanding the funding phalanx which a respect for public faith must protect, though it was engaged by false brethren."

Characterizing the makeup of the two parties, Jefferson started with the Federalists. "The Anti-republicans consist of: 1. The old refugees and tories. 2. British merchants residing among us, and composing the main body of our merchants. 3. American merchants trading on British capital. Another great portion. 4. Speculators and holders in the banks and public funds. 5. Officers of the federal government with some exceptions. 6. Office-hunters willing to give up principles for places. A numerous and noisy tribe. 7. Nervous persons, whose languid fibres have more analogy with a passive than active state of things."

Opposing the Federalists were Jefferson's Republicans. His description of them was more succinct. "The Republican part of our Union comprehends: 1. The entire body of landholders throughout the United States. 2. The body of labourers, not being landholders, whether in husbanding or the arts."

The Federalists were greatly outnumbered by the Republicans, Jefferson asserted. "The latter is to the aggregate of the former party probably as 500 to one." He was just guessing, quite optimistically. Yet the Federalists were stubborn and resourceful. "Trifling as are the numbers of the anti-republican party, there are circumstances which give them an appearance of strength and numbers. They all live in cities, together, and can act in a body readily and at all times. They give chief employment to the newspapers, and therefore have most of them under their command."

The Republicans were less successful than they should be. "The agricultural interest is dispersed over a great extent of country, have little means of intercommunication with each other, and, feeling their own strength and will, are conscious that a single exertion of these will at any time crush the machinations against their government." This last had lulled the Republicans into complacency, and let the Federalists defend their ground.


JEFFERSON RESPECTED ADAMS as a man more than he respected Hamilton, which was why he hoped to keep Adams from falling irretrievably under Hamilton's spell. "Mr. Adams and myself were cordial friends from the beginning of the revolution," Jefferson told James Madison. "Since our return from Europe, some little incidents have happened which were capable of affecting a jealous mind like his. The deviation from that line of politics on which we have been united has not made me less sensible of the rectitude of his heart."

To Adams himself, Jefferson reflected on the moral basis of republicanism, and its future in America. "Never was a finer canvas presented to work on than our countrymen," he said. "All of them engaged in agriculture or the pursuits of honest industry independent in their circumstances, enlightened as to their rights and firm in their habits of order and obedience to the laws. This I hope will be the age of experiments in government, and that their basis will be founded in principles of honesty, not of mere force." Americans of the current generation occupied a unique historical moment. "We have seen no instance of this since the days of the Roman republic, nor do we read of any before that. Either force or corruption has been the principle of every modern government. . . . If ever the morals of a people could be made the basis of their own government it is our case."

Jefferson expressed confidence that Adams agreed with him. "I am sure from the honesty of your heart you join me in detestation of the corruptions of the English government," he said. "No man on earth is more incapable than yourself of seeing that copied among us, willingly. I have been among those who have feared the design to introduce it here, and it has been a strong reason with me for wishing there was an ocean of fire between that island and us."

"But away politics," he concluded unconvincingly.

## 43

W HEN GEORGE WASHINGTON first considered retiring from the presidency, at the end of his first term, James Madison was still a confidant. The younger Virginian had helped write Washington's annual messages to Congress, and Washington enlisted him to draft a farewell address to the American people. Madison obliged, producing a document emphasizing the commonality of all Americans. "We may all be considered as the children of one common country," Madison wrote for Washington to deliver. "We have all been embarked in one common cause. We have all had our share in common sufferings and common successes. . . . We have established a common government."

Washington yielded to the pleas of Jefferson and Hamilton not to retire, and he filed Madison's draft away. Four years later, when he had had enough of what politics had become in America and decided definitively to retire, he took another look at Madison's draft. By this time Madison was the leader of the opposition in Congress, and the president sought friendlier counsel. Alexander Hamilton was busy with his law practice in New York, but he was happy to help his old mentor and especially to provide a counterweight to Madison.

The end product was an amalgam of Madison and Hamilton, and of Washington, who made final edits himself. Hamilton largely retained Madison's introductory paragraphs, in which Washington announced that he would not be a candidate again and that his retirement reflected no loss of interest in the future of the republic.

But the central thrust of the revised address revealed the degree to which American politics had changed during Washington's second term. In a message published in September 1796, the president cautioned Americans against "the baneful effects of the spirit of party." He granted that banding together in pursuit of shared interest was understandable in politics, being rooted in human nature. "It exists under different shapes in all governments, more or less stifled, controlled, or repressed," he said. "But in those of the popular form, it is seen in its greatest rankness, and is truly their worst enemy. The alternate domination of one faction over another, sharpened by the spirit of revenge, natural to party dissension, which in different ages and countries has perpetrated the most horrid enormities, is itself a frightful despotism. But this leads at length to a more formal and permanent despotism. The disorders and miseries which result gradually incline the minds of men to seek security and repose in the absolute power of an individual, and sooner or later the chief of some prevailing faction, more able or more fortunate than his competitors, turns this disposition to the purposes of his own elevation on the ruins of public liberty."

Washington conceded that parties could be a check on government. Such checks were essential in monarchical governments. "But in those of the popular character, in governments purely elective, it is a spirit not to be encouraged. From their natural tendency, it is certain there will always be enough of that spirit for every salutary purpose. And there being constant danger of excess, the effort ought to be by force of public opinion to mitigate and assuage it. A fire not to be quenched, it demands a uniform vigilance to prevent its bursting into a flame lest, instead of warming, it should consume."

Washington's second warning was against letting foreign countries intrude into American politics. "Observe good faith and justice towards all nations; cultivate peace and harmony with all," he said. "Religion and morality enjoin this conduct, and can it be that good policy does not equally enjoin it? It will be worthy of a free, enlightened, and at no distant period, a great nation, to give to mankind the magnanimous and too novel example of a people always guided by an exalted justice and benevolence."

Excessive attachment to any other nation would corrupt the example. "The nation which indulges towards another a habitual hatred or a habitual fondness is in some degree a slave. It is a slave to its animosity or to its affection, either of which is sufficient to lead it astray from

its duty and its interest. Antipathy in one nation against another dis-
poses each more readily to offer insult and injury, to lay hold of slight
causes of umbrage, and to be haughty and intractable when accidental
or trifling occasions of dispute occur." Undue sympathy was no better.
"A passionate attachment of one nation for another produces a variety
of evils. Sympathy for the favorite nation, facilitating the illusion of an
imaginary common interest in cases where no real common interest
exists, and infusing into one the enmities of the other, betrays the former into a participation in the quarrels and wars of the latter."

While making allowance for America's existing alliance with
France, Washington proposed a basic rule for American diplomacy: "It
is our true policy to steer clear of permanent alliances with any portion
of the foreign world."

## 44

THE CAMPAIGN FOR president proceeded confusingly. Time would prove the framers of the Constitution far-seeing in some things, but they couldn't have been more myopic when it came to choosing presidents. The system of electors, like Congress, was a compromise between the principles of state representation and of popular representation; also like Congress, it was a nod to the momentary needs of ratification. In the debate over ratification, various arguments were put forward to justify the electoral system and its provisions, but few believed the framers would have bothered with it absent the compulsion to bring all or nearly all the states aboard the new form of government.

The blind spot of the framers reflected three misapprehensions. One was that Americans would remain content to let their chief executive be chosen by electors insulated from the popular will. In fact the habit of deference had been more badly damaged by the revolution than the framers wanted to admit. Americans were happy enough to concede the presidency to Washington, the undisputed hero of the war, but after Washington retired they demanded a greater voice in choosing the one who would lead the country.

The second misapprehension was the assumption that the break from Britain had banished the role of parties from American politics. Parties had been something the framers identified with corrupt monarchies; most would have been horrified at the thought parties would spring up in republican America. But parties *did* spring up, and with each year after the midpoint of Washington's presidency, they grew stronger.

The third misapprehension was that the presidency wasn't a particular prize. The framers devoted most of their drafting attention to Article I, which describes the powers of Congress. Article II, regarding the presidency, was a comparative afterthought. Part of the casualness revealed exhaustion at the end of a long summer in Philadelphia; part indicated confidence in Washington as template-setter. But much reflected assumptions drawn from a century of parliamentary supremacy in British politics. Jefferson's finger-pointing at George III in the Declaration of Independence was tactical; he and everyone else in the Continental Congress knew America's problem was with Parliament, not the Crown. The framers of the Constitution intended to create a national government driven by the legislative branch and only administered by the executive; at the end of the summer, they thought they had done so. Even Hamilton, the most executive-minded of the framers, understood that his centralization schemes would stand or fall depending on his ability to muster majorities in Congress.

The flimsiness of the electoral system remained hidden during the first two rounds of voting. The Constitution gave each elector two ballots. In 1789 and again in 1792, George Washington received a ballot from every elector. John Adams received fewer ballots but more than anyone else besides Washington. Thus Washington became president and Adams vice president.

The fact that each elector cast two ballots reflected a belief that the states would instruct their electors to vote for favorite sons or regional candidates; the second ballots would be the ones that would determine the president. The states instructed their electors in different ways. Some allowed voters to guide the selection; others reserved selection to the state legislatures; still others employed hybrid schemes. The Constitution specified simply, "The states shall choose electors," and left the method of choosing to them.

THE STATES CHOSE electors for the third time during several weeks in the autumn of 1796. Adams was the candidate of the Federalists. Jefferson, after failing to persuade Madison to step forward, became the candidate of the Republicans.

Neither Adams nor Jefferson took an active part in campaigning. The slowness of travel and communication in those days would have made campaigning difficult and of dubious effect; more to the point, campaigning would have been unseemly. Washington had not campaigned, and although no one confused Adams or Jefferson with Washington, his negative example fairly forbade aspiring successors from touting themselves.

For both men, the aspirations were tepid at best. Such, at any rate, was how they presented themselves to family and friends. "The day after tomorrow is the great election," Adams wrote to John Quincy in early December, referring to the day when the electors would cast their ballots in their states. "I look upon the event as the throw of a die, a mere chance, a miserable meagre triumph to either party."

Jefferson's professed reluctance was even more pronounced. "The first wish of my heart was that you should have been proposed for the administration of the government," he wrote to Madison. "On your declining it, I wished anybody rather than myself." Even now, he resisted the idea that he might become president. "There is nothing I so anxiously hope as that my name may come out either second or third. These would be indifferent to me; as the last would leave me at home the whole year, and the other two-thirds of it."

If the preferences of the American people had determined the choice of the electors, Jefferson would have won handily. The House of Representatives, where the preferences of the people *were* determinative, swung sharply in the Republicans' favor. But the outsized influence of the states in the system of presidential electors rendered the race very close.

And the two-vote system made its outcome even harder to predict. Among the Republicans, Jefferson was the overwhelming first choice, with Aaron Burr of New York second. But while most of the Federalists favored Adams for president and Thomas Pinckney for vice president, others wanted Pinckney to come first. Yet because no distinction was made on the ballots themselves, some electors would have to throw their ballots away to register a preference. This might deprive both Adams and Pinckney of a majority and throw the race into the House of Representatives.

Jefferson could count votes as well as anyone—which was to say, not well at all. "I have no expectation that the eastern states will suffer

themselves to be so much outwitted as to be made the tools for bringing in Pinckney instead of Adams," he wrote to Madison. But the possibility remained that the race would go to the House, where the wishes
of the voters might be disregarded. "This is a difficulty from which the
Constitution has provided no issue," Jefferson said. A deadlock in the
House could produce a constitutional crisis. "It is both my duty and
inclination, therefore, to relieve the embarrassment, should it happen;
and in that case, I pray you and authorize you fully to solicit on my
behalf that Mr. Adams may be preferred," he told Madison. "He has
always been my senior, from the commencement of my public life, and
the expression of the public will being equal, this circumstance ought to
give him the preference. And when so many motives will be operating
to induce some of the members to change their vote, the addition of my
wish may have some effect to preponderate the scale."

"THIS IS the very day," Adams wrote to Abigail on December 7. "I
laugh at myself twenty times a day for my feelings and meditations
and speculations in which I find myself engaged. Vanity suffers. Cold
feelings of unpopularity. Humble reflections. Mortifications. Humiliation. Plans of future life. Economy. Retrenching of expences. Farm-
ing. Return to the bar. Drawing writs, arguing causes, taking clerks.
Humiliations of my country under foreign bribes. Measures to counteract them. All this miserable nonsense will come and go like evil into
the thoughts of gods or men, approved or unapproved."

He still couldn't decide if he wanted the job. "If my reason were to
dictate I should wish to be left out," he told Abigail. "A President with
half the continent upon his back besides all France and England, old
Tories and all Jacobins to carry will have a devilish load. He will be very
apt to stagger and stumble."

He tried to calculate how the electors might vote, but gave it up.
"It really seems to me as if I wished to be left out," he repeated. "Let
me see! Do I know my own heart? I am not sure." The worst would be
to lose and have to remain in government until the end of his current
term. "All that I seem to dread is a foolish, mortifying, humiliating,
uncomfortable residence here for two tedious months after I shall be
known to be shimmed, as my wallmen speak."

Adams prepared himself for the loss. "I can pronounce Thomas Jefferson to be chosen President of the United States with firmness and a good grace," he told Abigail. As president of the Senate, the announcement of the winner would be Adams's responsibility. "That I don't fear," he continued. "But here alone, abed, by my fireside, nobody to speak to, poring upon my disgrace and future prospects—this is ugly."

IT DIDN'T COME to that. When the electors' votes were gathered and tallied, Adams received 71 and Jefferson 68. Adams's total was one more than the required majority of 70 of the 138 electors.

On February 8, 1797, Adams addressed the Senate. "In obedience to the Constitution and law of the United States, and to the commands of both houses of Congress, expressed in their resolution passed in their present session, I now declare that John Adams is elected President of the United States for four years to commence with the fourth of March next," he said.

"And that Thomas Jefferson is elected Vice President of the United States for four years to commence with the fourth of March next.

"And may the Sovereign of the Universe, the ordainer of civil government on Earth for the preservation of liberty, justice and peace among men, enable both to discharge the duties of those offices, conformably to the Constitution of the United States, with conscientious diligence, punctuality and perseverance."

## 45

B Y THIS TIME Adams had learned something new about Jefferson. "I had a visit from Dr. Rush, whose tongue ran for an hour," he wrote to Abigail. "So many compliments, so many old anecdotes." One of Rush's stories got Adams's full attention. "He met Mr. Madison in the street and asked him if he thought Mr. Jefferson would accept the Vice Presidency. Mr. Madison answered there was no doubt of that. Dr. Rush replied that he had heard some of his friends doubt it. Mr. Madison took from his pocket a letter from Mr. Jefferson himself and gave it to the Dr. to read. In it he tells Mr. Madison that he had been told there was a possibility of a tie between Mr. Adams and himself. If this should happen, says he, I beg of you to use all your influence to procure for me the second place, for Mr. Adams's services have been longer, more constant and more important than mine."

As a lawyer, Adams was used to weighing evidence. He trusted Rush, and Rush had said he had seen and read the Jefferson letter. The evidence appeared sound. Perhaps the incoming vice president wasn't devoid of civic virtue after all.

Adams learned something else about the same time. In the final weeks of the election campaign, members of Adams's Federalist party had become discouraged about their prospects. Oliver Wolcott Jr., who had replaced Hamilton as treasury secretary, wrote to Hamilton from Philadelphia, "The Federal ticket is lost here. There are still hopes that Mr. Adams will be elected, but nothing more. I hope Mr. Pinckney will be supported as the next best thing which can be done. Pray write to our Eastern friends."

Hamilton responded at once with what appears to have been a form letter for circulation among influential Federalists. "Our excellent President, as you have seen, has declined a reelection," Hamilton wrote. "'Tis all important to our country that his successor shall be a safe man. But it is far less important who of many men that may be named shall be the person, than that it shall not be Jefferson. We have everything to fear if this man comes in, and from what I believe to be an accurate view of our political map, I conclude that he has too good a chance of success, and that good calculation, prudence, and exertion were never more necessary to the Federal cause than at this very critical juncture."

Federalist electors should weigh their choices very carefully. "All personal and partial considerations must be discarded, and everything must give way to the great object of excluding Jefferson," Hamilton said. "It appears to be a common opinion (and I think it a judicious one), that Mr. Adams and Mr. Pinckney (late minister to England) are to be supported on our side for President and Vice-President." Hamilton registered no objection of his own to this ordering of the two men. Yet others had questions about Adams, he said, and every Federalist must take this into account.

"New York will be unanimous for both," Hamilton continued. "I hope New England will be so too. Yet I have some apprehensions on this point, lest the fear that he may outrun Mr. Adams should withhold votes from Pinckney." Hamilton didn't want risk it. "Should this happen, it will be, in my opinion, a most unfortunate policy. It will be to take one only instead of two chances against Mr. Jefferson, and, well weighed, there can be no doubt that the exclusion of Mr. Jefferson is far more important than any difference between Mr. Adams and Mr. Pinckney."

Hamilton finally came to the point. "At foot is my calculation of chances between Adams and Jefferson. 'Tis too precarious. Pinckney has the chance of some votes southward and westward, which Adams has not. This will render our prospect in the main point, the exclusion of Jefferson, far better."

Hamilton didn't presume to tell electors how to vote; he simply wanted them to know the situation. "Relying on the strength of your mind, I have not scrupled to let you see the state of mine. I never was more firm in an opinion than in the one I now express."

Yet he didn't want this opinion of his widely shared. "In acting upon it there must be much caution and reserve," he said.

Hamilton's advice on voting was lost on the electors, who stuck with Adams. So was his caution about sharing his opinion, which apparently found its way to Adams. Perhaps Hamilton intended it to. Two years later Robert Troup, a longtime friend of Hamilton, wrote to Rufus King, a New York Federalist, "During the last election for president, Hamilton publicly gave out his wishes that Pinckney should be elected president. These wishes were communicated both privately and publicly to the president"—Adams.

The result was that at a moment when Adams was thinking better of Jefferson, his partisan foe, he was thinking worse of Hamilton, his putative ally. "Hamilton I know to be a proud, spirited, conceited, aspiring mortal always pretending to morality, with as debauched morals as old Franklin, who is more his model than any one I know," Adams wrote to Abigail. "As great an hypocrite as any in the United States. His intrigues in the election I despise. That he has talents I admit. But I dread none of them. I shall take no notice of his puppyhood but retain the same opinion of him I always had and maintain the same conduct towards him I always did—that is, keep him at a distance."

## 46

WHEN ADAMS MENTIONED Hamilton's "debauched morals," he had something specific in mind, something rumored in Philadelphia for several years but confirmed to the public only in 1797. The confirmer was James Callender, a journalist and pamphleteer who had fled his native Scotland after running afoul of Britain's sedition laws. Callender arrived in America in 1793 and got work recording the debates in Congress. He possessed a prickly temperament and soon annoyed his Federalist sponsors, but in doing so he endeared himself to Republicans seeking to counter Federalist propaganda with some of their own. Jefferson learned of Callender and encouraged his work, including a pamphlet titled *The History of the United States for 1796*. In this piece Callender revealed a scandal involving Alexander Hamilton that had been suppressed for several years. In Callender's pamphlet the story unfolded in a series of affidavits by James Monroe, then a senator from Virginia; Abraham Venable, a Virginia congressman; and Frederick Muhlenberg, a Pennsylvania congressman. The three were investigating allegations that Hamilton had been siphoning money from treasury accounts.

The allegations originated in legal proceedings against one James Reynolds, who had been charged with securities fraud. Muhlenberg's office was investigating that affair when Jacob Clingman, a clerk in the office, intimated he had special knowledge of Reynolds. "Clingman, *unasked,* frequently dropped hints to me that Reynolds had it in his power *very materially to injure the Secretary of the Treasury,* and that

Reynolds knew several very improper transactions of his," Muhlenberg recorded. Muhlenberg said he had paid little attention at first. "But when they were frequently repeated, and it was even added that Reynolds said *he had it in his power to hang the Secretary of the Treasury;* that he was *deeply concerned in speculation;* that he had frequently advanced money to him (Reynolds); and other insinuations of an improper nature, it created considerable uneasiness in my mind, and I conceived it my duty to consult with some friends on the subject." The friends were Venable and Monroe.

Together the three determined to pay a visit to James Reynolds. Hoping to find him at home, they waited until late in the evening. He was not there, but his wife, Maria Reynolds, was. "It was with difficulty we obtained any information from her on the subject," the three testified later. "But at length she communicated to us the following particulars. That since Colonel Hamilton was Secretary of the Treasury, and at his request, she had burned a considerable number of letters from him to her husband, and in the absence of the latter, touching business between them, to prevent their being made public." Mrs. Reynolds appeared not to know what was in the letters. She specifically denied that she had received any money from Hamilton.

The three questioned Clingman further. He reported encountering Hamilton at the Reynolds home, when James Reynolds was out but Maria Reynolds was in. Clingman asked her how long she had known Hamilton. "She replied, some months; that Colonel Hamilton had assisted her husband; that sometime before that he had received upwards of eleven hundred dollars of Colonel Hamilton," Clingman said.

The trio approached Hamilton. "Last night we waited on Colonel Hamilton," they wrote in December 1792. "He informed us of *a particular connection with Mrs. Reynolds;* the period of its commencement, and circumstances attending it; his visiting her at Inskeep's; the frequent supplies of money to her and her husband on that account; his duress by them from the fear of a disclosure; and *his anxiety to be relieved from it and them.*" Hamilton showed the three investigators letters from Maria and her husband, and he acknowledged letters they had acquired from Maria to be his, in a disguised hand.

Hamilton's explanation satisfied Monroe, Venable and Muhlenberg that Hamilton's missteps had been private and not public. They filed away their affidavits and dropped the matter.

But someone leaked the story to Callender, who published it for the reading world to see. Besides the affidavits, Callender included the disguised letters Hamilton had written to Maria and James Reynolds.

It was salacious stuff, served up in titillating manner. And yet it didn't satisfy Callender, who suggested that it was simply a cover-up. "Even admitting that his wife was the favourite of Mr. Hamilton, for which there appears no evidence but the word of the secretary, this conduct would have been eminently foolish," Callender wrote regarding the blackmail. "Mr. Hamilton had only to say that he was sick of the amour, and the influence and hopes of Reynolds at once vanished. Our secretary was far above the reach of his revenge. The accusation of an illicit amour, though sounded in notes louder than the last trumpet, could not have defamed the conjugal fidelity of Mr. Hamilton. It would only have been holding *a farthing candle to the sun.*"

CALLENDER'S EXPOSÉ CAUSED just the sort of stir Jefferson had hoped for when he brought Callender over to the Republican side. Callender's readers were invited to choose which kind of betrayal Hamilton had committed: against his wife or against his country.

Hamilton gave them help. He began with a blast against the Republican propaganda machine. "The spirit of Jacobinism, if not entirely a new spirit, has at least been clothed with a more gigantic body and armed with more powerful weapons than it ever before possessed," Hamilton wrote in a pamphlet of his own, published over his own name. "It is perhaps not too much to say that it threatens more extensive and complicated mischiefs to the world than have hitherto flowed from the three great scourges of mankind: War, Pestilence and Famine." Previously the Republicans had been content to defame public policies and principles; now they went after the private lives of individuals. "It is essential to its success that the influence of men of upright principles, disposed and able to resist its enterprises, shall be at all events destroyed."

Hamilton didn't know how Callender had got the affidavits and letters. But he had an idea. "The most profligate men are encouraged, probably bribed, certainly with patronage if not with money, to become informers and accusers." Character and evidence were no proof against the Republicans' attacks. "They still continue in corroding whispers to wear away the reputations which they could not directly subvert. If, luckily for the conspirators against honest fame, any little foible or folly can be traced out in one whom they desire to persecute, it becomes at once in their hands a two-edged sword, by which to wound the public character and stab the private felicity of the person. With such men, nothing is sacred. Even the peace of an unoffending and amiable wife is a welcome repast to their insatiate fury against the husband."

His enemies had long tried to blacken his reputation by baseless charges of fiscal impropriety, Hamilton said. As often as they had tried, they had failed. Yet they tried again, and in doing so they trod on ground where no gentleman would ever go. "The charge against me is a connection with one James Reynolds for purposes of improper pecuniary speculation. My real crime is an amorous connection with his wife, for a considerable time with his privity and connivance, if not originally brought on by a combination between the husband and wife with the design to extort money from me."

Having admitted his illicit affair, he proceeded: "This confession is not made without a blush. I cannot be the apologist of any vice because the ardour of passion may have made it mine. I can never cease to condemn myself for the pang which it may inflict in a bosom eminently intitled to all my gratitude, fidelity and love. But that bosom will approve, that even at so great an expence, I should effectually wipe away a more serious stain from a name, which it cherishes with no less elevation than tenderness. The public too will I trust excuse the confession. The necessity of it to my defence against a more heinous charge could alone have extorted from me so painful an indecorum."

Hamilton explained how the affair had come about. "Some time in the summer of the year 1791 a woman called at my house in the city of Philadelphia and asked to speak with me in private," he said. "I attended her into a room apart from the family. With a seeming air of affliction she informed that she was a daughter of a Mr. Lewis, sister to a Mr. G. Livingston of the state of New York, and wife to a Mr. Reynolds whose father was in the Commissary Department during the war with Great Britain; that her husband, who for a long time had treated her very cruelly, had lately left her, to live with another woman, and in so destitute a condition that though desirous of returning to her friends she had not the means; that knowing I was a citizen of New York, she had taken the liberty to apply to my humanity for assistance.

"I replied that her situation was a very interesting one; that I was disposed to afford her assistance to convey her to her friends, but this at the moment not being convenient to me (which was the fact) I must request the place of her residence, to which I should bring or send a small supply of money. She told me the street and the number of the house where she lodged. In the evening I put a bank bill in my pocket and went to the house. I inquired for Mrs. Reynolds and was shewn upstairs, at the head of which she met me and conducted me into a bedroom. I took the bill out of my pocket and gave it to her. Some conversation ensued from which it was quickly apparent that other than pecuniary consolation would be acceptable.

"After this, I had frequent meetings with her, most of them at my own house, Mrs. Hamilton with her children being absent on a visit to her father. In the course of a short time, she mentioned to me that her husband had solicited a reconciliation, and affected to consult me about it. I advised to it, and was soon after informed by her that it had taken place. She told me besides that her husband had been engaged in speculation, and she believed could give information respecting the conduct of some persons in the department which would be useful. I sent for Reynolds who came to me accordingly.

"In the course of our interview, he confessed that he had obtained a list of claims from a person in my department which he had made use of in his speculations. I invited him, by the expectation of my friendship and good offices, to disclose the person." Reynolds did so. But the man had left the employ of the Treasury Department, and Hamilton wasn't inclined to pursue him.

"Yet it was the interest of my passions to appear to set value upon it, and to continue the expectation of friendship and good offices," Hamilton continued. "Mr. Reynolds told me he was going to Virginia, and on his return would point out something in which I could serve him. I do not know but he said something about employment in a public office.

"On his return he asked employment as a clerk in the treasury department. The knowledge I had acquired of him was decisive against such a request. I parried it by telling him, what was true, that there was no vacancy in my immediate office, and that the appointment of clerks in the other branches of the department was left to the chiefs of the respective branches."

At this point in the story, Hamilton referred to a statement by Clingman printed by James Callender. Clingman said Reynolds had complained to him that Hamilton had promised him a job with the Treasury Department but had reneged. Hamilton cited this testimony as exculpatory of him—Hamilton. "Could I have preferred my private gratification to the public interest, should I not have found the employment he desired for a man, whom it was so convenient to me, on my own statement, to lay under obligations? Had I had any such connection with him, as he has since pretended, is it likely that he would have wanted other employment? Or is it likely that wanting it, I should have hazarded his resentment by a persevering refusal? This little circumstance shews at once the delicacy of my conduct, in its public relations, and the impossibility of my having had the connection pretended with Reynolds."

He went on with the story: "The intercourse with Mrs. Reynolds, in the meantime, continued; and, though various reflections, (in which a further knowledge of Reynolds' character and the suspicion of some concert between the husband and wife bore a part) induced me to wish a cessation of it, yet her conduct made it extremely difficult to disentangle myself. All the appearances of violent attachment, and of agonizing distress at the idea of a relinquishment, were played off with a most imposing art. This, though it did not make me entirely the dupe of the plot, yet kept me in a state of irresolution. My sensibility, perhaps my vanity, admitted the possibility of a real fondness, and led me to adopt the plan of a gradual discontinuance rather than of a sudden interruption, as least calculated to give pain, if a real partiality existed."

Maria Reynolds played her role well. "Her pen was freely employed, and her letters were filled with those tender and pathetic effusions which would have been natural to a woman truly fond and neglected."

One day she sent a letter saying her husband had discovered the affair. Hamilton didn't know what to think. "It was matter of doubt with me whether there had been really a discovery by accident, or whether the time for the catastrophe of the plot was arrived."

The shakedown unfolded. Reynolds came to Hamilton's office and accused him of taking advantage of Maria amid her distress. "I replied that he knew best what evidence he had of the alleged connection between me and his wife, that I neither admitted nor denied it—that if he knew of any injury I had done him, entitling him to satisfaction, it lay with him to name it."

Reynolds responded vaguely, but Hamilton caught his drift. "It was easy to understand that he wanted money, and to prevent an explosion, I resolved to gratify him."

Some days later Reynolds announced his price. "He was willing to take a thousand dollars as the plaister of his wounded honor," Hamilton paraphrased. "I determined to give it to him, and did so in two payments." The receipts had been printed by Callender.

Again Hamilton noted how the evidence proved an illicit personal affair rather than misfeasance of his public office. "It is a little remarkable that an avaricious speculating secretary of the treasury should have been so straitened for money as to be obliged to satisfy an engagement of this sort by two different payments!"

Reynolds wrote to Hamilton requesting that he—Hamilton—resume his visits to Maria. Hamilton hesitated. "If I recollect rightly, I did not immediately accept the invitation, nor 'till after I had received several very importunate letters from Mrs. Reynolds." But he did accept, though he realized now that the blackmail was the work of husband and wife together. "It was a persevering scheme to spare no pains to levy contributions upon my passions on the one hand, and upon my apprehensions of discovery on the other."

Hamilton explained the circumstances and import of the other published letters. They revealed him to be foolish and desperate, but they absolved him of mishandling public funds or betraying the public trust, he said. "These letters collectively furnish a complete elucidation of the nature of my transactions with Reynolds. They resolve them into an amorous connection with his wife, detected, or pretended to be detected by the husband, imposing on me the necessity of a pecuniary composition with him, and leaving me afterwards under a duress for fear of disclosure, which was the instrument of levying upon me from time to time forced loans."

Hamilton addressed Callender's intimation that embarrassment at being discovered in an extramarital affair wasn't motive enough for Hamilton's concession to blackmail—"that the dread of the disclosure of an amorous connection was not a sufficient cause for my humility, and that I had nothing to lose as to my reputation for chastity concerning which the world had fixed a previous opinion," in Hamilton's paraphrase.

It was a painful subject, but what remained of his honor required an answer. "I shall not enter into the question what was the previous opinion entertained of me in this particular, nor how well founded, if it was indeed such as it is represented to have been. It is sufficient to say that there is a wide difference between vague rumours and suspicions and the evidence of a positive fact. No man not indelicately unprincipled, with the state of manners in this country, would be willing to have a conjugal infidelity fixed upon him with positive certainty. He would know that it would justly injure him with a considerable and respectable portion of the society. And especially no man, tender of the happiness of an excellent wife, could without extreme pain look forward to the affliction which she might endure from the disclosure, especially a *public disclosure,* of the fact."

Yet he couldn't allow concern for his wife's feelings to prevent a refutation of the charges of public misbehavior. Hamilton apologized to readers for the length of his exposition. "Thus has my desire to destroy this slander completely led me to a more copious and particular examination of it than I am sure was necessary," he said. He believed he had succeeded, albeit at great cost. "The bare perusal of the letters from Reynolds and his wife is sufficient to convince my greatest enemy that there is nothing worse in the affair than an irregular and indelicate amour. For this, I bow to the just censure which it merits. I have paid pretty severely for the folly and can never recollect it without disgust and self-condemnation."

## 47

I F JEFFERSON WAS tempted to take pleasure at Hamilton's public shaming, he had reason to keep his sentiments to himself. Jefferson had a secret of his own. Jefferson had married Martha Wayles Skelton in 1772. They had six children together, of whom but two, Martha and Mary, survived past early childhood. The elder Martha herself died in 1782 after a lingering illness. The death of his wife left Jefferson distraught and disoriented. "Before that event my scheme of life had been determined," he lamented. "I had folded myself in the arms of retirement and rested all prospects of future happiness on domestic and literary objects. A single event wiped away all my plans."

Appointment by Congress to be the American minister to France, replacing Franklin, afforded new direction but raised new problems. His daughter Martha, known as Patsy in the family, was old enough to accompany him, but Mary, called Polly, was too young, being not quite six. She remained in Virginia with an aunt and uncle, the sister of Mary's mother and her husband.

Two years later Jefferson decided to bring Mary to France. To look after her, the aunt and uncle sent along fourteen-year-old Sally Hemings, who as a young child had been a slave in the household of Mary's grandfather John Wayles. It was generally understood that Sally was Wayles's daughter by an enslaved woman, which made Sally the half sister of Jefferson's wife. When Wayles died, Sally entered the Jefferson household. She became a nursemaid and then companion of Polly, and she accompanied Polly to France.

There she was reunited with her brother James Hemings, who had gone over with Jefferson earlier. The situation of James and Sally in France was ambiguous. Under French law they might have claimed their freedom. But they were economically dependent on Jefferson, and Sally was devoted to Polly. Jefferson paid for their education: James to learn the art of French cooking, Sally to acquire proficiency in sewing and other domestic practices. Both learned to speak French. Jefferson paid them a wage.

During the time they were in Paris, Jefferson commenced a sexual relationship with Sally. "My mother became Mr. Jefferson's concubine," said Madison Hemings, one of Sally's sons, many years later. Madison presumably got the story from his mother or from someone his mother told the story to. The relationship between Jefferson and Sally persisted through the end of Jefferson's term in Paris.

"When he was called home she was *enceinte*"—pregnant—"by him," Madison Hemings said. "He desired to bring my mother back to Virginia with him but she demurred. She was just beginning to understand the French language well, and in France she was free, while if she returned to Virginia she would be re-enslaved. So she refused to return with him."

Yet remaining in France was fraught with challenge for an unmarried young woman soon to be a mother. Perhaps Sally had realized this all along and simply wanted to make a point, or perhaps she seriously considered striking out on her own. In any event, Jefferson offered a deal. "He promised her extraordinary privileges and made a solemn pledge that her children should be freed at the age of twenty-one years," Madison said. When James informed her that he was going back to Virginia, Sally accepted Jefferson's offer.

"In consequence of his promises, on which she implicitly relied, she returned with him to Virginia," Madison Hemings said. "Soon after their arrival, she gave birth to a child, of whom Thomas Jefferson was the father. It lived but a short time. She gave birth to four others, and Jefferson was the father of all of them. Their names were Beverly, Harriet, Madison (myself), and Eston—three sons and one daughter."

Sally and the children were part of Jefferson's family at Monticello, although Jefferson didn't openly acknowledge them as such. "He was not in the habit of showing partiality or fatherly affection to us children," Madison Hemings recalled. Yet neither, apparently, did Jefferson have intimate relations with any woman besides Sally. "We were the only children of his by a slave woman," Madison said.

Jefferson's secret wasn't much of a secret around Monticello. Liaisons like his with Sally weren't unusual in the culture of plantations, and the fact that Sally's children, alone of Jefferson's slaves, were freed at adulthood seemed to confirm what was understood about her relationship with him.

All the same, this wasn't a relationship Jefferson wanted to have to acknowledge to the broader public. A sidelong reference to it was made amid the 1796 campaign. The *Gazette of the United States* printed a series of attacks by "Phocion" that were immediately gathered and published as a pamphlet titled *The Pretensions of Thomas Jefferson to the Presidency Examined.* The author, William Loughton Smith, a South Carolina Federalist, taxed Jefferson for inconsistency in his *Notes on the State of Virginia,* where Jefferson argued simultaneously for the emancipation of slaves and for their resettlement outside of Virginia, on account of what he considered the inability of whites and blacks to get along together in a condition of equality. Smith derided the argument and suggested that Jefferson got on *too* well with his slaves. "At one moment he is anxious to emancipate the blacks, to *vindicate the liberty of the human race*—at another he discovers that the blacks are of a *different race* from the *human race,* and therefore when emancipated must be instantly *removed* beyond the reach of mixture, lest he (or she) should *stain the blood* of his (or her) master; not recollecting what, from his situation and other circumstances he ought to have recollected— that this mixture may take place while the negro remains in slavery; he must have seen all around him sufficient marks of this *staining of blood* to have been convinced that retaining them in slavery would not prevent it; he must have been satisfied that the mixture would not be the less degrading from the emancipated state of the black."

If Jefferson read this, he probably was grateful for Smith's turgid style and the fact this glancing reference was buried in a hundred pages equally impenetrable. The exposé, such as it was, didn't catch on. William Smith was no James Callender, and Jefferson was glad he wasn't.

## 48

JOHN ADAMS HAD a tough act to follow, and he knew it. In his inaugural address, Adams sent Washington into retirement with the thanks of a grateful country. "May he long live to enjoy the delicious recollection of his services, the gratitude of mankind, the happy fruits of them to himself and the world, which are daily increasing, and that splendid prospect of the future fortunes of this country which is opening from year to year," he said.

Without dignifying the Republicans' allegations of monarchism against his party by mentioning them, Adams affirmed his devotion to republicanism. "To a benevolent human mind there can be no spectacle presented by any nation more pleasing, more noble, majestic, or august, than an assembly like that which has so often been seen in this and the other chamber of Congress, of a government in which the executive authority, as well as that of all the branches of the legislature, are exercised by citizens selected at regular periods by their neighbors to make and execute laws for the general good. Can anything essential, anything more than mere ornament and decoration, be added to this by robes and diamonds?" Certainly not. "Can authority be more amiable and respectable when it descends from accidents or institutions established in remote antiquity than when it springs fresh from the hearts and judgments of an honest and enlightened people?" Never. The American people should be pleased with what they had created. "The existence of such a government as ours for any length of time is a full proof of a general dissemination of knowledge and virtue throughout the whole body of the people. And what object or consideration more pleasing than this can be presented to the human mind? If national pride is ever justifiable or excusable, it is when it springs, not from power or riches, grandeur or glory, but from conviction of national innocence, information and benevolence."


ADAMS HADN'T BEEN sure he was going to survive the inaugural ceremony. "Your dearest friend never had a more trying day than yesterday," he wrote to Abigail afterwards. "I had not slept well the night before and did not sleep well the night after. I was unwell and I did not know whether I should get through or not." Washington's imposing figure loomed over the event. "A solemn scene it was indeed and it was made more affecting to me by the presence of the General, whose countenance was as serene and unclouded as the day. He seemed to me to enjoy a triumph over me. Methought I heard him think, Ay! I am fairly out and you fairly in! See which of us will be happiest."

Adams expected trouble ahead. Old friends, allies from the revolution, had come out against him. "It gives such a specimen of party spirit as is very disgusting, very shocking," he told Abigail. He thought he had become used to it, and he had, to some degree. But only to some degree. "These things do not shock me as they would have done when I had less experience. The inveteracy of party spirit is however indeed alarming at present."

The expense alone of being president was daunting. "I hope you will not communicate to anybody the hints I give you about our prospects, but they appear every day worse and worse," Adams told Abigail. "House rent at 2700 dollars a year. 1500 dollars for a carriage, 1000 for one pair of horses. All the glasses, ornaments, kitchen furniture. The best chairs, settees, plateaus etc. all to purchase. All the china, Delph or Wedgwood, glass and crockery of every sort to purchase. . . . I shall not pretend to keep more than one pair of horses for a carriage and one for a saddle. Secretaries, servants, wood, charities which are demanded as rights, and the million dittoes present such a prospect as is enough to disgust anyone. Yet not one word must we say. We cannot go back. We must stand our ground as long as we can."

It would be a difficult ground, and lonely. "John Adams must be an intrepid to encounter the open assaults of France and the secret plots of

England, in concert with all his treacherous friends and open enemies in his own country," he told Abigail.

HE PRESSED FORWARD. He circulated a memorandum among his cabinet—Timothy Pickering, secretary of state; Oliver Wolcott, secretary of the treasury; James McHenry, secretary of war; and Charles Lee, attorney general—asking for their opinions on the outstanding issues confronting the administration in foreign affairs.

"1st. Whether the refusal to receive Mr. Pinckney and the rude orders to quit Paris and the territory of the republic with such circumstances of indignity, insult and hostility as we have been informed of are bars to all further measures of negotiation? Or in other words will a fresh mission to Paris be too great an humiliation of the American people in their own sense and that of the world?

"2. If another mission be admissible, can any part, and what parts, of the articles of the treaty of amity and commerce with Great Britain be offered to France, or ultimately conceded to that power in case of necessity if demanded by her?

"3. What articles of the treaty of alliance and of the treaty of commerce with France should be proposed to be abolished?"

There were eleven more items on Adams's list, but they were subsidiary to these three, which summarized the parlous condition in which Washington had left American foreign policy. The Jay treaty had mollified Britain but enraged France, whose leaders concluded that the United States had become a de facto ally of Britain in the European war. The French government responded by treating American ships as though they were British ships and therefore targets of French warships and privateers. In short order French vessels seized more than three hundred American ships. After Washington sent Charles Cotesworth Pinckney to discuss the matter, the French government refused to receive him and declared him persona non grata. Adams's first question to his cabinet was how the United States should respond. Give up on negotiations and perhaps gird for war, or try diplomacy again?

His second question anticipated an obvious French demand in the event the French were willing to talk. The French would say that as an ally they ought to receive trading terms at least equal to those awarded the British.

The third question anticipated a failure of negotiations. If allies couldn't resolve their differences diplomatically, then perhaps the alliance should be revised or even ended.

AFTER HEARING FROM his advisers, Adams decided to pursue peace even as he prepared for war. "I have it much at heart to settle all disputes with France, and nothing shall be wanting on my part to accomplish it, excepting a violation of our faith and a sacrifice of our honor," he told Henry Knox. "Old as I am, war is even to me less dreadful than iniquity or deserved disgrace." For now he would make another attempt at negotiation.

This required choosing a negotiator. Knox had offered a suggestion. "Let Mr. Jefferson be sent to France," Knox said. If Adams was serious about peace, appointing Jefferson would impress the French with the administration's good faith. "Their pride would be gratified by the mission of the Vice President of the United States. This circumstance of rank, and the high estimation he is held in as the friend of the French revolution, would effect all the reconciliation that could possibly be effected by any measure whatever." Knox understood that Jefferson couldn't guarantee a result. But that didn't matter. "If the mission should be unsuccessful, his report upon his return would unite and brace the public mind to those exertions the case might require. In either event the glory and wisdom of the measure would redound to the President of the United States, who would be considered as having done *all* that was possible to serve the interests of his country."

Others seconded Knox's suggestion. "The proposal of appointing the Vice President to go as Envoy Extraordinary to Paris has arrived from so many quarters that I presume the thought is a natural one," Adams wrote to Elbridge Gerry in early April.

Adams himself was disinclined to appoint Jefferson, but he didn't want to be seen as thwarting peace. "I will tell you a secret, but I wish you to keep it a secret in your own breast," Adams continued to Gerry. "On the 3d of March"—the day before inauguration—"I had a conversation with Mr. Jefferson in which I proposed it to him, and frankly declared to him that if he would accept it, I would nominate him the next day, as soon as I should be qualified to do it. He as frankly refused, as I expected he would. Indeed I made a great stretch in proposing it, to accommodate to the feelings, views and prejudices of a party. I would not do it again, because upon more mature reflection I am decidedly convinced of the impropriety of it."

To send America's second-ranking civilian officer would impugn America's honor, Adams said. "The Vice President in our Constitution is too high a personage to be sent on diplomatic errands even in the character of an ambassador. We cannot work miracles. We cannot make nations respect ours or its government if we place before their eyes the persons answering to the first princes of the government in the low and subordinate character of a foreign minister. It must be a pitiful country indeed in which the second man in the nation will accept of a place upon a footing with the corps diplomatic."

Adams was relieved that Jefferson declined the appointment. He didn't exactly question Jefferson's patriotism, but he definitely distrusted Jefferson's judgment as to what patriotism entailed. He could imagine Jefferson bringing home a treaty that would be as unsatisfactory to Federalists, including Adams himself, as the Jay treaty had been to Jefferson and the Republicans. The Republicans would have another issue to use against Adams and his party, and Jefferson would be perfectly positioned to lead the charge.

Jefferson's declining doubtless reflected similar considerations, with the added reckoning, on Jefferson's part, that Adams would certainly reject anything the French could agree to. Jefferson would have wasted perhaps a year of his life.

Adams's animus toward the French increased by the day. "They consider nobody but themselves," he told Henry Knox. "Their apparent respect and real contempt for all men and all nations but Frenchmen are proverbial among themselves. They think it is in their power to give characters and destroy characters as they please, and they have no other rule but to give reputation to their fools and to destroy the reputation of all who will not be their fools." Adams deemed this a national trait. "To a Frenchman the most important man in the world is himself and the most important nation is France. He thinks France ought to govern all nations and that he ought to govern France. Every man and nation that agrees to this he is willing to *populariser*. Every man and nation that disputes it or doubts it he will *depopulariser* if he can."

The French seemed to be spoiling for war. Adams was ready. "Although peace be very desirable, and should be cultivated with zeal, there is such a thing as a just and necessary war," he wrote to a friend. A failed American peace effort would put the burden on France. "If we have a war, it will be forced upon us, much against our inclinations." Adams had faith in his country. "I know not that we need tremble before any nation at a thousand leagues distance, in a just cause."

## 49

ADAMS SUMMONED CONGRESS into special session. He re-counted the developments in American relations with France, emphasizing the rudeness and bellicosity of the French government. The rejection of Charles Cotesworth Pinckney was a grave insult to the United States, Adams said. "The right of embassy is well known and established by the law and usage of nations. The refusal on the part of France to receive our minister is, then, the denial of a right." And it was more. "The refusal to receive him until we have acceded to their demands without discussion and without investigation is to treat us neither as allies nor as friends, nor as a sovereign state." This latest assault on American honor was of a piece with the arrogance displayed by the French government since the efforts of Edmond Genêt to undermine American neutrality. "It evinces a disposition to separate the people of the United States from the government, to persuade them that they have different affections, principles, and interests from those of their fellow-citizens whom they themselves have chosen to manage their common concerns, and thus to produce divisions fatal to our peace."

The United States should not stand for this kind of treatment, Adams said. He as president *would* not stand for it. "Such attempts ought to be repelled with a decision which shall convince France and the world that we are not a degraded people, humiliated under a colonial spirit of fear and sense of inferiority, fitted to be the miserable instruments of foreign influence, and regardless of national honor, character, and interest."

Adams assured the members of Congress he would not be hasty. "I shall institute a fresh attempt at negotiation, and shall not fail to promote and accelerate an accommodation on terms compatible with the rights, duties, interests and honor of the nation." Yet he would not rely on talk alone. "While we are endeavoring to adjust all our differences with France by amicable negotiation, the progress of the war in Europe, the depredations on our commerce, the personal injuries to our citizens, and the general complexion of affairs render it my indispensable duty to recommend to your consideration effectual measures of defense."

The obvious first measure was the bolstering of America's naval defenses. "With a seacoast of near 2,000 miles in extent, opening a wide field for fisheries, navigation and commerce, a great portion of our citizens naturally apply their industry and enterprise to these objects. Any serious and permanent injury to commerce would not fail to produce the most embarrassing disorders. To prevent it from being undermined and destroyed it is essential that it receive an adequate protection." A strong navy should be second nature to Americans. "A naval power, next to the militia, is the natural defense of the United States."

The government must fund the construction of warships. These frigates would be able to match the French and any other maritime aggressors blow for blow. While these were being built, the government would rely on privateers—merchant vessels refitted for combat and authorized to capture and otherwise harass French craft.

A stronger navy must be complemented by a more powerful army. "The distance of the United States from Europe and the well-known promptitude, ardor and courage of the people in defense of their country happily diminish the probability of invasion," Adams acknowledged. "Nevertheless, to guard against sudden and predatory incursions the situation of some of our principal seaports demands your consideration. And as our country is vulnerable in other interests besides those of its commerce, you will seriously deliberate whether the means of general defense ought not to be increased by an addition to the regular artillery and cavalry, and by arrangements for forming a provisional army."

Adams hadn't forgotten the warning of Washington against embroilment in Europe's conflicts. "It is very true that we ought not

to involve ourselves in the political system of Europe, but to keep ourselves always distinct and separate from it if we can," he said. Yet it was
precisely to prevent embroilment that America must rearm. "However
we may consider ourselves, the maritime and commercial powers of the
world will consider the United States of America as forming a weight
in that balance of power in Europe which never can be forgotten or
neglected." That weight must not be at the mercy of any other country.
In a dangerous world, liberty must go armed.


JEFFERSON LIKED TO say that his succeeding Benjamin Franklin
at the court of France was an excellent school in humility. "On being
presented to any one as the minister of America, the commonplace
question, used in such cases, was 'C'est vous, Monsieur, qui remplace le
Docteur Franklin?' 'It is you, Sir, who replace Doctor Franklin?' I generally answered, 'No one can replace him, sir; I am only his successor.'"

In time Jefferson himself would be the one casting the long shadow.
At any rate, after Jefferson declined Adams's half-hearted offer of the
position of envoy to Paris, the president reckoned that three men—
Elbridge Gerry, Charles Cotesworth Pinckney and John Marshall—
would be necessary to take his place. Arriving in Paris in early October
1797, the three presented their credentials to the French foreign minister, Charles Maurice de Talleyrand-Périgord, via a secretary. Talleyrand
responded with an invitation to them to call on him two days later, at
one in the afternoon.

"Accordingly at that hour and day we waited on the minister at
his home where his office is held," Marshall explained in a letter to
Secretary of State Pickering. Talleyrand was not there, they were told;
they should return at three. "At which hour we called; the minister we
found was then engaged with the Portuguese minister, who retired in
about ten minutes, when we were introduced and produced the copy
of our letters of credence, which the minister perused and kept." Talleyrand said that the Directory—the central committee of the French
government—had required him to compile a report on relations with
the United States; the report would be complete in a few days. At that
time he would know what to tell the American envoys.

Six days later the three Americans received a message at third hand
from the foreign minister. "The Directory were greatly exasperated at

some parts of the president's speech at the opening of the last session of Congress, and would require an explanation of them from us," Marshall summarized to Pickering. "The particular parts were not mentioned." Later that day they received another message from Talleyrand, equally indirect. "It was probable we should not have a public audience of the Directory till such time as our negotiation was finished; that probably persons might be appointed to treat with us, but they would report to him, and he would have the direction of the negotiation."

At this point in his letter to Pickering, Marshall switched to an agreed-upon code, lest his report fall into French hands. Four more days went by. Pinckney was informed that a Monsieur Hottinguer, a banker with close connections to the foreign minister, wished to see him. "In the evening of the same day M. Hottinguer called on General Pinckney and after having sat some time in a room full of company whispered him that he had a message from M. Talleyrand to communicate when he was at leisure," Marshall wrote. "General Pinckney immediately withdrew with him into another room, and when they were alone, M. Hottinguer said that he was charged with a business in which he was a novice; that he had been acquainted with M. Talleyrand in America"—Talleyrand had taken refuge in America during the most violent phase of the French revolution—"and that he was sure he had a great regard for that country and its citizens; and was very desirous that a reconciliation should be brought about with France: that to effectuate that end, he was ready, if it was thought proper, to suggest a plan, confidentially, that M. Talleyrand expected would answer the purpose."

Pinckney replied that he would be pleased to hear what the foreign minister had to say.

"M. Hottinguer replied that the Directory, and particularly two of the members of it, were exceedingly irritated at some passages of the President's speech, and desired that they should be softened; and that this step would be necessary previous to our reception; that besides this, a sum of money was required for the pocket of the Directory and ministers, which would be at the disposal of M. Talleyrand; and that a loan would also be insisted on. M. Hottinguer said if we acceded to these measures, M. Talleyrand had no doubt that all our differences with France might be accommodated."

Pinckney asked for elaboration.

"M. Hottinguer could not point out the particular passages of the speech that had given offence, nor the quantum of the loan; but mentioned that the douceur"—bribe—"for the pocket was twelve hundred thousand livres, about fifty thousand pounds sterling."

Pinckney said he would have to speak to his colleagues, and that they all would need to have Hottinguer's proposal in writing. Hottinguer agreed, but when he delivered the proposal, the required bribe was wrapped in euphemism as "the customary distributions in diplomatic affairs."

At this stage, Hottinguer handed the matter over to a Monsieur Bellamy, said to be a "confidential friend" of Talleyrand. Bellamy reiterated that the Directory was incensed by the criticism President Adams had made of them in his speech, of which Bellamy produced a copy. "On reading the speech, M. Bellamy dilated very much upon the keenness of the resentment it had produced, and expatiated largely on the satisfaction he said was indispensably necessary as a preliminary to negotiation." The American president must retract his criticism. "But said he, gentlemen, I will not disguise from you, that this satisfaction, being made, the essential part of the treaty remains to be adjusted: 'il faut de l'argent—il faut beaucoup d'argent.' You must pay money—you must pay a great deal of money." Here he was referring to a secret loan to the French government. The bribe for Talleyrand stood separately. "Concerning the twelve hundred thousand livres, little was said, that being completely understood on all sides to be required for the officers of government, and therefore needing no further explanation."

Gerry, Pinckney and Marshall said they had neither authorization nor inclination to pay the bribe Talleyrand required. Hottinguer, again the foreign minister's agent, seemed to think they were playing hard to get. "M. Hottinguer again returned to the subject of money," Marshall reported. "Said he, Gentlemen you do not speak to the point; it is money; it is expected that you will offer money. We said we had spoken to that point very explicitly. We had given an answer. No, said he, you have not: what is your answer? We replied, it is no, no, not a six pence."

ADAMS COULDN'T HAVE wished for better if he had scripted the exchange himself. In fact someone friendly to the administration did improve the story, sharpening the riposte of the envoys to the bribe demand to "Millions for defense but not a penny for tribute." With this gloss, Adams released the Marshall document and some others that cast France in a venal and arrogant light. The names of Hottinguer, Bellamy and a third agent were replaced in the published version with the letters X, Y and Z, and the matter became known as the XYZ affair.

Adams further stoked the fires of hostility toward France. At every opportunity he denounced that country and its ruling group. "The pure principles which governed the commencement of their revolution I have never been able to discover," he remarked to one correspondent. The current regime was the worst. "Their entire disregard of our neutral rights, their piratical depredations on our lawful commerce and the marked contempt and insult with which our overtures for reconciliation are rejected have taught me that neither innocence nor friendship can protect us against the demands of that inordinate ambition and avarice that have triumphed over every mere principle and fair character from the beginning."

The French had fallen for the delusion that people could readily govern themselves. "A free and equal constitution of government has rarely existed among men," Adams said. "As almost all mankind from the earliest accounts which remain have deviated from the track, it is not surprising that foreigners in this age have not succeeded in the pursuit, especially as we knew they have all started wrong." In classical times republics might have been virtuous, but no longer. "The latter end of the eighteenth century has shewn us that every republic in Europe has lost its fundamental maxim," he wrote. "The virtues are gone." France epitomized the decline. "Republics founded on crimes and supported by crimes are a novelty in the universe. No delirium short of modern philosophy could have ever conceived the idea." In virtuous republics, the majority ruled. "But in all republics vicious and criminal, the minority always resorts to foreign influence for support and for assistance to overthrow and take vengeance on the majority. All the republics of former times were destroyed and all the republics in Europe which remained have fallen in the same manner, within a few months. Happy Americans, if you can learn wisdom from the experience of others."

Yet Adams increasingly worried that Americans were *not* learning from the experience of others. His biggest fear about France was that its example would corrupt America. "The best criterion by which a republic is to be tried, and the most infallible judgment of its duration, is to be formed from its unanimity against foreign influence and foreign hostility," Adams said. The Republican party was failing the test. The Republicans were more supportive of the French government than of their own, and the French were happy to reciprocate—to America's detriment. "The moment a party is formed abandoned enough to resort to foreign influence for support, that moment may be considered as the commencement of the decline and fall of a republic."

The XYZ affair showed the evil intertwining of French influence and Republican disloyalty. "When immense sums of money are demanded as the price of negotiation, a compliance would not only compromise our neutrality but debase our minds, corrupt our souls, and make our own government in a few years as profligate as theirs," Adams said. "It would be the beginning of an habit in the minds of our government and people of submission to insolence, injustice and disgrace. It would lay the foundation for employing our own money in corrupting our own elections. This very money would be employed in hiring venal writers and printers of scandal against virtue and panegyric upon vice. It would!"

A war against France would be a war for American virtue, Adams judged. A clergyman had written to him urging Christian forbearance; Adams responded, "The advent of the period when nations shall learn war no more is so uncertain to mortals that wisdom dictates to the ministers of the Prince of Peace, as well as to the agents of nations, to be always prepared for a state of hostility, because it is always uncertain when the unreasonable and infatuated leaders of some nation or other may compel us to take arms in support of our dearest rights."

A good war would benefit America's soul. "A war with France, if just and necessary, might wean us from fond and blind affections which no nation ought ever to feel towards another," Adams said.

## 50

A DAMS WASN'T SPEAKING to Hamilton these days, and Hamilton wasn't speaking to Adams. But Adams received the benefit of
Hamilton's efforts to make a villain of France in the American mind.
Again working without attribution, Hamilton published a series of
essays denouncing the French for insulting American honor and endan-
gering American interests. "The enlightened friend of America never
saw greater occasion of disquietude than at the present juncture," he
declared. "Our nation, through its official organs, has been treated with
studied contempt and systematic insult; essential rights of the country
are perseveringly violated, and its independence and liberty eventually
threatened, by the most flagitious, despotic and vindictive government
that ever disgraced the annals of mankind; by a government marching with hasty and colossal strides to universal empire, and, in the
execution of this hideous project, wielding with absolute authority the
whole physical force of the most enthralled but most powerful nation
on earth." Two decades earlier, Americans had bravely taken a stand
against British tyranny and in favor of American liberty. They faced a
similar choice now, between French tyranny and American liberty. "My
countrymen!" said Hamilton. "Can ye hesitate which to prefer? Can ye
consent to taste the brutalizing cup of disgrace, to wear the livery of
foreign masters, to put on the hateful fetters of foreign bondage?"

Hamilton linked the French danger abroad to Republican politics at
home. "The people of America are neither idiots nor dastards," he said.
"They did not break one yoke to put on another." Yet some had been

misled by compatriots who put the interests of France before those of America. Thankfully, most Americans saw through the baleful design. "The unfaithful and guilty leaders of a foreign faction, unmasked in all their intrinsic deformity, must quickly shrink from the scene, appalled and confounded. The virtuous whom they have led astray will renounce their exotic standard. Honest men of all parties will unite to maintain and defend the honor and the sovereignty of their country."

What, in particular, should be done? "Shall we declare war?" asked Hamilton. No; the fortunes of war were too uncertain. The despots of France might yet come to their senses. Rather: "Our true policy is, in the attitude of calm defiance, to meet the aggressions upon us by proportionate resistance, and to prepare vigorously for further resistance." To this end, the navy ought to be reinvigorated and an army raised.

The Republicans had opposed the administration's call for a standing army; its raising might provoke France to war, they said. Hamilton rejected this counsel of fear. "Being merely a precaution for internal security, it can in no sense tend to provoke war," he said of the army. And if limited war escalated, at France's insistence, to regular war, the nation would be prepared. "Suppose an invasion, and that we are left to depend on militia alone. Can it be doubted that a rapid and formidable progress would in the first instance be made by the invader? Who can answer what dismay this might inspire—how far it might go to create general panic—to rally under the banners of the enemy the false and the timid? The imagination cannot without alarm anticipate the consequences."

The test of Americans' love of country was the support they gave to the administration's worthy agenda, Hamilton declared. "It is the fervent wish of patriotism that our councils and nation may be united and resolute. The dearest interests call for it. A great public danger commands it." Every good citizen would rally to the cause. "Whoever does not do this consigns himself to irrevocable dishonor." The moment of trial was at hand. "Americans! Rouse! Be unanimous, be virtuous, be firm, exert your courage, trust in heaven and nobly defy the enemies both of God and man!"


WITH HAMILTON'S HELP, Adams got the money he wanted for ships and for an army of ten thousand soldiers.

The army required officers, and perhaps soon. In the autumn of 1797 the belligerents in the European war arranged an end, or at least an intermission, to the fighting. France enjoyed a freer hand than before to vent its anger at the Americans.

Adams turned to the obvious person for advice on matters military. "I am at an immense loss whether to call out all the old generals, or to appoint a young set," he wrote to George Washington. "If the French come here, we must learn to march with a quick step, and to attack, for in that way only they are said to be vulnerable. I must tax you, sometimes, for advice." And for more than advice: "We must have your name, if you in any case will permit us to use it," Adams said, thinking of possible problems in recruiting the army. "There will be more efficacy in it than in many an army."

As much as Adams sought the association of Washington with the army, the president did *not* relish bringing Hamilton aboard. Yet Hamilton insisted. He at once wrote to Washington, urging him in the most obsequious terms to accept command of the army. Hamilton pleaded patriotism and the national interest, but his greater concern was that otherwise the command would go to Henry Knox, who was very much less enamored of Hamilton than Washington was. "In such a state of public affairs it is impossible not to look up to you, and to wish that your influence could in some proper mode be brought into direct action," Hamilton wrote to Washington. "Among the ideas which have passed through my mind for this purpose, I have asked myself whether it might not be expedient for you to make a circuit through Virginia and North Carolina under some pretence of health etc. This would call forth addresses public dinners etc. which would give you an opportunity of expressing sentiments in answers, toasts etc. which would throw the weight of your character into the scale of the government and revive an enthusiasm for your person that may be turned into the right channel."

Hamilton went on: "You ought also to be aware, My Dear Sir, that in the event of an open rupture with France, the public voice will again call you to command the armies of your country; and though all who are attached to you will from attachment as well as public considerations deplore an occasion which should once more tear you from that repose to which you have so good a right, yet it is the opinion of all those with whom I converse that you will be compelled to make the sacrifice. All your past labour may demand, to give it efficacy, this further, this very great sacrifice."

When Washington didn't reject the idea of a last hurrah of command, Hamilton pressed his argument further. "It is a great satisfaction to me to ascertain what I had anticipated in hope, that you are not determined in an adequate emergency against affording once more your military services," he wrote. "There is no one but yourself that could unite the public confidence in such an emergency, independent of other considerations—and it is of the last importance that this confidence should be full and complete. As to the wish of the country, it is certain that it will be ardent and universal."

Washington knew Hamilton well enough to inquire what he—Hamilton—hoped to get out of this. Hamilton responded, "I have no scruple about opening myself to you on this point. If I am invited *to a station in which the service I may render may be proportioned to the sacrifice I am to make,* I shall be willing to go into the army. If you command, the place in which I should hope to be most useful is that of Inspector General with a command in the line. This I would accept."

Hamilton added the crucial element in his calculation: "I take it for granted the services of all the former officers worth having may be commanded, and that your choice would regulate the Executive." In other words, Washington should tell Adams that Hamilton was the man for the inspector general job. "With decision and care in selection, an excellent army may be formed."

A rumor that Washington might not accept the command after all elicited further flattery from Hamilton. "I use the liberty which my attachment to you and to the public authorises to offer my opinion that you should not decline the appointment," he said. "It is evident that the public satisfaction at it is lively and universal. It is not to be doubted that the circumstance will give an additional spring to the public mind, will tend much to unite and will facilitate the measures which the conjuncture requires. On the other hand, your declining would certainly produce the opposite effects, would throw a great damp upon the ardor of the country inspiring the idea that the crisis was not really serious or alarming."

Should Washington not feel up to a full campaign, something less would suffice. "Let me entreat you—and in this all your friends, indeed all good citizens will unite—that if you do not give an unqualified acceptance that you accept provisionally, making your entering upon the duties to depend on future events so that the community may look up to you as their certain commander."

This would satisfy the public craving; more important, it would still let Washington choose his subordinates. "The arrangement of the army"—including the selection of officers—"may demand your particular attention," Hamilton said. President Adams had no strong views on the matter. "And his prepossessions on military subjects in reference to such a point are of the wrong sort," Hamilton added. "It is easy for us to have a good army, but the selection requires care."

Hamilton couldn't make the point often enough: "If you accept, it will be conceived that the arrangement is yours, and you will be responsible for it in reputation. This and the influence of a right arrangement upon future success seem to require that you should in one mode or another see efficaciously that the arrangement is such as you would approve."

WASHINGTON ACCEPTED the command but on the condition that he not have to take the field unless actual hostilities impended. And he was willing to recommend Hamilton for inspector general, with the rank of major general.

This satisfied the first part of Hamilton's agenda—to wit, the right to be referred to as "General Hamilton." He had been "Colonel Hamilton" since the war, and while that honorific suited the young man he had been at war's end, in his early forties he needed something more dignified.

There remained the question of *relative* rank. By no stretch of anyone's imagination except his own should Hamilton have outranked Henry Knox. But Hamilton enlisted the support of the secretaries of war and state—James McHenry and Timothy Pickering—and most crucially Washington against Adams's preference for Knox. The effort did no credit to Hamilton, and it confirmed Adams in his belief that Hamilton always put himself before country or anything else. Yet Adams had other battles to fight, and Hamilton's persistence eventually won him the position he sought.

## 51

MADISON AND JEFFERSON were appalled at the momentum Adams and Hamilton were building for war. Madison had retired from Congress at the same time Adams was inaugurated president, and so observed the events from the distance of Virginia. Jefferson had a closer view geographically, being vice president, but was as much the outsider to administration thinking.

Jefferson thought a war against France would be lunacy. "It is quite impossible, when we consider all its existing circumstances, to find any reason in its favor resulting from views either of interest or honour, and plausible enough to impose even on the weakest mind," he wrote to Madison.

Madison concurred, vehemently. "Public opinion alone can now save us from the rash measures of our hot-headed Executive," he said. Madison had eventually disapproved of George Washington's policies, but he had never lost respect for Washington. Adams was a different story. "There never was perhaps a greater contrast between two characters than between those of the present president and of his predecessor, although it is the boast and prop of the latter that he treads in the steps of the former," Madison wrote to Jefferson. "The one cold, considerate and cautious, the other headlong and kindled into flame by every spark that lights on his passions; the one ever scrutinizing into the public opinion and ready to follow where he could not lead it, the other insulting it by the most adverse sentiments and pursuits; Washington a hero in the field yet over-weighing every danger in the cabinet, Adams without a single pretension to the character of soldier, a perfect Quixote as a statesman; the former chief magistrate pursuing peace everywhere with sincerity, though mistaking the means; the latter taking as much pains to get into war as the former took to keep out of it."

After Adams published the XYZ papers, Madison damned the French for giving the president such a gift. "The conduct of Talleyrand is so extraordinary as to be scarcely credible," he told Jefferson. "I do not allude to its depravity, which however heinous is not without examples. Its unparalleled stupidity is what fills one with astonishment. Is it possible that a man of sagacity as he is admitted to be, who has lived long enough in this country to understand the nature of our government, who could not be unaware of the impossibility of secrecy and the improbability of success in pursuing his propositions through the necessary forms, who must have suspected the Executive rather of a wish to seize pretexts for widening the breach between the two republics than to make use of any means however objectionable to reconcile their differences, who must have been equally suspicious of the probable inclination of some one or other of the envoys—is it possible, that such a man under such circumstances could have committed both his character and safety by such a proposition?" Madison wondered if Adams or John Marshall had fabricated or deliberately misconstrued what Talleyrand had said and done.

Even if that couldn't be proven, the administration's glee at the breakdown in negotiations showed it to be the chief obstacle to accommodation with France. "Whilst the Executive were pursuing ostensible plans of reconciliation and giving instructions which might wear that tendency, the success of them was indirectly counterworked by every irritation and disgust for which opportunities could be found, in official speeches and messages, answers to private addresses, harangues in Congress, and the vilest insults and calumnies of newspapers under the patronage of the government," Madison said.

The response of the public was disappointing. "The success of the war party in turning the despatches to their inflammatory views is a mortifying item against the enlightened character of our citizens," Madison told Jefferson. The opposition press was providing a partial remedy. "I am glad to find in general that everything that good sense and accurate information can supply is abundantly exhibited by the newspapers to the view of the public. It is to be regretted that these papers are so limited in their circulation, as well as that the mixture of indiscretions in some of them should contribute to that effect." The administration and its allies were trying to suppress this dissent. "It is to be hoped, however, that any arbitrary attacks on the freedom of the press will find virtue enough remaining in the public mind to make them recoil on the wicked authors. No other check to desperate projects seems now to be left. The sanguinary faction ought not however to adopt the spirit of Robespierre without recollecting the shortness of his triumphs and the perpetuity of his infamy."

Madison was counting on the future, because the present seemed so grim. "The successful use of the despatches in kindling a flame among the people, and of the flame in extending taxes armies and prerogative, are solemn lessons which I hope will have their proper effect when the infatuation of the moment is over," he said. "The management of foreign relations appears to be the most susceptible of abuse of all the trusts committed to a government, because they can be concealed or disclosed, or disclosed in such parts and at such times as will best suit particular views, and because the body of the people are less capable of judging and are more under the influence of prejudices on that branch of their affairs than of any other. Perhaps it is a universal truth that the loss of liberty at home is to be charged to provisions against danger real or pretended from abroad."

BENJAMIN BACHE's *Aurora* was the foremost of the papers Madison meant when he spoke of the struggling opposition. From the moment of publication of the XYZ dispatches, Bache's columns carried blistering reviews of the administration's performance. "The crisis is arrived which was foreseen by the philosopher and predicted by the friends of liberty and peace," declared a contributor writing as "Nestor." "Perhaps history cannot furnish an example of a nation rushing with such rapidity from prosperity to ruin, as that unhappily exhibited by our own country." Nestor attributed the decline to willful amnesia on the part of America's rulers. "In the day of our revolutionary difficulty, when we had to contend with a nation whose ferocity was commensurate to its power, a nation whose object and whose efforts were to subjugate the States, France extended her hand to us in friendship, and as an evidence of her sincerity bound herself to us in a treaty of alliance." Yet as soon as France ran into difficulty and required reciprocal aid, the government of the United States spurned her in favor of Britain. From denial of obligation to avowal of hostility was inevitable and swift; the current rush toward war against France was the natural outgrowth of this immoral policy.

The same issue of the *Aurora* carried an essay by one "Sidney" characterizing the publication of the XYZ papers as the "last link in the systematic chain of measures pursued by the Tories"—Federalists—"to alienate this country from France, draw its connection with Britain closer, and by strengthening the influence of that country here, pave the way for a subversion or total perversion of our constitution." Any other explanation was implausible, said Sidney. Some of the Federalists' defenders were claiming that the strong public reaction against France had been unforeseen; Sidney deemed this more of the deception the administration had been employing all along. "They cannot have been so dim-sighted as not to have perceived that it would have that effect," he wrote. "Is not their conduct an unparalleled example of the inveteracy and profligacy of their party spirit—to sacrifice, with their eyes open, the peace and prosperity of their country in an attempt to strengthen the influence of their party?"

Bache brought Nestor and Sidney back in subsequent issues. Nestor probed the history of the current crisis, treating the official neutrality of the Washington administration as a cynical cover for a blatantly pro-British and unconscionably anti-French policy. "The minister Genet was thwarted in every measure, embarrassments were multiplied upon him at every step he took," Nestor said of the awkward envoy. "Every artifice was employed to produce irritation in a mind keenly sensible of the interests of its country and alive to the great cause of humanity. The calculations were well conceived, the means certain of the end in view, and the effects were a natural result."

Sidney charged Gerry, Pinckney and Marshall with irresponsible diplomacy, connived in by the administration. "Suppose a French minister here had pursued a conduct parallel to that of our commissioners; had listened to persons calling themselves authorized or even in reality authorized by a *subordinate* of the government; that these persons had avowed themselves hostile to our administration; had predicted the downfall of our president; had declared that our executive preferred money to honor; that he totally disregarded justice and reason and could be approached only as the Dey of Algiers is, by presents or bribes—I say, suppose a French minister here should listen to, believe, reverberate and enlarge upon such suggestions; what would be our indignation?" wrote Sidney. "Suppose he should detail all this, affixing to it the seal of his faith to his government, and that government should publish it to the world, and its friends bring forward the correspondence as proof of the depravity and profligacy of our government. Would not all our indignation and resentment be roused against the nation who could thus, upon the bare assertion of two unknown unauthorized individuals, avowed enemies of our government, endeavour to stamp our administration with the most profligate and the most gangrenous corruption?"

The *Aurora*'s attacks went on for weeks. Jefferson and Madison took heart from their vigor. "The analysis of the despatches by Sidney cannot fail to be an effectual antidote, if any appeal to sober reflexion can prevail against occurrences which are constantly addressing their imaginations and feelings," Madison wrote to Jefferson. "The talents of this writer make it lucky that the task has not been taken up by other hands."

## 52

M Y DEAR SISTER," Abigail Adams wrote to Mary Cranch in May 1798. "I have not written you a word upon a subject which I know would have made you at least very uneasy. About three weeks ago a letter was sent, or rather brought here of a Sunday evening, by two young women of the city, one of whom said passing the house a few days before she took up a paper in a small alley which runs between our house and our neighbours." The house the Adamses occupied was the same one Washington had lived in, at the corner of Sixth and Market Streets. "It was wet by lying at the edge of a gutter which passes through the passage. The girl finding it in this way opened the letter and read it, but being alarmed at the contents knew not what to do. Her mother, who was absent at the time, returning and finding what she had done, directed the girl to bring it herself and relate the circumstances." The girl had enlisted a friend and they delivered the letter to the president.

Abigail Adams continued to her sister: "The purport of the letter was to inform the President that the French people who were in this city had formed a conspiracy with some unsuspected Americans, on the evening of the day appointed for the fast to set fire to the city in various parts and to massacre the inhabitants, entreating the President not to neglect the information and the warning given, though by an anonymous hand, signed a Real Though Heretofore a Misguided American." John Adams had proclaimed May 9 a day of fasting and prayer; his critics dubbed it a tawdry effort to wrap his bellicose policy in the robe of religion.

"The President conceived it to be an incendiary letter written to alarm and distress the inhabitants," Abigail said. "Another letter of the same purport was sent ten days after, thrust under the door of Mr. Otis's office." Samuel Otis was secretary of the Senate. "These with some rumours of combinations got abroad, and the mayor, aldermen etc. kept some persons upon the watch through all parts of the city, and the governor gave orders privately to have a troop of horse in case of need."

The supporters of the administration turned out in force. "There were assembled upon the occasion, it is said, ten thousand persons. This street"—Market Street—"as wide or wider than State Street in Boston, was full as far as we could see up and down," Abigail Adams wrote. "One might have walked upon their heads, besides the houses' windows and even tops of houses. In great order and decorum the young men with each a black cockade marched through the multitude and all of them entered the house preceded by their committee." The black cockade had been adopted by young Federalists as an emblem of support for the administration.

"The President received them in his levee room dressed in his uniform"—the outfit he had worn as diplomat to foreign governments— "and, as usual upon such occasions, read his answer to them, after which they all retired. The multitude gave three cheers and followed them to the State House yard, where the answer to the address was again read by the chairman of the committee. With acclamations they then closed the scene by singing the new song"—a patriotic air composed for the day—"which at 12 o'clock at night was sung by them under our windows, they having dined"—and apparently drunk—"together."

They weren't finished. "This scene burnt in the hearts of some Jacobins and they determined either to terrify or bully the young men out of their patriotism," Abigail Adams said. "Bache published some saucy pieces the young men resented, and he would have felt the effects of their resentment if some cooler heads had not interposed." In fact Benjamin Bache did feel the resentment, in the form of vandalism against his house.

After all this, the day of fasting and prayer finally came. "Yesterday was observed with much solemnity," Abigail Adams told her sister.

"The meetinghouses and churches were filled. About four o'clock, as is usual, the State House yard which is used for a walk, was very full of the inhabitants, when about 30 fellows, some with snow balls in their hats, and some with tri-couloured cockades, entered and attempted to seize upon the hats of the young men to tear out their cockades. A scuffle ensued when the young men became conquerors, and some of these tri-couloured cockades were trampled in the dust. One fellow was taken and committed to jail, but this was sufficient to alarm the inhabitants, and there were everywhere large collections of people. The light horse were called out and patrolled the streets all night. A guard was placed before this house, though through the whole of the proceedings, and amidst all the collection, the President's name was not once mentioned nor any one grievance complained of; but a foreign attempt to try their strength and to stir the inhabitants if possible was no doubt at the bottom."

Abigail Adams laid the blame at the feet of Benjamin Bache. "This Bache is cursing and abusing daily," she said. "If that fellow, and his agents, chronicle and all, is not suppressed, we shall come to a civil war."

Abigail Adams was not the only person telling her husband that Bache and other critics of the administration ought to be suppressed. But she had the president's ear in a way no one else did, and in a way she herself often had not. During much of John Adams's career, he and his wife were separated by hundreds or thousands of miles. In the Adams team, John took care of the public front as a diplomat or an elected official, while Abigail handled the home front, raising the children and running the farm. Occasionally she accompanied him on assignment. One of the reasons John disliked France so much was that Abigail couldn't stand the French men and especially women they encountered in Paris. Even during John's presidency, Abigail sometimes stayed in Quincy. But in 1798, amid the XYZ furor, she was with him in Philadelphia and gave him the daily benefit of her decided opinions.

As the spring of the year became summer, she grew more convinced that the Republicans were bent on destroying the government. "The Jacobins are plotting to raise the devil here," she wrote to her brother William in June. "There is an endeavour to raise a number of volunteers called *Republican Blues,* in opposition to Macpherson's Blues"—a Federalist militia named for its commander during the Whiskey Rebellion—"to excite a spirit of hostility against each other. Bache's brother the doctor"—William Bache—"is to be captain of it." Abigail Adams didn't mind a Federalist militia, which would defend the government and the status quo. But a Republican militia was illegitimate and subversive. "This measure of raising *Republican companies* is designed to defeat the other if possible, and to raise a spirit of hostility in the very bosom of the city," she said. "The *Republican Blues* will be *united Irishmen* and foreigners of all descriptions." Ireland was then a British colony, and Irish rebels against British rule received aid from France, making Irish republicans French agents in the minds of many American Federalists. "This system will be pursued in unison wherever they can disseminate their doctrine," Abigail Adams said.

She was glad her residence in Philadelphia was only temporary. "In New England we are a different kind of people from the Southern," she told William, putting all Americans south of New York in a single category. New Englanders were mostly good Federalists. In the rest of the country there were too many Republicans. "I believe it impossible for honesty and truth to reside in the breast of a Jacobin," she said.

Bache outraged her daily. "You see by the papers that Bache has begun his old billingsgate again," Abigail wrote to Mary Cranch after the *Aurora* had accused John Adams of nepotism in appointing his son John Quincy Adams to a foreign post. Bache and his partners in slander never rested. "There is no end to their audaciousness." They were doing the bidding of the French government. "French emissaries are in every corner of the union sowing and spreading their sedition," Abigail wrote. "We have *renewed information* that their system is to calumniate the President, his family, his administration until they oblige him to resign, and then they will reign triumphant, *headed by the Man of the People*"—her derisive term for Jefferson. "It behooves every pen and press to counteract them, but our countrymen in general are not awake to their danger. We are come now to a crisis too important to be languid, too dangerous to slumber, unless we are determined to submit to the fraternal embrace, which is sure and certain destruction as the poisoned shirt of Denarius"—which killed Heracles in Greek myth.

Abigail Adams saw French agents everywhere. "It would be difficult for you at the distance you are to conceive the change which has taken place in this city, the center of foreign influence and Jacobinism," she wrote to John Quincy Adams. The effect was most noticeable among the ordinary people. "The *real French* men, the *unprincipled Jacobin*, the *emissaries of France remain unchanged*, but real Americans who have been deceived and betrayed by falsehood and deception are the mass of the lower class of the people." Yet she hoped the true Americans might awake and strike back. "I would fain hope that the Hydra monster of Jacobinism is crushed never to rise with such mischievous effects again."

Again she blamed an unrestricted press for the troubles that vexed the nation. "As calumny and abuse upon the fairest characters and the best men in France was one of the most powerful engines employed to overturn one set of rulers and in setting up others who in their turn shared the same fate, so have their emissaries adopted the same weapons in this country," Abigail wrote to Mercy Otis Warren. "And the liberty of the press is become licentious beyond any former period. The good sense of the American people in general directs them right, where they can see and judge for themselves, but in distant and remote parts of the union, this continued abuse, deception and falsehood is productive of great mischief and tends to destroy that confidence and harmony which is the life, health and security of a republic."

"I wish the laws of our country were competent to punish the stirrer up of sedition, the writer and printer of base and unfounded calumny," Abigail Adams wrote. "This would contribute as much to the peace and harmony of our country as any measure." The enemies of America had neither honor nor shame. "Daringly do the vile incendiaries keep up in Bache's paper the most wicked and base, violent and calumniating abuse." In attacking the government, the *Aurora* undermined the essence of republicanism. "It insults the majesty of the sovereign people." The government must act. "Nothing will have an effect until Congress pass a sedition bill."

## 53

CONGRESS WAS LISTENING. In late June, a sedition bill was introduced in the Senate, where Federalists outnumbered Republicans by more than two to one. It passed easily and in early July was sent to the House, where the Federalist advantage was smaller. The most controversial part of the bill would criminalize "any false, scandalous and malicious writing or writings against the government of the United States, or either house of the Congress of the United States, or the President of the United States, with intent to defame the said government, or either house of the said Congress, or the said President, or to bring them, or either of them, into contempt or disrepute."

The proponents of the bill proclaimed a crisis of the republic resulting from an alliance of interests between the government of France and publishers like Benjamin Bache. "If ever there was a nation which required a law of this kind it is this," said John Allen of Connecticut. "Let gentlemen look at certain papers printed in this city and elsewhere and ask themselves whether an unwarrantable and dangerous combination does not exist to overturn and ruin the government by publishing the most shameless falsehoods against the representatives of the people." The barbarians were at the very gates, Allen declared. "I say, sir, a combination, a conspiracy against the Constitution, the government, the peace and safety of this country is formed and is in full operation. It embraces members of all classes, the representative of the people on this floor the wild and visionary theorist in the bloody philosophy of the day, the learned and ignorant."

Allen got specific. "In the *Aurora* of last Tuesday is this paragraph: 'Where a law shall have been passed in violation of the Constitution, making it criminal to expose the crimes, the official vices or abuses, or the attempts of men in power to usurp a despotic authority, is there any alternative between an abandonment of the Constitution and resistance?'" Referring to Bache as "this infamous printer," Allen asked how his "tocsin of insurrection" could be tolerated. "Are we bound hand and foot that we must be witnesses of these deadly thrusts at our liberty? Are we to be the unresisting spectators of these exertions to destroy all that we hold dear? Are these approaches to revolution and Jacobinic domination to be observed with the eye of meek submission?"

If this was freedom of the press, said Allen, America must reject it. "God deliver us from such liberty, the liberty of vomiting on the public floods of falsehood and hatred to everything sacred, human and divine!" Freedom of the press had produced all the baneful consequences of the French revolution. "If any gentleman doubts the effects of such a liberty, let me direct his attention across the water; it has there made slaves of thirty millions of men." Freedom of the press had been employed by French radicals as a tool to force their tyrannical views on the rest of the country. As in France, so in America if the opponents of this bill had their way. "The Jacobins of our country, too, sir, are determined to preserve in their hands the same weapon; it is our business to wrest it from them."

Albert Gallatin, the Pennsylvania Republican, rose to rebut Allen. The country had survived without a sedition law for more than two decades, Gallatin said. Why the sudden demand for one? "Does the situation of the country at this time require that any law of this kind should pass? Do there exist such new and alarming symptoms of sedition as render it necessary?" Had the administration suddenly lost confidence in its own arguments? "Was the gentleman afraid, or rather was the administration afraid, that in this instance error could not be successfully opposed by truth? The American government had heretofore subsisted, it had acquired strength, it had grown on the affection of the people; it had been fully supported without the assistance of laws similar to the bill now on the table. It had been able to repel opposition by the single weapon of argument." Allen and the other Federalists protested entirely too much. "At present, when out of ten presses in the country nine are employed on the side of the administration, such is their want of confidence in the purity of their own views and motives that they even fear the unequal contest and require the help of force in order to suppress the limited circulation of the opinions of those who do not approve all their measures." The proposed bill was not only pernicious, it was unnecessary. It deserved to be rejected.

BUT THE BILL was not rejected. It passed narrowly on a partisan vote. Three other measures, restricting the rights of resident aliens, who were often portrayed by the Federalists as actual or potential agents of the French government, were likewise passed during this period. Adams signed them all.

Of the Alien and Sedition Acts, as the measures were collectively called, the Sedition Act was the one that aroused the greatest furor. The Constitution said nothing about the rights of aliens, who in any case were ineffectively positioned to protest the new restrictions. But the First Amendment explicitly protected freedom of the press, and those targeted by the Sedition Act often had their own newspapers to complain in.

"The Constitution of the United States says that 'Congress shall make no law abridging freedom of speech or of the press,'" Bache wrote on the day the Sedition Act was approved. "But Congress have passed a law abridging the freedom of the press and therefore the Constitution is infracted. Quere: Of what efficacy is a law made in direct contravention of the Constitution?"

Bache's query was of direct importance to him. The law gave him new cause to assail the administration, which thereupon employed the law to arrest him for violating it. He wasn't alone; dozens of other administration critics were arrested at that time and in the following months. The Republican press didn't fall completely silent, but its voice became harder to hear—just as the sedition law intended.

THE QUESTION OF WHAT to do about a law that violated the Constitution was bigger than Bache and the editors, or even than the First Amendment. Until this point Congress and the president had interpreted the Constitution as they went along. Debates arose between the legislative and executive branches over their respective authorities—in the matter of which branch should declare neutrality between Britain and France, for example. But never yet had the legislature and the executive ganged up on the Constitution, jointly challenging the plain language of the charter.

Eventually the country would look to the third branch of the federal government, the judiciary, to defend the Constitution. But the Constitution offered no guidance on this subject. Article Six suggested that the federal judiciary could negate acts of the states that were contrary to the Constitution or federal law. Yet it said nothing about such a judicial power to negate acts of *Congress* that contravened the Constitution. Nor had the judiciary asserted such a power. Moreover, even if the judiciary did claim it, the legislature and the executive might not yield. And if the three branches of the government happened to align on a controversial issue—a sedition law, for instance—the states might deny the authority of the federal government as a whole.

Jefferson and Madison had been watching with concern as the Federalists ratcheted up their war on the Republican papers. "The object of that is the suppression of the Whig presses," Jefferson wrote to Madison. He feared that the Federalist strategy might work. "If these papers fall, republicanism will be entirely browbeaten."

Jefferson wasn't alarmist by nature, and he had faith in the American people. "Party passions are indeed high," he acknowledged to a correspondent who had written to that effect. "Nobody has more reason to know it than myself. I receive daily bitter proofs of it from people who never saw me, nor know anything of me but through Porcupine and Fenno"—flaming Federalists William Cobbett, writing as Peter Porcupine, and John Fenno. "At this moment all the passions are boiling over." Yet he hoped the passions would diminish. "The fever will not last," he predicted. The American people would regain their senses. "They are essentially republican. They retain unadulterated the principles of '75, and those who are conscious of no change in themselves have nothing to fear in the long run."

Yet in the meantime, the ruckus was threatening the union. One of Jefferson's informants suggested that New England had foisted its desires upon the country; Jefferson replied, "It is true that we are completely under the saddle of Massachusetts and Connecticut, and that they ride us very hard, cruelly insulting our feelings as well as exhausting our strength and subsistence. Their natural friends, the three other eastern states, join them from a sort of family pride, and they have the art to divide certain other parts of the Union so as to make use of them to govern the whole." But this wasn't new. "It is the old practice of despots: to use a part of the people to keep the rest in order. And those who have once got an ascendancy, and possessed themselves of all the resources of the nation, their revenues and offices, have immense means for retaining their advantage."

Jefferson reiterated that this was an anomaly. "Our present situation is not a natural one. The republicans, through every part of the Union, say that it was the irresistible influence and popularity of General Washington played off by the cunning of Hamilton which turned the government over to anti-republican hands, or turned the republicans chosen by the people into anti-republicans." Washington had retired, but things hadn't improved. "Very untoward events since, improved with great artifice, have produced on the public mind the impressions we see."

Some Republicans were suggesting that the only remedy was a separation of the Republican South from the Federalist Northeast. Jefferson saw nothing good coming from such thinking. "In every free and deliberating society, there must, from the nature of man, be opposite parties, and violent dissensions and discords; and one of these, for the most part, must prevail over the other for a longer or shorter time," he said. "Perhaps this party division is necessary to induce each to watch and delate"—report—"to the people the proceedings of the other. But if on a temporary superiority of the one party, the other is to resort to a scission of the Union, no federal government can ever exist. If to rid ourselves of the present rule of Massachusetts and Connecticut, we break the Union, will the evil stop there? Suppose the New England states alone cut off, will our nature be changed? Are we not men still to the south of that, and with all the passions of men? Immediately, we shall see a Pennsylvania and a Virginia party arise in the residuary confederacy, and the public mind will be distracted with the same party spirit."

Even absent actual separation, such talk could do grave damage. "What a game too will the one party have in their hands, by eternally threatening the other that unless they do so and so, they will join their northern neighbors," Jefferson said. "If we reduce our Union to Virginia and North Carolina, immediately the conflict will be established between the representatives of these two States, and they will end by breaking into their simple units."

Humans were simply quarrelsome, Jefferson said. "Seeing, therefore, that an association of men who will not quarrel with one another is a thing which never yet existed, from the greatest confederacy of nations down to a town meeting or a vestry; seeing that we must have some-body to quarrel with, I had rather keep our New England associates for that purpose, than to see our bickerings transferred to others."

Everyone should take a breath. "A little patience, and we shall see the reign of witches pass over, their spells dissolved, and the people recovering their true sight, restoring their government to its true prin-ciples," Jefferson said.

YET HE AND other Republicans had to do something, for one of those principles was respect for the Constitution, which the Federalists now flouted. "This bill and the alien bill both are so palpably in the teeth of the Constitution as to shew they mean to pay no respect to it," Jefferson wrote to Madison.

The question was: What could be done to enforce respect? Put oth-erwise: How could the states or the people rein in a federal government that trampled the Constitution?

Jefferson, working with Madison, proposed just such a mechanism. The Constitution balanced the powers of the states against those of the nation, with the Tenth Amendment reserving to the states—and the people—the powers not expressly delegated to Congress. Jefferson and Madison determined to employ the reserved authority of the states against the national government on the Alien and Sedition Acts. Their own judgment was that Congress and the president had overstepped, and they encouraged like-minded legislators in the states to pass reso-lutions to this effect.

Such resolutions would carry weight in themselves, but no less important were the consequences that would follow. The national government at this stage of its development had little in the way of enforcement capacity, which was why George Washington had had to summon state militiamen against the whiskey rebels in Pennsylvania. The central government relied on the states to facilitate federal opera-tions such as the delivery of mail and the collection of import duties. If a state refused to cooperate in the enforcement of a federal law, or if it actively resisted that law, it could exercise a de facto veto. And if several states joined in the refusal or resistance, the law might be effectively overturned.

Carrying out this plan was a delicate business. As vice president, Jefferson had a responsibility to the national government, and his plan involved an effort to undermine that government, or at least to undermine the authority claimed for it by the party that currently controlled it. By no means would his action constitute treason; the Constitution was very clear in its narrow definition of that crime. But Jefferson would be engaged in the sort of obstruction the Sedition Act was designed to prevent.

He moved carefully. He assumed his mail was being read by postmasters, who owed their jobs to the Federalist administration. "Always examine the seal before you open my letters," he wrote to James Monroe. To John Taylor, a Virginia friend and political ally, Jefferson remarked, "The infidelities of the post office and the circumstances of the times are against my writing fully and freely. . . . I know not which mortifies me most, that I should fear to write what I think, or my country bear such a state of things." To Madison, whom Jefferson enlisted as a partner in the endeavor, he simply sent nothing by mail about the project, saving communication for when they could meet in person.

To Taylor, Jefferson laid out his thinking on the strategy of opposition. "For the present, I should be for resolving the alien and sedition laws to be against the constitution and merely void, and for addressing the other states to obtain similar declarations," he said. "And I would not do anything at this moment which should commit us further, but reserve ourselves to shape our future measures or no measures, by the events which may happen. It is a singular phenomenon, that while our state governments are the very *best in the world*, without exception or comparison, our general government has, in the rapid course of 9 or 10 years, become more arbitrary, and has swallowed more of the public liberty than even that of England."

JEFFERSON DRAFTED a protest against the Alien and Sedition Acts. He cast it as a series of resolutions, beginning with the most philosophical. "Resolved: That the several states composing the United States of America are not united on the principle of unlimited submission to their general government; but that by a compact under the style and title of a Constitution for the United States, and of amendments thereto, they constituted a general government for special purposes, delegated to that government certain definite powers, reserving, each state to itself, the residuary mass of right to their own self-government; and that whensoever the General government assumes undelegated powers, its acts are unauthoritative, void, and of no force; that to this compact each state acceded as a state, and is an integral party, its co-states forming, as to itself, the other party; that the government created by this compact was not made the exclusive or final judge of the extent of the powers delegated to itself, since that would have made its discretion, and not the Constitution, the measure of its powers, but that, as in all other cases of compact among powers having no common judge, each party has an equal right to judge for itself, as well of infractions as of the mode and measure of redress."

The final assertion here, that the central government could not be the judge in its own case, was obvious to Jefferson. When governments became the judges of their own actions, they quickly devolved into despotism. By making the states the judges of the actions of the central government, Jefferson would forestall this.

His second resolution cited the Tenth Amendment specifically as reserving undelegated powers to the states and to the people. Because the Constitution had not delegated the powers claimed by the Alien and Sedition Acts, those acts were "altogether void and of no force."

Jefferson's third resolution adduced the First Amendment's protection of free speech and press. Because the Sedition Act contradicted this amendment, it too was "altogether void and of no force."

The fourth resolution assailed the Alien Act as usurping the powers of the states over voting and other rights within their borders, without the express approval of the Constitution. It was, therefore, "altogether void and of no force."

Four more resolutions culminated in an assertion of state authority to veto measures adopted by the general government but unsupported by the Constitution. "Where powers are assumed which have not been delegated, a nullification of the act is the rightful remedy,"

Jefferson declared. "Every state has a natural right, in cases not within the compact (casus non foederis) to nullify of their own authority all assumptions of power by others within their limit." Nullification would forestall more-dire consequences. "These and successive acts of the same character, unless arrested at the threshold, necessarily drive these states into revolution and blood, and will furnish new calumnies against republican government, and new pretexts for those who wish it to be believed that man cannot be governed but by a rod of iron."


JEFFERSON OFTEN FOUND himself in the middle of controversy, but he rarely sought out such ground. He preferred calm and quiet, being no Patrick Henry or Samuel Adams. In the present case he sidestepped the debate by disguising his authorship of the resolutions against the Alien and Sedition Acts. As long as he lived he never definitively acknowledged his role in drafting them. He didn't wish to incur more criticism than he was receiving already; no less to the point, he had no authority in the adoption of such resolutions. He was merely offering suggestions to state legislators who agreed that they might play a part in restraining the federal government as it was being directed by the Federalists.

The legislators who took him up were Kentucky's. Republicans there controlled the state assembly, and in November 1798 they approved a set of resolutions drawn directly from Jefferson's. The Kentucky resolutions copied Jefferson's repeated use of the phrase "void and of no force," applied to acts of Congress deemed unsupported by the Constitution. In the editing process, the Kentucky lawmakers elided "nullify" and "nullification" from their version. However, a streamlined resolution approved by the Kentucky assembly in 1799 followed Jefferson all the way to "nullification," declaring it to be the rightful remedy against the aggrandizements of the general government.

The question of word choice would pique interest decades later, when John Calhoun of South Carolina and others developed a more comprehensive theory of nullification and its corollary, secession. In 1798, no one noticed the omission of the term in the Kentucky resolutions, not least because almost no one knew of Jefferson's role in drafting the model the Kentuckians employed. Consequently no one asked

Jefferson to elaborate on nullification or to explain what *he* thought its corollaries might be.

MADISON ADOPTED a more cautious line. While agreeing with Jefferson on the unconstitutionality of the Alien and Sedition Acts, Madison thought the Republicans should take care not to fall into the Federalists' trap by letting themselves be portrayed as promoting disunion. As the first in a series of resolutions he drafted for the Virginia legislature, which duly approved them, Madison wrote: "Resolved, that the General Assembly of Virginia doth unequivocally express a firm resolution to maintain and defend the constitution of the United States, and the constitution of this state, against every aggression, either foreign or domestic, and that they will support the government of the United States in all measures warranted by the former."

Madison's second resolution echoed the first but got more to the point: "That this Assembly most solemnly declares a warm attachment to the Union of the States, to maintain which it pledges all its powers; and that for this end, it is their duty to watch over and oppose every infraction of those principles which constitute the only basis of that union, because a faithful observance of them can alone secure its existence and the public happiness."

Although disavowing anything hinting of disunion, Madison articulated the principle that would form the basis of secessionist thought: "That this Assembly doth explicitly and peremptorily declare that it views the powers of the federal government as resulting from the compact to which the states are parties." The theory of American government as a compact of states started from the simple observations that the states had existed before the federal government and had created the federal government, and proceeded to the conclusion that the states might un-create the federal government by withdrawing.

Madison didn't draw out this implication; he left that for others. But he did say that the powers of the federal government were "limited by the plain sense and intention of the instrument"—the Constitution—"constituting that compact; as no farther valid than they are authorised by the grants enumerated in that compact, and that in case of a deliberate, palpable and dangerous exercise of other powers not granted by the said compact, the states who are parties thereto have the right, and are in duty bound, to interpose for arresting the progress of the evil, and for maintaining within their respective limits, the authorities, rights and liberties appertaining to them." Here Madison eschewed Jefferson's "nullify" in favor of the less categorical and more nebulous "interpose."

Yet Madison left nothing vague in the displeasure the Virginia legislature felt about the direction of Federalist policies. "The General Assembly doth also express its deep regret that a spirit has in sundry instances been manifested by the federal government to enlarge its powers by forced constructions of the constitutional charter which defines them; and that indications have appeared of a design to expound certain general phrases (which having been copied from the very limited grant of powers in the former Articles of Confederation were the less liable to be misconstrued) so as to destroy the meaning and effect of the particular enumeration, which necessarily explains and limits the general phrases; and so as to consolidate the states by degrees into one sovereignty, the obvious tendency and inevitable consequence of which would be, to transform the present republican system of the United States into an absolute, or at best a mixed monarchy."

Madison made use of the fact that Virginia's ratifying convention had called for a bill of rights. He didn't mention that he had opposed that call at the Virginia convention, but with the zeal of the convert and the jealousy of the author of the Bill of Rights, he asserted Virginia's responsibility to the rights specified therein. "It would mark a reproachful inconsistency and criminal degeneracy if an indifference were now shewn to the most palpable violation of one of the rights thus declared and secured," he said.

In Madison's words, Virginia summoned other states to protest the recent unconstitutional legislation. "The General Assembly doth solemnly appeal to the like dispositions of the other states, in confidence that they will concur with this commonwealth in declaring, as it does hereby declare, that the acts aforesaid are unconstitutional, and that the necessary and proper measures will be taken by each for cooperating with this state in maintaining unimpaired the authorities, rights and liberties reserved to the states respectively, or to the people."

## 54

I N AUGUST 1798, Adams sent an order to the commanders of American warships. "You are hereby authorized, instructed and directed to
subdue, seize and take any armed French vessel or vessels sailing under
authority, or pretence of authority, from the French Republic which
shall be found within the jurisdictional limits of the United States or
elsewhere on the high seas," the president said.

Adams was ordering the American navy to war. He did so without
a declaration of war by Congress, although he did cite congressional
authorization to defend American ships against French depredations.
Conspicuously Adams did not order the army to war, partly because he
wanted to contain the conflict with France and partly because the army
wasn't ready to fight.

Adams had found what he considered the appropriate balance
between diplomacy and war in the face of French attacks on American rights and property. Diplomacy unaided by force had failed so far;
now he would add a measure of force. But not too much: the French
offenses had been confined to the high seas, and so the American
response would be confined to the high seas. If the French escalated,
for example to attacks on American ports, then Adams could escalate too and attack French islands in the West Indies. He didn't think
it would come to that, and he hoped it wouldn't. Adams didn't want
a general war. He wanted the French to end the naval war they had
started. And he wanted to terminate the alliance with France that still
hung around America's neck.

There was another reason Adams didn't want a regular war. He was an unlikely and uncomfortable commander in chief. Anyone would have been, coming after Washington. And Adams's interest and experience had been in law, diplomacy and politics, not in war and the martial arts.

A naval war he could leave to the navy men. In preparation, Adams had persuaded Congress to add a fifth member to the cabinet, a navy secretary. Benjamin Stoddert was a Maryland merchant who had fought in the Revolutionary War. His mercantile experience had attuned him to matters maritime, and his time in the army to the affairs of war. Adams relied on Stoddert to ready the navy for battle and to direct naval strategy.

Adams intervened when naval affairs intersected larger issues. The British decided that their interest for the moment lay in helping the Americans against the French; Adams was willing to accept the help but only when necessary and then quietly. "The French 60 or 80 privateers out of Guadeloupe must be generally very small and trifling I should think," Adams wrote to Stoddert not long after the American campaign began. "We shall be very indiscreet if we depend on the English to protect our commerce or destroy French privateers." Yet English assistance would be appreciated all the same. "Whether their ships in the West Indies have been sickly, or whatever has been the cause of their inactivity, it has been very remarkable. We must depend on God and our right as well as the English."

For their part the French, still at peace with Britain, hoped to employ their recent and age-old enemy against their current one. "The sentiment of Beauvarlet that it is incumbent on all Europe to unite for the purpose of checking the progress of the United States, no doubt he thought very profound," Adams remarked to Stoddert. "It is true, there is an European jealousy against America, but we have one fortunate resource—One half of Europe is always pitted against the other, and in the last resort, we can join ourselves with one moiety or other. Britain and France united against America! This will not happen as long as Britain's power, revenue and being depends so much on American commerce."

Adams let Stoddert choose the officers for the navy, but he occasionally supplied a suggestion as to their management. Undeclared war, by its nature, was a complicated business, and participants sometimes had trouble determining where the line lay between acceptable and unacceptable behavior. Captain Thomas Truxtun erred on the side of aggressiveness, thereby worrying Stoddert. Adams told him not to fear. "I wish all the other officers had as much zeal as Truxton," Adams said. The navy could use more energy. "If you correct Truxton's ardor a little, as you ought to do, I pray you to do it very gently and with great delicacy. I would not have it damped for the world."

Adams urged greater energy in American strategy as a whole. After several months of what was being called the "quasi-war," the French government hinted at a desire to end it. Adams told Stoddert to press America's advantage. "Some of our fast sailing vessels might be employed to advantage in a cruise on the coasts of Spain and France during the hurricane season in the West Indies," he said. Let the French and their allies feel the taste of war near home. "Nor do I think we ought to wait a moment to know whether the French mean to give us any proofs of their desire to conciliate with us. I am for pursuing all the measures of defence which the laws authorize us to adopt, especially at sea, with as much zeal and to as great an extent as if we knew the first vessels would bring us a declaration of war against us from Paris."

YET ADAMS NEVER considered escalating to general war. He had been happy to enlist Washington as a figure around which the country might rally, but he foresaw little need to send him into the field. The French wouldn't be foolish enough to attack the United States frontally when war in Europe might break out again at any moment. "At present there is no more prospect of seeing a French army here than there is in Heaven," Adams wrote to James McHenry in October 1798. And when the European war did resume the following month, the prospect became slimmer still.

Adams was relieved. The army was becoming a financial burden on the government and another source of partisan friction. The Republicans had long accused the Federalists of wanting to create a standing army, which would be a constant temptation to corruption as elected officials channeled funds to favored vendors. More alarmingly, the army might be used to intimidate opponents of the administration, as the state militias had intimidated the whiskey rebels.

Adams was thrifty by nature and as opposed to corruption in government as any Republican. He didn't pick political fights except on principle. Supporting a standing army didn't qualify. The provisional army had never met its recruiting quotas, and Adams was happy to let it die. "There has been no rational plan that I have seen as yet formed for the maintenance of the army," he wrote to McHenry. "One thing I know, that regiments are costly articles everywhere and more so in this country than in any other under the sun." For the Federalists to continue to fund the army was a losing proposition all around. "If this nation sees a great army to maintain without an enemy to fight, there may arise an enthusiasm"—uproar—"that seems to be little foreseen."

The demise of the army disappointed the jobbers who had hoped to batten on it, and perhaps their sponsors in Congress. Others had mixed feelings. Alexander Hamilton had just won his contest to be appointed Washington's second in command when the resumption of war in Europe killed any chance of gallantry on horseback. But on the positive side it eliminated any chance of being killed on horseback.

Hamilton got what he wanted most—the rank and title of general—even without seeing action. And he received a bonus after Washington relinquished command upon realizing there would be no fighting. Hamilton made a point of staying longer than Washington, so that for a few months he was the highest-ranking officer in the army of the United States. He did not, however, receive the rank of commanding general of the army; Adams denied him that.

# PART VIII

# The Revolution of 1800

## 55

THE ELECTION CAMPAIGN of 1800 began in early 1799. Jefferson's diffidence toward office had disappeared amid the fight over the Alien and Sedition Acts, when he concluded that American republicanism was in real peril. John Adams, far from being a bulwark against the radical Hamiltonians, had fallen into league with them in ravaging the Constitution. He had led the country to war against France, circumventing the requirement that Congress, not the president, should wield this most fateful of government powers. And in doing so, he endangered republicanism not merely in America but in Europe too.

Jefferson consulted with Madison and James Monroe. They planned his campaign with care—and with caution. "I shall seldom write to you, on account of the strong suspicions of infidelity in the post offices," he told Madison. "Always examine the seal before you open my letters, and note whether the impression is distinct."

Jefferson gave no speeches; candidates for office still did not do so. But he did describe his views in letters to influential persons, including Elbridge Gerry, who had asked where Jefferson stood on various issues. Federalist papers had been imputing to Jefferson ideas and convictions he didn't hold; often he ignored the misrepresentations, but not always. "In confutation of these and all future calumnies, by way of anticipation, I shall make to you a profession of my political faith, in confidence that you will consider every future imputation on me of a contrary complexion, as bearing on its front the mark of falsehood and calumny," he wrote to Gerry.

"I do then, with sincere zeal, wish an inviolable preservation of our present federal constitution, according to the true sense in which it was adopted by the states, that in which it was advocated by its friends, and not that which its enemies apprehended, who therefore became its enemies," Jefferson said. "And I am opposed to the monarchising its features by the forms of its administration, with a view to conciliate a first transition to a President and Senate for life, and from that to a hereditary tenure of these offices, and thus to worm out the elective principle." From this followed his belief in the legitimate balance between the different arms of government. "I am for preserving to the states the powers not yielded by them to the Union, and to the legislature of the Union its constitutional share in the division of powers; and I am not for transferring all the powers of the states to the general government, and all those of that government to the Executive branch."

Government power must constantly be restrained. "I am for a government rigorously frugal and simple, applying all the possible savings of the public revenue to the discharge of the national debt; and not for a multiplication of officers and salaries merely to make partisans, and for increasing, by every device, the public debt, on the principle of its being a public blessing," Jefferson wrote. He opposed a standing army and a large navy. "I am for relying, for internal defence, on our militia solely, till actual invasion, and for such a naval force only as may protect our coasts and harbors from such depredations as we have experienced; and not for a standing army in time of peace, which may overawe the public sentiment; nor for a navy which, by its own expenses and the eternal wars in which it will implicate us, grind us with public burthens, and sink us under them."

America's foreign policy should be modest. "I am for free commerce with all nations; political connection with none; and little or no diplomatic establishment. And I am not for linking ourselves by new treaties with the quarrels of Europe; entering that field of slaughter to preserve their balance, or joining in the confederacy of kings to war against the principles of liberty."

The power of government must be checked wherever it encroached on the liberty of citizens. "I am for freedom of religion, and against all maneuvres to bring about a legal ascendancy of one sect over another; for freedom of the press, and against all violations of the Constitution to silence by force and not by reason the complaints or criticisms, just or unjust, of our citizens against the conduct of their agents."

He acknowledged his support of the French revolution when it stood for republican principles. "I was a sincere well-wisher to the success of the French revolution, and still wish it may end in the establishment of a free and well-ordered republic." But he gave no carte blanche to the French government. "I have not been insensible under the atrocious depredations they have committed on our commerce."

Yet France was secondary. "The first object of my heart is my own country. In that is embarked my family, my fortune, and my own existence. I have not one farthing of interest, nor one fibre of attachment out of it, nor a single motive of preference of any one nation to another, but in proportion as they are more or less friendly to us. But though deeply feeling the injuries of France, I did not think war the surest means of redressing them. I did believe, that a mission sincerely disposed to preserve peace, would obtain for us a peaceable and honorable settlement and retribution."

"These, my friend, are my principles," Jefferson concluded to Gerry. "They are unquestionably the principles of the great body of our fellow citizens." He added, in words to Gerry but meant equally for other moderates, "I know there is not one of them which is not yours also. In truth, we never differed but on one ground, the funding system; and as, from the moment of its being adopted by the constituted authorities, I became religiously principled in the sacred discharge of it to the uttermost farthing, we are united now even on that single ground of difference." The principles they shared had not guided American policy during much of the previous several years, but Jefferson sensed a turning. "The unquestionable republicanism of the American mind will break through the mist under which it has been clouded, and will oblige its agents to reform the principles and practices of their administration."

Jefferson said more in this letter, intended for Gerry's eyes only. And he cautioned Gerry to be careful with this letter. "Besides the accidents which might happen to it even under your care, considering the accident of death to which you are liable, I think it safest to pray you, after reading it as often as you please, to destroy at least the 2d and 3d leaves. The 1st contains principles only, which I fear not to avow; but the 2d and 3d contain facts stated for your information, and which, though sacredly conformable to my firm belief, yet would be galling to some, and expose me to illiberal attacks. I therefore repeat my prayer to burn the 2d and 3d leaves."

Jefferson marveled at what politics had come to. "Did we ever expect to see the day when, breathing nothing but sentiments of love to our country and its freedom and happiness, our correspondence must be as secret as if we were hatching its destruction! Adieu, my friend, and accept my sincere and affectionate salutations. I need not add my signature."

TO OTHER ALLIES, Jefferson wrote urging action. Edmund Pendleton was now chief justice of Virginia, still active at almost the end of his eighth decade. "Your patriarchal address to your county is running through all the republican papers, and has a very great effect on the people," Jefferson complimented Pendleton, speaking of a recent message to the residents of Caroline County. "It is short, simple, and presents things in a view they readily comprehend. The character and circumstances too of the writer leave them without doubts of his motives." Jefferson hoped Pendleton would turn his wisdom and eloquence to a larger audience. "You know what a wicked use has been made of the French negotiation; and particularly the XYZ dish cooked up by Marshall, where the swindlers are made to appear as the French government." Pendleton was just the man to write a rebuttal. "Nobody in America can do it so well as yourself, in the same character of the father of your county, or any form you like better, and so concise, as omitting nothing material, may yet be printed in hand bills, of which we could print and disperse 10 or 20,000 copies under letter covers, through all the U.S., by the members of Congress when they return home." Such an effort would go far toward putting the country back on its true course. "If the understanding of the people could be rallied to the truth on this subject, by exposing the dupery practiced on them, there are so many other things about to bear on them favorably for the resurrection of their republican spirit, that a reduction of the administration to constitutional principles cannot fail to be the effect."

Jefferson took heart from responses to the resolutions he and Madison had written for Kentucky and Virginia. "Petitions and remonstrances against the alien and sedition laws are coming from various parts of New York, New Jersey, and Pennsylvania, some of them very well drawn," he wrote to Madison. "I am in hopes Virginia will stand so countenanced by those states as to repress the wishes of the government to coerce her, which they might venture on if they supposed she would be left alone." Yet the Republicans must move carefully. "Firmness on our part, but a passive firmness, is the true course. Anything rash or threatening might check the favorable dispositions of these middle States, and rally them again around the measures which are ruining us."

Jefferson judged that Adams and the Federalists had overreached. "The violations of the Constitution, propensities to war, to expense, and to a particular foreign connection, which we have lately seen, are becoming evident to the people, and are dispelling that mist which XYZ had spread before their eyes," he told Edmund Pendleton. "This state"—Pennsylvania: he was writing from Philadelphia—"is coming forward with a boldness not yet seen. Even the German counties of York and Lancaster, hitherto the most devoted"—to Federalism— "have come about, and by petitions with 4,000 signers remonstrate against the Alien and Sedition laws, standing armies, and discretionary powers in the President. New York and Jersey are also getting into great agitation."

Yet again he urged caution. "In this state, we fear that the ill designing may produce insurrection. Nothing could be so fatal. Anything like force would check the progress of the public opinion and rally them round the government. This is not the kind of opposition the American people will permit. But keep away all show of force, and they will bear down the evil propensities of the government, by the constitutional means of election and petition. If we can keep quiet, therefore, the tide now turning will take a steady and proper direction. Even in New Hampshire"—a Federalist bastion—"there are strong symptoms of a rising inquietude."

Jefferson employed the moment to renew his call to Pendleton to enter the arena. "In this state of things, my dear sir, it is more in your power than any other man's in the U.S., to give the *coup de grâce* to the ruinous principles and practices we have seen. In hopes you have consented to it, I shall furnish to you some additional matter which has arisen since my last."

To another Republican, Jefferson wrote, "The spirit of 1776 is not dead. It has only been slumbering. The body of the American people is substantially republican. But their virtuous feelings have been played on by some fact with more fiction; they have been the dupes of artful maneuvres, and made for a moment to be willing instruments in forging chains for themselves. But time and truth have dissipated the delusion, and opened their eyes." The inroads in the middle states were especially heartening. "Pennsylvania, Jersey and New York are coming majestically round to the true principles. In Pennsylvania, 13 out of 22 counties had already petitioned on the alien and sedition laws. Jersey and New York had begun the same movement, and though the rising of Congress stops that channel for the expression of their sentiment, the sentiment is going on rapidly, and before their next meeting those three states will be solidly embodied in sentiment with the six Southern and Western ones."

## 56

B Y THE AUTUMN of 1799, Jefferson was confident enough of his presidential chances to begin drawing an electoral map. "Georgia, North Carolina, Tennessee, Kentucky, Virginia, Maryland and Pennsylvania choose their electors by the people directly," he observed to Wilson Nicholas, an Albemarle County neighbor bound for the Senate and later the governorship of Virginia. "In Massachusetts the choice is, first by the people in districts; but if a candidate had not a majority of all the qualified voters of the district, it devolves on the legislature to appoint the elector for that district. Besides, as they have but 14 districts (laid off for some state purpose) and are entitled to 16 electors, the legislature name the two extra ones in the first instance. Again, if any of those elected either by the people or legislature die, or decline to act, the residue of the electors fill up the vacancies themselves. In this way the people of Massachusetts chose 7 electors on the last occasion, and the legislature 9. In New Hampshire, Rhode Island, Connecticut, Vermont, New York, Jersey, Delaware and South Carolina, the legislature name electors."

The states with the popular vote for electors were mostly southern and western, and were already Republican, with the exception of Pennsylvania, which Jefferson hoped was becoming so. The states where the legislatures chose electors were mostly northern and eastern, and leaned Federalist. This was fitting, Jefferson thought: the Federalists didn't trust the people. Jefferson couldn't imagine New England turn-

ing Republican overnight, but he looked with hope to Pennsylvania
and New York, two states that might decide the election.

The calculations grew more intricate as the election approached.
And Jefferson took greater care than ever. "I have today had a conversation with 113 who has taken a flying trip here from New York,"
Jefferson wrote to James Monroe in January 1800. "113" was the code
for Aaron Burr, who again would be Jefferson's running mate. Jefferson
valued Burr primarily for his political acumen, which Jefferson hoped
would suffice to deliver New York. "He says they have really now a
majority in the house of representatives"—the New York assembly—
"but for want of some skillful person to rally round, they are disjointed,
and will lose every question. In the senate there is a majority of 8 or 9
against us. But in the new election which is to come on in April, three
or four in the senate will be changed in our favor; and in the house of
representatives, the county elections will still be better than the last; but
still all will depend on the city election, which is of 12 members." Burr
had expressed confidence regarding the city vote, and he gave Jefferson
confidence. "At present there would be no doubt of our carrying our
ticket there," Jefferson told Monroe. "Nor does there seem to be time
for any events arising to change that disposition. There is therefore the
best prospect possible of a great and decided majority on a joint vote
of the two houses."

In this letter to Monroe, Jefferson wondered if his ambition was
showing. "Perhaps it will be thought I ought in delicacy to be silent
on this subject," he said. "But you, who know me, know that my private gratifications would be most indulged by that issue which should
leave me most at home. If anything supersedes this propensity, it is
merely the desire to see this government brought back to its republican
principles."

STARTLING REPORTS FROM Europe threatened to overturn Jefferson's calculations. Napoleon Bonaparte was said to have seized the
French government, replacing the Directory with what he called the
Consulate, a body he declared to be more representative of the will of
the French people. Jefferson was skeptical. "Should it be really true that
Buonaparte has usurped the government with an intention of making
it a free one, whatever his talents may be for war, we have no proofs

that he is skilled in forming governments friendly to the people," Jefferson wrote to Thomas Randolph, his son-in-law. "Wherever he has meddled we have seen nothing but fragments of the old Roman government stuck into materials with which they can form no cohesion; we see the bigotry of an Italian to the ancient splendour of his country, but nothing which bespeaks a luminous view of the organization of rational government."

Jefferson didn't rule out improvement. "This may end better than we augur, and it certainly will if his head is equal to true and solid calculations of glory. It is generally hoped here that peace may take place." A peace settlement would be a blessing, to America no less than to Europe. "We have great need of this event, that foreign affairs may no longer bear so heavily on ours. We have great need for the ensuing twelve months to be left to ourselves."

Absent peace, Jefferson feared an American Bonaparte, probably Hamilton. "The enemies of our constitution are preparing a fearful operation, and the dissensions in this state are too likely to bring things to the situation they wish, when our Buonaparte, surrounded by his comrades in arms, may step in to give us political salvation in his way." Peace in Europe would make an American coup d'état less likely. Even so, Americans must be vigilant. "It behooves our citizens to be on their guard, to be firm in their principles, and full of confidence in themselves. We are able to preserve our self-government if we will but think so."

Jefferson knew that Napoleon's actions, if they proved despotic, would be charged against Republicans in America, on account of the Republicans' not having sided with Britain against France. Jefferson interpreted matters differently. "I fear our friends on the other side of the water, laboring in the same cause, have yet a great deal of crime and misery to wade through," he wrote of the French to Samuel Adams in Boston. "My confidence has been placed in the head, not in the heart of Buonaparte. I hoped he would calculate truly the difference between the fame of a Washington and a Cromwell. Whatever his views may be, he has at least transferred the destinies of the republic from the civil to the military arm. Some will use this as a lesson against the practicability of republican government. I read it as a lesson against the danger of standing armies."

·　　·　　·

THE FEDERALISTS GOT little mileage out of Napoleon. Rather, they continued to lose ground. "The Federalists begin to be very seriously alarmed about their election next fall," Jefferson wrote to Madison in March 1800. "Their speeches in private, as well as their public and private demeanor to me, indicate it strongly."

But Jefferson wasn't ready to celebrate. Much might still happen. Yet though he couldn't be sure the Republicans would carry the presidency at the coming election, he was certain their cause would prevail before long. "Whatever it may be, and my experience of the art, industry, and resources of the other party has not permitted me to be prematurely confident, yet I am entirely confident that ultimately the great body of the people are passing over from them," he wrote in late April. "This may require one or two elections more, but it will assuredly take place. The madness and extravagance of their career is what ensures it. The people through all the states are for republican forms, republican principles, simplicity, economy, religious and civil freedom."

Jefferson believed the Federalist project was doomed to fail. "Our country is too large to have all its affairs directed by a single government," he declared. "Public servants at such a distance, and from under the eye of their constituents, must, from the circumstance of distance, be unable to administer and overlook all the details necessary for the good government of the citizens, and the same circumstance, by rendering detection impossible to their constituents, will invite the public agents to corruption, plunder and waste."

Republicanism recognized and countered this tendency, Jefferson said. "The true theory of our constitution is surely the wisest and best, that the states are independent as to everything within themselves, and united as to everything respecting foreign nations. Let the general government be reduced to foreign concerns only, and let our affairs be disentangled from those of all other nations, except as to commerce, which the merchants will manage the better, the more they are left free to manage for themselves, and our general government may be reduced to a very simple organization, and a very unexpensive one; a few plain duties to be performed by a few servants."

## 57

A s THE CAMPAIGN careened toward its end, the attacks on Jefferson mounted. His advocacy of freedom of religion, and in particular the disestablishment of the Episcopal church in Virginia, had earned him the enmity of many ministers of established churches throughout the country, including Connecticut, where the Congregational church continued to receive taxpayer support. Timothy Dwight was the most prominent Congregational minister in Connecticut, besides being president of Yale College. Dwight regularly preached on the danger posed to the Christian faith by infidels in politics like Jefferson. "The sins of these enemies of Christ and Christians are of numbers and degrees which mock account and description," he said. "All that the malice and atheism of the dragon, the cruelty and rapacity of the beast, and the fraud and deceit of the false prophet, can generate or accomplish swell the list. No personal or national interest of man has been uninvaded; no impious sentiment or action against God has been spared; no malignant hostility against Christ and his religion has been unattempted."

Dwight here declined to mention Jefferson by name, whether from political delicacy or belief that the name of the beast must not be spoken. But his congregants and students, and the larger Federalist community of New England, understood to whom he was referring. Nor was Dwight exactly providing election counsel, but the implication was clear. "For what end shall we be connected with men of whom this is the character and conduct? Is it that we may assume the same character and pursue the same conduct? Is it that our churches may become temples of reason, our Sabbath a decade"—the tenth day of the French revolutionary calendar—"and our psalms of praise Marseillois hymns? Is it that we may change our holy worship into a dance of Jacobin phrenzy, and that we may behold a strumpet personating a goddess on the altars of Jehovah? Is it that we may see the Bible cast into a bonfire, the vessels of the sacramental supper borne by an ass in public procession, and our children, either wheedled or terrified, uniting in the mob, chanting mockeries against God, and hailing in the sounds of *Ca ira*"—a French revolutionary anthem—"the ruin of their religion and the loss of their souls? Is it that we may see our wives and daughters the victims of legal prostitution, soberly dishonoured, speciously polluted, the outcasts of delicacy and virtue, and the loathing of God and man? Is it that we may see in our public papers a solemn comparison drawn by an American mother club between the Lord Jesus Christ and a new Marat, and the fiend of malice and fraud exalted above the glorious Redeemer? Shall we, my brethren, become partakers of these sins? Shall we introduce them into our government, our schools, our families? Shall our sons become the disciples of Voltaire, and the dragoons of Marat; or our daughters the concubines of the Illuminati?"

William Linn, a New York Presbyterian minister, devoted a disquisition to Jefferson's heresies. Jefferson denied the miracles recounted in the Bible and derided what Christians held sacred, Linn said. He related at third hand a story of a visitor to Monticello who went riding with Jefferson. The visitor observed the dilapidated condition of a church they passed. Jefferson replied, "It is good enough for him that was born in a manger." Linn remarked, "Such a contemptuous sling at the blessed Jesus could issue from the lips of no other than a deadly foe to his name and his cause." Jefferson had long championed freedom of religion; Linn was horrified. "Would this not be a nation of atheists? Is it not natural, after the free declaration of such a sentiment, to suspect the man himself of Atheism?" Linn tolerated freedom of conscience as a matter of law, but Jefferson took things too far. "Though neither the constitution nor any law forbids his election, yet the public opinion ought to disqualify him. On account of his disbelief of the Holy Scriptures and his attempts to discredit them, he ought to be rejected from the presidency." Americans must consider what would happen if Jefferson were elected. "The effects would be to destroy religion, introduce immorality and loosen all the bonds of society," Linn said. "Let the first magistrate be a professed infidel, and infidels will surround him. Let him spend the Sabbath in feasting, in visiting or receiving visits, in riding abroad, but never in going to church; and to frequent public worship will become unfashionable. Infidelity will become the prattle from the highest to the lowest condition in life, and universal dissoluteness will follow. 'The wicked walk on every side when the vilest men are exalted.'"

JEFFERSON WAS DISINCLINED to respond to most of the charges leveled against him. "As to the calumny of atheism, I am so broken to calumnies of every kind, from every department of government, executive, legislative and judiciary, and from every minion of theirs holding office or seeking it, that I entirely disregard it," he wrote to James Monroe. "It has been so impossible to contradict all their lies that I have determined to contradict none; for while I should be engaged with one, they would publish twenty new ones."

Yet he felt obliged to say something, if only in private. "I have a view of the subject which ought to displease neither the rational Christian nor Deists, and would reconcile many to a character they have too hastily rejected," Jefferson wrote to Benjamin Rush, who couldn't keep a secret, as Jefferson knew. Jefferson's philosophy of belief was simple, he said. "I have sworn upon the altar of god, eternal hostility against every form of tyranny over the mind of man." This formula affirmed Jefferson's belief in God, on whose altar he swore. It simultaneously insisted that all people be free to worship—or not worship—as they saw fit.

## 58

A DAMS SUFFERED his own share of slander, not least at the hands of Jefferson's slanderer-for-hire James Callender. The author of the exposé on Hamilton's affair with Maria Reynolds found himself a prime target for prosecution under the Sedition Act. He skipped ahead of the law from Philadelphia to Richmond, where he found newspaper work while composing a takedown of Adams in time for the 1800 election campaign. Callender faulted Adams for innumerable failures of policy, but he warned voters to pay particular attention to Adams's character. "Ye will judge without regard to the prattle of a president, the prattle of that strange compound of ignorance and ferocity, of deceit and weakness, without regard to that hideous hermaphroditical character, which has neither the force and firmness of a man, nor the gentleness and sensibility of a woman."

This time the prosecutors caught up with Callender, and he was convicted, fined and sent to prison for his unwelcome words. By then, though, Adams had a more formidable print antagonist: Alexander Hamilton.

Hamilton's opposition began as an elaboration of the sabotage he had attempted in 1796. Elections in New York City returned a majority of Republicans. "The moral certainty therefore is that there will be an Anti-Federal majority in the ensuing legislature," Hamilton observed to John Jay, now New York's governor. Because the legislature would choose New York's presidential electors, this was bad news for the Federalist ticket. "The very high probability is that this will bring *Jefferson* into the Chief Magistracy, unless it be prevented by the measure which I shall now submit to your consideration, namely the immediate calling together of the existing legislature." What Hamilton was proposing was to defeat the will of the people by having the repudiated legislature choose the electors.

"I am aware that there are weighty objections to the measure; but the reasons for it appear to me to outweigh the objections," Hamilton said. "And in times like these in which we live, it will not do to be over-scrupulous. It is easy to sacrifice the substantial interests of society by a strict adherence to ordinary rules."

Hamilton said he wasn't asking Jay to act dishonestly. "I shall not be supposed to mean that anything ought to be done which integrity will forbid, but merely that the scruples of delicacy and propriety, as rela-tive to a common course of things, ought to yield to the extraordinary nature of the crisis. They ought not to hinder the taking of a *legal* and *constitutional* step to prevent an *Atheist* in Religion and a *Fanatic* in politics from getting possession of the helm of the state."

Hamilton guessed that Jay wasn't as convinced as he was of the malignity of the Republicans. "You do not know them as well as I do," Hamilton said. "'Tis a composition indeed of very incongruous mate-rials but all tending to mischief—some of them to the overthrow of the government by stripping it of its due energies, others of them to a revo-lution after the manner of Buonaparte. I speak from indubitable facts, not from conjectures and inferences. In proportion as the true character of this party is understood is the force of the considerations which urge to every effort to disappoint it. And it seems to me that there is a very solemn obligation to employ the means in our power."

Jay read Hamilton's letter and rejected his scheme. At the bottom of the letter, the governor jotted, "Proposing a measure for party purposes which I think it would not become me to adopt."

Hamilton turned his efforts in another direction. As he had done in 1796, he urged Federalist electors to demote Adams on the Federalist ticket, in this case favoring Charles Cotesworth Pinckney. Again as he had done, he at first proposed putting the two Federalist candidates on an equal footing. "To support Adams and Pinckney equally is the only thing that can possibly save us from the fangs of Jefferson," he wrote to Theodore Sedgwick, a Massachusetts Federalist.

Before long, Hamilton's implicit preference for Pinckney became explicit. Sedgwick had responded with testimony from a fellow Federalist who argued that Adams remained a favorite among party members. Hamilton challenged Sedgwick's informant. "He is I am persuaded much mistaken as to the opinion entertained of Mr. Adams by the Federal party," Hamilton said. "Were I to determine from my own observation I should say, *most* of the *most influential men* of that party consider him as a very *unfit* and *incapable* character."

Speaking for himself, Hamilton continued, "My mind is made up. I will never more be responsible for him by my direct support, even though the consequence should be the election of *Jefferson.* If we must have an *enemy* at the head of the government, let it be one whom we can oppose and for whom we are not responsible, who will not involve our party in the disgrace of his foolish and bad measures. Under *Adams* as under *Jefferson* the government will sink. The party in the hands of whose chief it shall sink will sink with it, and the advantage will all be on the side of his adversaries."

Hamilton declared that support for Adams represented a failure of what the Federalists stood for. "'Tis a notable expedient for keeping the Federal party together to have at the head of it a man who hates and is despised by those men of it who in time past have been its most efficient supporters. If the cause is to be sacrificed to a weak and perverse man, I withdraw from the party and act upon my own ground— never certainly against my principles, but in pursuance of them in my own way. I am mistaken if others will not do the same. The only way to prevent a fatal schism in the Federal party is to support General Pinckney in good earnest."

Hamilton took his campaign against Adams on the road. Arthur Fenner, the governor of Rhode Island, received a visit from Hamilton at his home in Newport. "General Hamilton was very familiar, open and candid," Fenner later recounted. "He at once began the election of the President, supposing, as he said, that I should be one of the electors, to which no reply was made by me at that moment respecting my not being one. He observed that he had been to the eastward upon the business, and that it was concluded upon to run for Adams and Charles Cotesworth Pinckney; that all New England would vote for them, and that the electors to the southward that voted for Adams would vote for Pinckney, and a number to the southward that voted for Jefferson would also vote for Pinckney, by which Mr. Pinckney would certainly succeed.

"I then asked him what Mr. Adams had done that he should be tipped out of the tail of the cart," Fenner continued. "He answered, that Mr. Adams could not succeed, and that it was better to lose the man than the measures. I replied that my attachment for Mr. Adams was much greater now than it was before when I gave him my vote"—in 1796—"that he had sent envoys to France to endeavor to reconcile the two countries and that there were great prospects of a happy issue; that he had disbanded an unnecessary army, and dismissed his secretaries who were opposed to his pacific measures, and that his eyes were now opened and he saw the danger he had run by being led by a set of men who were, in my opinion, under the influence of the British, and that it was my opinion Mr. Pinckney was too much attached to the British interest to be our chief magistrate."

Hamilton differed vehemently. "He observed that as I had no acquaintance with Mr. Pinckney he would inform me that he was *all* before Mr. Jefferson for president. Mr. Jefferson was a man of no judgment; he could write a pretty book, it was true, and gave some hard words; that if I should hear the two converse together he was sure of my judgment coinciding with his."

Fenner told Hamilton he missed the point. "My reply was that I had said nothing respecting Jefferson; all that I had said was in favor of Adams."

Hamilton again told Fenner he was wrong. "He replied, Adams is out of the question, it is Pinckney and Jefferson."

"I asked him if that was really the case; he answered in the affirmative; my reply was that if that was really the case, if I was an elector, if a hundred votes were my proportion to give, they would all be given for Jefferson in preference to Pinckney, for the British yoke I abhorred."

THIS WAS HARDLY the first time Hamilton had been called a catspaw for the British, but now it annoyed him more than ever. And he thought he knew the one to blame. "I have serious thoughts of writing to the *President* to tell him that I have heard of his having repeatedly mentioned the existence of a British faction in this country and alluded to me as one of that faction," Hamilton wrote to Oliver Wolcott. "His friends are industrious in propagating the idea to defeat the efforts to unite for Pinckney. The inquiry I propose may furnish an antidote and vindicate character. What think you of the idea?" Hamilton added, "For my part I can set malice at defiance."

Wolcott didn't talk him out of it, and Hamilton went ahead. "Sir," he wrote to Adams, conspicuously omitting "dear" or other polite adjective. "It has been repeatedly mentioned to me that you have on different occasions asserted the existence of a *British faction* in this country, embracing a number of leading or influential characters of the *Federal Party* (as usually denominated) and that you have sometimes named me, at other times plainly alluded to me, as one of this description of persons. And I have likewise been assured that of late some of your warm adherents, for electioneering purposes, have employed a corresponding language."

Hamilton invited Adams to deny the reports. "I must, sir, take it for granted, that you cannot have made such assertions or insinuations without being willing to avow them and to assign the reasons to a party who may conceive himself injured by them. I therefore trust that you will not deem it improper that I apply directly to yourself, to ascertain from you, in reference to your own declarations, whether the information I have received has been correct or not, and if correct what are the grounds upon which you have founded the suggestion."

Hamilton waited for a reply. None came.

"The time which has elapsed since my letter of the first of August was delivered to you precludes the further expectation of an answer," he wrote to Adams on October 1. "From this silence, I will draw no inference; nor will I presume to judge of the fitness of silence on such an occasion on the part of the Chief Magistrate of a republic towards a citizen who without a stain has discharged so many important public trusts. But this much I will affirm, that by whomsoever a charge of the kind mentioned in my former letter may, at any time, have been made or insinuated against me, it is a base wicked and cruel calumny, destitute even of a plausible pretext to excuse the folly or mask the depravity which must have dictated it."

As Hamilton and Adams well knew, the language of Hamilton's two letters was of a tenor often followed by a challenge to a duel. Even had his office not precluded it, Adams was of no mind to give Hamilton such satisfaction. So Hamilton sought satisfaction otherwise.

In late October a very long letter written by Hamilton was printed in pamphlet form, addressed to an unspecified "sir." Hamilton might initially have intended to circulate this letter among a select group of Federalists, perhaps the Federalist electors and those most influential with them. Yet he must have known that the chances of limiting its circulation were slim. And indeed when Aaron Burr got wind of the printing, he arranged to have the more provocative portions published in the *Aurora*. Thereupon Hamilton decided to release the whole thing to the public, which might have been his intention all along.

In contrast to Hamilton's many anonymous writings, this letter displayed a tone that was patently personal. "Some of the warm personal friends of Mr. ADAMS are taking unwearied pains to disparage the motives of those Federalists who advocate the equal support of Gen. PINCKNEY at the approaching election of President and Vice-President," Hamilton wrote. As readers would have known, Hamilton headed this group. The allegations against them were varied but always derogatory. "Sometimes they are versatile, factious spirits, who cannot be long satisfied with any chief, however meritorious," he said, paraphrasing one of the criticisms leveled against him. "Sometimes they are ambitious spirits, who can be contented with no man that will not submit to be governed by them. Sometimes they are intriguing partisans of Great Britain, who, devoted to the advancement of her views, are incensed against Mr. ADAMS for the independent impartiality of his conduct."

Hamilton observed that his critics claimed that his dissatisfaction with Adams resulted from the president's refusal to make him commanding general of the army. This was entirely wrong, Hamilton said. His disappointment long antedated any recent actions by the president, however spiteful those might have been. Hamilton said he had originally admired Adams for his early role in promoting independence from Britain. "My imagination had exalted him to a high eminence as a man of patriotic, bold, profound and comprehensive mind." But he had discovered his error soon enough. "In the progress of the war, opinions were ascribed to him which brought into question, with me, the solidity of his understanding. He was represented to be of the number of those who favored the enlistment of our troops annually, or for short periods, rather than for the term of the war—a blind and infatuated policy directly contrary to the urgent recommendation of General WASHINGTON, and which had nearly proved the ruin of our cause."

Other misjudgments had followed, Hamilton said. Yet revelation of the true character of Adams—his arrogance and selfishness—awaited the end of the war and the adoption of the Constitution. In the first presidential contest, everyone understood that Washington should be president, and many were willing for Adams to be second. "Great was my astonishment, and equally great my regret, when, afterwards, I learned from persons of unquestionable veracity, that Mr. ADAMS had complained of unfair treatment in not having been permitted to take an equal chance with General WASHINGTON, by leaving the votes to an uninfluenced current. The extreme egotism of the temper which could blind a man to considerations so obvious as those that had recommended the course pursued cannot be enforced by my comment. It exceeded all that I had imagined, and shewed, in too strong a light, that the vanity which I have ascribed to him existed to a degree that rendered it more than a harmless foible."

When Washington retired, Adams became the Federalists' choice to be his successor. But the choice was not an enthusiastic one. "By this time, men of principal influence in the Federal Party whose situation had led them to an intimate acquaintance with Mr. ADAM's character began to entertain serious doubts about his fitness for the station," Hamilton wrote. "Yet his pretensions in several respects were so strong that after mature reflection they thought it better to indulge their hopes than to listen to their fears." Even then, Adams had resented efforts to promote Thomas Pinckney on an equal basis with himself. The irony was not lost on Hamilton, though it escaped Adams. "Mr. ADAMS, who had evinced discontent because he had not been permitted to take an equal chance with General WASHINGTON, was enraged with all those who had thought that Mr. PINCKNEY ought to have had an equal chance with him."

As president, Adams's weakness were never more apparent than in his inconsistent handling of the diplomatic mission to France. "The desolutoriness of his mind is evinced by the very different grounds upon which, at different times, he has defended the propriety of the mission," Hamilton said. "Sometimes he has treated with ridicule the idea of its being a measure which would terminate in peace, asserting that France would not accommodate on terms admissible by the United States, and that the effect to be expected from the mission was the demonstration of this truth and the union of public opinion on the necessity of war. Sometimes, and most frequently, he has vindicated the measure as one conformable with the general and strong wish of the country for peace, and as likely to promote that desirable object."

Adams's inconsistencies were chronic, and they reflected his "ungovernable temper," Hamilton said. "It is a fact that he is often liable to paroxysms of anger, which deprive him of self command, and produce very outrageous behaviour to those who approach him. Most if not all his ministers and several distinguished members of the two houses of Congress have been humiliated by the effects of these gusts of passion."

Adams dismissed able cabinet secretaries for no good reason, Hamilton said. James McHenry was one. "A prominent charge was that the secretary in a report to the House of Representatives had *eulogized General Washington,* and had attempted to eulogize General *Hamilton,* which was adduced as one proof of a combination in which the secretary was engaged to depreciate and injure him, the President. Wonderful! passing Wonderful! that an eulogy of the dead patriot and hero, of the admired and beloved WASHINGTON, consecrated in the affections and reverence of his country, should in any shape be irksome to the ears of his successor! Singular, also that an encomium on the officer"—Hamilton—"first in rank in the armies of the United States, appointed and continued by Mr. ADAMS, should in his eyes have been a crime in the head of the War Department, and that it should be necessary, in order to avert his displeasure, to obliterate a compliment to that officer from an official report."

Though Hamilton had denied his own mistreatment as grounds for his criticism of Adams, he took the opportunity to set straight the record on that subject. "The circumstances of my late military situation have much less to do with my personal discontent than some others," Hamilton wrote. "In respect to them, I shall only say that I owed my appointment to the station and rank I held, to the *express stipulation* of General WASHINGTON when he accepted the command of the Army, afterwards *peremptorily insisted upon* by him in *opposition* to the *strong wishes* of the President; and that, though second in rank, I was not promoted to the first place, when it became vacant, by the death of the

Commander in Chief. As to the former, I should have had no cause to complain if there had not been an apparent inconsistency in the measures of the President; if he had not nominated me *first* on the list of major generals, and attempted afterwards to place me *third* in rank. As to the latter, the chief command, not being a matter of routine, the not promoting me to it, cannot be deemed a wrong or injury; yet certainly I could not see in the omission any proof of good will or confidence, or of a disposition to console me for the persecutions which I had incessantly endured. But I dismiss the subject, leaving to others to judge of my pretensions to the promotion and of the weight, if any, which they ought to have had with the President."

Hamilton claimed to have been injured more recently. "I was accused of having contributed to the loss of the election in New York, out of ill will to Mr. ADAMS." This charge was ludicrous. "Who is so blind as not to see that if actuated by such a motive, I should have preferred, by the success of the election, to have secured the choice of electors for the state of New York who would have been likely to cooperate in the views by which I was governed?"

Yet this was the way the mind and soul of Adams worked. "To those who have not had opportunities of closely inspecting the weaknesses of Mr. ADAMS's character, the details of this extraordinary interview would appear incredible," Hamilton wrote. "But to those who have had these opportunities, they would not even furnish an occasion of surprise. But they would be, to all who knew their truth, irrefragable proofs of his unfitness for the station of Chief Magistrate."

## 59

J EFFERSON HADN'T EXPECTED such help from Hamilton, and he might not have needed it. The voting broke much as Jefferson had predicted before the Hamilton pamphlet appeared. The Republican ticket carried everything south of Pennsylvania, except Delaware's three electors and four of North Carolina's twelve. The Federalist ticket swept New England. Of the three middle states, the Republicans won New York and the Federalists New Jersey, and the two parties split Pennsylvania, which cast eight Republican votes and seven Federalist. The totals were 73 for the Republicans and 65 for the Federalists.

But the result came with a complication. The Republican electors voted in lockstep, giving Jefferson and Aaron Burr 73 votes each. The aim had been for at least one Republican elector to withhold a vote from Burr, but neither Jefferson nor other party leaders specified which elector it would be. No vote was withheld, and Jefferson and Burr tied, sending the contest to the House of Representatives. The Republicans swamped the Federalists in the elections to the House, but the new members wouldn't take office until after the vote for president. The Federalists in the House, smarting from their ouster and tempted to mischief, would decide which Republican—Jefferson or Burr—would become president.

BURR ASSURED JEFFERSON that he understood his subordinate position. The Republicans had intended that Jefferson be president, and

Burr would honor that intention. "My personal friends are perfectly informed of my wishes on the subject and can never think of diverting a single vote from you," he wrote to Jefferson. "On the contrary, they will be found among your most zealous adherents." In the House, each state's delegation would cast a single vote. Nine votes would make a majority. "I see no reason to doubt of you having at least nine states," Burr said. The Republicans were united behind Jefferson, and would remain so. "It is the unanimous determination of the Republicans of every grade to support your administration with unremitted zeal."

Burr's assurances didn't prevent various Federalists from hatching plots to deny Jefferson the presidency. They dangled the prize of the office before Burr, hoping to win concessions from him in exchange.

Jefferson wasn't surprised at the intriguing. "It was to be expected that the enemy would endeavor to sow tares between us, that they might divide us and our friends," he wrote to Burr in February. He expressed his confidence in Burr. "Every consideration satisfies me you will be on your guard against this, as I assure you I am strongly."

But he sent a warning. "I hear of one stratagem so imposing and so base that it is proper I should notice it to you. Mr. Munford, who is here, says he saw at New York before he left it, an original letter of mine to Judge Breckenridge in which are sentiments highly injurious to you. He knows my handwriting and did not doubt that to be genuine. I enclose you a copy taken from the press copy of the only letter I ever wrote to Judge Breckenridge in my life. The press copy itself has been shewn to several of our mutual friends here. Of consequence the letter seen by Mr. Munford must be a forgery, and if it contains a sentiment unfriendly or disrespectful to you, I affirm it solemnly to be a forgery; as also if it varies from the copy enclosed. With the common trash of slander I should not think of troubling you; but the forgery of one's handwriting is too imposing to be neglected."

Jefferson concluded, "A mutual knowledge of each other furnishes us with the best test of the contrivances which will be practised by the enemies of both. Accept assurances of my high respect and esteem."

Burr reiterated that Jefferson had nothing to worry about. "It was so obvious that the most malignant spirit of slander and intrigue would be busy that, without any inquiry, I set down as calumny every tale calculated to disturb our harmony," he wrote to Jefferson. "My friends are often more irritable and more credulous. Fortunately I am the deposi-tory of all their cares and anxieties, and I invariably pronounce to be a lie everything which ought not to be true. My former letter should have assured you of all this by anticipation."

In any case, Burr said, he hadn't encountered the particular ploy Jefferson had described. "Munford never told me what you relate, and if he had, it would have made no impression on me. Your solicitude on this occasion, though groundless, is friendly and obliging."

HAMILTON HAD HOPED to be kingmaker, but between Adams and Pinckney. That effort had failed. Yet he still wanted to matter, to have a seat at the table of decision. He might never reach the head of the table, not after the Maria Reynolds affair. But who knew? If the coun-try continued on its downward course, the people might turn to a man of energy and talent, even one with a private blemish on his record.

In the meantime he would be kingmaker between Jefferson and Burr. He had said that if the country were to sink, better that it sink under Jefferson. Now that the Federalists had lost, he was sure it was going to sink. So, indeed, better under Jefferson.

Under no circumstances should Burr win the presidency. As much as Hamilton despised Jefferson, he hated and feared Burr. The rivalry ran back decades, to when Hamilton was first climbing the ladder of New York society and politics. Burr had much of what Hamilton wanted: social position, personal connections, political friends. And Burr was clever—as clever as Hamilton but in a smoother, less pushy way. Burr glided past opponents where Hamilton knocked them down. Burr made allies easily; Hamilton couldn't help making enemies. When Hamilton looked to the future—*his* future—he didn't worry about Adams and Jefferson, his seniors by twenty years and twelve years respectively. They would be gone in time for him to mount a come-back, if such were possible. But Burr, born within months of Hamilton, might forever block his way.

So Hamilton launched a ferocious assault on Burr. In letters to key Federalists, Hamilton declared Burr a danger to the country and an individual utterly unfit to be president. "His private character is not defended by his most partial friends," Hamilton wrote to Oliver Wolcott. "He is bankrupt beyond redemption except by the plunder of his country. His public principles have no other spring or aim than his own aggrandisement per *fas* et *nefas*"—by fair means or foul. "If he can, he will certainly disturb our institutions to secure to himself *permanent power* and with it *wealth*. He is truly the *Cataline* of America." To Gouverneur Morris, Hamilton said of Burr, "He is sanguine enough to hope everything—daring enough to attempt everything—wicked enough to scruple nothing. From the elevation of such a man heaven preserve the country!" In another letter to Morris, Hamilton declared, "It is a fact that Mr. Burr is now in frequent and close conference with a Frenchman who is suspected of being an agent of the French government, and it is not to be doubted that he will be the firm ally of Buonaparte." To James Bayard of Delaware, Hamilton wrote, "The maintenance of the existing institutions will not suit him, because under them his power will be too narrow and too precarious." To Theodore Sedgwick: "The appointment of Burr as President would disgrace our country abroad. No agreement with him could be relied upon. His private circumstances render disorder a necessary resource. His public principles offer no obstacle. His ambition aims at nothing short of permanent power and wealth in his own person. For heaven's sake let not the Federal party be responsible for the elevation of this man."

Hamilton stressed the responsibility argument in a second letter to Wolcott. "If Jefferson is president, the whole responsibility of bad measures will rest with the Anti-federalists," he said. "If Burr is made so by the Federalists, the whole responsibility will rest with them. The other party will say to the people: We intended him only for Vice President. Here he might have done very well or been at least harmless. But the Federalists to disappoint us and a majority of you took advantage of a momentary superiority to put him in the first place. He is therefore their president and they must answer for all the evils of his bad conduct." The Federalists must not let this happen, Hamilton said. "Adieu to the Federal Troy if they once introduce this Grecian Horse into their citadel."

In all these letters, Hamilton concluded by declaring that Jefferson would be the lesser evil. "There is no doubt but that upon every virtuous and prudent calculation Jefferson is to be preferred," he summarized to Wolcott. "He is by far not so dangerous a man and he has pretensions to character." To Gouverneur Morris, Hamilton posed and answered the determinative question: "*Jefferson* or *Burr?*—the former without all doubt." To James Bayard, Hamilton insisted that under no circumstances should Burr be elevated past Jefferson. "For Heaven's sake, my dear sir, exert yourself to the utmost to save our country from so great a calamity."

HAMILTON'S BARRAGE PRODUCED no clear effect for several weeks. The Federalists in the House delayed a vote, desperate to squeeze as much political effect as possible from their final moments in control. A constitutional crisis loomed. Adams's term would expire, and if no president were in place, the powers of office might fall to John Marshall, currently secretary of state. To some Federalists, this outcome appeared preferable to handing the presidency to a Republican.

Any such scheme would require the cooperation or at least the acquiescence of the president. Adams observed the scheming and weighed his options. He was as convinced as Hamilton that the ascendancy of Jefferson and the Republicans would be the downfall of America. The Federalists he continued to correspond with told him so. "I dread the effect of those political evils that surround us, especially of that disunion which I now hold as inevitable, in every sense that can be annexed to disunion," a Boston lawyer and old friend wrote to Adams. Another Federalist stalwart declared in anguish, "To see mock patriots, learned cheats and weak rogues mingling their lies and leading an host of dupes to retail them in every street and corner to trample down merit honour and patriotism clouds the morning of the new century." This writer blamed the American people for choosing radical Jefferson over reliable Adams. "That the successful efforts of a whole life, arduous as dangerous, through the untried scenes of a mighty revolution, from dependence to empire, should so lightly touch the springs of reason or gratitude, as that talents in embryo and merit unborn could assume the reins of supreme rule sickens the mind and dims the regions of hope. Events so unworthy the national character are ominous of its future destiny."

Adams's son Thomas pronounced a plague on both parties, starting with Hamilton's wing of the Federalists. "The adherents of Mr. Hamilton are men of violence, impetuous in their resentments and utterly regardless of the ties of gratitude," Thomas wrote to Adams. "They can discern no title to favor or support in any but devoted partisans. In general they are hostile to our present institutions, and therefore feel no obligation imposed upon them to promote the success of them. They imagine that opposition is the only means to effect a change more consonant to their wishes." The Jeffersonians were no better. "The Democrats, who are a vast majority when compared with this small band, profess that the design and scope of their opposition is to restore the government of the Country to old, original principles. The plausibility of their doctrines is irresistibly persuasive with the multitude, who have in all ages been gulled out of their liberties by such gilded artifices. They yield to the siren song of these base and profligate seducers, who no sooner have robbed them of their chastity than they desert them, or impose heavier shackles than they wore before."

Elbridge Gerry wrote to say he worried that the political name-calling and partisan warring would tear the country apart. The president should proceed cautiously. Gerry said he had preferred Adams for president above the other candidates, but now that the voters had spoken the president should not dignify any efforts to keep Jefferson from office. In particular he should steer clear of the schemes to put Burr ahead of Jefferson or to deadlock the House vote. "Although the elevation to the chair of Mr. Burr, if accomplished, will be perfectly constitutional, and will demand the support of every friend to the Union, it will serve to increase the exasperation which has threatened its destruction," Gerry said. "And if faction in our counsels should so far prevail as to prevent the choice of either of the candidates, it will present to our view the dreary prospect of a political convulsion."

Adams took Gerry's counsel seriously. "I lament with you the arbitrary application of party nicknames and unpopular appellations," he said. Yet he didn't think anything he did or refrained from doing would make much difference. "I heartily wish, yet I cannot say I hope, that the wickedness of the wicked will come to an end. On the contrary it appears to me, that unlike the rising light which shineth more and more to the perfect day, the darkness will thicken till it may be felt."

Nor did Adams think the danger would be lessened by anything the House did. "I know no more danger of a political convulsion if a President pro tem of the Senate or a Secretary of State or Speaker of the house should be made President by Congress than if Mr. Jefferson or Mr. Burr is declared such," he told Gerry. "The President would be as legal in one case as in either of the others, in my opinion, and the people as well as satisfied. This however must be followed by another election and Mr. Jefferson would be chosen. I should in that case decline the election. We shall be tossed at any rate in the tempestuous sea of liberty for years to come, and where the bark can land but in a political convulsion I cannot see." Adams could only pray for the best. "I wish the good ship to her desired harbor."

PERHAPS ABIGAIL ADAMS HEARD the metaphor of the stormy sea from her husband; perhaps Adams got it from her; or perhaps it was just in the turbulent air of the capital in early 1801. Whatever the case, Abigail employed it in a letter she wrote to Thomas Adams in late January. "I have enclosed you a curious conversation, which though at table, was not heard by anyone but ourselves, as we spoke low," she said. Her interlocutor was Jefferson, the setting a dinner hosted by Adams. "You will draw this inference from it, that there are certain persons who carry everything they hear, and I dare say many things they make"—fabricate—"to the ear of Mr. Jefferson. If only what is said by the party"—the dinner party—"be told, his prospect is not a summer sea."

Abigail Adams reproduced for her son the dialogue between "Mr. J." and "Mrs. A."

Mr. J. "Pray, who is that gentleman who sits next but one to the President?"

Mrs. A. "That is Mr. Waln of Pennsylvania"—a merchant and Federalist congressman.

Mr. J. "I never saw him to know him before. Pray who is the next?"

Mrs. A. "That is Mr. Holmes. You surely know him." She smiled. "He is a Democrat."

Mr. J. "No, I do not."

Mrs. A. "I know nearly all the gentlemen of both houses, a few violent Democrats excepted who have excluded themselves from our table."

Mr. J. "I do not know one in twenty. They complain and say that I will not take my hat off to them when I pass them, but I cannot help it. I have no means of knowing them. I never see them but at your table."

Mrs. A. "Do you never go into the House of Representatives?"

Mr. J. "No, I cannot. I am sure there are persons there who would take a pleasure in saying something purposely to affront me."

Mrs. A. "I cannot answer for them. I wished myself to have gone last winter when one or two interesting questions were before the House, but was restrained by the same consideration. Party spirit is much alike upon both sides the question."

Mr. J. "I think there is more candor and liberality upon one side than there is upon the other."

Mrs. A. "I differ from you, sir. Yet I do not deny but that there is a difference amongst those who profess the same sentiments. Some are mere brutes, others are gentlemen. But party spirit is a blind spirit. I was at the House today for the first time; I would have gone into the Senate, but was obliged to return home."

Mr. J. "I wish you had been there. Mr. Gouverneur Morris really made an eloquent speech upon the subject of the mausoleum"—a proposed tomb for George Washington. "And Mr. Cocke tried for his life to make one too. It was really diverting."

Mrs. A. "Pray, sir, what do the Senate design to do with the convention?" The Convention of 1800 was a recently concluded agreement with France that would end both the naval war and the French alliance.

Mr. J. "Upon my soul, I believe they will reject it."

Mrs. A. "I am surprised at that. The mercantile interest in the great states are in favour of it."

Mr. J. "I have information from the South that they are so."

Mrs. A. "There have always been a party determined to defeat it from the first sending the mission. I mean the Hamiltonians; they must abide the consequences."

Mr. J. "Pray is not your new Senator Mason of that party?"

Mrs. A. "I think he is."

Mr. J. "Foster, I think, is not."

Mrs. A. "There, sir, you are mistaken. Foster was brought into Senate by that party, to the exclusion of Mr. Sewall, who ought to have been senator. Mr. Foster is not one of the violent party men. His brother, however, votes and thinks differently from him."

Mr. J. "I think Chipman as bitter a man as any in Senate."

Mrs. A. "I know very little of Mr. Chipman. I never see him but at public dinners, and he is a very silent man. Mr. Paine I am well acquainted with. He is a sensible, well-informed, candid man, and as free from party spirit as any gentleman I know."

Mr. J. "I wonder what they mean to do? They have some daring projects on foot."

At this point in her letter, Abigail Adams remarked to Thomas Adams: "As I supposed this referred to the election, I replied, 'I do not know. That is a subject which I do not choose to converse upon.'"

She proceeded to tell Jefferson a story: "I have heard of a clergyman who upon some difficulty amongst his people took a text from these words—'and they knew not what to do'—from whence he drew this inference, that when a people were in such a situation that they do not know what to do, they should take great care that they do not do they know not what."

"At this he laughed out," said Abigail Adams. "And here ended the conversation."

## 61

O N FEBRUARY 11 the House voted. Adams got the news from James Bayard of Delaware. "The House of Representatives has balloted seven times and the result of each ballot was 8 votes for Mr. Jefferson, 6 for Mr. Burr and 2 divided," Bayard wrote in the late afternoon of that day. A winner required a majority of the sixteen state votes. "We have allowed ourselves an hour for refreshment and at the end of that time are to proceed with the ballot. There is a prospect that our confinement will continue during the night."

The confinement lasted longer than that night. The House voted again and again over several days, thirty-five times in all, without breaking the deadlock. In merely the second contested presidential election under the Constitution, the system seemed to have broken down.

Adams had decided by default not to cooperate in resolving the issue. Instead he chose another route for extending Federalist influence beyond the deadline the voters had established. At the president's behest, the departing Federalist Congress approved a new judiciary law reorganizing and expanding the federal court system and creating sixteen new judgeships. In the two-and-a-half weeks before his term ran out, Adams hastened to fill the positions with judges who shared his Federalist views and would interpret the law accordingly long after Adams had left office.

For good measure, Adams filled a vacancy on the Supreme Court by nominating John Marshall to be chief justice. Senate confirmation precluded Marshall's stepping into the presidency should the House deadlock remain unbroken at the time Adams's term expired. Adams had decided against conspiring in any attempt to deny the Republicans the presidency, and he reasoned that the relatively young—forty-five years old—Marshall would serve Federalist values better and longer in a lifetime appointment to the Supreme Court.

WITH NO SUPPORT from Adams, and with Hamilton hectoring them to abandon Burr, the Federalist holdouts against Jefferson finally gave way. On the thirty-sixth ballot, James Bayard, the sole member of the Delaware delegation, changed his Burr vote to abstention, depriving Burr of that state. Other key Federalists moved their states from the divided column into the Jefferson camp or, in the case of South Carolina, from Burr to undecided. The result was ten states for Jefferson and four for Burr, with two undecided.

## 62

I S THIS the violent democrat, the vulgar demagogue, the bold atheist and profligate man I have so often heard denounced by the Federalists?" asked Margaret Smith after her first meeting with Jefferson. "Can this man, so meek and mild, yet dignified in his manners, with a voice so soft and low, with a countenance so benignant and intelligent, can he be that daring leader of a faction, that disturber of the peace, that enemy of all rank and order?"

Margaret Smith had arrived in Washington city, the new national capital, at the same time Congress moved there from Philadelphia, in the autumn of 1800. Her husband was a Republican and had spoken well of Jefferson, but her Federalist friends had prepared her for the worst. "I did believe that he was an ambitious and violent demagogue, coarse and vulgar in his manners, awkward and rude in his appearance, for such had the public journals and private conversations of the Federal party represented him to be," she recalled. The reality of the matter caught her unawares. "In December, 1800, a few days after Congress had for the first time met in our new metropolis, I was one morning sitting alone in the parlour, when the servant opened the door and showed in a gentleman who wished to see my husband. The usual frankness and care with which I met strangers were somewhat checked by the dignified and reserved air of the present visitor; but the chilled feeling was only momentary, for after taking the chair I offered him, in a free and easy manner and carelessly throwing his arm on the table near which he sat, he turned towards me a countenance beaming with an expression of benevolence and with a manner and voice almost femininely soft and gentle, entered into conversation on the commonplace topics of the day, from which, before I was conscious of it, he had drawn me into observations of a more personal and interesting nature. I know not how it was, but there was something in his manner, his countenance and voice that at once unlocked my heart, and in answer to his casual enquiries concerning our situation in our *new home,* as he called it, I found myself frankly telling him what I liked or disliked in our present circumstances and abode. I knew not who he was, but the interest with which he listened to my artless details, induced the idea he was some intimate acquaintance or friend of Mr. Smith's and put me perfectly at my ease; in truth so kind and conciliating were his looks and manners that I forgot he was not a friend of my own, until on the opening of the door, Mr. Smith entered and introduced the stranger to me as *Mr. Jefferson.*"

During four decades in Washington, Margaret Smith would learn to become unflappable, but as a new bride of twenty-two and a recent arrival in the city, she found herself embarrassed. "I felt my cheeks burn and my heart throb, and not a word more could I speak while he remained. Nay, such was my embarrassment I could scarcely listen to the conversation carried on between him and my husband." Margaret Smith had been a student of politics even before moving to Washington. Jefferson had intrigued her. "For several years he had been to me an object of peculiar interest. In fact my destiny, for on his success in the pending presidential election, or rather the success of the democratic party (their interests were identical), my condition in life, my union with the man I loved, depended." Samuel Smith had moved to Washington to open a Republican newspaper, the *National Intelligencer.* "In addition to this personal interest, I had long participated in my husband's political sentiments and anxieties, and looked upon Mr. Jefferson as the corner stone on which the edifice of republican liberty was to rest, looked upon him as the champion of human rights, the reformer of abuses, the head of the republican party, which must rise or fall with him, and on the triumph of the republican party I devoutly believed the security and welfare of my country depended."

These hopes and beliefs hadn't kept back the doubts sown by the Federalists. "Eager as I was for his success, I retained my previously conceived ideas of the coarseness and vulgarity of his appearance and manners and was therefore equally awed and surprised on discovering the stranger whose deportment was so dignified and gentlemanly, whose language was so refined, whose voice was so gentle, whose countenance was so benignant, to be no other than Thomas Jefferson. How instantaneously were all these preconceived prejudices dissipated, and in proportion to their strength, was the reaction that took place in my opinions and sentiments. I felt that I had been the victim of prejudice, that I had been unjust. The revolution of feeling was complete and from that moment my heart warmed to him with the most affectionate interest and I implicitly believed all that his friends and my husband believed and which the after experience of many years confirmed. Yes, not only was he great, but a truly good man!"

On this occasion, Jefferson had come to see Samuel Smith about publishing a manual he—Jefferson—had compiled on the operations of Congress. Drawn from Jefferson's experience presiding over the Senate and from his observations of the House, it served as a primer for new members and a repository of the institutional memory of the legislature. Margaret Smith got a look at Jefferson's manuscript. "The original was in his own neat, plain, but elegant handwriting. The manuscript was as legible as printing and its unadorned simplicity was emblematical of his character."

"After the affair of business was settled," Margaret Smith continued, "the conversation became general and Mr. Jefferson several times addressed himself to me; but although his manner was unchanged, my feelings were, and I could not recover sufficient ease to join in the conversation. He shook hands cordially with us both when he departed, and in a manner which said as plain as words could do, 'I am your friend.'"

Margaret Smith learned where Jefferson resided while in Washington. "Conrad's boarding house was on the south side of Capitol Hill and commanded an extensive and beautiful view," she wrote. "It was on the top of the hill, the precipitous sides of which were covered with grass, shrubs and trees in their wild uncultivated state. Between the foot of the hill and the broad Potomac extended a wide plain, through which the Tiber"—a creek—"wound its way. The romantic beauty of this little stream was not then deformed by wharves or other works of art. Its banks were shaded with tall and umbrageous forest trees of every variety, among which the superb tulip-poplar rose conspicuous;

the magnolia, the azalea, the hawthorn, the wild-rose and many other indigenous shrubs grew beneath their shade, while violets, anemonies and a thousand other sweet wood-flowers found shelter among their roots from the winter's frost and greeted with the earliest bloom the return of spring." Margaret Smith thought Jefferson had chosen Conrad's boardinghouse in part because of the view.

In the house he insisted on being treated like the other guests. "He had a separate drawing-room for the reception of his visitors; in all other respects he lived on a perfect equality with his fellow boarders, and ate at a common table. Even here, so far from taking precedence of the other members of Congress, he always placed himself at the lowest end of the table. Mrs. Brown, the wife of the senator from Kentucky, suggested that a seat should be offered him at the upper end, near the fire, if not on account of his rank as vice-president, at least as the oldest man in company. But the idea was rejected by his democratic friends, and he occupied during the whole winter the lowest and coldest seat at a long table at which a company of more than thirty sat down. Even on the day of his inauguration when he entered the dining-hall no other seat was offered him by the gentlemen. Mrs. Brown from an impulse which she said she could not resist, offered him her seat, but he smilingly declined it, and took his usual place at the bottom of the table. She said she felt indignant and for a moment almost hated the levelling principle of democracy, though her husband was a zealous democrat." Margaret Smith agreed with Mrs. Brown. "Certainly this was carrying equality rather too far; there is no incompatibility between politeness and republicanism; grace cannot weaken and rudeness cannot strengthen a good cause, but democracy is more jealous of power and privilege than even despotism."

Margaret Smith followed the tortuous dealings in the House that finally gave the election to Jefferson. "It was an awful crisis," she wrote. "The people, who with such an overwhelming majority had declared their will would never peaceably have allowed the man of their choice to be set aside, and the individual they had chosen as vice president, to be put in his place. A civil war must have taken place, to be terminated in all human probability by a rupture of the Union." Crowds of Republicans thronged Washington to ensure that their champion not be denied his due. "The citizens of Baltimore, who from their proximity were the first apprised of this daring design, were with difficulty restrained from rushing on with an armed force to prevent—or if they could not prevent, to avenge—this violation of the people's will and in their own vehement language to hurl the usurper from his seat."

She marveled at Jefferson's composure amid the turmoil. "Mr. Jefferson, then president of the Senate, sitting in the midst of these conspirators, as they were then called, unavoidably hearing their loudly whispered designs, witnessing their gloomy and restless machinations, aware of the dreadful consequences which must follow their meditated designs, preserved through this trying period the most unclouded serenity, the most perfect equanimity. A spectator who watched his countenance would never have surmised that he had any personal interest in the impending event."

Margaret Smith enjoyed an unusual vantage. Married to a Republican confidant of Jefferson, she was the cousin and adopted sister of James Bayard, the Delaware Federalist whose change of vote broke the deadlock in the House, in Jefferson's favor.

She attended the inauguration with her husband. "Let me write to you, my dear Susan, e'er that glow of enthusiasm has fled which now animates my feelings," Margaret wrote to her sister-in-law that evening. "Let me congratulate not only you, but all my fellow citizens, on an event which will have so auspicious an influence on their political welfare. I have this morning witnessed one of the most interesting scenes a free people can ever witness. The changes of administration, which in every government and in every age have most generally been epochs of confusion, villainy and bloodshed, in this our happy country take place without any species of distraction, or disorder. This day has one of the most amiable and worthy men taken that seat to which he was called by the voice of his country. I cannot describe the agitation I felt while I looked around on the various multitude and while I listened to an address, containing principles the most correct, sentiments the most liberal, and wishes the most benevolent, conveyed in the most appropriate and elegant language and in a manner mild as it was firm. If doubts of the integrity and talents of Mr. Jefferson ever existed in the minds of any one, methinks this address must forever eradicate them. The Senate chamber was so crowded that I believe not another creature could enter. On one side of the house the Senate sat, the other was resigned by the representatives to the ladies. The roof is arched, the room half circle, every inch of ground was occupied. It has been conjectured by several gentlemen whom I've asked, that there were near a thousand persons within the walls. The speech was delivered in so low a tone that few heard it. Mr. Jefferson had given your brother a copy early in the morning, so that on coming out of the house, the paper was distributed immediately. Since then there has been a constant succession of persons coming for the papers. I have been interrupted several times in this letter by the gentlemen of Congress, who have been to bid us their adieus; since three o'clock there has been a constant succession of persons coming for the papers."

## 63

THE SPEECH THEY WANTED to read was one of the rare public addresses of Jefferson's life. It was his first as president, and
nearly his last. He had never liked to speak other than in conversation.
He winced under public scrutiny. But he couldn't avoid the inaugural address, the precedent for which had been established by George
Washington.

The speech read better than it sounded, featuring the rambling
sentences Jefferson favored. He must have paused for breath several
times mid-sentence. As Margaret Smith noted, his oratorical effort was
wasted on those not in the nearest rows to where he stood—which
explained the rush to purchase copies of the speech from her husband.
Yet for all his being no Patrick Henry, Jefferson got his message across.

"Friends and fellow citizens," he began. "Called upon to undertake
the duties of the first Executive office of our country, I avail myself of
the presence of that portion of my fellow citizens which is here assembled to express my grateful thanks for the favor with which they have
been pleased to look towards me, to declare a sincere consciousness that
the task is above my talents, and that I approach it with those anxious
and awful presentiments which the greatness of the charge and the
weakness of my powers so justly inspire."

He scarcely looked up from his reading. "A rising nation, spread
over a wide and fruitful land, traversing all the seas with the rich pro-
ductions of their industry, engaged in commerce with nations who feel
power and forget right, advancing rapidly to destinies beyond the reach

of mortal eye—when I contemplate these transcendent objects, and see the honour, the happiness, and the hopes of this beloved country committed to the issue and the auspices of this day, I shrink from the contemplation and humble myself before the magnitude of the under-taking. Utterly indeed should I despair, did not the presence of many whom I here see remind me that in the other high authorities provided by our Constitution, I shall find resources of wisdom, of virtue, and of zeal, on which to rely under all difficulties." To these men, and to the others in the chamber, Jefferson asked for guidance and support.

Jefferson's was not a combative temperament; he had no desire to retrace the steps that had finally resulted in his election. But neither could he ignore them. He cast the whole matter as an aspect of politics in a free society, even as he prayed his listeners to put the controversy aside. "During the contest of opinion through which we have passed, the animation of discussions and of exertions has sometimes worn an aspect which might impose on strangers unused to think freely, and to speak and to write what they think," he said. "But this being now decided by the voice of the nation, announced according to the rules of the Constitution, all will of course arrange themselves under the will of the law, and unite in common efforts for the common good."

He would do his part for reconciliation. "Though the will of the majority is in all cases to prevail, that will, to be rightful, must be rea-sonable," he said. "The minority possess their equal rights, which equal laws must protect, and to violate would be oppression." He called on his listeners to join him. "Let us reflect that having banished from our land that religious intolerance under which mankind so long bled and suf-fered, we have yet gained little if we countenance a political intolerance as despotic, as wicked, and capable of as bitter and bloody persecutions."

"Every difference of opinion is not a difference of principle," Jeffer-son explained. "We have called by different names brethren of the same principle. We are all Republicans; we are all Federalists." Difference of opinion should be celebrated, not proscribed. *He* would not proscribe even the deepest difference. "If there be any among us who would wish to dissolve this Union, or to change its republican form, let them stand undisturbed as monuments of the safety with which error of opinion may be tolerated where reason is left free to combat it."

He articulated the principles that would guide his presidency: "Equal and exact justice to all men, of whatever state or persuasion, religious or political. Peace, commerce, and honest friendship with all nations, entangling alliances with none. The support of the state governments in all their rights, as the most competent administrations for our domestic concerns, and the surest bulwarks against anti-republican tendencies. The preservation of the general government in its whole constitutional vigor, as the sheet anchor of our peace at home, and safety abroad. A jealous care of the right of election by the people, a mild and safe corrective of abuses which are lopped by the sword of revolution where peaceable remedies are unprovided. Absolute acquiescence in the decisions of the majority, the vital principle of republics, from which is no appeal but to force, the vital principle and immediate parent of the despotism. A well disciplined militia, our best reliance in peace, and for the first moments of war, till regulars may relieve them. The supremacy of the civil over the military authority. Economy in the public expence, that labor may be lightly burthened. The honest payment of our debts and sacred preservation of the public faith. Encouragement of agriculture, and of commerce as its handmaid. The diffusion of information, and arraignment of all abuses at the bar of the public reason. Freedom of religion; freedom of the press; and freedom of person, under the protection of the habeas corpus. And trial by juries impartially selected."

Jefferson requested the patience and assistance of his fellow citizens. "I shall often go wrong through defect of judgment. When right, I shall often be thought wrong by those whose positions will not command a view of the whole ground. I ask your indulgence for my own errors, which will never be intentional; and your support against the errors of others, who may condemn what they would not if seen in all its parts." With their help, and God's, he would do all he could for America. "I advance with obedience to the work, ready to retire from it whenever you become sensible how much better choices it is in your power to make. And may that infinite power, which rules the destinies of the universe, lead our councils to what is best, and give them a favorable issue for your peace and prosperity."

ADAMS SKIPPED JEFFERSON'S inauguration. He rose early and started the journey north to home before the crowds began arriving for the ceremony. He had reconciled himself to his political defeat; what weighed on his heart was the recent death of his and Abigail's son Charles, at the age of thirty after long troubles with alcohol. "The melancholy decease of your brother is an affliction of a more serious nature to this family than any other," Adams wrote to Charles's brother Thomas. "Oh! that I had died for him if that would have relieved him from his faults as well as his disease."

Abigail Adams had gone before him, to prepare the house they expected to occupy—permanently together, for a welcome change— for the rest of their lives. "I arrived here about half after six, without any accident but beat and banged enough," she wrote from Baltimore. "I do not wish for the present a severer punishment to the Jacobins and half Feds who have sent me home at this season, than to travel the roads in the sans-cullotes style just now." Thrifty Abigail traveled economy class. "The roads were hard-frozen, points up, all the way. We were four hours making our first stage, and then commenced a violent snow storm. When we made our second stage, which was Spurriers"—a tavern between Washington and Baltimore—"we found ourselves so late that we could not stop but to change our horses, and came through without taking a mouthful of refreshment."

A letter from Jefferson followed Adams home. It proved to be merely a note forwarding some papers to Adams that had arrived late at the executive mansion. But the cordial tone of the note—Jefferson conveyed "the homage of his high consideration and respect"—caused Adams to respond in kind. "Had you read the papers enclosed they might have given you a moment of melancholy or at least of sympathy with a mourning father," Adams said. "They relate wholly to the funeral of a son who was once the delight of my eyes and a darling of my heart, cut off in the flower of his days amidst very flattering prospects by causes which have been the greatest grief of my heart and the deepest affliction of my life. . . . I sincerely wish you may never experience anything in any degree resembling it."

Adams added, "This part of the Union is in a state of perfect tranquility, and I see nothing to obscure your prospect of a quiet and prosperous administration, which I heartily wish you."

MADISON'S CAREER IN government resumed the day after Adams's ceased. Jefferson called him to Washington to become secretary of state. Until this point the path to the presidency had run through the vice presidency, but it had done so most awkwardly. The recent imbroglio in the House prompted demands to change the manner of electoral voting. While that change still pended, Jefferson determined to chart a new route for his successor. By making Madison secretary of state, Jefferson would employ Madison's talents even while grooming him for the presidency.

Jefferson knew he would need all the talent he could muster in the first big battle of his administration. Republicans already derided the "midnight judges" appointed by Adams on his way out the door, and Jefferson ordered that any appointments not officially completed be halted at once. William Marbury's commission lay undelivered on the desk of the secretary of state, and the president's directive caused it to remain there. Marbury, a Maryland Federalist, wanted the job, and he sued Madison to receive it.

The case found its way to the Supreme Court, where John Marshall now sat as chief justice. Marshall was Jefferson's second cousin, and he was one of the few men Jefferson feared. "When conversing with Marshall, I never admit anything," Jefferson told a lawyer who knew them both. "So sure as you admit any position to be good, no matter how remote from the conclusion he seeks to establish, you are gone. So great is his sophistry, you must never give him an affirmative answer or you will be forced to grant his conclusion. Why, if he were to ask me if it were daylight or not, I'd reply, 'Sir, I don't know, I can't tell.'"

In the Marbury case, Marshall justified Jefferson's fear, handing the president a cunningly poisoned victory. Marshall and the court ruled that Marbury should not receive his commission, but not because it had not been delivered on time. Rather it should not be delivered because the salient part of a 1789 statute governing such matters was unconstitutional.

It was a powerful stroke for the unelected judicial branch against the elected legislative branch. In that regard it was a slap in the face to Jefferson's philosophy of popular rule. And it was brilliant in leaving Jefferson no riposte. Jefferson and Madison had won; Marbury did not receive his commission. The case was closed.

Marshall never again found a federal law unconstitutional. Indeed, not until a half century had passed would the Supreme Court strike down another statute. Yet the precedent established in *Marbury v. Madison* would become a cornerstone of judicial supremacy and a lasting reproof to the first Republican president.

THE COLLAPSE HAMILTON HAD predicted under the Republicans did not come. Jefferson's party strengthened its hold on the government, increasing its majorities in Congress and driving the Federalists to the brink of inconsequence. Hamilton heard himself blamed for the party's decline, for having attacked its own president and delivering the office to Jefferson.

He took solace in the eclipse of Aaron Burr. Jefferson soon revealed that Burr had been an ally of convenience to him; having served his purpose, the vice president was set aside. Burr found himself as unoccupied as Jefferson and Adams had been as vice president before him. Rather than wait to be tossed from the ticket in the next election, Burr made a run for New York governor. Hamilton attacked him with the same vigor and some of the same words he used against Burr during the House contest for president.

Burr lost the governor's race and afterward accused Hamilton of traducing his honor. Much as Hamilton had demanded satisfaction from Adams, Burr now demanded satisfaction from Hamilton. Unlike Adams, Hamilton didn't think he could ignore the challenge.

On the morning of July 11, 1804, the two met on the dueling ground of Weehawken, New Jersey. Both men fired. Burr wasn't hit, but Hamilton was severely wounded. He died the next day.

JEFFERSON DELIVERED the presidency to Madison after two terms. The Twelfth Amendment split the voting by the electors into separate categories for president and vice president. There would be no repeat of the muddle of 1800. Madison found himself as vexed by the European war as Adams had been, but rather than fight a half war against France, he fought a full war against Britain. In the process he came to appreciate something he had rejected when proposed by Hamilton: a federal bank. The charter for Hamilton's bank having expired, Madison got Congress to charter a new one.

Madison retired after two terms in favor of James Monroe, his secretary of state. By this time grumblings against a "Virginia dynasty" were common. Monroe deflected them by appointing as secretary of state, and presumptive next president, John Quincy Adams. With the demise of the Federalists, the old labels had lost their edge; indeed Monroe's presidency was dubbed the "era of good feelings." And when Monroe, the heir of Republicans Jefferson and Madison, anointed and was then succeeded by Quincy Adams, the son of Federalist Adams, the description seemed apt.

The good feelings were confirmed by the reconciliation of Adams and Jefferson. The two had said little to each other during their presidencies, with Federalist Adams excluding his Republican vice president from policy matters and then Jefferson, after declaring Americans all Republicans and all Federalists, running his administration as a Republican fiefdom. But once the two entered the most exclusive society in America, as the only living former presidents, they found it easier to recall the time when they had been allies in the service of American independence.

They swept away the fog of partisanship that had obscured what they held in common. They observed the extension of religious freedom when Connecticut demoted Congregationalism, and found they agreed more than they differed. "Twenty times in the course of my late reading have I been upon the point of breaking out, 'This would be the best of all possible worlds if there were no religion in it!!!'" Adams wrote. "But in this exclamation I should have been as fanatical as Bryant or Cleverly"—a priest and a schoolmaster Adams had known as a boy. "Without religion this world would be something not fit to be mentioned in polite company—I mean Hell."

Jefferson responded, "I join you therefore in sincere congratulations that this den of the priesthood is at length broken up, and that a protestant popedom is no longer to disgrace the American history and character." He added, "If, by *religion*, we are to understand *Sectarian dogmas*, in which no two of them agree, then your exclamation on that hypothesis is just, that this would be the best of all possible worlds if there were no religion in it. But if the moral precepts innate in man and made a part of his physical constitution as necessary for a social being, if the sublime doctrines of philanthropism and deism taught us by Jesus of Nazareth in which all agree, constitute true religion, then, without it, this would be, as you again say, 'something not fit to be named, even indeed a Hell.'"

Yet Adams, still the more conservative, remarked on the slowness of human progress. "I cannot contemplate human affairs, without laughing or crying," he wrote to Jefferson. "I choose to laugh. When people talk of the freedom of writing, speaking or thinking, I cannot choose but laugh. No such thing ever existed. No such thing now exists: but I hope it will exist. But it must be hundreds of years after you and I shall write and speak no more."

The most basic human experiences brought them closer together. Jefferson, having lost his own wife decades earlier, commiserated on learning of the death of Abigail Adams. "Tried myself in the school of affliction by the loss of every form of connection which can rive the human heart, I know well and feel what you have lost, what you have suffered, are suffering, and have yet to endure," he wrote to Adams. "The same trials have taught me that for ills so immeasurable, time and silence are the only medicines. I will not therefore, by useless condolences, open afresh the sluices of your grief nor, although mingling sincerely my tears with yours, will I say a word more where words are vain, but that it is of some comfort to us both that the term is not very distant at which we are to deposit, in the same cerement, our sorrows and suffering bodies, and to ascend in essence to an ecstatic meeting with the friends we have loved and lost and whom we shall still love and never lose again. God bless you and support you under your heavy affliction."

A crisis over Missouri distressed them both. "The clouds look black and thick, assembling from all points threatening thunder and lightning," Adams wrote. Jefferson likened the crisis to an angry wave. "The Missouri question is a breaker on which we lose the Missouri country by revolt, and what more God only knows," he said. "From the battle of Bunker's Hill to the treaty of Paris we never had so ominous a question." It made him appreciate old age. "I thank god that I shall not live to witness its issue."

The country survived the Missouri crisis, but each man still worried for the future. As the aging do, they found solace in the past. Adams was fondest of the period that yielded the decision for independence. Other episodes blurred in his memory, but his recollection of those weeks, when he stood out as the stalwart for American freedom, remained sharp.

Jefferson took pride in "the revolution of 1800," as he called the change of government produced by the election of that year. "That was as real a revolution in the principles of our government as that of '76 was in its form, not effected indeed by the sword, as that, but by the rational and peaceable instrument of reform, the suffrage of the people."

"I am certainly very near the end of my life," Adams wrote in his last letter to Jefferson. "I am very far from trifling with the idea of death, which is a great and solemn event. But I contemplate it without terror or dismay. Aut transit, aut finit"—I cross, or I come to an end. "If finit, which I cannot believe, and do not believe, there is then an end of all. But I shall never know it and why should I dread it, which I do not. If transit, I shall ever be under the same constitution and administration of Government in the Universe and I am not afraid to trust and confide in it."

Jefferson's last to Adams introduced his grandson Thomas Randolph, who was visiting Boston and hoped to meet Adams. "Like other young people, he wishes to be able in the winter nights of old age to recount to those around him what he has heard and learnt of the Heroic age preceding his birth, and which of the Argonauts particularly he was in time to have seen," Jefferson said. "Gratify his ambition then by receiving his best bow, and my solicitude for your health by enabling him to bring me a favorable account of it. Mine is but indifferent, but not so my friendship and respect for you."

As the jubilee—fiftieth anniversary—of independence drew near, Americans looked to the remaining signers of the Declaration. Of the fifty-six, only three survived: Jefferson, Adams, and Charles Carroll of Maryland. Carroll was the oldest but seemed likely to live forever; Jefferson and Adams were fading. The country watched and wished them strength to reach the great day.

They held on just long enough. Both awoke on the morning of July 4, 1826. Both died before nightfall.

MADISON LIVED a decade longer, almost. During the presidency of Andrew Jackson, which was made possible by Jackson's victory in the last battle of Madison's War of 1812, Madison opposed the nullification threatened by South Carolina over a tariff it didn't like. Madison carefully explained how the ideas he had put forward in the Virginia resolutions of 1798 were being misused, and he denounced John Calhoun's doctrine as illegitimate and unconstitutional. "A plainer contradiction in terms or a more fatal inlet of anarchy cannot be imagined," he declared.

His health, never robust, grew worse. As the sixtieth anniversary of the Declaration of Independence approached in 1836, many Americans looked toward Montpelier to see if Madison would be taken in the same timely fashion as Adams and Jefferson. He had no such ambition. The Declaration was their document; his was the Constitution. He was the last survivor of its signers, but there was no way he would live to its jubilee, fifteen months hence. His mind was clear and his soul composed as his heart ticked down and finally stopped, on June 28.

George Washington's farewell address hadn't caught on as presidential practice, yet Madison left something similar as he bade farewell to life. "As this advice, if it ever see the light, will not do it till I am no more, it may be considered as issuing from the tomb where truth alone can be respected, and the happiness of man alone consulted," he wrote. "It will be entitled therefore to whatever weight can be derived from good intentions, and from the experience of one who has served his country in various stations through a period of forty years, who espoused in his youth and adhered through his life to the cause of its liberty, and who has borne a part in most of the great transactions which will constitute epochs of its destiny."

At the time of the deaths of Adams and Jefferson, it had been possible for Madison to think he had been wrong about the inevitability of parties. No new party had arisen to replace the Federalists; the Republicans governed unchallenged.

But the era of good feelings turned out to be a mere moment. The same dynamics of interest and ambition that had given birth to the Republicans and the Federalists spawned a second duopoly of political power: the Democrats and the Whigs. The former claimed descent from the Republicans; the latter were reconfigured Federalists. If Madison reread his essay about parties now, he must have thought himself right after all.

The new parties aggravated divisions over issues, just as the old ones had. In his prime Madison had been a feisty, if sometimes reluctant, partisan. Age and, finally, approaching death caused him to rethink his priorities. His last words placed the nation above party and everything else. "The advice nearest to my heart and deepest in my convictions is that the Union of the states be cherished and perpetuated," he said. "Let the open enemy to it be regarded as a Pandora with her box opened, and the disguised one as the serpent creeping with his deadly wiles into Paradise."

# Sources

## PROLOGUE

1  "Desperate as some . . . all parties": Madison to Jefferson, Jan. 10, 1801, Founders Online, https://founders.archives.gov/. Where no other repository is cited below, this is to be understood.
2  "Reason first": Adams to Timothy Pickering, Aug. 2, 1822.
3  "I know . . . I cannot see": Adams to Elbridge Gerry, Feb. 7, 1801.
4  "His politics": Hamilton to James Bayard, Jan. 16, 1801.
5  "I feel no impulse": Jefferson to Mary Jefferson Eppes, Feb. 15, 1801.

## PART 1 THE MAKING OF A CONTINENTALIST

### 1.

9  "Folly, caprice . . . entire confidence": Hamilton to Clinton, Feb. 13, 1778.
11 "Shall I speak . . . think with me": Hamilton to Clinton, Mar. 12, 1778.
12 "The fundamental defect . . . or with system": Hamilton to Duane, Sept. 3, 1780.
14 "a convention of all the states . . . confidence in others": Hamilton to Duane, Sept. 3, 1780.

### 2.

16 "It would be . . . VIOLENT END": "Continentalist 1," July 12, 1781.
18 "In federal governments . . . encourage it": "Continentalist 2," July 19, 1781.
19 "Political societies . . . and security": "Continentalist 3," Aug. 9, 1781.
19 "The three first . . . the principal": "Continentalist 4," Aug. 30, 1781.
20 "The vesting Congress . . . people at all": "Continentalist 5," Apr. 18, 1782.
22 "We may preach . . . of thy tranquility!": "Continentalist 6," July 4, 1782.

### 3.

25  "I take the liberty . . . may cooperate": Hamilton to Washington, Feb. 13, 1783.
26  "I shall pursue": Washington to Hamilton, Mar. 4, 1783.
26  "I was among": Washington address, Mar. 15, 1783.
27  "As to any combination": Hamilton to Washington, Mar. 17, 1783.
27  "The question": Hamilton to Washington, Apr. 8, 1783.

### PART II  BLESSING OR CURSE?

### 4.

31  "Among the various . . . the public relief": Madison to Jefferson, Mar. 27, 1780.
32  "Each State retains": Article 2, Articles of Confederation.
32  "All charges of war": Article 7, Articles of Confederation.
33  "The necessity . . . northern brethren": Madison to Jefferson, Apr. 16, 1781.
34  "Every State": Article 13, Articles of Confederation.
34  "the said United States": Proposed amendment, Mar. 12, 1781.
35  "unless nine States assent": Article 9, Articles of Confederation.
35  "As it is a rule": Madison to Jefferson, Nov. 18, 1781.

### 5.

36  "A detachment": Hamilton to Jackson, June 19, 1783.
37  "The mutinous soldiers . . . might be stipulated": Madison notes, June 21, 1783.
38  "The conduct of the executive": Hamilton to Clinton, June 29, 1783.
39  "Congress remain": Madison to Randolph, July 8, 1783.

### 6.

40  "The confederation . . . want of support": Hamilton draft resolution, July 1783.
41  "The great object . . . or a curse": Washington to the states, June 8, 1783.

### 7.

44  "Are your people": Washington to Lincoln, Nov. 7, 1786.
44  "Many of them . . . hourly decreasing": Lincoln to Washington, Dec. 4, 1786–Mar. 4, 1787. Lincoln's letter included his exchanges with Shays and Bowdoin.
48  "The suppression": Washington to Lincoln, Mar. 27, 1787.
49  "Good God!": Washington to Knox, Dec. 26, 1786.
49  "If three years ago": Washington to Knox, Feb. 3, 1787.
49  "Our affairs": Washington to Knox, Feb. 25, 1787.

### 8.

50  "The homilies": McHenry to Hamilton, Oct. 22–23, 1783.
51  "I am far": Madison to James Monroe, Mar. 14, 1786.
52  "to take into": Hamilton address at Annapolis convention, Sept. 14, 1786.

## PART III  CONSPIRACY AT PHILADELPHIA

### 9.

55  "The appointments": Madison to Jefferson, Mar. 19, 1787.

55  "for the sole and express": *Journals of the Continental Congress,* Feb. 21, 1787.

55  "What may be ... bend to them": Madison to Jefferson, Mar. 19, 1787.

57  "I am glad ... will ensue": Madison to Randolph, Apr. 8, 1787.

60  "Dear sir ... sea or land": Madison to Washington, Apr. 16, 1787.

### 10.

61  "Mr. Madison": William Pierce in *The Records of the Federal Convention of 1787,* edited by Max Farrand (1911), 3:94–95.

61  "Monday last ... to be wished": Madison to Jefferson, May 15, 1787.

62  "I am in possession": Read to Dickinson, May 21, 1787, William Thompson Read, *Life and Correspondence of George Read* (1870), 443–44.

63  "We have here": Franklin to Thomas Jordan, May 18, 1787.

63  "I have yielded": Washington to Lee, May 20, 1787.

63  "General Washington": Madison journal, *Records,* 1:3–4.

64  "Delaware restrained": Yates journal, *Records,* 1:6.

64  "Governor Randolph": McHenry notes, *Records,* 1:24.

64  Randolph elaborated: The Virginia plan is in the notes of Madison, Yates, McHenry and William Paterson in *Records,* 1:passim.

64  "He candidly confessed": Yates notes, *Records,* 1:24.

65  "When the convention ... owned the paper": Pierce anecdote, *Records,* 3:86–87.

### 11.

67  "Mr. Charles Pinckney": Madison notes, *Records,* 1:33–34.

67  "When the convention": John Fine to Martin Van Buren, Apr. 30, 1857, in Martin Van Buren, *Inquiry into the Origin and Course of Political Parties in the United States,* edited by "His Sons" (1867), 105–6. Fine heard the story from William Burnet, who said he had it from Hamilton.

68  "the former being": Madison notes, *Records,* 1:34.

68  "Mr. Mason": Madison notes, *Records,* 1:34.

69  "that a national government": *Records,* 1:30.

69  "That the Articles": *Records,* 1:33. There is some question about the precise number and content of Paterson's resolutions. A careful reckoning is at *Records,* 3:611–15.

69  "He preferred ... thought of?": *Records,* 1:250–52.

### 12.

71  "Colonel Hamilton": Pierce in *Records,* 3:89.

71  "Mr. Hamilton ... proposes": Madison notes, *Records,* 1:282–91.

78  "What even": Yates notes, *Records,* 1:293.

## 13.

79  "First, to preserve ... to the whole": Madison notes, *Records*, 1:317–22.

82  "He had not been understood": Madison notes, *Records*, 1:323.

82  "He concurred": Madison, *Records*, 1:424.

## 14.

83  "This tavern ... going to tell": *Life, Journals and Correspondence of Rev. Manasseh Cutler, L.L.D.*, edited by William Parker Cutler and Julia Perkins Cutler (1888), 1:253–69.

## 15.

88  "It is impossible to judge how long": Mason to George Mason Jr., May 27, 1787, *Records*, 3:28.

88  "It is impossible to judge when": Mason to George Mason Jr., June 1, 1787, *Records*, 3:32.

89  "They are now": Washington to Hamilton, July 10, 1787.

89  "The convention continue": Madison to Jefferson, July 18, 1787.

89  "Mr. President ... that service": *Records*, 1:450–52.

91  "I confess ... that this is just?": *Records*, 1:474–75.

91  "The diversity": *Records*, 1:488.

93  "The states": *Records*, 1:486–87.

94  "He thought the blacks": *Records*, 1:542.

94  "He thought the admission": *Records*, 1:586.

94  "Mr. Wilson": *Records*, 1:587.

94  "Mr. Govr. Morris": *Records*, 1:588.

95  "It was inconsistent": *Records*, 2:364.

95  "Religion and humanity": Ibid.

95  "Let every state": Ibid.

95  "South Carolina": *Records*, 2:364–65.

96  "this infernal traffic": *Records*, 2:370.

96  "This widening": *Records*, 2:375.

96  "a bargain": *Records*, 2:374.

96  "It was better": Ibid.

96  "Mr. Madison": *Records*, 2:417.

96  "Mr. President ... our names": *Records*, 2:641–43.

### PART IV  PATRICK HENRY SMELLS A RAT

## 16.

101  "We have now ... most ardent wish": Washington to President of Congress, Sept. 17, 1787.

102  "What reception": Madison to James Madison Sr., Sept. 30, 1787.

103  "It appeared ... a miracle": Madison to Jefferson, Oct. 24, 1787.

### 17.

105 "To the People ... your happiness": Hamilton, Federalist 1, https://guides.loc
.gov/federalist-papers.

106 "The undertaking": Madison note cited in *The Federalist: A Commentary
on the Constitution of the United States,* edited by John C. Hamilton (1864),
lxxxv.

107 "It is too true": Federalist 4.

107 "Men are ambitious ... violent propensities": Federalist 6.

107 "Precisely the same": Federalist 7.

108 "The want of fortifications": Federalist 8.

109 "By a faction ... republican government": Federalist 10.

111 "If men were angels": Federalist 51. Like all the Federalist essays, this one was
published over the nom de plume "Publius." There is some doubt whether Madison or Hamilton was the author, but the balance of evidence seems to favor Madison. See https://founders.archives.gov/documents/Hamilton/01-04-02-0151
-0001.

112 "Energy in the executive": Federalist 70.

112 "I go further": Federalist 84.

### 18.

114 "When the public ... in their way": Brutus, Oct. 18, 1787, in *The Complete Anti-
Federalist,* edited by Herbert J. Storing (1998), 2.9.1–2.9.9.

116 "Could there ... abused and enslaved": Martin to the Citizens of the United
States, Mar. 30, 1788, *The Documentary History of the Ratification of the Constitution,* edited by Merrill Jensen et al. (1976–), 12:512.

### 19.

118 "The establishment ... probable result": Lee to Randolph, Oct. 18, 1787, *Documentary History,* 8:61–64.

119 "Colonel Mason": Madison to Jefferson, Oct. 24, 1787.

120 "There is no declaration ... one or the other": *Documentary History,* 8:43–46.

121 "It is a national government ... small territories": *Documentary History,* 9:936–40.

### 20.

123 "Let us not ... give me death": William Wirt, *The Life and Character of Patrick Henry* (1817), 138–42. This account includes the eyewitness testimony of
Judge Tucker. Henry's speech was not transcribed at the time; Wirt re-created it
from the recollections of people who heard it. If not precisely what Henry said,
Wirt's rendition captured the tenor of Henry's oration and the effect it had on
listeners.

125 "I smelt a rat": Hugh Blair Grigsby, *The History of the Virginia Federal Convention
of 1788* (1890), 1:32.

125 "Mr. Chairman ... perilous innovation": *Documentary History,* 9:929–31.

126  "Here is a revolution . . . small minority": Ibid., 9:951–68.

127  "What is the inference . . . the determination": *Documentary History*, 10:1474–1506.

129  "The decision": Archibald Stuart in *Life of Henry*, 312–13.

130  "Mr. Mason": Extract in *Carlisle Gazette*, Sept. 24, 1788, *Documentary History*, 10:1561.

130  "Previous to . . . be mistaken": *Virginia Independent Chronicle*, July 9, 1788, ibid., 1560–61.

131  "It was him": *Virginia Independent Chronicle*, Apr. 1, 1789, ibid., 1562.

131  "The birth": "Anecdotes of Patrick Henry: From the manuscripts of the late David Meade Randolph," *Southern Literary Messenger* (1835), 1:332.

2 1 .

132  "As Clinton . . . liberally paid": Hamilton to Madison, May 19, 1788.

133  "They have . . . our politics": Hamilton to Madison, June 8, 1788.

134  "Our chance": Hamilton to Madison, June 25, 1788.

134  "Our arguments": Hamilton to Madison, July 2, 1788.

134  "Our only chance": Hamilton to Madison, June 27, 1788.

134  "It was at about noon . . . ratification by Virginia": from the *Poughkeepsie Daily Eagle*, Feb. 18, 1888, in *Documentary History*, 21:1218.

135  "All that conviviality . . . hope for from you": *New York Daily Advertiser*, July 5, 1788, in *Documentary History*, 21:1275–77.

136  "When the news . . . despaired of": *New York Journal*, July 14, 1788, *Documentary History*, 21:1268–69.

137  "I felicitate you . . . rational recommendations": Hamilton to Madison, July 8, 1788.

138  "Everything possible . . . break up the party": Hamilton to Madison, July 19, 1788.

138  "I am sorry . . . a rejection": Madison to Hamilton, July 20, 1788.

139  "Mr. Hamilton . . . than before": *New York Daily Advertiser*, July 16, 1788, in Papers of Hamilton.

139  "The terms . . . have adopted it": Hamilton speeches, July 24, 1788, in ibid.

140  "We, the members": New York convention circular letter, July 28, 1788, *The Debates in the State Conventions on the Adoption of the Federal Constitution*, edited by Jonathan Elliott (1891), 2:413–14.

PART V THE LANGUAGE OF REPUBLICANISM

2 2 .

143  "Dear sir": Adams to Jay, July 18, 1788.

143  "He is not qualified": Jonathan Sewall letter in Alice Brown, *Mercy Warren* (1896), 223–24.

144  "The decision of the convention": Adams to Jay, July 18, 1788.

144  "The accession of Virginia": Adams to Lee, July 18, 1788.

144 "I am apprehensive": Adams to Theophilus Parsons, Nov. 2, 1788.

145 "If my future employment": Adams to Abigail Adams Smith, Nov. 11, 1788.

145 "My mind": Adams to Abigail Adams, Dec. 2, 1788.

145 "The few months": Adams to Jean Luzac, Dec. 2, 1788.

145 "We had a review": Adams to William Smith, Nov. 11, 1788.

146 "Our fellow citizens . . . suffrages of freemen": Adams to Jefferson, Jan. 2, 1789.

147 "It may be found": Adams to Jefferson, Mar. 1, 1789.

147 "The constancy": Adams to Thomas Hollis, Dec. 3, 1788.

148 "The people": Adams to Warren, Mar. 2, 1789.

148 "Invited to this . . . just expectations": Adams address, Apr. 21, 1789.


23.

150 "I like the organization . . . blood was spilt": Jefferson to Madison, Dec. 20, 1787.

151 "It seems pretty . . . in most instances": Jefferson to Madison, July 31, 1788.


24.

154 "The dictates of humanity": Madison speech, May 13, 1789.

154 "I do not conceive titles": Madison speech, May 11, 1789.

154 "This house . . . states respectively": Madison speech, June 8, 1789.

157 "I am inclined . . . produce that effect": Ibid.


25.

159 "The revolution . . . to public liberty": Jefferson to Madison, May 9, 1789.

161 "I received one day . . . of the constitution": Jefferson Autobiography, 153–55, Jefferson papers.

162 "Charter of Rights": Proposed charter for France, June 3, 1789.

163 "When the king": Jefferson to Jay, June 24, 1789.

163 "It began": Jefferson to Jay, June 29, 1789.

163 "The people rushed . . . liberty of the nation": Jefferson to Jay, July 19, 1789.

165 "The spirit of tumult": Jefferson to Jay, July 23, 1789.

165 "The city is": Jefferson to Jay, Aug. 12, 1789.

166 "It is impossible . . . in the latter": Jefferson to Madison, Aug. 28, 1789.

167 "We think in America": Jefferson to L'Abbé Arnoud, July 19, 1789.

167 "The question whether . . . not of right": Jefferson to Madison, Sept. 6, 1789.


26.

170 "these plain and undeniable . . . jealousy and opposition": "Report Relative to a Provision for the Support of Public Credit," Jan. 9, 1790.


27.

174 "We have been told . . . inconsistent language": Madison speech, Apr. 22, 1790.

176 "The question of assumption": Jefferson to Lee, Apr. 26, 1790.

176   "Congress has been . . . rather than separate": Jefferson to Monroe, June 20, 1790.
178   "The assumption . . . at Philadelphia": Jefferson memorandum, February 1793.

28.

180   "A national bank . . . importance to the state": Report on a National Bank,
      Dec. 13, 1790.
183   "I consider . . . would be nugatory": Jefferson, "Opinion on the Constitutionality
      of the Bill for Establishing a National Bank," Feb. 15, 1791.
184   "A period . . . this government": Madison speech, Feb. 8, 1791.
185   "I object . . . become subscribers": Madison to Washington, Feb. 21, 1791.
186   "The constitutionality . . . the time elapsed": Madison memo, c. Jan. 31, 1820.

29.

188   "The measures": *Gazette of the United States,* Mar. 2, 1791.
189   "a paper": Jefferson to Thomas Randolph, May 15, 1791.
189   "The *National Gazette*": *National Gazette,* Oct. 31, 1791.
190   "Here then": "Consolidation," *National Gazette,* Dec. 3, 1791. Also in Papers of
      Madison, where the editors explain how Madison subsequently acknowledged
      authorship of this essay and the others he wrote for the paper.
190   "Public opinion . . . is favorable to liberty": *National Gazette,* Dec. 19, 1791.
191   "In monarchies . . . intermediate governments": *National Gazette,* Dec. 31, 1791.
192   "All dependent countries": *National Gazette,* Dec. 12, 1791.
192   "In every political society . . . existing vices": *National Gazette,* Jan. 23, 1792.
194   "The life . . . society itself": *National Gazette,* Mar. 5, 1792.
195   "The Union . . . and monarchy": *National Gazette,* Apr. 2, 1792.
196   "It appears . . . our government": *National Gazette,* Feb. 27, 1793.

30.

197   "I have long": Adams to William Tudor, Mar. 15, 1791.
198   "Gratitude": Adams to Charles Storer, Mar. 16, 1791.
198   "It has appeared . . . support me": Adams to John Trumbull, Mar. 31, 1791.
199   "I have a dozen times . . . never shall": Jefferson to Adams, July 17, 1791.
199   "I give full . . . seen in this country": Adams to Jefferson, July 29, 1791.
202   "having a tendency": Jefferson notes of conversation, Aug. 13, 1791.

31.

203   "The winter": Adams to Jay, Jan. 4, 1792.
203   "If intrigues": Adams to Nathaniel Hazard, Mar. 10, 1792.
204   "We are ruined": Jefferson to Monroe, Apr. 17, 1791.
204   "The bank filled": Jefferson to Monroe, July 10, 1791.
204   "Ships are lying idle": Jefferson to Edward Rutledge, Aug. 29, 1791.
204   "It is computed": Jefferson to Thomas Randolph, Apr. 19, 1792.
205   "The rage of gambling": Jefferson to J. P. P. Derieux, Jan. 6, 1792.

205 "This nefarious business": Jefferson to William Short, Mar. 18, 1792.

205 "I learn with real concern": Jefferson to Francis Eppes, Apr. 14, 1792.

206 "When you first mentioned . . . you to hang on": Jefferson to Washington, May 23, 1792.

### 32.

209 "I have lost . . . public good": Hamilton to Washington, July 30–Aug. 3, 1792.

210 "How unfortunate . . . have been erecting": Washington to Jefferson, Aug. 23, 1792.

211 "Differences . . . it is withheld": Washington to Hamilton, Aug. 26, 1792.

### 33.

215 "The elections": Jefferson to Pinckney, Dec. 3, 1792.

216 "In the struggle . . . as it now is": Jefferson to William Short, Jan. 3, 1793.

217 "We surely cannot deny": Jefferson to Morris, Mar. 12, 1793.

218 "In the early periods . . . estimate it rightly": Hamilton essay on the French Revolution, undated (1794).

### 34.

221 "No country": Jefferson to Morris, Apr. 20, 1793.

221 "the duty and interest": Washington proclamation, Apr. 22, 1793.

222 "As attempts . . . state of war": *Gazette of the United States,* June 29, 1793.

223 "The alliance between . . . England and Spain": *Gazette of the United States,* July 3, 1793.

223 "All contracts": *Gazette of the United States,* July 6, 1793.

224 "It is at this shrine": *Gazette of the United States,* July 10, 1793.

224 "those who love France": *Gazette of the United States,* July 13–17, 1793.

224 "It ought to teach": *Gazette of the United States,* July 17, 1793.

225 "For god's sake": Jefferson to Madison, July 7, 1793.

225 "I have forced": Madison to Jefferson, July 30, 1793.

226 "I am extremely": Madison to Jefferson, Aug. 11, 1793.

226 "Several pieces . . . a tyranny": *Gazette of the United States,* Aug. 24 and 28, 1793.

227 "The power of the legislature": *Gazette of the United States,* Sept. 7 and 11, 1793.

227 "We are to regard . . . *hereditary* magistrate": *Gazette of the United States,* Sept. 14, 1793.

### 35.

229 "Great Britain is still . . . *our public paper*": Jefferson to Monroe, Apr. 17, 1791.

230 "free bottoms make free goods": Jefferson opinion on neutral trade, Dec. 20, 1793.

230 "This article . . . independent country": Jefferson to Pinckney, Sept. 7, 1793.

231 "The French have been guilty": Jefferson to Randolph, June 24, 1793.

232 "incompatible": Jefferson to Genêt, June 5, 1793.

232   "Genet has thrown down": Jefferson to Madison, Aug. 25, 1793.

232   "hot-headed, all imagination": Jefferson to Madison, July 7, 1793.

232   "His conduct": Jefferson to Monroe, July 14, 1793.

233   "As the right": Hamilton memorandum, May 15, 1793.

233   "The good sense . . . true policy": Hamilton draft message, May 14–16, 1793.

234   "A committee": *Gazette of the United States,* May 18, 1793.

234   "painful necessity": Jefferson to Morris, Aug. 23, 1793.

235   "While you are exterminating": Jefferson to Lafayette, June 16, 1792.

235   "The zealous apostles": Jefferson to Jean Pierre Brissot de Warville, May 8, 1793.

235   "Would you believe": Jefferson to Paine, June 19, 1792.

236   "Parties seem": Jefferson to Monroe, June 4, 1793.


36.

237   "I sincerely regret": Madison to Rush, Oct. 1, 1792.

237   "The history": Adams to Rush, Apr. 4, 1790.

238   "The precursors . . . of the night": Benjamin Rush, *An Account of the Bilious Remitting Yellow Fever as it Appeared in the City of Philadelphia in the Year 1793* (1794).

241   "I have myself": Hamilton to College of Physicians, Sept. 11, 1793.

242   "This is to certify": Note to Hamilton to Abraham Yates Jr., Sept. 23, 1793.

242   "I have long": Madison to Jefferson, undated (after Sept. 8, 1793).

242   "It afforded": Rush, *Account.*


37.

244   "The prospects . . . harmony in America": Adams to Abigail Adams, Jan. 9, 1794.

244   "Jefferson went off": Adams to Abigail Adams, Jan. 6, 1794.

244   "The motives . . . no soldier": Adams to John Quincy Adams, Jan. 3, 1794 (inadvertently dated 1793).

245   "He might have": Adams to Charles Adams, Jan. 2, 1794.

245   "My country . . . individuals in this country": Adams to Abigail Adams, Dec. 19, 1793.

246   "The present . . . to the nation": Hamilton to Washington, Apr. 14, 1794.

247   treasury secretary wrote instructions: Enclosure in Hamilton to Washington, Apr. 23, 1794.

248   "We are both . . . commercial adventure": Hamilton to Jay, May 6, 1794.


38.

251   "On the evening . . . of his gun": Hugh H. Brackenridge, *Incidents of the Insurrection in the Western Parts of Pennsylvania in the Year 1794* (1795) 5–6, 18–19.

253   "The whole country . . . molest no one": Ibid., 41–58.

256   "It has from . . . *your own power*": *Dunlap and Claypoole's American Daily Advertiser,* Aug. 23, 1794.

257 "Shall the majority . . . this perishes": Ibid., Aug. 26, Aug. 28 and Sept. 2, 1794.

258 "The essential interests": Washington proclamation, Aug. 7, 1794.

259 "The moment": Washington proclamation, Sept. 25, 1794.

259 "You will forward": Hamilton to Hodgdon, Sept. 17, 1794.

259 "For the Virginia": Hamilton to Hodgdon, Sept. 15, 1794.

259 "Mr. Hamilton": Hamilton to Hodgdon, Sept. 25, 1794.

260 "Upon full reflection": Hamilton to Washington, Sept. 19, 1794.

260 "Nothing from": Hamilton to King, Sept. 17, 1794.

260 "There is a large": Hamilton to Lee, Sept. 18, 1794.

260 "The disease": Hamilton to Lee, Sept. 17, 1794.

260 "Though severity": Hamilton to Lee, Sept. 24, 1794.

261 "A certain John Holcroft . . . the excise law": *Incidents*, 79.

262 "The one . . . shot the boy mortally": William Findley, *History of the Insurrection in the Four Western Counties of Pennsylvania in the Year 1794* (1796), 143–44.

263 "The president . . . against the laws": Ibid., 170–71.

264 "The time": Ibid., 178.

264 "Perhaps the most . . . point of view": Ibid., 223–25.

### 39.

267 "My opinion": Jay to Randolph, Nov. 19, 1794.

268 "We are still uninformed": Jefferson to Monroe, May 26, 1795.

268 "Resolved": Boston citizens to Washington, July 13, 1795.

269 "In every act . . . opinions of others": Washington to Boston selectmen, July 28, 1795.

269 "misconception, jealousy": "The Defence No. 1," July 22, 1795, Hamilton Papers.

### PART VII ALIENS AND SEDITIONISTS

### 40.

274 "Mr. Bache": *Aurora General Advertiser,* June 29, 1795.

274 "Awakened . . . public evils": *Aurora General Advertiser,* Sept. 11, 1795.

276 "As the faith": Adams to Washington, Aug. 10, 1795.

276 "You will see": Adams to Jefferson, Feb. 5, 1795.

276 "A battle royal": Adams to Abigail Adams, Feb. 9, 1795.

276 "treacherous publication": Adams to John Quincy Adams, Aug. 25, 1795.

277 "If those patriots . . . impracticable": Adams to John Quincy Adams, Sept. 19, 1795.

278 "If elections . . . himself popular": Adams to John Quincy Adams, Nov. 17, 1795.

279 "By one section": *Annals of Congress,* 4th Congress, 1st session, 466–74.

280 "The nature . . . be preserved": Washington message, Mar. 30, 1796, American Presidency Project, https://www.presidency.ucsb.edu/documents/message-the-house-representatives-regarding-documents-relative-the-jay-treaty.

280 "According to": Madison to Jefferson, Apr. 4, 1796.

281 "Under that idea": Madison to Jefferson, Apr. 11, 1796.

281   "The banks": Madison to Jefferson, May 1, 1796.
281   "The people": Madison to Jefferson, May 9, 1796.


## 41.

282   "It must be kept . . . disgraced in it": Adams to Abigail Adams, Jan. 5, 1796.
282   "Happy is . . . opposite boxes": Adams to Abigail Adams, Jan. 7, 1796.
284   "It is probable . . . *checkmate*": *Aurora General Advertiser*, Jan. 15, 1796.
285   "I wish": Washington to Tobias Lear, Apr. 12, 1791.
286   "The democrats": Adams to Abigail Adams, Jan. 15, 1796.
286   "The southern gentry": Adams to Abigail Adams, Jan. 23, 1796.
286   "All this": Adams to Charles Adams, Jan. 31, 1796.
286   "I see daily . . . in the people": Adams to Abigail Adams, Feb. 2, 1796.
287   "I would not": Adams to Abigail Adams, Feb. 6, 1796.
287   "The world": Adams to Abigail Adams Smith, Feb. 6, 1796.
287   "We are happy": *Aurora General Advertiser*, Feb. 10, 1796.
288   "The enclosed slip . . . of our country": Adams to Abigail Adams, Feb. 10, 1796.
288   "The subject . . . nor of public": Adams to Abigail Adams, Feb. 15, 1796.
289   "I hate": Adams to Abigail Adams, Mar. 1, 1796.


## 42.

290   "The campaign": Jefferson to Monroe, July 10, 1796.
290   "Hamilton is really . . . their patron-nation": Jefferson to Henry Tazewell, Sept. 13, 1795.
291   "The people of America . . . against their government": Jefferson notes on letter of Christoph Ebeling, undated (after Oct. 15, 1795).
294   "Mr. Adams and myself": Jefferson to Madison, Jan. 30, 1797.
294   "Never was a finer canvas . . . But away politics": Jefferson to Adams, Feb. 28, 1796.


## 43.

296   "We may all": Enclosure in Madison to Washington, June 20, 1792.
297   "the baneful effects . . . foreign world": Washington farewell address, Sept. 17, 1796 (published Sept. 19, 1796), American Presidency Project.


## 44.

301   "The day": Adams to John Quincy Adams, Dec. 5, 1796.
301   "The first wish": Jefferson to Madison, Dec. 17, 1796.
301   "I have no expectation": Jefferson to Madison, Dec. 17, 1796.
302   "This is the very day . . . this is ugly": Adams to Abigail Adams, Dec. 7, 1796.
303   "In obedience . . . and perseverance": Adams proclamation to Senate, Feb. 8, 1797.

## 45.

304 "I had a visit": Adams to Abigail Adams, Jan. 1, 1797.

304 "The Federal ticket": Wolcott to Hamilton, Nov. 6, 1796.

305 "Our excellent . . . caution and reserve": Hamilton to unidentified addressees, Nov. 8, 1796.

306 "During the last election": Troup to King, Nov. 16, 1798, in *The Life and Correspondence of Rufus King,* edited by Charles R. King (1895), 2:466.

306 "Hamilton": Adams to Abigail Adams, Jan. 9, 1797.

## 46.

307 "Clingman": Muhlenberg affidavit, undated, in Callender, *The History of the United States in 1796* (1797), 209–10. The italics presumably were Callender's.

308 "It was with difficulty": Affidavit by Muhlenberg, Monroe and Venable, undated, in ibid., 211–12.

308 "She replied": Clingman affidavit, Dec. 13, 1792, in ibid., 213.

308 "Last night": Affidavit by Monroe, Venable and Muhlenberg, Dec. 15, 1792, in ibid., 217.

309 "Even admitting": Ibid., 222.

309 "The spirit of Jacobinism . . . self-condemnation": *Observations on Certain Documents Contained in No. V & VI of "The History of the United States for the Year 1796," In Which the Charge of Speculation Against Alexander Hamilton, Late Secretary of the Treasury, is Fully Refuted. Written by Himself* (1797), 3–36.

## 47.

315 "Before that event": Jefferson to Chastellux, Nov. 26, 1782.

316 "My mother . . . slave woman": Recollections of Madison Hemings, "Life Among the Lowly, Number 1," *Pike County Republican,* Mar. 13, 1873.

317 "At one moment": *The Pretensions of Thomas Jefferson to the Presidency Examined* (1796), 7. "Phocion" was initially thought by some to be Hamilton, who had used the persona previously. But William Smith's authorship emerged within weeks. "Cousin Smith is said to have written Phocian," Adams wrote to Abigail on Dec. 7, 1796, citing by-then-conventional wisdom. On Smith and "Phocion," see "William Loughton Smith," in *South Carolina Encyclopedia.* Ron Chernow in *Hamilton* (2005) revived the Hamilton-as-Phocion claim, but he is in a distinct minority among scholars. For what it is worth, Smith was a staunch Hamilton ally, as was Oliver Wolcott, who apparently contributed to the Phocion project.

## 48.

318 "May he long live . . . and benevolence": Adams inaugural address, Mar. 4, 1797, American Presidency Project.

319 "Your dearest friend": Adams to Abigail Adams, Mar. 5, 1797.

319 "It gives such": Adams to Abigail Adams, Dec. 12, 1796.

319  "I hope you": Adams to Abigail Adams, Feb. 4, 1797.

319  "John Adams": Adams to Abigail Adams, Dec. 30, 1796.

320  "1st. Whether . . . be abolished": Adams to Pickering, March 1797 (no day given).

321  "I have it": Adams to Knox, Mar. 30, 1797.

321  "Let Mr. Jefferson": Knox to Adams, Mar. 19, 1797.

321  "The proposal . . . corps diplomatic": Adams to Gerry, Apr. 6, 1797.

322  "They consider nobody": Adams to Knox, Mar. 30, 1797.

322  "Although peace": Adams to William Heath, Apr. 19, 1797.

### 49.

324  "The right of embassy . . . forgotten or neglected": Adams speech to Congress, Mar. 16, 1797, American Presidency Project.

326  "On being presented": Jefferson to William Smith, Feb. 19, 1791.

326  "Accordingly . . . no further explanation": Marshall to Pickering, Oct. 22, 1797, Papers of John Marshall Digital Edition, https://rotunda.upress.virginia.edu/founders/JNML.html.

328  "M. Hottinguer": Marshall to Pickering, Nov. 8, 1797, ibid.

329  "The pure principles": Adams to Stephen Temple, June 6, 1798.

329  "A free and equal": Adams to James Wood, June 10, 1798.

329  "The best criterion": Adams to Caleb Newbold, June 11, 1798.

330  "When immense sums": Adams to Isaac LeBaron, June 8, 1798.

330  "The advent": Adams to James Cogswell, June 7, 1798.

330  "A war with France": Adams to William Prentis, June 6, 1798.

### 50.

331  "The enlightened friend . . . of their country": *Commercial Advertiser*, March 30, 1798.

332  "Shall we declare . . . God and man!": Ibid., Apr. 19, 1798.

333  "I am at an immense": Adams to Washington, June 22, 1798.

333  "In such a state . . . very great sacrifice": Hamilton to Washington, May 19, 1798.

334  "It is a great . . . may be formed": Hamilton to Washington, June 2, 1798.

334  "I use the liberty . . . you would approve": Hamilton to Washington, July 8, 1798.

### 51.

336  "It is quite impossible": Jefferson to Madison, Mar. 21, 1798.

336  "Public opinion": Madison to Jefferson, Feb. 18 or 19, 1798.

337  "The conduct . . . of the government": Madison to Jefferson, Apr. 15, 1798.

337  "The success of the war party": Madison to Jefferson, May 5, 1798.

338  "The successful use": Madison to Jefferson, May 13, 1798.

338  "The crisis is arrived": *Aurora General Advertiser*, Apr. 14, 1798.

339  "last link in the systematic chain": *Aurora General Advertiser*, Apr. 14, 1798.

339  "The minister Genet": *Aurora General Advertiser*, Apr. 16, 1798.

339 "Suppose a French minister": *Aurora General Advertiser,* Apr. 16, 1798.
340 "The analysis": Madison to Jefferson, May 5, 1798.

## 52.

341 "My dear sister . . . a civil war": Abigail Adams to Mary Cranch, May 10, 1798.
343 "The Jacobins . . . of a Jacobin": Abigail Adams to William Smith, June 9, 1798.
344 "You see": Abigail Adams to Mary Cranch, Mar. 20, 1798.
344 "It would be difficult": Abigail Adams to John Quincy Adams, Apr. 21, 1798.
345 "As calumny": Abigail Adams to Mercy Otis Warren, Apr. 25, 1798.
345 "I wish the laws": Abigail Adams to Mary Cranch, May 26, 1798.
345 "Daringly do": Abigail Adams to Mary Cranch, Apr. 26, 1798.

## 53.

346 "any false": *Statutes at Large,* 1:596.
346 "If ever there . . . wrest it from them": *Debates and Proceedings in the Congress of the United States,* 5th Congress, 2093–98.
347 "Does the situation": Ibid., 2107–11.
348 "The Constitution": *Aurora General Advertiser,* July 14, 1798.
349 "The object of that": Jefferson to Madison, Apr. 26, 1798.
349 "Party passions": Jefferson to James Lewis, May 9, 1798.
349 "It is true . . . true principles": Jefferson to John Taylor, June 1, 1798.
351 "This bill": Jefferson to Madison, June 7, 1798.
352 "Always examine": Jefferson to Monroe, May 21, 1798.
352 "The infidelities . . . that of England": Jefferson to Taylor, Nov. 26, 1798.
353 "Resolved . . . rod of iron": Fair copy of Kentucky resolutions, before Oct. 4, 1798.
354 "void and of no force": Kentucky resolutions, Nov. 16, 1798, and Dec. 3, 1799, at "Virginia and Kentucky Resolutions," Jack Miller Center, https://jackmiller center.org/cd-resources/virginia-kentucky-resolutions/.
355 "Resolved . . . to the people": Virginia resolutions, Dec. 21, 1798, at ibid.

## 54.

357 "You are hereby": Adams to Benjamin Stoddert, Aug. 10, 1798.
358 "The French 60": Adams to Stoddert, Aug. 31, 1798.
358 "The sentiment": Adams to Stoddert, Apr. 8, 1799.
359 "I wish all": Adams to Stoddert, Apr. 22, 1799.
359 "Some of our": Adams to Stoddert, May 19, 1799.
359 "At present . . . little foreseen": Adams to McHenry, Oct. 22, 1798.

## PART VIII THE REVOLUTION OF 1800

## 55.

363 "I shall seldom": Jefferson to Madison, Jan. 16, 1799.
363 "In confutation . . . add my signature": Jefferson to Gerry, Jan. 26, 1799.

366 "Your patriarchal address": Jefferson to Pendleton, Jan. 29, 1799.

366 "Petitions and remonstrances": Jefferson to Madison, Jan. 31, 1799.

367 "The violations ... since my last": Jefferson to Pendleton, Feb. 14, 1799.

368 "The spirit of 1776": Jefferson to Thomas Lomax, Mar. 12, 1799.

## 56.

369 "Georgia, North Carolina": Jefferson to Nicholas, Sept. 5, 1799.

370 "I have today ... republican principles": Jefferson to Monroe, Jan. 12, 1800.

370 "Should it be ... but think so": Jefferson to Randolph, Feb. 2, 1800.

371 "I fear our friends": Jefferson to Samuel Adams, Feb. 26, 1800.

372 "The Federalists begin": Jefferson to Madison, Mar. 4, 1800.

372 "Whatever it may be": Jefferson to Edward Livingston, Apr. 30, 1800.

372 "Our country is too large ... a few servants": Jefferson to Gideon Granger, Aug. 13, 1800.

## 57.

373 "The sins ... the Illuminati?": Timothy Dwight, *The Duty of Americans, at the Present Crisis* (1798), 20–21.

374 "It is good enough": William Linn, *Serious Considerations on the Election of a President* (1800), 17–26.

375 "As to the calumny": Jefferson to Monroe, May 26, 1800.

375 "I have a view": Jefferson to Rush, Sept. 23, 1800.

## 58.

376 "Ye will judge": James Callender, *The Prospect Before Us* (1800–1), 2:57.

376 "The moral certainty ... to adopt": Hamilton to Jay, May 7, 1800, with Jay note at bottom.

377 "To support Adams": Hamilton to Sedgwick, May 4, 1800.

378 "He is I am ... in good earnest": Hamilton to Sedgwick, May 10, 1800.

378 "General Hamilton ... I abhorred": Conversation with Arthur Fenner, June 25–26, 1800, Hamilton papers.

379 "I have serious thoughts": Hamilton to Wolcott, July 1, 1800.

380 "Sir ... the suggestion": Hamilton to Adams, Aug. 1, 1800.

380 "The time": Hamilton to Adams, Oct. 1, 1800.

381 "Some of the warm ... Chief Magistrate": *Letter from Alexander Hamilton Concerning the Public Conduct and Character of John Adams* (1800), 3–41.

## 59.

386 "My personal friends": Burr to Jefferson, Dec. 23, 1800.

386 "It was to be expected ... respect and esteem": Jefferson to Burr, Feb. 1, 1801.

386 "It was so obvious ... friendly and obliging": Burr to Jefferson, Feb. 12, 1801.

387 "His private character": Hamilton to Wolcott, Dec. 16, 1800.

388 "He is sanguine enough": Hamilton to Morris, Dec. 24, 1800.

388  "It is a fact": Alexander Hamilton to Morris, Jan. 13, 1801.

388  "The maintenance": Hamilton to Bayard, Dec. 27, 1800.

388  "The appointment of Burr": Hamilton to Sedgwick, Dec. 22, 1800.

388  "If Jefferson is president": Hamilton to Wolcott, undated (December 1800).

388  "There is no doubt": Hamilton to Wolcott, Dec. 16, 1800.

389  "*Jefferson* or *Burr?*": Hamilton to Morris, Dec. 24, 1800.

389  "For Heaven's sake": Hamilton to Bayard, Dec. 27, 1800.

### 60.

390  "I dread the effect": William Tudor Sr. to Adams, Jan. 9, 1801.

390  "To see mock patriots": Joseph Ward to Adams, Jan. 22, 1801.

391  "The adherents": Thomas Adams to Adams, Jan. 20, 1801.

391  "Although the elevation": Gerry to Adams, Jan. 26, 1801.

391  "I lament . . . desired harbor": Adams to Gerry, Feb. 7, 1801.

392  "I have enclosed . . . ended the conversation": Abigail Adams to Thomas Adams, with enclosure, Jan. 25, 1801.

### 61.

395  "The House of Representatives": Bayard to Adams, Feb. 11, 1801.

### 62.

397  "Is this the violent democrat . . . your friend": Mrs. Samuel Harrison Smith (Margaret Bayard), *The First Forty Years of Washington Society*, edited by Gaillard Hunt (1906), 5–8.

399  "Conrad's boarding house . . . even despotism": Ibid., 10–13.

400  "It was an awful crisis . . . for the papers": Ibid., 22–26.

### 63.

403  "Friends and fellow citizens . . . peace and prosperity": Jefferson inaugural address, Mar. 4, 1801, American Presidency Project.

### 64.

406  "The melancholy decease": Adams to Thomas Adams, Dec. 17, 1800.

406  "I arrived here": Abigail Adams to Adams, Feb. 13, 1801.

407  "the homage": Jefferson to Adams, Mar. 8, 1801.

407  "Had you read . . . heartily wish you": Adams to Jefferson, Mar. 24, 1801.

407  "When conversing with Marshall": Joseph Story quoting Jefferson in Charles Warren, *The Supreme Court in United States History* (1924), 1:182.

410  "Twenty times": Adams to Jefferson, Apr. 19, 1817.

410  "I join you": Jefferson to John Adams, May 5, 1817.

410  "I cannot contemplate": Adams to Jefferson, July 15, 1817.

410  "Tried myself": Jefferson to John Adams, Nov. 13, 1818.

411 "The clouds": Adams to Jefferson, Nov. 23, 1819.

411 "The Missouri question": Jefferson to Adams, Dec. 10, 1819.

411 "the revolution of 1800": Jefferson to Spencer Roane, Sept. 6, 1819.

411 "I am certainly": Adams to Jefferson, Jan. 14, 1826.

411 "Like other young people": Jefferson to Adams, Mar. 25, 1826.

412 "A plainer contradiction": Madison remarks on nullification, December 1834.

412 "As this advice . . . into Paradise": "Advice to My Country," December 1830.

# Index

## Illustration Credits

## THE LAST CAMPAIGN
*Sherman, Geronimo and the War for America*

William Tecumseh Sherman and Geronimo were keen strategists and bold soldiers, ruthless with their enemies. Over the course of the 1870s and 1880s these two war chiefs would confront each other in the final battle for what the American West would be: a sparsely settled, wild home where Indian tribes could thrive, or a more densely populated extension of the America to the east of the Mississippi. Sherman was a well-connected son of Ohio who attended West Point and rose to prominence through his scorched-earth campaigns in the Civil War. Geronimo grew up among the Apache people, hunting wild game for sustenance and roaming freely on the land. After the brutal killing of his wife, children and mother by Mexican soldiers, he became a relentless avenger, raiding Mexican settlements across the American border. When Sherman rose to commanding general of the Army, he was tasked with bringing Geronimo and his followers onto a reservation where they would live as farmers and ranchers and roam no more. But Geronimo preferred to fight. *The Last Campaign* is a powerful retelling of a turning point in the making of our nation and a searing elegy for a way of life that is gone.

History


## THE ZEALOT AND THE EMANCIPATOR
*John Brown, Abraham Lincoln
and the Struggle for American Freedom*

John Brown was a charismatic and deeply religious man who heard the God of the Old Testament speaking to him, telling him to destroy slavery by any means. When Congress opened Kansas territory to slavery in 1854, Brown raised a band of followers to wage war. In 1859 Brown and his men assaulted the federal arsenal at Harpers Ferry, Virginia, hoping to arm slaves for a race war that would cleanse the nation of slavery. Brown's violence pointed ambitious Illinois lawyer and former officeholder Abraham Lincoln toward a different solution to slavery: politics. Lincoln shrewdly threaded the needle between the opposing voices of the fractured nation and won election as president. But the time for moderation had passed, and Lincoln's fervent belief that democracy could peacefully resolve its moral crises faced its ultimate test.

History

THE FIRST AMERICAN
*The Life and Times of Benjamin Franklin*

Wit, diplomat, scientist, philosopher, businessman, inventor, and bon vivant, Benjamin Franklin's "life is one every American should know well, and it has not been told better than by Mr. Brands" (*The Dallas Morning News*). From penniless runaway to highly successful printer, from ardently loyal subject of Britain to architect of an alliance with France that ensured America's independence, Benjamin Franklin came from obscurity to become one of the world's most admired figures, whose circle included the likes of Voltaire, Hume, Burke, and Kant. Drawing on previously unpublished letters and a host of other sources, acclaimed historian H. W. Brands has written a thoroughly engaging biography of the eighteenth-century genius. *The First American* is a work of meticulous scholarship that provides a magnificent tour of a legendary historical figure, a vital era in American life, and the countless arenas in which the protean Franklin left his legacy.

Biography

ALSO AVAILABLE
*The Age of Gold*
*American Colossus*
*Andrew Jackson*
*The General vs. the President*
*The Heartbreak of Aaron Burr*
*Heirs of the Founders*
*Lone Star Nation*
*The Man Who Saved the Union*
*The Murder of Jim Fisk for the Love of Josie Mansfield*
*Our First Civil War*
*Reagan*
*Traitor to His Class*

VINTAGE BOOKS
Available wherever books are sold.
vintagebooks.com